2010

THE BEST 10-MINUTE PLAYS

Smith and Kraus's
Short Plays and 10-Minute Play Collections

Christopher Durang Vol. I: 27 Short Plays
Frank D. Gilroy Vol. II: 15 One-Act Plays
Israel Horovitz Vol. I: 16 Short Plays
Romulus Linney 17 Short Plays
Terrence McNally Vol. I: 15 Short Plays
Lanford Wilson: 21 Short Plays
Act One Festival 1995: The Complete One-Act Plays
Act One Festival 1994: The Complete One-Act Plays
Boston Theater Marathon XI: 2009 Anthology of 10-Minute Plays
EST Marathon: The Complete One-Act Plays, annual anthologies from 1995–1999
HB Playwrights Short Play Festival
- 2003 The Subway Plays
- 2002 The Beach Plays
- 2001 The Hospital Plays
- 2000 The Funeral Plays
- 1999 The Airport Plays
- 1998 The Museum Plays
- 1997 The Motel Plays

Twenty One-Acts from 20 Years at the Humana Festival 1975–1995
The Women's Project and Productions Rowing to America and Sixteen Other Short Plays
8 TENS @ 8 Festival: 30 10-Minute Plays from the Santa Cruz Festivals I–VI
30 Ten-Minute Plays from the Actors Theatre of Louisville for 2 Actors
30 Ten-Minute Plays from the Actors Theatre of Louisville for 3 Actors
30 Ten-Minute Plays from the Actors Theatre of Louisville for 4, 5, and 6 Actors
2004: The Best 10-Minute Plays for Two Actors
2004: The Best 10-Minute Plays for Three or More Actors
2005: The Best 10-Minute Plays for Two Actors
2005: The Best 10-Minute Plays for Three or More Actors
2006: The Best 10-Minute Plays for Two Actors
2006: The Best 10-Minute Plays for Three or More Actors
2007: The Best 10-Minute Plays for Two Actors
2007: The Best 10-Minute Plays for Three or More Actors
2008: The Best 10-Minute Plays for Two Actors
2008: The Best 10-Minute Plays for Three or More Actors
2009: The Best 10-Minute Plays for Two or More Actors

2010

The Best 10-Minute Plays

Edited by Lawrence Harbison

CONTEMPORARY PLAYWRIGHT SERIES

A Smith and Kraus Book
Hanover, New Hampshire

Published by Smith and Kraus, Inc.
177 Lyme Road, Hanover, NH 03755
www.SmithandKraus.com
(888) 282-2881

First Edition: September 2010
10 9 8 7 6 5 4 3 2 1

Manufactured in the United States of America
Cover and text design by Julia Hill Gignoux, Freedom Hill Design

ISBN-13: 978-1-57525-772-3 // ISBN-10: 1-57525-772-6
ISSN 1550-6754
Library of Congress Control Number: 2010931602

Contents

PLAYS FOR THREE OR MORE ACTORS

Foreword

Again this year, Smith and Kraus has combined its two annual ten-minute play books into this one volume, divided into two sections: Plays for Two Actors and Plays for Three or More Actors. Now, you can get the best ten-minute plays produced during the 2009–2010 theatrical season all in one book!

In years past, playwrights who were just starting out wrote one-act plays of thirty to forty minutes in duration. One thinks of writers such as A. R. Gurney, Lanford Wilson, John Guare and several others. Now, new writers tend to work in the ten-minute play form, largely because there are so many production opportunities. Fifteen years ago, there were none. Actors Theatre of Louisville used to commission playwrights to write ten-minute plays for their apprentice company. When I was senior editor at Samuel French, it occurred to me that there might be a market for these very short plays, so I compiled and edited an anthology of ten-minute plays from Actors Theatre, which did so well that Samuel French has now published six such anthologies. For the first time, ten-minute plays were now widely available, and they started getting produced. There are now a multitude of ten-minute play festivals, not only in the U.S. but all over the world.

In this volume you will find a plethora of ten-minute plays, culled from the hundreds I read last year. All have been produced successfully. Some have even won awards. These plays are written in a wide variety of styles. Some are realistic, some are not. Some are comic (laughs); some are dramatic (no laughs). I think this form lends itself well to experimentation in style and subject matter. A playwright can have fun with a device which couldn't be sustained as well in a longer form. Many of these plays employ such devices.

What makes a good ten-minute play? Well, first and foremost I have to like it. Isn't that what we mean when we call a play, a film, a novel "good?" We mean it effectively portrays the world *as I see it.* Aside from this obvious fact, a good ten-minute play has to have the same things any good play has — conflict, interesting characters and compelling subject matter. It also has to have a clear beginning, middle and end. Many of the plays I read for this book were scenes, not complete plays — well-written scenes, but scenes nonetheless. They left me wanting more. I chose plays which were complete in and of themselves; full-length plays which happen to be about ten minutes long. Also, I chose plays which I knew would interest those of you who produce ten-minute plays; because if a play isn't produced it's the sound of a tree falling in the forest, far away. In the back of this book you will find information on whom to contact when you decide which plays you want to produce.

There are a few plays in this book by playwrights who are fairly well-known, such as Don Nigro, Carson Kreitzer, Elaine Romero, Bridgette A. Wimberly, Richard Vetere and P. J. Gibson; but most are by terrific new writers you never heard of, playwrights destined without a doubt to become far better known when their full-length plays get produced by major theatres. And you read their work first here!

Lawrence Harbison
Brooklyn, New York

PLAYS FOR TWO ACTORS

PLAYS FOR ONE MAN AND ONE WOMAN

Goat

Don Nigro

Goat was first presented by Theatre NXS in Columbia, Missouri, on June 19, 2009. Cast: Lil — Nora Dietzel; Goat — Christopher Gould. Director: L. R. Hults. Stage Manager: Samantha Jones. Sound Designer: Bruce Humphries. Set Pieces: David Summers and Linda Smith. Promotion: Megan Clark and Clayton Coffman.

CHARACTERS

GOAT, perhaps a man in his late thirties.

LIL, perhaps a woman of thirty.

SETTING

Deep in an abandoned part of the underground. Now and then we can hear the clatter of what may be subway cars going by overhead somewhere. Most of what we see is darkness.

• • •

In the darkness, we can hear the metallic clatter and roar of what might be subway trains passing somewhere in the distance, above. We can see the faint orange flickering of a fire on the craggy face of a dark man who sits before it, staring into the fire, or perhaps just past it, and trying to warm his hands. After a moment, we see the dim glow of a weak flash light approaching, held by Lil. She sees the man and stops. His back is to her. She hesitates, then speaks.

LIL: Goat?

(The man doesn't answer, doesn't turn.)

Are you Goat?

(No response.)

I'm looking for somebody. They said he'd be way down here where nobody comes. Some of them called him Goat. Are you the one I'm looking for? Do they call you Goat?

GOAT: Not to my face they don't.

LIL: I'll call you anything you like. But I need to speak to you.

GOAT: Go away.

LIL: It's very important.

GOAT: Creatures like you are defiled and eaten down here every night. Gutted and roasted on spits.

LIL: I can take care of myself. I'm stronger than I look. You look strong. You look like you're still strong.

GOAT: What do you want?

LIL: I want you to do something for me.

GOAT: You want a favor?

LIL: Not a favor. I'll pay you.

GOAT: You'll pay.

LIL: Anything you want. I'll give you anything you want.

GOAT: I don't want anything.

LIL: That's not what I heard.

GOAT: Who have you been talking to about me?

LIL: Some of your friends.

GOAT: I don't have friends.

LIL: Ones who live down here.

GOAT: They'd kill me if they could.

LIL: I just need you to do this one thing.

GOAT: You better watch where you step down here. Snakes. There's snakes everywhere.

LIL: I'm not afraid of snakes.

GOAT: Sometimes I kill them and eat them. I make boots out of the skin. Using your hands to make things can keep you from going insane so fast. A lesson someone taught me.

LIL: I don't think you're insane.

GOAT: You are. You're out of your mind to come down here. Nobody comes down here. Why would you come here? What could possibly be worth descending to this lost place?

LIL: You came here.

GOAT: I was cast out.

LIL: Then you and I have something in common.

GOAT: I don't think so.

LIL: We both have a grievance.

GOAT: A grievance.

LIL: This could be in your interest as well as mine.

GOAT: Interest.

LIL: It's about my ex-husband.

GOAT: Your ex-husband? Do you think I give a shit about your ex-husband? Don't know him. Don't care to know him. Don't care to know anything about him.

LIL: You know him. And you know his brother. And his father. You know his father very well.

GOAT: I don't know anybody's father. I don't know anybody.

LIL: His father is your father.

GOAT: *(A burst of sudden and genuinely terrifying anger directed towards her which causes her to retreat a step or two in spite of herself.)* Don't talk to me about fathers. I have no father.

LIL: I know you hate him. I know you can't forgive him for what he did to you. Well, you're not the only one. I hate them, too. I hate the whole rotten bunch. I know the story. It's an ancient story. There were three brothers.

GOAT: Don't tell me any stories. There are no more stories in this place.

LIL: You were the oldest. Things seemed fine, for a while. Until the second one came along.

GOAT: *(Reaching out and putting his hand around her throat.)* Don't talk to me about that one. Don't you mention that one. Don't you come into my place and mention that bastard to me. This is my place. Don't foul it with his name.

(A moment in which their eyes meet while he holds her throat with one hand. Then he lets go.)

Comes along. Thinks he knows everything. Tries to tell me how to behave. Thinks he's better than me. He's the good son. Hypocritical cocksucker.

LIL: He took your place. He pushed you aside. You were cast out. And he got everything. And the the third son was my husband. The baby. Adam. My husband, Adam.

GOAT: He's a moron.

LIL: It's true. He is a moron. But I loved him, at first. I don't know why. Perhaps I felt sorry for him. And all the while the old man watched us, his great rheumy bloodshot eyes, always looking at us. Knowing what would happen. Knowing everything that would happen. But allowing himself to misplace the knowledge just enough to keep being interested. Like somebody watching bugs. We were like his ant farm.

GOAT: I don't want to talk about this any more.

LIL: Do you have bad dreams? I still have dreams. The old man peeping in dirty windows.

GOAT: Falling. I dream about falling. From an impossibly great height. Somebody kicks me, hard, and I fall down the steps. Out into the night. Into the abyss. Arms extended. Clawing the dark. I fall and fall.

LIL: I dream about the garden. That's what I miss the most. Not him, so much. We were never happy, exactly. Lust kept it going. The old man could tell about us. He spied on us through keyholes and peepholes and holes in the floorboards. Now he watches them. The new one. The new wife. But it must be disappointing, because they don't even do it. They just kiss and cuddle and hold hands like a couple of cretins. She's dumb as dirt. They didn't even tell her about me. She thinks he's a virgin. She's seen the animals. She must know she could do it too. But she's afraid of it. I don't know what his problem is. Maybe I scared him off it forever. He still thinks about me, I know. Unless the old man gave him something to make him forget. I've always suspected brain damage, there. And the old man is capable of anything. Any indignity. Any atrocity. But you know that. Look what he did to you.

GOAT: Why were you cast out?

LIL: I terrified them. I looked the old man in the eye. I was the only one. I wanted to be on top. So did you.

GOAT: And look where it got us. I can't even remember that other place. I try, but it only comes to me in fragments. There is no time in that place. Past and future are hopelessly confused there. I wanted it to be different. I wanted direction. Sequence. Narrative. Time. But time is suffering, said my brother. Then let there be suffering, I said. And the old man watched and listened like a great malicious crab. To him, we were all just pieces of his own demented being. Yet he had emotions. He could be cold, then suddenly strange and violent. He loved the gentle son, but he hated me. I was too much like him, so he cast me out. And then he made the garden, and put the youngest one, the idiot boy, there, to amuse himself. That was my idea. Not his. The son of a bitch stole my idea.

LIL: You had creative differences.

GOAT: It was mine. He stole my idea and cast me into the abyss.

LIL: Then help me.

GOAT: Help you what? It's all over. Everything is over now. Everything is lost.

LIL: No. It's just begun. Listen to me. The new wife is a fool. She's the way to get at him, to get to them both, to get them all. She's bored with the idiot boy. Who wouldn't be? So she walks in the garden. And she always goes to the apple trees. The old man ordered them to stay away from his apple trees. He's got special ones he planted, they're not supposed to touch. He's messing with their minds. She goes there every evening, and looks at those apple trees. She likes the orchardy smell. She's horny, but she doesn't know it. She reaches out her hand towards those stupid apples. Then at the last second she pulls it back. She's afraid. She just needs a little push.

GOAT: How do you know what she does?

LIL: I've been spying on them.

GOAT: Lurking behind the trees, have you? Like the old man?

LIL: I go in disguise.

GOAT: What kind of disguise? A false mustache?

LIL: I'm disguised as an owl.

GOAT: An owl?

LIL: Yes.

GOAT: You go to the garden disguised as an owl, and she doesn't notice?

LIL: She notices. She thinks I'm an owl. I'm very good. That's not the point. You could find her alone there. Almost any evening.

GOAT: And what am I supposed to do when I find her? Do you want me to kill her? Is that what you want?

LIL: A long, slow death is better. She's like a child. She'll trust you. She'll be attracted to you. She's never met anybody like you, except for the old man.

GOAT: She hates the old man.

LIL: Passion is passion. Part of her worships what she hates and fears the most. You'll seem dangerous and exciting and mysteriously familiar to her. And you'll have her.

GOAT: But what's the purpose in it? I have nothing against this pathetic creature. Why bother at all?

LIL: Because they belong to him. They belong to the old man. They're his possessions. And he's a jealous, jealous old monster. You don't have to kill her yourself. That's the beauty of it. Seduce her. Get her to betray him. Get her to break the rules. She'll drag the husband into it. The old man will be enraged. He'll kill them for us. And your brother, the one you hate so much, will try to intervene, to preach forgiveness, and the old man will kill him, too.

GOAT: He won't kill his son.

LIL: He'll nail him to a tree. He cast you out, didn't he? I know what it's like to be cast out. I know exile is death. I've wandered the streets like a stray dog at night. He banished me to the waste places, like he banished you, recast the play, erased what he wrote and started over. Make him pay for it. Make him suffer for what he's done. You're the only one who can. You're the only one.

(Pause. He stares into the fire.)

GOAT: I don't know what I am. I was something once. I was my father's son. I don't know what I am now.

LIL: Take action. Fashion mortal consequences. You'll begin a relentless chain reaction. Clocks will tick. Creatures will die. It will all be unspeakably obscene and beautiful.

(He stares into the fire, thinking about it.)

GOAT: My brother's wife. The garden.

LIL: You can wear your snake skin boots.

(Sound of the subway above, something violent and terrible going by, loud. The light fades on them and goes out.)

END OF PLAY

Gunning for Life

WILLIAM BORDEN

Produced by Stageworks/Hudson, Hudson, New York, in their 13th Annual Play By Play Festival Of New One Acts, performances September 30 to October 11, 2009 and at Proctors, Schenectady, New York, October 14 to 18, 2009.

CHARACTERS

ABBY, about fifty, possibly a little younger. Her dress is practical. She's practical—with a down-home wit and repartee.

ROSCOE, older than Abby. He wears pajamas, an old robe, wool socks, old slippers. His crankiness is more a consequence of his situation than anything else.

SETTING

Minimally, all that's necessary is a cabinet with drawers. A more elaborate set might include a door to the outside and a door to another room and the suggestions of a kitchen.

TIME

The present.

• • •

Roscoe, in a wheelchair, a shotgun in his hand, rummages through drawers. Abby enters. She watches him for a moment. She's accustomed to his idiosyncrasies. Their banter is long established, irascibility flavored by long-lasting, well-tested love.

ABBY: What are you looking for?
ROSCOE: Shells.
ABBY: Shells?
ROSCOE: For my gun.
ABBY: For your gun?
ROSCOE: Are you hard of hearing?
ABBY: You're going hunting in a wheelchair?
ROSCOE: Don't be stupid.
ABBY: You're going to shoot me?
ROSCOE: It crosses my mind.
ABBY: That's why I threw out the shells. Years ago.
(He starts for the door.)
Now where are you going?
ROSCOE: Buy some shells.
(He exits. She waits. He enters.)
Drive me.

ABBY: I won't drive you.

ROSCOE: When you go to the grocery. Drop me at Bradley's Guns and Ammo.

ABBY: You want to sit out in the yard and shoot at beer cans?

ROSCOE: *(Making it up.)* Yes.

ABBY: With a *shotgun*?

ROSCOE: My aim's not so good anymore.

ABBY: What's going on?

ROSCOE: I'm gonna die.

ABBY: We're all gonna die.

ROSCOE: I'm gonna die first.

ABBY: We've always known that. You're older than I am.

ROSCOE: At the end I'll be in pain, I'll be doped up, I'll be smelling like those rotten potatoes we found last year. I'll be shitting the bed and puking my pablum — I'll be disgusting.

ABBY: So you're going to shoot yourself.

ROSCOE: While I still have my wits about me.

ABBY: It's too late for that.

ROSCOE: Go out clean. With dignity.

ABBY: When?

ROSCOE: Haven't decided. I want to be ready. Double-ought buckshot should do the trick. Eat the barrel, top of the head pops off. Side of the head, the shell just bounces around the skull, leaves you on life support, a big rutabaga hooked to tubes, you don't want that.

ABBY: Top of the head.

ROSCOE: Smithereens.

ABBY: Blood all over the place.

ROSCOE: Brains, bone, the works.

ABBY: Haven't I cleaned up enough of your messes?

ROSCOE: You gonna bring up Janice Winterbottom again? That was sixteen years ago, for chrisake.

ABBY: Fifteen.

ROSCOE: And she's dead.

ABBY: She lives in your heart.

ROSCOE: Cancer.

ABBY: Something else in common.

ROSCOE: I haven't thought about her for years.

ABBY: You went to her funeral.

ROSCOE: It was the least I could do.

ABBY: Remind her husband? In his hour of grief?

ROSCOE: *You* live in my heart. You know that. Better get some oil and cleaning stuff. I want it to go smoothly, no hitches — wham, bam, thank you ma'am.

ABBY: That sounds familiar.

ROSCOE: Now wait a minute —

ABBY: Blood and brains all over the walls and ceiling for me to clean up?

ROSCOE: Don't be silly. You'll hire the Merry Maids.

ABBY: You could do it in the yard. Out by the incinerator.

ROSCOE: What if it's winter?

ABBY: You're afraid you'll freeze to death?

ROSCOE: That's one solution.

ABBY: And have them arrest me for neglect and abuse?

ROSCOE: If it's winter I can't get my wheelchair through the snow.

ABBY: I'll push you.

ROSCOE: I could wear a hat.

ABBY: And your winter coat.

ROSCOE: I mean inside. A hat so the blood and brains don't splatter all over.

ABBY: They'd just go through the hat.

ROSCOE: I could buy an army helmet. At the surplus store.

(He finds a pot, puts it on his head.)

ABBY: I thought you wanted to go out with dignity.

ROSCOE: This is the gun Hemingway used.

ABBY: To shoot lions?

ROSCOE: To shoot himself.

ABBY: You never told me that.

ROSCOE: I never saw the need.

ABBY: That's what you said about Janice.

ROSCOE: For chrisake it only lasted a year or two.

ABBY: You said a month.

ROSCOE: More or less.

ABBY: Two years?

ROSCOE: It wasn't a steady thing, just now and then, just once in a while, just — where are you going?

ABBY: Buy those shotgun shells.

ROSCOE: So you agree I should do it myself. When the time comes.

ABBY: *I'm* going to shoot you.

ROSCOE: Over Janice?
ABBY: Over lying to me.
ROSCOE: Lying is what keeps a marriage together.
ABBY: Really?
ROSCOE: I ask, "Did you come?" You say, "Oh, yes, it was fantastic!" You ask, "Did you like my bean soup?" I say, "It was delicious!" If people lied more, we'd see fewer divorces.
ABBY: You don't like my bean soup?
ROSCOE: It's OK.
ABBY: What's wrong with my bean soup?
ROSCOE: It's *OK.*
ABBY: What else have you lied about?
ROSCOE: If I wanted to go to confession, I'd join the Catholics.
ABBY: Do you want a funeral?
ROSCOE: No.
ABBY: Cremation?
ROSCOE: On the woodpile, behind the barn. Like that poet who drowned.
ABBY: Memorial service?
ROSCOE: Invite Janice's husband.
ABBY: Obituary? "Loving husband, dutiful father, doting grandfather"?
ROSCOE: Be sure to mention Janice Winterbottom.
ABBY: Hemingway's gun?
ROSCOE: The very one.
ABBY: Where'd you get it?
ROSCOE: eBay.
ABBY: You've had that gun for years. Before there even was an eBay.
ROSCOE: It's *like* Hemingway's gun.
ABBY: You're so full of shit.
ROSCOE: Is that why you married me?
ABBY: I thought you liked my bean soup.
ROSCOE: It's too salty. And you put some herb in it that's weird.
ABBY: Why didn't you tell me?
ROSCOE: I didn't want to hurt your feelings.
ABBY: Which herb?
ROSCOE: How would I know?

(He stifles a groan.)

ABBY: It's every day now, the pain.
ROSCOE: It's in new places.

ABBY: Did you take the pills?

ROSCOE: They make my brain fuzzy.

(He groans.)

ABBY: The pain's getting worse.

ROSCOE: You're giving me a news flash?

ABBY: We have morphine.

ROSCOE: I don't want to spend the rest of my life doped up. That's not life. I don't want that.

ABBY: I know you don't.

ROSCOE: I'll be too doped up to pull the god damn trigger. I'll aim for my head and shoot my foot.

ABBY: Or me.

ROSCOE: We could go together.

ABBY: I wouldn't get your social security. Take that trip to Hawaii I've been counting on.

ROSCOE: Have a good time.

ABBY: I will.

ROSCOE: Learn the hula.

ABBY: I wish we'd gone.

ROSCOE: Me, too.

(He grimaces in pain. She gets a syringe, bottle.)

ABBY: The morphine will help.

ROSCOE: I have to keep my wits about me!

ABBY: You can't think when you're in pain. Let me give you a shot, for the pain.

ROSCOE: And when it gets worse? When it's all the time?

ABBY: I'll do whatever you want.

ROSCOE: The bottle's empty.

ABBY: No, it's full. See?

ROSCOE: It's empty.

(She sees his look, understands his meaning.)

ABBY: I'll tell the doctor we need more. I'll tell him you're using it all the time now.

ROSCOE: There won't be a problem?

ABBY: Only if you shoot me.

(She takes the gun.)

ROSCOE: You could sell that on eBay.

ABBY: Hemingway's?

ROSCOE: Why not?
ABBY: Why not, indeed.
ROSCOE: What's for dinner?
ABBY: Bean soup. I'll leave out the savory.

END OF PLAY

High Speed Disconnect

CHRIS WIDNEY

High Speed Disconnect was first produced by the Emerging Artists Theatre Company as part of their "Fall EATfest," November, 2008. Artistic Director: Paul Adams. Cast: Martha — Sarah Miriam Aziz; David — Dan Barnhill. Director: Aimee Howard.

CHARACTERS

MARTHA, twenty-seven. Neurotic, works too much. Dates often but has no time to waste on dead ends. Wants answers quick.

DAVID, twenty-nine. A workaholic investment banker. Always in the middle of a deal. Studied Chinese for a year so that he could develop emerging markets in Southeast Asia.

PLACE

A bar.

TIME

Present. Night.

• • •

At Rise: David sits on a stool next to a table near the bar. There are two glasses of white wine on the table. David listens intently on his cell phone as Martha arrives. She is also on her cell phone and completely self-absorbed.

MARTHA: *(On cell.)* I'm here now.

DAVID: *(On cell, engrossed.)* Uh-huh.

MARTHA: *(To David while covering phone.)* Hi, I'm Mar — . You're — ?

(She tries to shake hands while indicating that she is on the phone.)

DAVID: Da — . I —

(Indicating that he is also on the phone.)

Yeah.

(He motions for her to sit and gestures toward the wine.)

MARTHA: *(On cell.)* Stacey, I literally just arrived.

DAVID: *(To Martha.)* Ordered you a — .

MARTHA: *(Tasting.)* Chablis, nice.

(On cell to Stacey.)

He ordered a Chablis.

DAVID: *(On cell.)* Tell the Wongs that doesn't help anybody.

MARTHA: *(On cell to Stacey, tasting wine.)* It's fine. Hang on.

(Clicks her call waiting.)

I don't know yet. Mom, I just sat down.

DAVID: *(On cell.)* My date just arrived.

MARTHA: *(On cell to Mom.)* So far? Good.

DAVID: *(On cell but toward Martha.)* Thus far I'd say it looks much more promising than the situation in China.

(Refocusing on cell call, concerned.)

They said what?!

(To Martha.)

I'm sorry, I just have to — .

MARTHA: *(On cell to Mom.)* At this point things look promising. Let me jump, Ma, I have Stace on the other — . Call me back.

DAVID: *(On cell, he speaks in Chinese obviously conducting some type of business transaction. Right now he is calm and professional.)*

MARTHA: *(Call waiting back to Stacey.)* He's cute. And multi-lingual. Up to now we've been getting along very well.

DAVID: *(To Martha, hand over cell.)* We're about to close on the first ever automotive parts distribution center in Quin-huang-dao. Just outside of Beijing?

(He suddenly goes back to his call in a flurry of Chinese.)

MARTHA: *(On cell to Stacey.)* The conversation's going well.

DAVID: *(To Martha.)* Do you — ? Bruscetta? Anything?

(Before she can answer he goes back to Chinese on his cell.)

MARTHA: *(On cell to Stacey.)* He's attentive to my needs.

DAVID: *(Half to Martha, half on cell.)* Huh?

MARTHA: *(To David.)* Finish your —

DAVID: *(On cell, nervous.)* Huh? Wha?

(He blathers in Chinese.)

MARTHA: *(On cell to Stacey.)* He's a good listener.

DAVID: *(On cell to business partner.)* You have to make them understand that it is a win-win situation. Call me back.

MARTHA: *(On cell to Stacey.)* Lemme jump.

DAVID: *(Finally hanging up.)* Whew! Gosh.

MARTHA: Yeah. Crazy.

DAVID: I'm so —

MARTHA: — No. Me, too.

DAVID: Well, whew!

MARTHA: Double whew!

DAVID: Finally.

MARTHA: Yes.

DAVID: So . . .

(Awkward silence.)

MARTHA: So . . .

(More awkward silence is broken by the ringing of Martha's cell phone.)

MARTHA: Oh, geez, I better —

(David's cell phone rings.)

DAVID: *(Pulling out his cell.)* Here we go.

MARTHA: *(On cell.)* Stace, Oh my God, this is really going well.

(Reacts to call waiting.)

That's my mother.

DAVID: *(On cell.)* Dude, this woman is hot.

MARTHA: *(On cell.)* Mom, don't get hysterical but at this point I feel a very deep, very real connection.

DAVID: *(On cell.)* I want her to bear my children.

MARTHA: *(On cell to Mom.)* It's something — . He gets me. Call me back.

(She clicks her call waiting.)

DAVID: *(On cell.)* What's going on with the Wongs? Uh-huh. Uh-huh.

MARTHA: *(On cell to Stacey as David remains oblivious on his cell.)* Stace, I can't explain it and I know it's crazy but I can see myself fashioning a life with this man. Lemme jump.

(She hangs up and waits attentively to talk to David.)

DAVID: *(On cell.)* Give me Papa Wong.

(In Chinese, David begins calmly but grows increasingly agitated. Martha goes from gushing and beaming toward the new love of her life to slight concern. David becomes more frustrated, now fuming and shouting in Chinese. Martha smiles and waves, trying to get his attention but David is too focused on his call. Martha pulls back and auto-dials.)

MARTHA: *(On cell, near tears.)* Mom?

(Sniffling.)

I don't know what's happening.

DAVID: *(On cell now screaming in Chinese.)*

MARTHA: *(On cell to Mom as David continues.)* It was going so well. Now I don't know. We never talk any more. It's all about his business.

(Reacts to call waiting.)

That's Stace.

(On cell to Stacey.)

Do I want to start a life with a man who's obsessed with his work?

DAVID: *(On cell in Chinese, now soothing and professional, maybe even laughing a bit.)*

MARTHA: *(On cell with Stacey now completely absorbed in her conversation.)*

What about my career? I'm supposed to drop everything and birth babies while he jets off to Quin-huang-dao every weekend?

DAVID: *(On cell with business partner.)* OK, the Wongs are in.

MARTHA: *(On cell with Stacey.)* I raise kids and get fat while he's gone, gone, gone.

DAVID: *(On cell but noticing Martha.)* Regarding that other transaction there seems to be a possible neediness situation.

MARTHA: *(On cell with Stacey.)* Who knows what they do over there? China? That's one short hop to Thailand. And we all know what that means; Sex tours.

(Call waiting.)

Hang on.

DAVID: *(On cell with business partner.)* OK, possible psychotic episode in progress.

MARTHA: *(On cell with Mom.)* Mom, Stacey and I are ninety percent certain that my "DreamDate.com" is a sex addict.

DAVID: *(To Martha as he hangs up his cell.)* Look . . .

MARTHA: *(On cell with Mom.)* Call you back.

(To David, agreeing.)

Yeah . . .

DAVID: I just think we're two very different —

MARTHA: *(Agreeing.)* — at two very different times in our —

DAVID: — Yes.

(Their cell phones both ring.)

MARTHA: *(On cell.)* It's over, Mom.

DAVID: *(On cell to business partner.)* Things didn't work out.

MARTHA: *(On cell.)* We'll always be good friends.

DAVID: *(On cell.)* She's still hot.

MARTHA: *(On cell.)* I love him but I am no longer in love with him.

DAVID: *(On cell, toward Martha.)* She's still hot.

MARTHA: *(On cell, toward David.)* There's no denying the attraction.

(They stare at each other briefly then begin making out like teenagers.)

DAVID: *(On cell.)* Dude, we're sucking face at the bar, check it out!

(He takes their picture with his cell.)

MARTHA: *(On cell, in between tonguing David.)* Yes, mother, I know that this is a repeating pattern of self-destructive behavior. Perhaps brought about by my need to replace an absent father who was driven away by your neurosis before I was two. Hence the resulting nymphomania. Here we go.

(She growls and licks David's face. He pulls back.)

DAVID: *(On cell.)* This girl's weird, Dude.

MARTHA: *(On cell.)* He's pulling away.

DAVID: *(On cell.)* She could never understand what it's like to be raised by a man who'd "pop in" between business trips. Who'd meagerly dole out love based on achievement, on being the best or making the most. Which, of course, manifested itself in a compulsive work disorder in order to suppress never having had a real relationship with my father.

MARTHA: *(On cell.)* He has no clue what it's like to never know your father.

DAVID: *(On cell.)* I gotta get out of here.

MARTHA: *(On cell.)* I gotta get back into therapy.

DAVID: *(On cell, pretending to receive urgent news.)* What?! The Wongs will only accept the deal if I can make it to Quin-huang-dao in less than twenty-four hours?

MARTHA: *(On cell, also pretending.)* Mom! Elevate the limb and apply pressure directly to the wound.

DAVID: *(To Martha but indicating his cell.)* I — . Next available flight.

MARTHA: *(To David but indicating her cell.)* Can opener gone wild.

DAVID: *(To Martha as he gets up to leave.)* But it was really nice meeting you . . .

(Not knowing her name.)

MARTHA: Yes . . .

(Not knowing his name.)

DAVID: *(Lying.)* We'll stay in touch.

MARTHA: *(Also lying.)* Definitely.

BOTH: *(Big, fake smiles.)* Yeah.

(They both turn to leave and immediately go back to their cell phones.)

DAVID: *(On cell.)* Hello?

MARTHA: *(On cell.)* Mom? Stace?

DAVID: *(On cell, pressing buttons.)* Dude, are you there?

MARTHA: *(On cell.)* Hello?

DAVID: *(On cell.)* Hello?

MARTHA AND DAVID: *(On cell, growing desperate.)* Is anybody there?!

(Black out.)

END OF PLAY

Jesse

P. J. GIBSON

Original production by the Ensemble Studio Theatre and Going to the River as part of Going to the River 2009. Director: Lydia Fort. Cast: Tauna Randolph — Maya Lynne Robinson; Gareth Randolph — Christopher Burris. Artistic Director (Ensemble Studio Theatre): William Carden. Executive Director (Ensemble Studio Theatre): Paul Alexander Slee. Artistic Director (Going to the River): Elizabeth Van Dyke. Executive Producer (Going to the River): Jamie Richards.

Playwright's Biography

P. J. Gibson holds an M.F.A. from Brandeis University, studying under a Shubert Fellowship. Published and widely produced, she has penned thirty-seven plays, many works of fiction and poetry; the compilation *Destiny's Daughters: 9 Voices of P. J. Gibson,* 1st Books Library Publisher is one her latest play publications; other publishers include *Long Time Since Yesterday* — Samuel French, Inc., *Brown Silk and Magenta Sunsets* — New American Library, and several plays, poetry and fiction in Alexander Street Press Collections, Third World Publishing, Mentor Books, Applause Theatre Books, Meta Press and Doubleday. She has been the recipient of many honors including the 2008 Black Women Playwright Group's *Whisper, Laugh, Shout Tell The Story* Award; Audelco *VIV Pioneer Award;* the National Black Theatre Festival's *August Wilson Playwright Award;* the Bushfire Theatre of Performing Arts Seventh Annual "Walk of Fame," *Celebrated Playwright* at The Ensemble Studio Theatre's *Going to the River 2003* festival, and a number of fellowships, grants, awards and eight commissions, the most recent is for the Diana Sands story. Gibson is a tenured professor of English at John Jay College of Criminal Justice in New York City.

Characters

Tauna Randolph, an attractive, successful Black woman professional in her mid thirties. Wife to Gareth.

Gareth Randolph, a handsome, successful Black professional male in his mid thirties. Husband to Tauna.

Note

Pronunciation Guide:
Tauna — Tah/nah
Gareth — Gair/ith

• • •

The stage is divided into two levels. Each representing the playing areas of the characters. Down stage is the playing area for Tauna Randolph. On a small table rest the props needed for her scenes: a cell phone, a bottle of champagne wrapped in a huge bow, a pair of stiletto heels, a thin notebook computer, papers, files. Upstage is the playing area for Gareth Randolph. It has a valet which allows him to hang his suit jacket. A small table holds his props a cell phone, an attaché case, a stack of legal briefs. Lights rise on Tauna Randolph, an attractive, successful Black woman professional in her mid thirties. She is dressed fashionably, yet professional. The attire should be a cutaway, able to accommodate two outfits a Moroccan belly dancer outfit, and a sexy bra and panties set.

TAUNA: *(To Audience.)* It was all about a surprise.

(Lights rise on Gareth Randolph, a handsome, successful Black professional male in his mid thirties. He dresses in a stylish double breast suit.)

GARETH: *(To Audience.)* I've never been one for surprises. Most of the time they backfire, with the surpriser becoming the surprisee.

TAUNA: *(To Audience.)* As a couple . . . we've been blessed. Money isn't a concern, and that all unto itself is a true blessing. We have all we need and most of what we want. I got myself a superb education . . .

GARETH: *(To Audience.)* I Graduated Magna Cum Laude U.C. Berkeley Boalt Hall in law.

TAUNA: *(To Audience.)* I graduated Suma Cum Laude from Duke. Earned myself a comfortable and lucrative position as a Merger Specialist.

GARETH: *(To Audience.)* Partnered early with Lathin, Warner and Beers.

TAUNA: *(To Audience.)* We're doing well.

GARETH: *(To Audience.)* Chose to hold off on having children . . .

TAUNA: *(To Audience.)* To settle in on enjoying each other.

GARETH: *(To Audience.)* Life's good.

TAUNA: *(To Audience.)* Really good. Anyway, October 12, 2002 I got the bright idea to give Gareth a special, special birthday present.

GARETH: *(To Audience.)* We always make birthdays special.

TAUNA: *(To Audience.)* Really special. Isn't this simply precious.

(She shows audience a charm she wears on a gold necklace.)

It's a tree. Specifically, the tree we met beneath. A symbol of our bond, deep roots and sturdy wood.

(She throws a kiss to Gareth. He catches it and places it on his heart.)

Anyway . . . October 12th, 2002 I dressed up like a Moroccan belly dancer. Took lessons for that birthday gift.

GARETH: *(To Audience.)* Can you believe? She took lessons . . . And she's good.

TAUNA: *(To Audience.)* Yeah . . . I am good. Anyway . . .

GARETH: *(To Audience.)* October 12th, 2002 Tauna phones me in a panic.

(Lights shift.)

TAUNA: *(Into cell phone.)* Gareth, we have a problem.

GARETH: *(To Audience.)* I could tell something was wrong. It was all in her voice.

(Into his cell phone.)

What's wrong? You OK? . . .

TAUNA: *(Into cell phone.)* I am, but . . . We've got a real big problem in the bedroom.

GARETH: *(Into cell phone.)* What do you mean problem?

TAUNA: *(Into cell phone.)* The skylight.

GARETH: *(Into cell phone.)* What about the skylight?

(To Audience.)

Now you need to know it's pouring outside.

TAUNA: *(To Audience.)* The proverbial buckets upon buckets of . . .

GARETH: *(To Audience.)* Water, water, everywhere.

TAUNA: *(To Audience.)* Raining like you can't believe. Roads are turning into ponds.

GARETH: *(To Audience.)* It's a bad storm.

TAUNA: *(To Audience.)* Really bad.

GARETH: *(To Audience.)* Lightening struck a tree; killed a family of three right in front of their house. One minute they're sitting in their car, and the next . . . dead. It's a really bad storm. Transportation slowed down to a "no go" speed. Things are bad, and I get this call from Tauna saying . . .

TAUNA: *(Into phone.)* The sky light's leaking. I covered the bed with a tarp, but . . .

GARETH: *(To Audience.)* She didn't have to say more. We had an emergency.

TAUNA: *(To Audience.)* You see we had our bed specially made with ebony wood.

GARETH: *(To Audience.)* Now one of the rarest woods in the world.

TAUNA: *(To Audience.)* Truly a beautiful piece of craftsmanship.

GARETH: *(To Audience.)* Now, I don't want to sound trite, but . . .

TAUNA: *(To Audience.)* He love's that bed.

GARETH: *(To Audience.)* I love that bed.

TAUNA: *(To Audience.)* He really loves that bed.

GARETH: *(To Audience.)* It's strong and firm and . . .

TAUNA: *(To Audience.)* What he means is it has four intricately carved posts, which serve for more than aesthetic appeal.

GARETH: *(To Tauna.)* Ahh . . . come on Tauna.

TAUNA: *(To Audience.)* When we wanna spice up the sexing . . . Well, we can actually do a few of those Kama Sutra swinging positions. He likes to call them . . .

GARETH: *(To Audience.)* Page number 137, 199, and 271.

TAUNA: *(To Audience.)* Ladies, you simply must try number 199 and 271. Talk about deep, full penetration.

(She holds her heart.)

Be still my heart.

GARETH: *(To Audience.)* So, I fly home. Speeding like I'm in training for Nascar. I hit the door, turn the key and step into . . .

TAUNA: *(To Audience.)* Rose petals.

GARETH: *(To Audience.)* Everywhere.

TAUNA: *(To Audience.)* Everywhere. Leading up the stairs to our master bedroom.

GARETH: *(To Audience.)* There she is . . .

(Tauna sheds her outer attire, revealing a Moroccan belly dancer outfit. Belly dancing music rises as Tauna moves seductively to the rhythms.)

GARETH: *(To Audience.)* My God . . . My God . . . Oh, My God . . . Had the skylight really been leaking . . . Well, let's just say . . . You look at her. Look at her. I loved her right on through to the morning light.

TAUNA: *(To Gareth.)* Did you have a happy, happy birthday?

GARETH: *(To Tauna.)* I believe in instant replays.

TAUNA: *(To Audience.)* That was October 12th, 2002.

GARETH: *(To Audience.)* October 12th, 2003 . . .

TAUNA: *(To Audience.)* I had to work.

GARETH: *(To Audience.)* In Japan.

TAUNA: *(To Audience.)* Heading problems off at the pass is what I do. That's why I make the big bucks. But I did feel really bad. Birthdays are special for us. For my 2002 birthday, he took me to Bahamas, for the week-end. Full moonlit strolls along the beach. Full body massages . . .

(To Gareth.)

You've got really good hands suggah.

GARETH: *(To Tauna.)* Oh yeah? That what you want this year?

TAUNA: *(To Gareth.)* Hey . . . No complaints on last year's gift. No complaints whatsoever.

(To Audience.)

Anyway . . . 2003, I'm in Japan. I've never missed his birthday, ever.

GARETH: *(To Audience.)* I've never missed her's.

TAUNA: *(To Gareth.)* You did though miss a Thanksgiving, once.

GARETH: *(To Tauna.)* But never a birthday.

TAUNA: *(To Gareth.)* Thanksgivings are also important.

GARETH: *(To Tauna.)* It wasn't a birthday . . .

TAUNA: *(To Gareth.)* But it was a Thanksgiving. And not just any Thanksgiving.

GARETH: *(To Audience.)* One of my clients had barricaded himself in on his ranch, out of state . . . Oklahoma. The problem? . . . He was supposed to have been in court, giving a last minute deposition. I had to go to . . .

GARETH AND TAUNA: *(Simultaneously.)* Oklahoma.

GARETH: *(To Tauna.)* Anyway . . . You know what year that was. Thanksgiving with the entire Taylor clan.

(To Audience.)

And I do mean the *entire* Taylor clan.

TAUNA: *(To Audience.)* He has in-law problems.

GARETH: *(To Audience.)* They hate me.

TAUNA: *(To Gareth.)* Actually, daddy's ambivalent.

GARETH: *(To Audience.)* Like I said . . . They hate me.

TAUNA: *(To Audience.)* They think he's a little too good to be true.

GARETH: *(To Audience.)* I'm a decent guy, and I'm too good to be true. Her mom has this philosophy . . .

TAUNA: *(To Audience.)* She believes a successful marriage is rooted in her belief that the man ought to love . . .

GARETH: *(To Audience.)* The wife more than the reverse.

TAUNA: *(To Audience.)* That a woman should never, ever . . .

GARETH: *(To Audience.)* Never, ever . . .

TAUNA: *(To Audience.)* Marry a pretty face.

GARETH: *(To Audience.)* Now that's a description I'd never been linked to, until Mrs. Taylor. To my face she tells me . . .

"Pretty men are nothing but problems laying in wait."

TAUNA: *(To Audience.)* I married him anyway.

GARETH: *(To Audience.)* Despite her mother's and Aunt Lany's warnings. And I've been living by the Napoleonic Code, ever since. Jesus! . . . Talk about a spoon always stirring up something. My mother-in-law . . . Mother Taylor.

TAUNA: *(To Audience.)* He got a new assistant.

GARETH: *(To Audience.)* Oh that went over well. Like I had much of a say. She was John Beer's niece.

TAUNA: *(To Audience.)* And beautiful.

GARETH: *(To Audience.)* And qualified.

TAUNA: *(To Audience.)* And on sexual overload.

GARETH: *(To Audience.)* And qualified.

TAUNA: *(To Audience.)* And . . . extraordinarily pleasing to the eye.

GARETH: *(To Audience.)* Did I mention she was John Beer's niece?

TAUNA: *(To Audience.)* The problem, you ask? October 12th, 2003 . . . Ms. Attractive Assistant . . .

GARETH: *(To Audience.)* Along with George Patterson, Ming Wa, and, might I also add, Mr. John Beers, himself . . .

TAUNA: *(To Audience.)* Celebrated Gareth's thirty-fourth at the Shangri-La.

GARETH: *(To Audience.)* Mother Taylor's . . .

TAUNA: *(To Audience.)* Favorite restaurant.

GARETH: *(To Audience.)* You fill in the blanks.

TAUNA: *(To Audience.)* I'm in Japan, and I get a call about the . . .

GARETH: *(To Audience.)* "Husband thief celebrating Gareth's birthday."

(To Tauna.)

It was a working dinner, that coincidently happened on my birthday.

TAUNA: *(To Audience.)* Coincidently . . . So, this year I'm thinking on how to bury 2003, erase it from the books; pull something big out of the hat to knock him off his feet. I'm doing some serious contemplating, 'cause we're way past the sweaters, ties, guy toys, belly dancing and such.

GARETH: *(To Audience.)* I know she's working on something big.

TAUNA: *(To Audience.)* I get a call, September 20th.

(Tauna turns her back to audience as she speaks into cell phone.)

GARETH: *(To Audience.)* Canada . . . Montreal, Canada to be specific. Tauna's fluent in French and . . .

(Tauna puts on a stylish raincoat, gathers her computer, hand bag and airplane ticket.)

TAUNA: *(To Audience.)* Fires . . . We had a potentially serious fire. And the Flaubert's hold to a little language bias. They want the negotiations done in French. Did he tell you I'm fluent in French?

GARETH: *(To Audience.)* And I'm locked into the court calendar, so . . . joining me in . . .

GARETH AND TAUNA: *(Simultaneously.)* Montreal's out.

TAUNA: *(To Audience.)* I'm trying my best but . . .

GARETH: *(To Audience.)* Canada. She's in Canada.

(Lights dim on Tauna.)

GARETH: *(To Audience.)* I know she felt bad. We're now talking about two years in a row. First Japan and now Canada. And we're still rather new in this marriage thing . . . Birthdays are special.

TAUNA: *(To Audience.)* Really special.

GARETH: *(To Audience.)* October 9th I get a call.

TAUNA: *(Into cell phone.)* I'm so sorry. We ran into more smoke . . .

GARETH: *(Into cell phone. Disappointed.)* Hey . . . I understand.

TAUNA: *(To Audience.)* I heard his disappointment.

(To Gareth.)

I love you.

GARETH: *(Into cell phone.)* Love you too.

(To Audience.)

October 11th I get another call.

TAUNA: *(Into cell phone.)* I promise I'm going to make this up to you.

GARETH: *(Into cell phone.)* Hey babe . . . You just drown those flames, and come on home as soon as possible.

TAUNA: *(Into cell phone.)* I love you.

GARETH: *(Into cell phone.)* Love you too.

TAUNA: *(Into cell phone.)* Happy early birthday.

GARETH: *(Into cell phone.)* Thanks. Now, get on back to work.

(To Audience.)

So . . . she's not going to be home, and me . . . Well, I guess it's just me, these briefs . . .

(He indicates the legal briefs.)

a little wine and the bed.

(Gareth takes off his shirt. Lights dim on Gareth.)

TAUNA: *(To Audience.)* I know he's feeling bad, and I've got just the right surprise. Me. I'm not in Canada . . . We'll I am, but I'm on the plane, on the runway heading home. I'm ready to blow his mind. I'm wearing . . .

(Tauna opens her raincoat. She is scantly clad in expensive, stylish, sexy, red silk and lace bra and panties, a garter belt, silk stockings and stiletto high heels.)

TAUNA: *(To Audience.)* I have a limo waiting at the airport, once I land. A bottle of champagne on ice, and I plan to love my man on into the middle of tomorrow. How's that for a happy birthday?

(Sound of the faint sound of keys. The opening a closing of a door.)

TAUNA: *(To Audience.)* I hit the door.

(Gareth's area is bathed in darkness.)

GARETH: Shit! . . .

(*To Audience.*)

I heard the door.

TAUNA: (*To Audience.*) The lights were out. Except for at the top of the stairs. Low light spilled out of our bedroom.

(*Sound Slow, sultry, music comes from behind Gareth.*)

GARETH: (*To Audience.*) I cross to the top of the landing. I hear someone. Who?

TAUNA: (*To Audience.*) I hear him . . . See him . . . He steps out of the bedroom, stands at the top of the landing, goes back to the bedroom, comes back and . . .

GARETH: (*To Audience.*) A silhouette stands at the bottom of the stairs.

TAUNA: (*To Audience.*) I step into the stream of light filtering down from the skylight.

GARETH: Shit! . . .

(*To Audience.*)

I don't say it out loud, but . . . Shit!

TAUNA: (*To Audience.*) He's standing at the top of the stairs in the silk pajama bottoms I got him for Christmas. The light from the skylight reveals . . .

GARETH: (*To Audience.*) Tears . . . I felt them rise up and spill . . . tears.

TAUNA: (*To Audience.*) Tears . . . Rolling down his cheeks. Tears. I come home, just moments before midnight, October 12th, 2004 to find my man frozen at the top of the stairs, bare chest in the pajama bottoms I bought him, and he's crying. In the background I can hear an old mellow slow drag tune. My mother's words are swarming around my head. "Never, ever marry a handsome man . . . " I climb the stairs.

(*Tauna moves up towards Gareth. She carries the champagne bottle.*)

GARETH: (*To Audience.*) I don't say a word as she mounts the stairs.

TAUNA: (*To Audience.*) He doesn't say a word.

GARETH: (*To Audience.*) I can't move.

TAUNA: (*To Audience.*) He doesn't move.

GARETH: (*To Audience.*) She can't know what this surprise of her's has done. My God . . . My God . . . My legs are weak.

TAUNA: (*To Audience.*) My legs are weak, but I climbed. One step after the other.

GARETH: (*To Audience.*) She moves up the stairs, getting closer. God . . . She has no idea how much I love her, how this moment may have . . . I can't think of my life without her. I wanna scream how stupid, how stupid.

TAUNA: *(To Audience.)* I stand in front of him. He doesn't move. The music's spilling out of the dimly lit bedroom. He doesn't move.

GARETH: *(To Audience.)* I can't move. She can't possibly understand.

TAUNA: *(To Audience.)* His arms don't embrace me. His lips don't kiss me. His eyes don't speak of joy. His arms, hands . . . locked behind his back. Hiding . . . what? . . . Wine glasses?

(To Gareth.)

I guess the surprise is on me.

(To Audience.)

He still didn't speak. I wanted to run. Turn around, race down those stairs, run out into the street; let the rain drops drown my tears. I wanted to turn back the clock, to be in Canada, to still be working on their fires, but I was here . . . Here . . . In front of him, and . . . I dug for courage.

(To Gareth.)

Happy Birthday Honey.

(To Audience.)

My words were bathed in an acidic water. I tried not to gag. God . . . God . . . Why doesn't he move?

Why doesn't he say anything?

GARETH: *(To Tauna.)* Tauna . . .

TAUNA: *(To Gareth.)* Momma always told me my surprises were gonna some day bite me in the ass.

GARETH: I thought you were in Canada.

TAUNA: Yeah . . . Well, that went over as planned. I was on the plane. Surprise.

(She looks over his shoulder to the bedroom.)

So . . . What you got there behind you?

GARETH: Behind me?

TAUNA: Umm.

(Gareth swallows hard and then reveals a hand gun.)

TAUNA: Jesse? . . . What are you doing with Jesse?

GARETH: I heard someone at the door. I just spoke with you; you were in Canada. I heard someone, saw someone . . .

TAUNA: So you got Jesse?

GARETH: I thought someone had broken in . . . Baby, you know how close I came to using her? I almost . . . No more surprises Tauna.

TAUNA: Well . . . just one.

(Tauna drops her coat. She stands before him in the red silk and lace bra and panties, garter belt and stiletto heels.)

TAUNA: Happy Birthday 2004.

(They embrace. Tauna holds a bottle of champagne. Gareth holds the gun.)

(Lights dim to black.)

(Curtain.)

END OF PLAY

Labor Day Weekend

Jon Spano

Labor Day Weekend was produced by Emerging Artists Theatre for their Fall One-Act Play Festival and ran from November 11 to 22, 2009, at TADA! 15 West 28th Street, in New York City. Cast: Jason — Tommy Day Carey; Andrea — Andrea Alton. Director: Dan Dinero.

Characters

JASON, a transman in his early thirties.

ANDREA, Jason's wife, also early thirties.

Setting

Jason and Andrea's bedroom. Their bed.

Time

Today.

• • •

In the dark, a man screams in agony.

JASON: Ah Ah Ah AHH AAAAAAAAAAAHHHHHHHHHHH!

(Lights up on Jason, sweaty and breathless, lying in bed beneath a white sheet. His four limbs are tied to the bedposts. Andrea, wearing a nurse's outfit, sits facing forward, between Jason's legs so he can't be fully seen. Andrea, nonchalant but a bit sinister, files her nails. She also has a bit of the deadpan about her. The setting is macabre, like something from a Stephen King novel. A wicker picnic basket is near the bed. Hidden behind the headboard is a stack of white towels.)

ANDREA: *(Rapture; deaf ears to Jason's scream.)* Too bad you can't join me for a holiday picnic, baby. I made German-style potato salad and . . . baked beans.

JASON: *(Sheer agony.)* OH OH OHHHH — GOOOOOOOOOOD-DDD *DAMN*!!!

ANDREA: *(More nail filing; getting off on Jason's pain.)* It's been such a long hot summer hasn't it? I can't *wait* to get to the lake.

JASON: Please Please honey baby darling don't do this! *Please!*

ANDREA: Stop your whining you pig. No I shouldn't call you a pig. That's an insult to pigs.

JASON: You've gotta let me go!

ANDREA: No Jason I *don't* gotta.

JASON: Andrea *please* I beg you just loosen the —

ANDREA: You *beg* me? I'm laughing so hard I could bust a gut.

JASON: No, *I'm* going to bust a gut!

ANDREA: After everything I've had to put up with the last two years! My patience! My my my *resolve*!

JASON: Yeah but —

(Quoting.)

"Love is the the river th-th-that washes away the scourge of of everyday hatred." Remember when you said that?

ANDREA: I'll say anything after a few beers in a bowling alley on a Saturday night.

JASON: No you said it the night I proposed to you. At the Olive Garden.

ANDREA: Must have been something in the manicotti.

(Sigh.)

Christ. — I was *so* much happier when you were still a woman.

(Andrea rises and walks away to reveal Jason's protruding stomach. He's been having labor contractions.)

JASON: *(Panic!)* Oh shit!

ANDREA: What?

JASON: My water just broke.

ANDREA: I thought it *had.*

JASON: No. That was pee. — Andrea, why are you doing this?

ANDREA: Because I want an explanation. Not some baloney about an an an *in vitro* mix up at the clinic while you were under anesthesia. I mean *honestly!*

JASON: But I've told you over and over! I didn't *know.* If I *had* known, I would've postponed the wedding. But since I'd already had the breast reconstruction I . . . I mean I was *so* close! I was *finally* on my way to becoming a real —

ANDREA: But you had to go get yourself knocked up! So we had to interrupt the transition. After all that planning with the doctors. The battles with the insurance company. The snickers behind our backs. The hate mail. The taunting by those people from the church: "Tranny lover! Burn in hell you *freaks!*" — Not to mention the fights with my father. And just to remind you, Jason: I've been disinherited. I stood to inherit *millions.* But I tossed it all aside. For *you.*

JASON: I know I know. I'm sorry.

ANDREA: *(Holding back her tears.)* Sorry? You still haven't answered my question! I want to know who he was! I want you to *tell* me, you two-timing son-of-a-bitch!

JASON: Andrea I *can't.*

ANDREA: You mean you *won't!* And that's why I've tied you to the bedposts! That's why I'm not letting you go!

JASON: If you feel this way, if you really think I cheated on you, why haven't you divorced me? Or gotten an annulment?

ANDREA: Oh no! No no no no no! That's too easy. I'll torture you the way you've tortured *me* with your lies. In matters of revenge Jason, *timing* is everything.

JASON: If you only knew the truth.

ANDREA: That's what I'm trying to find out! The *truth!* Now for the last time! What was his name?

JASON: I SAID I *CAN'T!*

ANDREA: You mean there've been so many you can't even remember?

JASON: I don't *like* men. You k*now* that.

ANDREA: You could've kept this all a secret you know. Gotten rid of it and spared my feelings and this whole mess. You've had so many operations, why not one more little procedure?

JASON: I didn't get an abortion because we talked about having kids anyway. Getting a donor. Raising a child together. Wasn't that the plan?

ANDREA: It wasn't only the plan, Jason. It was the *dream.* I wanted the white picket fence. A bungalow on Main Street. A Labradoodle.

JASON: We can still have the dream, Andrea. We can *raise* this child.

ANDREA: I won't raise a child with a man who's unfaithful to me!

JASON: So what do we do with the baby, then? Once it's born?

ANDREA: Well. I guess we'll put it up for adoption. And *then* I'll divorce you. *(Jason's cellphone rings. Andrea grabs it.)*

JASON: Hey that's *my* phone!

ANDREA: *(Reacting to caller ID.)* It's *HER* again! I told you not to give her your number!

(Answering.)

What gives Oprah . . . ?! Shouldn't your rep be calling to discuss this . . . ? The "Pregnant Man" story is a little *tired* don't you think . . . you *did* it already OKAY!? — Yeah well up your ass *too* bitch!!

(Disconnects.)

Someone needs to *stop* that woman!

JASON: Was she calling about the follow-up?

ANDREA: What else?

JASON: But I already committed to it!

ANDREA: Well say ta-ta to fame!

JASON: *(Another contraction.)* Ah Ah AHH AHHHHH AHHHHHHHHH! GOOODD GOOODDDDD!

(Crying; trying to catch breath.)

Oh oh oh oh . . . They're getting closer now. You've got to get me to a hospital. You don't want to hurt an innocent baby do you?

ANDREA: I'm a registered nurse who works in a maternity ward Jason! I think I know how to deliver a goddamned baby!

JASON: I need an epidural!

ANDREA: No.

JASON: Pethadine? Diamorphine? Something!

ANDREA: Sorry. And wipe that pout off your face. You deserve this!

JASON: No, Andrea. I don't. I don't. Please. Let's do this the *right* way.

ANDREA: This is the *only* way, Jason. Unless you tell me. Now out with it or I won't let you go!

JASON: No, Andrea!

(To get him to reveal the truth, Andrea starts to tickle Jason's feet, one foot then the other. She'll soon pounce on the bed and meanly tickle Jason, who squirms in pain.)

ANDREA: Tell me . . . Tell me. Tell me . . . Tell me tell me tell me who did you screw behind my back you little scumbag!

JASON: No No Don't Don't St st stop Ow ow ow no no no That hurts!

ANDREA: Tell me!

JASON: Y-y-you don't want to to know! S-s-s-stop it please! Ah ah ah Oh god stop!

ANDREA: TELL ME! TELL ME OR I SWEAR I'LL TICKLE YOU TO DEATH!

JASON: Please just try to to to Don't make me I-I-I've got to AH I SAID STOP! ALRIGHT! ALRIGHT!

(Andrea stops tickling. A standoff.)

Alright.

(Gasping for breath; spent.)

You're going to hate me for this. But don't say I didn't warn you.

ANDREA: *Out with it!*

JASON: O-o-o-OK . . . Re-re-remember last Thanksgiving when you went to visit your brother in Denver?

ANDREA: How could I forget? When I got back, a thousand dollars was missing.

JASON: *(Difficult to tell this.)* While you were gone, a a pipe broke in the upstairs apartment. Water was pouring in everywhere. I mean it it was like a flash-flood in here. And so I-I call the super and and and he sends over this plumber.

ANDREA: Plumber? Why didn't you tell me? *That's* probably who stole my money!

JASON: No no just *listen* a second . . . So the plumber comes over and he keeps pointing to the ceiling and laughing and saying *"Mucho Agua! Es muy malo!"* And with no complaint he sops up the mess and replaces the tiles and installs new pipes and —

ANDREA: I didn't ask for a recap of "Bathroom 911"!

JASON: *(Spanish said without accent.)* But the super had to turn off the heat for the repairs. It's so cold that the windows are frosting over and we can even see our own breath. So I ask the plumber, *"Vino rojo?"* And he says, *"Si! Vino rojo. Con mucho gusto!"*

ANDREA: You got him *drunk*?!

JASON: One glass. No it was two. We each had *two* small glasses of red wine and got to talking about stuff. About Columbia.

ANDREA: He goes to Columbia?

JASON: No he's *from* Columbia. And we talked about his family and how he had no money, no *dinero* to send back home to his parents. And we sort of . . . hit it off . . . speaking our, our Spanglish together.

ANDREA: How cozy! Or should I say, "How cozito!"?

JASON: So without even realizing what was happening, this quite virile and amazing looking young man and I were . . . flirting.

ANDREA: *How* amazing?

JASON: What?

ANDREA: How amazing looking was he?

JASON: You know that Jesus guy that Madonna is "dating?"

ANDREA: *(Hurt and jealous.)* You had sex with a pin-up model in *our* bed?! An *immigrant* no less?!

JASON: I prefer the term "undocumented worker."

ANDREA: *(Accusatory.)* I prefer the term *Puta*!

JASON: No it wasn't . . . it wasn't *vulgar* like you're thinking. It's was . . . exploratory.

ANDREA: "Space" is exploratory, Jason! "Surgery" is exploratory. But "procreation" between consenting adults is simply meiosis. Biology!

JASON: Anyway we're finishing our wine and suddenly I just blurt out, *(Imperfect Spanish.)*

"Yo quiero ser un hombre con una mujer." I want to be a man with a woman. And he laughed and said, *"Entiendo."* I understand. So then I said, *"Ayudame."* Help me. And he said sweetly, boyishly, *"Seguro. Cuantos?"*

ANDREA: *"Cuantos."* That means "how much."

JASON: I thought a thousand dollars was a pretty reasonable offer.

ANDREA: *AAAAHHHHHI'MGOINGTOKILLYOUUUU!* THAT MONEY WAS FOR OUR HONEY *MOOON!* We were aiming for Paris and wound up in Paramus!

JASON: I thought that Holiday Inn on Route 17 was quite nice.

ANDREA: The point is you *paid* him like a prostitute! With *my* money! And you didn't even use protection!

JASON: Rodrigo said —

ANDREA: So you *do* know his name!

JASON: He said, *"Un bebe no es posible. Soy impotente!"*

ANDREA: Well obviously he *wasn't* "impotente!" He could have had a dis*ease*! He could have had Swine *Flu*! — So where is he now?

JASON: He got deported.

ANDREA: That's not *fair*!

JASON: No. I agree our government really should step up to the plate and allow those people to—

ANDREA: THAT'S NOT WHAT I *MEANT*!

JASON: Don't be upset.

ANDREA: Don't tell me not to be upset! My husband's baby's *father* is an illegal alien plumber!

(Andrea turns away, broken. Silence.)

JASON: *(Tenderly.)* Didn't you say on our wedding night how much our lovemaking had improved? Didn't you say I was the manliest man you'd ever been with? Didn't you say you felt safe and warm in my arms? That my kisses had grown more tender with time? That my touch was even kinder with each passing day?

ANDREA: *(Pause: remembering fondly, slowly.)* Yes. Yes I did, didn't I? On our wedding night. On Route 17 . . . Because . . . because it was . . . *true.* I meant it. Every word. But now everything's —

(Andrea listens. She grows compassionate, taking in Jason's every heartfelt word.)

JASON: Better. Everything's *better.* — I did something *strange* Andrea: I had a sexual experience with a member of what was *once* the opposite sex. I'd never slept with a *man* before. You *know* that.

ANDREA: Then *why*?

JASON: I was intimate with Rodrigo to better understand a man's body. For *your* sake.

ANDREA: For my — ?

JASON: Yes.

ANDREA: You mean you did all that to . . . to please *me*?

JASON: To *love* you. And to be more secure with who I'm actually becoming.

ANDREA: Who you're be*com*ing.

JASON: Who I *am.*

ANDREA: Who you . . . *Oh!*

JASON: Who *we* are. Rodrigo truly taught me . . . how to be a *man.* I wish he were here now. I'd like to thank him.

(Long pause as Andrea considers: recognition. Then, through her tears she remembers:)

ANDREA: *(Slowly.)* "Love is the river that washes away the scourge of everyday hatred."

(Pause.)

Oh Jason . . . Oh no . . . Oh God . . . I've been . . . I've been such a fool!

(Goes to him; melting.)

Can you *ever* forgive me?

JASON: No. Can you ever forgive *me*? For being too scared to tell you sooner. For fear that you'd leave me forever.

ANDREA: I won't ever leave you. You truly *are* the most remarkable person I've ever met! From the very first time I saw you on the M41 reading *A Room of One's Own*, I knew we were meant to be together.

JASON: Andrea? — Can, can you unfasten the restraints?

ANDREA: *(Darting up; realizing!)* What?! Oh dear! Oh my! I'm so — !

(Unfastening the restraints.)

I-I-I have to get you to a hospital!

JASON: No . . . I think it's too late.

ANDREA: No we'll leave right now.

JASON: *(Overlapping.) (A contraction; agonizing.)* No it's too It's too Ah Ah Ah AH AH AHHHHHHH! *AHHHHHHHHHHH!* IT'S COMING ANDREA! THE BABY! IT'S COMING!

ANDREA: *(Overlapping.) (Frenzied, forced now to deal with the baby.)*

OH! OH NO! NOT! OH DEAR! OH! JUST BREATHE. JUST BREATHE. AND PUSH!

(Andrea grabs a few of the white towels. She aids Jason as he ad-lib's his pain. Jason breathes and pushes.)

Don't worry my love! The water's boiling!

(Puts on a pair of latex gloves, stands between Jason's legs and prepares to deliver.)

C'mon! THAT A *BOY! PUSH!!* JUST BREATHE! PUSH . . . ! *PUSH!* That's it! *PUUUSSSSHH!* I love you darling!

JASON: *(Agonizing: the worst and loudest one!)* I — LOOOOVE — YOUU-UU — *TOOOOOOOOOOOOOOOOOOOOO!*

(Blackout.)

END OF PLAY

Ladybug Gonna Getcha

Kara Lee Corthron

Produced at the Ensemble Studio Theatre's Going to the River Festival, September 10 to 27, 2009 (full festival). Producing Artistic Director: Elizabeth Van Dyke. Cast: Ladybug — Toks Olagundoye; Cockroach — Adam Couperthwaite. Director: Pat Golden.

CHARACTERS

LADYBUG, well past her prime . . . for a rocker (somewhere in her thirties), desperate for her big break. She's from Queens and a woman of color, ideally African American.

COCKROACH: Ladybug's manager, oily as his hair. Younger than she is (late twenties to early thirties.). He speaks with a thick Bronx accent though he may secretly hail from Greenwich, Connecticut. This is a white dude.

ANNOUNCER: a voice-over recording, which sounds like the guy that announces the prizes on "Wheel of Fortune."

NOTE

Certain lines of dialogue do not end with a punctuation mark and this means that the thought keeps moving until there is a punctuation mark, i.e. no internal pauses — this play moves fast.

PLACE

A notorious, yet beloved rock club in the East Village of New York City.

TIME

Two years into Jimmy Carter's presidency.

• • •

Lights up on Ladybug in a filthy, disgusting, backstage dressing room. The wall containing one single, cracked mirror, should be covered in graffiti. Ladybug stares at herself in the mirror. From beyond the dressing room, the sounds of random rock music and general loud cavorting can be heard. Ladybug brushes her big wig (the wig's colors should be off-putting; perhaps platinum blonde with black stripes) and freshens her makeup. Ladybug is a giant, punk wannabe, but with some discordant elements thrown in: i.e. black lipstick, glitter eye shadow; baby doll dress with the anarchy symbol spray-painted across the front; fishnet stockings with silver platforms. Be creative: She's a mess.

LADYBUG: *(To herself in the mirror, speaking:)*
Look at you — with your long eyelashes and your healed-up rashes.
You're a star

'Bug.
It's a coups — with your shaven fanny, it's really uncanny!
You're a star
'Bug!

ANNOUNCER: *(Off Stage voice.) (The Announcer only exists in Ladybug's head.)* It is my unparalleled joy to introduce you to our next, most fabulous, most perfect performer! You may remember her from such films as *Satan, My Love, Snuff it Like You Mean it,* and countless other masterpieces not intended for distribution in the United States, Canada, or the British Isles. Well, here she is again! Three-time participant of Alphabet City's Sharon Tate Look-a-like Contest — Heeeeeeeere's LADYBUG!!!! *(The first few notes of the "Overture" from "Gypsy" are played, then cut out abruptly as:)*

LADYBUG: *(Singing with all grave seriousness and not the best voice:)*
My fa-vor-ite
My fa-vor-ite
My fa-vor-ite
Thing is a ta-ta-ta taco.
Taco!
My fa-vor-ite
My fa-vor-ite
My fa-vor-ite
Thing is a ta-ta-ta taco.
Taco!
With guacamole
With guacamole
And pepper jack cheese
I'm on my knees
This taste is hol-ay.
Hol-ay.
I said hol —
(Ladybug attempts to hit a high screechy note and her voice cracks horribly. Cockroach enters.)
Dammit! I was so close —

COCKROACH: 's OK, babe.

LADYBUG: It's just hittin' that high C

COCKROACH: You dunno nothin' about no high C don't even worry about it.

LADYBUG: I wanna be on pitch

COCKROACH: Make it loud and fast, this crowd won't care if you spurt High-C outcha anis.

LADYBUG: Speaking of liquids, Sam from the butcher shop collected a gallon a pig's blood for me in this pail.

COCKROACH: That's real swell, babe. Where's the rest a the band?

LADYBUG: Huffin' glue. That's their new warm-up. Anyways, I was figurin' Jerry could dump the piggie's blood on my head at the end of "Pork Me" as a clever double entendre, but also as a reference to that Carrie movie so that I'm makin' a statement.

COCKROACH: Again with the statements?

LADYBUG: No, it's a good one, Roachie. It's like a fuckoff to all proms and prom queens and anybody who likes that shit. And then I thought I'd borrow your gun —

COCKROACH: You're not touchin' my gun

LADYBUG: But fill it with blanks

COCKROACH: You're not touchin' my gun

LADYBUG: And pretend to shoot my head off for the finale.

COCKROACH: You didn't rehearse that.

LADYBUG: I just thought of it like thirty seconds ago! I gotta stand out tonight!

COCKROACH: Fuck all a that noise! You're the Queen a the East Village. You don't need no lousy gimmicks.

LADYBUG: You know, that is true.

I was just lookin' at myself in the mirror and, Roachie, I looked so damn good, I got a little moist.

COCKROACH: Hot

LADYBUG: I feel good

COCKROACH: Babe

LADYBUG: I feel excited

COCKROACH: *Babe!*

LADYBUG: I feel like — ya know — the sexiest bitch around!

COCKROACH: Yeah.

LADYBUG: Like — ya know — Cheryl Ladd's prettier sister!

COCKROACH: Yeah!

LADYBUG: Like — ya know — my pussy is tighter than the Tin Man's asshole!

COCKROACH: Settle down.

LADYBUG: Decca Records. This is it. This is my last shot. They have to see

COCKROACH: They got eyes

LADYBUG: They have to believe

COCKROACH: They *will* believe

LADYBUG: That I am the planet's greatest undiscovered star and I alone can save their fledgling label. No more failures. No more giggin' at Polish food fairs or Wiccan weddings. Tonight, *I* — I mean "we," I mean . . . the band. Tonight the band will finally get the respect we deserve.

COCKROACH: You sure are somethin'.

(Ladybug makes a kiss sound at herself in the mirror and heads for the exit.)

There's just one thing.

(Ladybug freezes.)

LADYBUG: What thing? There is no thing that can extinguish me. I am on fire, my dear cockroach. 4 alarm!

COCKROACH: I know, but —

LADYBUG: No "thing!" Decca Records, bitch! Decca Records!

COCKROACH: Last minute schedule change. Teeny thing.

LADYBUG: How teeny?

COCKROACH: You guys have to follow Blondie.

(Dead silence.)

LADYBUG: But but but but but . . . That's simply not possible! *You* told me they had a gig in Pittsburgh. *You* told me they'd be far, far, *far* away!

COCKROACH: Cancelled. Blizzard.

LADYBUG: But but but but but . . . We cannot go after them! We'll look —

COCKROACH: Terrible!

LADYBUG: Cockroach!

COCKROACH: Like amateurs.

LADYBUG: You're my fuckin' MANAGER! You're s'posed ta protect me from things like this!

COCKROACH: Well — you all — especially *you*, babe. You know you're my number one

LADYBUG: I know I'm the best thing you have.

COCKROACH: Believe me: I did everything in my power to make sure you'd be playin' here on a Blondie-free night. But what can I tell ya? It snowed.

LADYBUG: I AM the world's most magnificent undiscovered star. I have no doubts about this.

However, Blondie? *Her?* How can I compete with that?

COCKROACH: There's the rub. Her voice is amazing

LADYBUG: Not helping

COCKROACH: And that *face*. It is *so* pretty. She's like a goddamn angel!

LADYBUG: Punk is not supposed to be pretty!!!!

COCKROACH: Don't get upset, babe. You don't have to be pretty to compete wit her. You gotcha own thing. A flair.

LADYBUG: A flair? In case ya ain't noticed, I'm aging. *Larry.*

COCKROACH: Don't get personal.

LADYBUG: I *need* a record deal! I need my face on the cover of *Rolling Stone*, my home full of Warhol-esque sychophants, my daily life invaded by the paparazzi. And I need these things NOW. For fuck sake, the seventies are almost over! What if the eighties are all futuristic and mathematic and white and sterile and shit?! I ain't sterile, Roachie! I'll never make it.

COCKROACH: You're clean enough.

(Beat.)

LADYBUG: Blondie. God help me they're so fucking commercial. I'm not. I'm just too hard to categorize. And I refuse to alter my artistic vision to fit some pencil-dick executive's marketing ideas. It's a conundrum, Cockroach.

(Tragic:) It is torment to know how sublime I am when no one else sees it. How do I make people understand that if they'd only give me a chance, it would be obvious that I am far better then they are.

COCKROACH: You know, they say superiority complexes can give ya hemorrhoids.

LADYBUG: Only for the deluded.

COCKROACH: Let's be real: you ain't the best singer out there or the best face. But you ain't so bad, babe. Not if I squint a little. And maybe if you laid off the tacos for awhile —

(Ladybug grabs Cockroach by his collar as she howls in fury. It is a long and earth-shattering howl and it ROCKS! She stops and everything is silent. For a moment, even the music and ruckus in the club ceases.)

COCKROACH: Holy shit.

LADYBUG: Was that *me*?

COCKROACH: *(Genuine shock:)* Oh my God. You have talent.

LADYBUG: Yeah.

COCKROACH: Did you swallow Annie Wilson? 'Cuz babe, you are a SIREN!

LADYBUG: I AM a siren!

COCKROACH: I mighta misjudged you.

(Beat. The noise beyond resumes.)

LADYBUG: With great belt voice, comes great responsibility.

COCKROACH: Huh?

LADYBUG: What the Hell? I'll be the bigger person. I am clearly a force of astonishing proportions. I can tango with a lil' Jersey girl.

COCKROACH: Sure ya can.

LADYBUG: But I have my pride.

COCKROACH: Can't deny that.

LADYBUG: I will not, under any bullshit circumstances, share my dressin' room with her.

COCKROACH: Of course not!

LADYBUG: And YOU will announce me tonight. Not some hophead, wannabe comedian.

COCKROACH: No question.

LADYBUG: And — just for tonight, Roachie, just for tonight — we are not the Lesbian Marsupial Experiment.

COCKROACH: You changin' the name a the band?!

LADYBUG: No, darling.

(A big ol' flip of the hair.)

Tonight, we are *Ladybug* . . . and the Lesbian Marsupial Experiment.

COCKROACH: Aw, babe. You got real class.

LADYBUG: Thank you. I know.

Why don't you run along and round up the others? I need a few moments of "me" time.

(Cockroach starts to leave, but turns back.)

COCKROACH: I just wanna say: workin' wit you is a real joy. You know? I mean, even if tonight — even if this end's up bein' what they call a swan song for youse guys? Just know, babe, just know that I truly value you. You got somethin' special.

(Beat. Cockroach pats his hair helmet in the mirror. Ladybug stares at him.)

LADYBUG: You sold me out. Didn't ya?

COCKROACH: *What*? Babe! Thass thass crazy talk!

LADYBUG: This "last minute schedule change." Wasn't no accident, was it?

(Cockroach quickly kisses Ladybug on the mouth. It's kinda creepy and not at all sensual.)

COCKROACH: You know I love ya. You're bein' paranoid.

LADYBUG: *(Desperate:)* I'm the brightest star you got!

(Cockroach nods.)

COCKROACH: *(To himself:)* For now.

(As he begins to exit:) Just get out there and do your best, babe. Thass all anyone can ask of ya.

(This is a dagger in the gut!)

LADYBUG: *(Roar:)* My — *best?!*

(We hear the opening chords of "One Way Or Another" on stage. The crowd loses its mind!)

COCKROACH: Jesus they can work a crowd!

(Ladybug can't take it. Suddenly, she rips open Cockroach's jacket, pulls out his gun and runs on stage. Shots are heard followed by screaming and pandamonium from the club.)

(Blackout.)

(Lights up: same night, a bit later. Cockroach and Ladybug sit in a brightly lit room, hands cuffed behind their backs. They face forward. Ladybug's wig is gone and her makeup is streaking all over her face. Long silence. Then:)

COCKROACH: I can't believe you shot Debbie Harry.

LADYBUG: You should know by now, Roachie. Never cross a Scorpio with Leo tendencies.

COCKROACH: *You killed Blondie!*

LADYBUG: Make sure to ask the peace officer for a copy of my mug shot. It screams punk. Perfect album cover. After a little air brushing. And fuck Decca Records. I'm an international headline. Time to talk to Columbia.

COCKROACH: You're gonna fry. I'll see to it.

ANNOUNCER: *(Off Stage voice.)* She's back, Ladies and Gentleman! After an extended vacation on New York City's lovely Riker's Island, back with a full-body tan, that naughty, naughty girl you just can't help but love — heeeeeeeere's . . .

(Announcer sharply cuts out.)

LADYBUG: I am a *star.*

(Smash to black.)

END OF PLAY

A Modest Proposal

STEVE KOPPMAN

A Modest Proposal was produced by PianoFight Productions as part of its ShortLived 2.0 festival from April 17, 2009 through May 23, 2009, at the Off-Market Theater, Studio 250, 965 Mission Street, San Francisco, California. The festival lasted from April through June, in six rounds. This play was featured in rounds 2, 3 and 4 of the festival. Director: Eric Reid. Cast: She — Christy Crowley; He — Rob Ready.

CHARACTERS

HE AND SHE, both thirties.

SETTING

A bedroom. Night.

• • •

Scene: A man and a woman are lying in a large bed. She has her eyes closed, apparently sleeping or trying to. He is awake. He sighs. She turns over. Long pause. He sighs again. She turns over violently.
Pause. He sighs again.

SHE: What is it?

(Pause. He sighs again.)

SHE: *(Eyes still closed.)* WHAT?

HE: What do you mean?

SHE: What is it?

HE: What is what?

SHE: Why are you sighing?

HE: *(Looking off into distance.)* Oh, I don't know.

(Long pause. He sighs again.)

SHE: *(Angrily.)* What is it?

(Long pause.)

HE: It's just — I'm having these feelings.

SHE: Feelings?

HE: Yeah —

SHE: What kind of feelings?

HE: They're kind of — *(Pause.)* —

SHE: What?

(Pause.)

HE: Inchoate. They're kind of — *(Pause.)* inchoate.

SHE: I mean, are — inchoate — feelings — a good reason to keep me up all night?

HE: *(Sighing.)* No. *(Pause.)* No. I'm sorry. I didn't — realize —

(Pause. He sighs again.)

SHE: STOP! *(Pause.)* Do you want to say anything more about these feelings?

HE: *(Nodding.)* They're really, really — inchoate.

SHE: *(Turning over.)* Can we talk about this tomorrow?

HE: I guess.

(Pause. He sighs loudly.)

SHE: WHAT IS IT?

(Pause.)

HE: It's just — I just wonder — sometimes — if — I'm — really — fully — living.

SHE: What do you mean?

HE: I mean — We don't want to live our lives and — find — at the end — we haven't — really lived.

SHE: No.

(He sighs.)

SHE: *(Totally losing it.)* STOP THAT!

HE: I'm sorry.

SHE: What is this about? I mean — in what way are you afraid you aren't living? What do you have to do?

(Pause.)

HE: I think it's — somehow — about — *(Pause.)* people.

SHE: People.

HE: All real living is meeting, right?

SHE: Maybe.

HE: So it has to be that our most profound concerns are about — the nature of our being — in relationship with — people.

SHE: What do you mean? What — people — are you suddenly so concerned about being — "in relationship" — with?

HE: I don't know — *(Pause.)* well — different — *(Pause.)* people.

SHE: So there isn't any particular variety of people you have in mind?

(Long pause.)

HE: *(Nodding.)* Women.

SHE: *(Her eyes finally opening decisively:)* Women?

HE: Yes. *(Pause.)* I know you understand. It's just — I feel like — I haven't — *(Struggling.)*

SHE: What kind of — I mean — what is it you want? You suddenly want to get to know women better?

HE: Yeah.

SHE: Like, relate to them, really understand them better?

HE: Well, sure. I mean, that's part of being — in relationship. *(Pause.)* I mean, really, though, not so much, though. I'm not fanatical about that.

SHE: So what is it?

(He sighs.)

So — you don't *(Pause.)* want to — *(Pause.)* just, for example — *(Pause.)* fuck them?

(Pause. He sighs.)

HE: Oh, I don't know.

SHE: You don't know?

HE: I would never put it that way.

SHE: But you do want to fuck them?

HE: Not in so many words.

SHE: But you do?

(Pause.)

HE: Yes.

(Pause.)

SHE: Any particular women?

HE: Oh, no. No. Certainly not. No one in particular.

SHE: Just women — in general?

HE: I don't know. *(Pause.)* Maybe.

SHE: You want me to fuck other men — in general? *(Pause.)* Or in particular?

HE: Can't we keep this about me, please?

(Pause.)

SHE: Well, how many women do you all of a sudden want to fuck?

HE: I don't know how you would exactly put a number to it.

SHE: As many as you can get your hands on?

(Pause.)

HE: That's probably as good an estimate as I've heard.

SHE: OK. So, now that I've heard this deep, important, sublime thought, can I go back to sleep? *(Positioning herself to go back to sleep.)*

(Pause.)

HE: *(Sighing.)* I mean, though, we all have to remember: Life is an ongoing process.

SHE: WHAT?

HE: Just what I said. I just mean, it's a function of time.

SHE: But what do you mean?

HE: Time has no beginning and no end, right?

SHE: It doesn't? What? *(Pause.)* So? Oh, my God. What more can go wrong tonight?

HE: I'm just saying, things can't necessarily be rightly conceived of as starting or ending at one particular moment.

SHE: WHAT?

HE: In other words: Life is a river.

SHE: A river?

HE: Time can't be looked at as inherently a totally fixed and independent variable. It's all part of the larger — process.

(Pause.)

SHE: You mean you've already fucked as many women as you could get your hands on?

HE: No, no. *(Pause.)* Not — as many.

SHE: But some.

HE: Quite a few.

SHE: But you want more?

(Pause.)

HE: Yes.

SHE: Many — more?

(Pause.)

HE: Yes. Yes.

SHE: So who have you fucked?

HE: That's not what it's about at all.

SHE: What do you mean?

HE: No one benefits from excavating the past. Hashing over all the dreary details. That's not what it's about. Not at all.

SHE: Who?

HE: You're missing the whole point. This isn't what I'm trying to get across to you.

SHE: WHO HAVE YOU FUCKED? I WANT TO KNOW! WHO? WHO? WHO?

HE: You're sounding like an owl. Please stop.

SHE: *(Attacking him physically.)* Tell me who they are!

HE: You don't even know all of them.

SHE: So tell me some of them.

HE: I can't even remember all their names. Don't you see, that's not the issue.

SHE: What is the issue? Who have you fucked? Tell me their names!

HE: Rachel, Carla, Sara *(At this point actor should simply repeat every female first name he can think of, at least dozens, one after the other, in no particular order, ending with:)* But it was nothing.

SHE: *(At wit's end.)* I cannot believe this. Where am I in all this? What about me?

HE: Why are we always talking about you?

SHE: We're not!

HE: Doesn't it sometimes seem like it? Can't we concentrate on one thing at a time?

SHE: One thing affects other things! What are you talking about? How would you feel if I went out fucking other men?

HE: I could understand your wanting to do that.

SHE: But how would you feel?

HE: I don't know. That would depend. If you could do it in the same spirit — as me.

SHE: What do you mean?

HE: What I do has nothing to do with our relationship. *(Pause.)* We've been together — for what, eleven years now? And you didn't have the slighest idea till this moment.

SHE: How would you feel if I went out and fucked everyone in the whole wide world?

HE: How would you ever do that?

SHE: I don't know. But I promise you — I will try.

HE: You can't. So you're going to pick and choose.

SHE: I will try!

HE: Would you still stay with me?

SHE: I don't know.

HE: You see, there's the difference! It means something totally different to you than it does to me. *(Pause.)* What I've done has no impact on our relationship. What you would do would totally destroy our relationship.

SHE: *(Overlapping.)* No impact — ?

HE: No. I was just hoping — desperately — for some understanding from you. I wanted to talk to you about it. I want for you to know me. I really do want to be closer to you. I want you to really truly understand me. The way I really am. Deep down. In my heart. I just so desperately want us to really, truly understand each other.

SHE: Let me just go back to sleep, OK? Maybe we'll get up tomorrow and we can both agree this was all a bad dream.
(She lies back down and appears to be preparing to go to sleep. Pause.)
And you think — what you're telling me — has no impact on our relationship.

HE: *(Frustrated beyond endurance.)* Oh, God! It's my fault. I shouldn't have talked about it. Maybe I'm just no good. But I love you. I really do. What I want from other girls has nothing at all to do with us. You've got to understand that! That's absolutely crucial to your really understanding what I'm about. It really is. I love you.

SHE: OK, look. I'll try to understand. I don't now. This whole subject makes me feel like throwing up blood. But I am too tired and too depressed right now to even do that.

(Pause.)

HE: Look — if it makes you feel better: You want to get married tomorrow?

(Pause.)

SHE: I can't. Tomorrow I'm going to go out and fuck everyone in the entire world.

(Pause.)

HE: How about Wednesday?

(Pause.)

SHE: *(Pulling blanket over head.)* Let me get back to you.

END OF PLAY

Mrs. Jansen Isn't Here Now

STEVEN KORBAR

Mrs. Jansen Isn't Here Now premiered as part of the Spring Eatfest in February 2009 at the TADA Theatre in New York City. Director: Vivian Meisner. Cast: Mary Margaret — Elizabeth Bell; Chris — Dan Barnhill.

CHARACTERS

MARY MARGARET, thirty to forty. Tough, tawdry and provocatively dressed. Appears to be a little drunk.

CHRIS, thirty to forty. Handsome and athletically built, but seems fragile and unsure of himself. His clothing is a bit out of date.

SETTING

A cheap bar late at night.

• • •

Chris, a handsome, though rather unfashionably dressed man in his thirties is standing at a bar nursing, a drink. He seems shy to the point of fragility. Down the bar is Mary Margaret; also thirties. She is dressed rather provocatively, has a whisky soaked voice and looks like she's been around more than once. She is huddled over her drink, a little sloshed.

CHRIS: *(A long moment to build up his courage.)* Hi . . .

MARY MARGARET: *(Turning to him slowly, completely dead pan.)* . . . Ya think? *(Turns away.)*

CHRIS: . . . Would it be, I mean, is it, could I . . . would you mind if I bought you a drink?

MARY MARGARET: *(Looking him up and down.)* Just off the slacks alone, I'm thinking no.

CHRIS: *(Nervously.)* That's alright. I understand. I just thought since we were both alone.

MARY MARGARET: You're alone. I'm in a long term, committed relationship with this Vodka Gimlet.

CHRIS: That's cute. You have a very nice sense of humor.

MARY MARGARET: Yeah, why don't you just go share the hilarity with somebody to your right.

CHRIS: My name's Chris, by the way.

MARY MARGARET: Mine's Mary Margaret; you can remember it cause it rhymes with 'Bye-bye'.

CHRIS: *(Smiling to himself.)* Mary Margaret. I don't mean to laugh; it's just that that's really very ironic. Somehow I'm betting you must be a Catholic.

MARY MARGARET: And exactly what business is that of yours?

CHRIS: None, none at all. Not anymore.

MARY MARGARET: *(Loudly.)* And just when was I ever your business!? I don't know you from Adam. I don't need you bothering me. What are you, some kind of stalker? A girl can't even go out for a drink without . . .

CHRIS: No, no please; don't get angry. I didn't mean that you were my business. I wasn't talking about that. I was . . . what I was talking about is . . . Catholicism.

MARY MARGARET: *(Stopped. A little befuddled.)* So what are you telling me; you work at one of those 'big box' stores that cater to people with twelve kids?

CHRIS: No.

MARY MARGARET: You're connected with that Pinkberry shop in the Valley, where the Virgin Mary's face suddenly appeared in the frozen yogurt? *(Chris shakes his head.)*

MARY MARGARET: *(Continued.)* Well I know you're not the Pope; he wears a funny hat.

CHRIS: No. No, I am hardly his Holiness, that's for sure. I can guarantee you they wouldn't let the likes of me anywhere near the Vatican at this point. The closest I ever came was St. Andrews over in the Valley. That was my Parish.

MARY MARGARET: *(Joking.)* So what are you trying to say; that you're some kind of a priest or something?

CHRIS: *(Solemnly.)* No. No, I'm not. I'm saying that I was. Up until about six weeks ago.

MARY MARGARET: . . . You were a priest?

CHRIS: Yes. I was. Until I decided it was better for everybody that I leave.

MARY MARGARET: *(Looking around the room.)* . . . Boy . . . slooooow night . . . you aren't just screwing with me, are you?

CHRIS: No.

MARY MARGARET: I mean you're a real priest; not like from one of those crackpot, splinter groups waiting up in the hills for spaceships to take 'em to Jesus?

CHRIS: No.

MARY MARGARET: So a real, honest to God, Roman Catholic priest? Just like the kind I had when I was in parochial school.

(Looking him over, becoming more interested.)

The kind who would hear our sins and make us ashamed of our raging adolescent hormones and all us girls would follow around the playground and giggle about behind your backs and fill us with so much fear and awe and . . . all the rest of that?

CHRIS: I suppose so.

MARY MARGARET: And now here you are; stripped of your vestments. Just like any other man. And you're reduced to sitting in a crummy bar late at night desperately trying to pick up strange women.

CHRIS: *(Terribly Shamed.)* Yes. I guess that that's the truth of it. I can see that I've upset you. I'm sorry. I won't make you suffer my presence any longer. I'll go.

(Beginning to go.)

MARY MARGARET: *(Grabbing his arm like a shot.)* No. I mean, you don't have to leave just because I'm here. Of course as a Catholic, I'm shocked and sickened by what you've done. But, I mean really, what the hell can I do; this ain't the Reformation. You can still finish your drink.

CHRIS: I'm almost done anyway.

MARY MARGARET: OK, ease off. Enough with the high pressure. If you really want to buy me a Gimlet I won't stop you. I don't want to make your debasement any worse.

CHRIS: *(Plaintively.)* I know that I did this all wrong. I apologize. I went into the seminary very young; I've never had any experience with the secular world. I'm afraid that I'm really just completely helpless and naive. I know that must seem very funny to you.

MARY MARGARET: *(A low, extremely lascivious chuckle.)*

CHRIS: I'm very embarrassed and humiliated. I just can't believe that I'm in this place, that I've come to this, that I . . .

(On the verge of tears.)

will you excuse me a minute, I've got to go to the . . .

(Exits quickly.)

MARY MARGARET: *(Waits a moment, then pulls out her cell phone and dials. Very excited.)* Hi, it's me. Oh my God, I am having the best night! I can hardly even believe it, Gene; every filthy, schoolgirl sex dream I ever had just walked through the door and sat down next to me in front of the Pabst Blue Ribbon sign! No I'm not overdoing it as usual, this is the big one; the Super Lotto of dirty, sacrilegious wish fullfillment! My all-time favorite sexual fantasy thrown directly into my waiting lap; seducing a spiritually conflicted, yet undeniably heterosexual Catholic priest! Why is that my all-time fantasy? Why do you think it is ya dumbbell, because I'm a Catholic, that's why!

(Looks for Chris.)

Oh, OK, OK, I'm going to go now; we can talk about this more later. Yes, we can go into all the details, but not right now. Right now I'm going to go hit that defrocked badboy like I just caught him stealing from the collection plate — oh my God Gene; this is even better than that dream where I pick up the Amish hitchhiker after his horse goes lame!

CHRIS: *(Entering. More composed.)* Sorry. I apologize for leaving you here like that.

MARY MARGARET: Oh that's alright; you're forgiven

(Giggles; flips open another button on her blouse.)

CHRIS: You've been very kind and patient with me; I want to thank you.

MARY MARGARET: Well you're very welcome Father.

CHRIS: Chris.

MARY MARGARET: Father Chris.

CHRIS: Just plain Chris.

MARY MARGARET: We can work that out later. So, tell me a little about yourself. Where are you from, what are you into, how did you get from the holy alter of God to 'Benny's Zebra Lounge' in six short weeks.

CHRIS: Well, that's a complicated question I'm not sure I can even answer to myself. All I know is I've been on a spiritual journey and at some point along the path I began to suspect I was no longer being really true to myself . . .

MARY MARGARET: Um hmm, uh hmm; and did they let you keep the collar?

CHRIS: . . . Well no; of course it would be completely inappropriate for me to ever wear that again

MARY MARGARET: . . . We can work that out later too.

CHRIS: I guess I just had a crisis of faith, and didn't know what to do with the roiling inner conflict I was forced to deal with.

MARY MARGARET: It looks like maybe you worked a lot of it off in the ole rectory gym.

CHRIS: I didn't know if I could serve God best by leading a congregation or having a family. How to balance my love for Jesus with the love I might feel for a woman.

MARY MARGARET: *(A low, sexy growl.)* Yeah, I bet you know how to make a woman feel like she was Jesus.

CHRIS: I don't know why I'm bothering you with all this. I know it's not your problem. But for some reason I feel like I can trust you.

MARY MARGARET: You are putting yourself in the right hands. In fact, why don't you and I get out of this unholy atmosphere and go some place where we can really talk religion. You know, my apartment is only three blocks from here and the elevator is almost always empty at this time of night . . .

CHRIS: Oh, I don't know.

MARY MARGARET: *(Tempting.)* Oh com'on, it'll be nice; I'll light some candles, poor some wine.

CHRIS: That's always good.

MARY MARGARET: Tell you what, you think about it. And, if you want, when I get back from the ladies room, I'll take you to a place I think that you might really learn to like. My apartment's only five short minutes away . . .

(Seductively.)

and I think I may still have some of my Christmas decoration up . . .

(Exits.)

CHRIS: *(Waits a moment. Then pulls out his cell phone and dials. Very excited.)* Yeah, it's me. Holy crap you were right, it's working like a charm. This tormented ex-priest routine is the biggest pootie magnet you and I have ever come up with! It's amazing; I mean, I've never seen a woman this worked up! All these years, I've wasted my time slogging through foreplay and it turns out all I ever needed was a couple of phrases of reasonably believable Latin-dead language my ass! Of course I'm going to play it through to the end, are you crazy?! If we can find another girl and I can figure out a way to mention Lourdes a couple of times, this could turn into some honest to goodness three-way action! Oh, I gotta sign off now; I think it's about that time. Oh yeah, we're going to talk more about this later. I am telling you, we have hit on a gold mind here; sure thing babe-candy. Holy shit, that St. Thomas Aquinas must have just been beating the chicks off with a stick! Yeah, OK, right, I got you; I'll talk to you later.

(Hangs up.)

(Mary Margaret re-enters looking different. She's buttoned up her blouse, put on a sweater and removed much of her make up.)

CHRIS: *(Continued.) (Again earnest.)* I wasn't sure you would come back. I'm glad . . .

(A bit too dramatic.)

though I would have understood if you'd chosen to shun me

(Turns away.)

MARY MARGARET: Maybe you would have been better off if I had.

CHRIS: Oh no, you are a good and kind woman Mary Margaret. And that is why I know when you bring me back to your place, you will take into account that I am a healthy, athletically built young man who's been celibate since the age of consent and you will let your principles be your guide.

MARY MARGARET: My principles aren't what's been paying my bar tab, padre. Infact, you probably didn't even know that women like me exist. I've been on more men then you've been on bus trips with your grandma. Old men, young men. Poor men, rich men; the undocumented. It doesn't matter. It's just the way I am. I just looked at myself in the ladies room mirror, and thought of you out here waiting for me to wipe that new car smell off a ya and I just couldn't deny it anymore . . . and for the first time in my life . . . I was truly ashamed of myself.

CHRIS: *(A beat. His smile fading.)* . . . Huh?

MARY MARGARET: It made me sick to look at what I've become. After seeing a man who's lived his life on such a high plane, I finally understand how meaningless this stream of sleazy one-night stands really is.

CHRIS: No. No, no. No.

MARY MARGARET: Oh you don't know the kind of perverted things I've let men do to me.

CHRIS: Well, but you could tell me, couldn't you?

MARY MARGARET: Oh no, it's just too depraved.

CHRIS: That's OK. I can keep a secret. For cryin' out loud, I used to be a priest.

MARY MARGARET: But I think that meeting you may be a turning point for me, that it's some kind of a sign to repent.

CHRIS: You know, signs are really a pagan superstition that predate Christianity. Now if we were to go back to your place and kneel in prayer . . .

MARY MARGARET: Oh no, no, I know now that I could never be clean enough for you. You should only be with respectable women.

CHRIS: You know what that kind of thinking is? What that is, is the hypocritical sexual practices of the Church. And that is just really wrong and you should protest that injustice and make up your mind to go on being just as big a skank as you ever were.

MARY MARGARET: Well, I do really think you're right that the Church should modernize some of its thinking.

CHRIS: Yes; modernize. Reform. Vatican II! You know what the real sin is now; abstinence.

MARY MARGARET: But do you really think that God can forgive all the wanton, immoral things I've done?

CHRIS: Yes. This near to closing time; I do.

MARY MARGARET: Well, I guess it is true that Jesus was able to befriend Mary Magdalene despite her sordid past. What is it he says to her in the Bible?

CHRIS: . . . Hey Mary . . .

(Vamping lamely.)

no worries.

MARY MARGARET: Well, I suppose if you really think it's OK, it must be. I mean, you should know.

CHRIS: Yes. Yes.

MARY MARGARET: And you really don't mind about my slutty, whorish past?

CHRIS: Noooo.

MARY MARGARET: And you truly think God could absolve me of my sins?

CHRIS: Absofreakinlutely.

MARY MARGARET: Then I guess it must really be alright for us to be together. If you can accept me the way that I am?

(Chris nods.)

MARY MARGARET: *(Continued.)* Even though I'm a sinner?

(Chris shakes his head.)

MARY MARGARET: *(Continued.)* And a sex addict?

(Chris shakes his head.)

MARY MARGARET: *(Continued.)* And promiscuous and profane and morally bankrupt and preoperative . . .

CHRIS: *(A long beat.)* . . . Huh?

MARY MARGARET: Well don't look so worried, silly; I mean with the injections and everything I'm all but technically a woman.

CHRIS: *(Looks at her for a long beat, then smiles politely.)* . . . Will you excuse me a minute?

(Calmly pulling out his cell phone and dialing. After a moment, Mary Margaret's cell rings. She gives him a look and then answers. Speaking to her over the phone:)

CHRIS: *(Continued.)* Um umm, no, forget it. Doesn't work for me.

MARY MARGARET: Oh, you are just such a weenie. The minute anything even slightly homoerotic comes up, you completely bail on me.

CHRIS: You know how I feel about that stuff.

MARY MARGARET: But it was going so great, Gene.

CHRIS: You know the rules; if you cross the boundaries it's your own fault. We'll just have to start again with something new. What about sexy nurse and appendectomy patient?

MARY MARGARET: Again?

CHRIS: Harry Potter gets private lessons from McGonagall?

MARY MARGARET: We left the wand at home.

CHRIS: What about Hilary and the angry OPEC Oil Minister?

MARY MARGARET: You know, it's getting late, why don't we just call it a night? I've been up since seven and Justin's got T-ball in the morning and I promised the sitter we would be home by eleven.

CHRIS: I know, I've still got the recycling to put out. Oh I alright. I'll just go ahead and pay the check.

(Hanging up his phone. Then teasing a bit.)

Maybe I can at least do that without ruining everything.

MARY MARGARET: *(Hanging up her cell and then immediately redialing.)* Hi Teena? It's Mrs. Jansen. Listen, we're just leaving and we should be home in about twenty minutes. Why don't you call your Mom and tell her that Mr. Jansen will drive you home as soon as we get there, alright? Thanks sweetie, we'll see you soon.

CHRIS: Why do I always have to drive that girl home, she only lives a few blocks away?

MARY MARGARET: Because she's 17 and still doesn't have her permit yet, and she sure can't be walking home at this hour in those skimpy outfits she wears; as if you haven't noticed them.

CHRIS: *(A guilty little chuckle.)* I have no idea what you're referring to.

MARY MARGARET: *(A beat. She looks at Chris for a moment, then effects the breathy voice of a coquettish teenage girl.)* . . . And besides, Mr. Jansen; you're so big and strong and manly, I always feel extra safe whenever I'm around you.

CHRIS: *(A beat, then catching on; smiling.)* Well . . . maybe you shouldn't Teena, a pretty, pretty little girl like you.

MARY MARGARET: Oh Mr. Jansen. What are you saying? I don't understand; I thought you loved your wife.

CHRIS: Oh, I do. Very, very much. I find the woman endlessly amusing. But you know what Teena; Mrs. Jansen isn't here now. It's just you and me. So why don't you be a good girl and go wait for me in the back of the

Mini-van; and if anyone should ask you who I am . . . you just tell them I'm your uncle . . .
(Chris smiles at Mary Margaret, she smiles back.)

END OF PLAY

Public Relations

Andrew Biss

Produced in May of 2009 by The Curan Repertory Company (Ken Terrell, Artistic Director) as part of its Notes from the Underground festival. Director: Gretchen Page. Location: American Theatre of Actors, 314 West 54th Street, New York, New York.

CHARACTERS

SARAH, pleasant, easygoing personality. Thirties/forties.

TIM, affable, gregarious, with a mercurial quality. Twenties/thirties.

SETTING

A city street.

TIME

Late afternoon. The present.

• • •

Tim enters stage left and proceeds to cross stage right. Simultaneously, Sarah enters stage right and crosses stage left. As they pass each other, Tim suddenly stops and turns.

TIM: Wait!

(Sarah continues walking.)

TIM: Wait . . . Sarah?

(Sarah stops and turns.)

SARAH: Yes?

TIM: *(Crossing back towards centre stage.)* Sarah! Good God, it *is* you! Well, I thought it was but . . . well, I wasn't a hundred percent.

SARAH: *(With a smile, somewhat confused.)* Ah!

TIM: Thought I was about to make a total fool of myself — not for the first time, I might add — ha, ha, ha! Well, how on earth are you?

(Sarah slowly crosses back toward Tim, working hard to mask her embarrassment at not being able to place him.)

SARAH: Oh, I'm . . . I'm very well . . . thank you.

TIM: You look well. God, how long has it been?

SARAH: I . . . I'm not sure.

TIM: Well, I can't expect you to remember, but it's certainly been a while, that's for sure.

SARAH: *(Still desperately trying to conceal her embarrassment.)* Yes, it . . . it must've been.

TIM: So, how's Paul?

SARAH: Paul? Oh, he's um . . . he's — he's doing well.

TIM: Good, good. Still working at, uh . . . what's it called?

SARAH: Yes, yes, still there. He's um . . . he's thinking of going back to college, actually — finishing his Masters.

TIM: Good for him. Bit of a strain on you though, no?

SARAH: Well, I'll be the main bread winner for a while, so we'll have to tighten our belts a bit, but . . .

TIM: But worth it in the long run, right?

SARAH: Exactly . . . exactly.

TIM: Give him a bit of a leg up the old corporate ladder.

SARAH: Well, that's exactly it. I mean, the way things are there's not much room for him to advance.

(Tim nods in agreement. Beat.)

TIM: Well, you haven't changed a bit, I must say. Not that it's been *that* long, but you know.

SARAH: *(With a feigned laugh.)* No, no . . . but, um . . . as you say.

(Pause.)

SARAH: So, um . . . how are *you* doing?

TIM: Me? Oh, I'm fine. Can't complain. Well, I could, but who'd listen? Ha, ha, ha!

(Sarah laughs along with him, though not entirely convincingly. Beat.)

SARAH: Well, it's um . . . it's been lovely bumping into you again. Anyway, I'd better —

TIM: Yes, yes, it has. Listen, by the way, whatever happened with that spare room business?

SARAH: Spare room?

TIM: Yes, yes, now let me see . . . as I remember, Paul wanted to turn it into a games room and Justine was hell-bent on converting it into an artist's studio . . . or something like that.

SARAH: Oh, God yes! The spare room fiasco. I thought I'd never hear the end of that one.

TIM: So who won?

SARAH: *(Beginning to relax a little.)* Well, nobody really. We sort of reached an uneasy compromise. For the time being it'll be a games room, which placated Paul and made him feel like he got his way as usual.

TIM: Doesn't he always?

SARAH: Just about. And anyway, it would've been silly turning it into an art studio — I mean, for heaven's sake, Justine's only fourteen; she doesn't know what she wants to do yet.

TIM: Probably want to be an astronaut next week.

SARAH: Well, that's exactly it. *But* we did agree that when she gets closer to leaving school, if she decides she wants to go to art college and study it properly, then Paul's games will be confined to the garage and Justine can lock herself in there and paint away until the cows come home.

TIM: Family diplomacy?

SARAH: Something like that.

TIM: Justine's a feisty one.

SARAH: Don't I know it. She gets it from Paul, of course, not me. When those two lock horns it's best just to step out of the way.

TIM: You don't have to tell me — I've seen it enough times.

(Beat.)

SARAH: Yes.

TIM: In fact — and don't take this the wrong way — but I don't think you should let her talk to you the way she does sometimes.

SARAH: I'm sorry?

TIM: It's not good for them. I know she's just being a typical teen and the rest of it, but you have to draw the line somewhere, Sarah — especially with the girls.

(Beat.)

SARAH: Well, I . . . I'm not sure that I . . .

(Composing herself.)

Actually . . . Oh God, I feel like such an idiot. I don't . . . I don't think there's any way I can say this without sounding like a complete and utter fraud, but . . .

(Screwing up her face in embarrassment.)

Would you ever be able to forgive me if I told you that I've been trying for the life of me to recall your name, but for some ridiculous reason it's just not coming. I'm so, *so* sorry. Please don't be angry with me.

TIM: Angry? Why would I be angry?

SARAH: *Because!* Because I've been behaving like a social philistine. Because you obviously know so much about us, and you clearly know Paul and Justine *very* well, and because . . . well, I've been so insanely busy lately, and — and I don't mean this as an excuse — but honestly, I meet so many people in my line of work — public relations, as hard as that is to believe — and sometimes it's just hard to keep track of it all, and . . . well, actually I suppose I do mean that as an excuse, even if it is a poor one. But the fact is I do — meet so many people, that is. Not that that makes it any the less excusable. I mean, why didn't I just come clean from the outset?

(Beat.)

I don't know. God, I'm so embarrassed.

TIM: Sarah, *please*, why should you be? You don't know me — I'm nobody.

SARAH: Oh, now don't make me feel worse than I do.

TIM: But who am I? — just little old me. I'm one of thousands . . . millions, maybe — who knows? If you think about the odds, it's actually something close to an act of God that we bumped into each other in the first place.

SARAH: Oh God, please don't rub it in. I'm sorry, I really am . . . *I am.*

TIM: Well, don't be. But if it makes you feel any better, the name's Tim.

SARAH: *(With feigned recognition.)* Tim! God, of course, Tim! Tim, Tim, Tim!

(With a sigh.)

Well, Tim, if it makes *you* feel any better I think I can safely say I've just sealed my fate in hell.

TIM: Then I'll be in good company.

SARAH: *(With a laugh.)* God, it's ridiculous, isn't it? I mean, why do we do that? Why couldn't I have come straight out and said, "I'm sorry, but at this precise moment I have absolutely no idea who you are," instead of play-acting some polite charade, which only serves to make everything far more confusing anyway? Not to mention humiliating.

TIM: Well, none of us wants to give ourselves away, do we? Not unless we really have to.

SARAH: I suppose not, but even so . . .

TIM: And I was serious about Justine.

SARAH: I'm sorry?

TIM: You give her too much rope, Sarah.

SARAH: Well, I . . . I try to —

TIM: And it's not just the way she talks to you, which is bad enough because you're a very nice person — at least, from my experience — but it's her whole attitude.

SARAH: Well, it's . . . it's just a stage, isn't it? You know kids. I'm just biding my time. She'll work through it — it's just her age.

TIM: Well, if you ask me, you'll live to regret it. This is a very formative period in her life — now is when she needs to learn.

SARAH: Yes, but she'll grow out of it. They all do eventually.

TIM: Ah, but will she? And it's not just the way she treats you and Paul. When she's alone in her room . . .

(Rolling his eyes.)

Well, that's another story altogether.

SARAH: What on earth do you mean?

TIM: I'm talking about the dildo, Sarah. I mean, I like to see some action, but Jeez, when she starts at it — Christ, she's like a thing possessed.

(Beat.)

SARAH: What?

TIM: She's like an animal. She whacks that thing into her like there's no tomorrow.

(Beat.)

SARAH: *(Completely at a loss.)* What . . . I . . . what are you talking about?

TIM: Justine. I'm talking about Justine. She treats it like it was a . . . a thing . . . like an object. Which it is, of course, but that's hardly the point, is it? It's not the fact that it's a piece of plastic, or rubber, or what have you — it's the principle. It's a control thing with her. And that's not healthy, Sarah.

SARAH: *(Uncomprehending.)* What in God's name are you saying?

TIM: *(Patiently.)* Sarah, all I am saying is that she fucks that plastic cock with all the appreciation of a rube at an opera recital, and if you're not careful you're going to end up with a very dysfunctional child.

SARAH: I —

TIM: And I know what you're going to say, but you know as well as I do, that that sort of behaviour bodes very poorly for a healthy sex life, let alone a successful marriage. You really need to start thinking about her future, Sarah; you are her mother, after all.

SARAH: I . . . I — I don't understand. Who are you?

TIM: Granted, Sarah, it's not necessarily my place to say these things, but the fact is, if I don't who will? I know many people would step aside and let things take their course — or intercourse, if you will — for good or for worse; but the fact is — God, I keep saying that, don't I? — but the fact is, Sarah, I feel like I almost know you. I'd even go so far to say that, in a very post-modern way — though heaven knows that sounds passé nowadays — I feel a . . . a bond with your family; almost as if it were my own. And I cannot stand by and watch things devolve without trying to . . . well, yes, help . . . in my own way. Not when I have you right in front of me.

SARAH: Is . . . is this some sort of joke? Because if it is, it's . . . whoever did it . . . I don't like it, and it's not funny . . . not to me — not at all.

TIM: Nor should it be. It's not a laughing matter. We are, after all, talking about Justine — your daughter — and I, for one, am very concerned. But . . .

(Suddenly clasping his hands to his face.)

Oh no!

SARAH: What?

TIM: Oh, God!

SARAH: *What?*

TIM: I've just realised . . . I've been going on and on about Justine and her dildo, and her future, and her potential marriage — or lack thereof — and it's just struck me . . . you have absolutely no idea what I'm talking about, do you?

SARAH: *No!* No, I don't.

TIM: God, now *I* feel like such a fool — just like you did earlier. But it's true, I . . . I've come to feel like such a part of your lives. I feel so close to you; you and Paul and Justine — and it's hard sometimes to . . . to . . .

(Slicing the air with his hands.)

draw the difference — does that make any sense? To separate it all. I mean, here I am, giving you all this carefully considered advice and insight, and . . . and yet you don't know a thing about me, let alone about Justine's dildo, or . . . or anything else for that matter.

SARAH: *(Becoming angry.)* What are you doing?

TIM: What?

SARAH: Who did this?

TIM: Well you don't have to put that accusatory tone in your voice. I didn't *do* anything. All I've ever done is look.

SARAH: Look?

TIM: *(Patronizingly.)* Yes, *look — with my eyes.* There's nothing weird about that is there? We all do it: A landscape painting, a perfect rose, a puppy, a car crash, a dead body, other people having sex — we all look. We can't help ourselves — it's in our nature. It's just who we are. And don't tell me that you don't, or I'll tell you the plain and simple truth, and that would be that you're a big, fat, fucking liar.

SARAH: What!

TIM: You heard.

SARAH: Look, I . . . I don't know who you are or, or . . . or what you are, but I . . . I'm not going to stand here —

TIM: Don't start getting all haughty with me, lady. I'm not the one who rigged up your house. I'm the one trying to help — remember?

(Beat.)

Justine — ring a bell?

SARAH: Rigged up? Rigged up what?

TIM: God, you people are so judgemental. I just look, OK — what's the big deal!

SARAH: At me?

TIM: Yes, at you . . . at Paul . . . at Justine — *especially* Justine. But you can't blame me for that, can you? Or can you? Maybe you can . . . who knows? But I'm only human . . . and she's only fourteen.

SARAH: I . . . I don't understand this. I have no idea who you are, or why you're doing this to me, but . . . but whatever your part in this — whatever this is — you should feel . . . ashamed, because . . . because this isn't funny. It may have been intended that way — in some sick, stupid way — but it isn't.

TIM: Look, "*Sarah*," don't blame me if you don't like your little slice of celebrity. I was trying to be nice about it. I was trying to help out. I didn't put the cameras there, and I don't like your attitude. Yes, I watch the feedback — so what? That doesn't make me a criminal, it just makes me a member of the viewing public, the same as anyone else, so don't start getting all cocky and full of yourself with me.

SARAH: *(Entreating.)* Please stop this now. Stop it and tell me who you are!

TIM: *(Upon reflection.)* My name . . . is Michael Caine.

SARAH: What?

TIM: Yes, yes, yes, it all makes sense now. Of course you wouldn't have known about the dildo — how could you? — she's behind closed doors . . . to you, at least. And God forbid you should know about the rest of what she shoves up there. I won't tell you, that's for sure — wouldn't want to give you the creeps. But suffice to say if you ever invite me over to dinner, I'll skip the vegetable plate, if you know what I mean.

(Beat.)

Politely, of course.

SARAH: I don't believe a single word you're saying. Unless you tell me who you are, I swear I'm going to call the police.

TIM: *(Mockingly.)* Ooh, no — please don't do that. Now you've got me all nervous.

(Beat.)

And they'll send me down for what? A bad joke? Logging on to someone else's peek-a-boo website? Offering my insights into your daughter's vaginal veggie intake? And by the way, since we're back on that subject, I'm quite adamant on my feelings on that, Sarah; it really is something that needs to be addressed.

SARAH: Website? Do you mean that I've —

TIM: Naturally, I'm sure you'd much rather have her ram some tuber or piece of man-made material up there than have her banging every Tom, Cock and Harry at her school, all riddled with disease and parasites and baby-making sperm — although, thinking about it, some of those vegetables have more bugs and chemicals clinging to them than you could shake a stick at, and at the rate she's going, she's on track to be the proud mother of the world's first half-human, half-turnip hybrid. Now there's a thought — and not a very tasty one. But I digress . . .

(Beat.)

So, actually, yes, in retrospect, plastic is the way to go. But whatever it is, it deserves to be treated with a little respect, don't you think? Because it's not what it is, it's what it represents. I think even you would agree with me there, Sarah.

SARAH: Oh my God, you've been watching us!

TIM: Ding-dong! Hello? Haven't you been paying attention? I told you I have. We all have. We watch all of you . . . whoever "we" are?

SARAH: Oh my God! My God, you have cameras in my house!

TIM: *(Irritably.)* No I don't! I told you I don't. I didn't put them there. I just look. And like they say . . . there's no harm in looking.

SARAH: Then who did?

TIM: *(Rolling his eyes.)* As if I would know — you think I'm psychic? Maybe a nosey neighbour; maybe a curious landlord; maybe a URL gifted air conditioning repairman? Your guess is as good as mine. How do I know you didn't put them there — trying to get a little screen time for that body you plaster in age-defying lotions so desperately every night? "Get it while it's still hot!"

SARAH: *(Almost to herself.)* You've been watching all this time.

TIM: Not all the time — just when I feel like it. I do have a life outside of your kinky family, you know. No, but then, you wouldn't know, would you? Well, I do. Anyway, like I said . . . oh, no I didn't say, did I? Well, like I meant to say, my computer crashed for what seems like an eternity ago. A real mess. Just got it back. They took *forever*, the useless bastards, and charged me a small fortune, to boot. That's why I haven't seen you in a while. Well, now I'm *really* seeing you, of course, but you know what I mean . . . in your natural habitat, as it were.

SARAH: Oh my God, you're . . . you're sick!

TIM: Excuse me? *I'm* sick? *You* are calling *me* sick? Look, Sarah, I've been very restrained about this so far, wouldn't you say? But let's face some facts here: I'm not the one who smells their toilet paper after they've wiped themselves for the umpteenth time after taking a shit — I mean, if you're that worried about your ass smelling, why don't you just wash it, for God's sake? And it's not me tweaking their nipples with the family shampoo while masturbating in the bathtub, is it? And, in closing, I'm not the person who shoves their index finger up their husband's ass every time they "make love" — which isn't very often, by the way. And since we're on the subject, I've never quite figured that one out. Do you do it because he gets off on it and you tolerate it, or vice versa? Or verse vica?

SARAH: Oh my God!

(As she runs off stage, left.)

Oh my God!

TIM: *(Calling after her.)* Wait . . . Sarah! . . . There's no need to over react. It's just a few people looking at you.

(Beat. To no one in particular.)

And there's always *someone* looking at you.

(Curtain.)

END OF PLAY

Rainbow Sprinkles

STACEY LANE

Rainbow Sprinkles was produced in May and June of 2009 by EMU Theatre at the Lawrence Arts Center in Lawrence, Kansas, with director Jerry Salisbury. Cast: Miranda — Janette Salisbury; Rainbow Sprinkles — David Butterfield; Voice on Machine — Jaymie Maus.

CHARACTERS

MIRANDA GILES-HAMPTON, thirty-seven-year-old prim and proper businesswoman.

RAINBOW SPRINKLES, sixty-eight-year-old kind-hearted birthday party clown.

VOICE ON MACHINE, pre-recorded voice of young female secretary.

SCENE

An ornate, classy office of an executive lawyer in a well-known firm.

TIME

The present.

• • •

Miranda Giles-Hampton, a businesswoman with sharp features, sits at her desk hurriedly eating a salad and leafing through a few pieces of paper.

VOICE ON MACHINE: Mrs. Giles-Hampton, your noon appointment is here.

MIRANDA: *(Pushing the intercom button on her phone.)* Thank you, Jessy. Please send him in.

VOICE ON MACHINE: Yes, Mrs. Giles-Hampton.

(Miranda picks up the papers and puts them in a neat stack off to the side of her desk. She pushes her salad to the side as well. There is a knock at the door.)

MIRANDA: Come in.

(Rainbow Sprinkles, an elderly clown in full costume and make-up, enters. He has a long overcoat, a hat, and a scarf, which shield most of his strange attire.)

SPRINKLES: Good day!

MIRANDA: *(She searches for the proper legal pad and initially does not look up.)* Hello, Mr. Noman. Thank-you again for coming out here on such short notice. As I mentioned on the phone, my —

(Rainbow Sprinkles has now removed his coat, hat, and scarf. Miranda looks up and for the first time gets a glimpse of him dressed as a clown. She lets out a small shriek.)

MIRANDA: Oh, I beg your pardon. I didn't realize that you would come dressed as a clown.

SPRINKLES: I am a clown, ma'am.

MIRANDA: Well, yes, of course, I knew that. I just assumed that . . . well . . . Never mind. Um, please have a seat Mr. Noman.

SPRINKLES: Please call me Sprinkles.

(Sprinkles tosses confetti into the air with gusto.)

MIRANDA: Excuse me.

SPRINKLES: That's my name, Rainbow Sprinkles.

(Sprinkles again tosses confetti into the air.)

MIRANDA: Yes, of course.

SPRINKLES: Pleased to meet you, ma'am.

MIRANDA: Likewise. My name is Miranda Giles-Hampton.

SPRINKLES: Nice to meet you, Miranda.

MIRANDA: Please call me Mrs. Giles-Hampton.

SPRINKLES: Certainly.

(He notices a photograph of a ten-year-old boy on her desk. He picks it up.)

SPRINKLES: So this must be the lucky birthday boy.

MIRANDA: Yes, that's my son, Benjamin. He's my pride and joy.

SPRINKLES: Well, he looks just like a perfect angel. Just look at that grin! Is Benjamin your only child?

MIRANDA: Yes. He's my one and only little baby and now he's about to turn the big double digits. He's so excited. He can't stop talking about it. I want Benjamin's tenth birthday party to be the best he has ever had. That's where you come in, Mr. Noman.

SPRINKLES: Sprinkles.

(Sprinkles tosses confetti into the air.)

MIRANDA: Yes, Mr. *Sprinkles.*

(Sprinkles tosses confetti into the air.)

MIRANDA: In the past, I have always organized his birthday parties completely on my own, but this year, being his tenth, I decided to do something extra special. I want to make it a day he will never forget.

SPRINKLES: And that's exactly what we'll do. I absolutely love spending time with children on their birthdays. They are always so truly blissfully happy. It's inspiring. That's why I love my job.

MIRANDA: Indeed. Now, let's just get down to business. I jotted down a few questions for you. Just standard information, really.

SPRINKLES: Of course.

MIRANDA: Please explain to me what your general birthday party clown act consists of.

SPRINKLES: Well, as I greet the children, as they arrive, I tell them jokes and —

MIRANDA: What kind of jokes?

SPRINKLES: Oh you know, kid jokes, like —

MIRANDA: As I am sure you are aware, Mr. Noman, humor is a very sensitive topic nowadays. What may be funny to one individual, may be quite offensive to another. To joke is to poke fun at something or someone and well, Mr. Noman, we don't want to hurt anyone's feelings.

SPRINKLES: My jokes are just children's jokes, to make them laugh and smile. I assure you, ma'am, that my jokes will not offend anyone.

MIRANDA: Mr. Noman, you never can know for certain what will offend people these days and I for one am simply not willing to take that risk at my son's party. I think that it would just make my heart feel much more at ease, if we just cancelled the joke portion of the afternoon. I am sure you understand.

SPRINKLES: Ma'am, I don't see how —

MIRANDA: Well, I am glad that that is settled. Now, let's see. What else does your clown act consist of?

SPRINKLES: Well, typically after we eat the cake and open the presents, I paint faces.

MIRANDA: Hhhhmmm . . . I see. And what exactly do you paint on faces?

SPRINKLES: Oh, whatever the kid wants.

MIRANDA: Whatever the kid wants! Mr. Noman, I think you give children a tad too much credit. What if the child wants a pentagram or a swastika on his or her face? Or what if he or she wants a cross and that offends the Jewish child at the party or the Jewish child wants a Star of David and that offends the Christian child?

SPRINKLES: Kids usually ask for balloons, smiley faces, flowers, hearts, things like that.

MIRANDA: Hearts! Do you think that little ten-year-old girls at my son's party need to have hearts on their faces, as if they are just begging for a romantic relationship at such a young and impressionable age?

SPRINKLES: I am sure that is not what they mean by —

MIRANDA: Not to mention, the chance of a child having an allergic reaction to the make-up you put on him or her.

SPRINKLES: I use high quality make-up and have never had a problem before —

MIRANDA: Furthermore, it's not quite sanitary, using the same make-up on each child.

SPRINKLES: I clean the brush between each use.

MIRANDA: With what?

SPRINKLES: Water.

MIRANDA: Make it some sort of non-scented hypoallergenic sanitizer and I suppose that should appease most of the mothers. I will tell you what I will do for you, Mr. Noman. You can draw me some basic images that you might want to paint and I will approve the politically correct ones.

SPRINKLES: Well, I suppose that maybe —

MIRANDA: On second thought, some of your face paintings might come out nicer than others and then the children may not feel like equals. The parents may feel that you are playing favorites. It would probably be in the best interest of all involved if we just cut the face painting from our little party line up.

SPRINKLES: But, ma'am, I —

MIRANDA: Now, Mr. Noman, you seem to be a reasonable gentleman and I am sure you understand my situation as a parent and my desire to take all precautions to ensure that my son has the best birthday party he or anyone else on the block has ever had. I am glad that that matter is settled. Now, what else do you have on your agenda?

SPRINKLES: Well, after the kids have had a chance to play on their own a little, I usually sit them down for the big event, my magic show. I must say that I am quite proud of it. It is one of the best that I have ever seen.

MIRANDA: Do you use a rabbit?

SPRINKLES: Actually, yes, I do. Mr. Hoppity. He has been with me for five years now.

MIRANDA: Cut the rabbit. The animal rights activists would have a field day with that one.

SPRINKLES: But ma'am, Mr. Hoppity has been part of the grand finale of my magic show for the past —

MIRANDA: To be perfectly honest, there is a bit of an ethical dilemma with the whole idea of a magic show, Mr. Noman.

SPRINKLES: I beg your pardon.

MIRANDA: When the children ask you how you do a trick what do you say?

SPRINKLES: "It's magic!"

(Sprinkles pulls a bouquet of flowers out of his sleeve and hands it to Miranda.)

MIRANDA: Exactly. You lie to them.

SPRINKLES: Well, I wouldn't call it that. It's part of —

MIRANDA: Mr. Noman, as you and I both know, "magic" does not exist. If you tell a child that you just performed "magic", you are indeed lying to him or her.

SPRINKLES: Ma'am, I would never lie to a child as long as I live.

MIRANDA: Well, I appreciate your sentiments, but the fact of the matter remains. It's a lie and I won't allow you to tell it.

SPRINKLES: Mrs. Hampton, please listen to yourself. This is ridiculous. It's just a magic act. It's fun. It makes the children happy. That's all I am trying to do.

MIRANDA: Now, Mr. Noman, please do not misunderstand me. I believe that your intentions are good, but misled. I, myself, do not personally share many of the concerns that I have voiced to you today, but I know that there are people out there who do. I am simply looking out for the best interest of all involved. I am sure you can understand my delicate situation. Mr. Noman, are you a parent?

SPRINKLES: No, ma'am.

MIRANDA: Well if you were a parent, I am sure you would feel the same way I do. Now, let's move on. You won't be doing the magic act, but I am sure there are many other things that you have planned for the party that you can do.

SPRINKLES: No, actually, there is just one more.

MIRANDA: And that is?

SPRINKLES: Balloon animals.

MIRANDA: Balloon animals? Why that's wonderful. I love balloon animals.

SPRINKLES: You do?

MIRANDA: Yes. Ever since I was a child and my family took me to the circus for the first time.

SPRINKLES: *(Digging into his pocket and producing a long pink balloon and a hand air-pump.)* Then, I just happen to have a little treat for you. Consider it a free sample.

(He begins to blow up the balloon and twist it into a "Weiner dog".)

MIRANDA: Well, see Mr. Noman, I knew that we could agree on a common ground of some sort. There is certainly nothing objectionable about balloon animals. They are actually quite adorable and children love-

(Sprinkles has made the two bubble legs of the "Weiner dog". He holds the long pink balloon in his lap, as he twists the bubbles into place.)

MIRANDA: Why, Mr. Noman! I am shocked and appalled!

SPRINKLES: I beg your pardon.

MIRANDA: You are making a phallic symbol.

SPRINKLES: No it's just a "Weiner" —

MIRANDA: *(Overlapping.)* Exactly!

SPRINKLES: — dog.

MIRANDA: Well, after that demonstration, I certainly cannot allow you to make balloon animals at my ten-year old's party. What more, I feel that I have been robbed of some sort of childhood innocence. My circus memory is now forever tainted.

SPRINKLES: *(Defeated.)* It's just a dog.

(He finishes it.)

See.

(He hands it to her.)

MIRANDA: Oh, I apologize Mr. Noman. I do not mean to blame you, but as I am sure you can understand, I simply cannot allow children to be subjected to that. Now, you said that you do not have any other planned activities for the party.

SPRINKLES: None that haven't been cut, no. So I guess I will be going. I am sorry that things didn't work out. I would have very much liked to bring joy to your son on his birthday.

MIRANDA: Now, Mr. Noman, where are you going? I like you very much. You seem a decent gentleman and I would like to hire you for my son's party.

SPRINKLES: But ma'am, I don't have an act to perform, anymore.

MIRANDA: Well, that's all right, I suppose. Children do like clowns. Why don't you just come to the party and mingle with the children, help cut the cake, and pass out presents, and so forth. It's probably much safer that you don't actually do any sort of "act" anyway.

SPRINKLES: Well, I don't know. I always have a prepared act, but I suppose that I might be able to do that.

MIRANDA: Great. We are all set then. 2 P.M. Saturday. Oh, there is just one more tiny matter that I need to discuss with you.

SPRINKLES: Yes.

MIRANDA: Well, there is the matter of your clown make-up.

SPRINKLES: I beg your pardon.

MIRANDA: Well, I couldn't help but notice that you have an icon of a rainbow on your cheek.

SPRINKLES: Yes. That's my trademark. My name is, after all, Rainbow Sprinkles.

(Sprinkles tosses confetti into the air.)

MIRANDA: Well, I understand that, but some people, not myself of course, but others, more conservative types, might interpret that to be a, how shall I put this? Well . . . a homosexual symbol.

SPRINKLES: That's crazy.

MIRANDA: And the upside down triangles under your eyes don't help either. Now, of course, these suggestive symbols do not offend me personally, but they might not sit well with some of the parents at this party.

SPRINKLES: Mrs. Hampton, that is the most ridiculous thing I have ever heard. This is my clown face. It's me. It doesn't symbolize anything but me.

MIRANDA: I understand that, Mr. Noman. But I am sure that you can see my position on this matter. Nonetheless, it's easily resolved. Just change your make-up to something different for Benjamin's party. That's all. It won't be a problem.

SPRINKLES: No, ma'am.

MIRANDA: I'm sorry?

SPRINKLES: No. I will not change my clown face for you, ma'am. I have been wearing my clown make-up exactly like this for forty-nine years. A clown's face is his trademark. It is his clown personality and his clown soul exposed for all the world to see. I will not change it for you or anyone else.

MIRANDA: Well, Mr. Noman, then I am afraid we are at an unfortunate impasse. If only you could realize that I am trying to protect the fragile innocence of the children, I am sure you could see it my way.

SPRINKLES: I pray to God that I never see it your way. You are not protecting the fragile innocence of children. You're robbing them of their childhood and their innocence. You are truly a sad human being.

(He walks to the coat rack and collects his scarf, hat, and coat, but does not put them on.)

MIRANDA: I am sorry that things did not work out. Goodbye Mr. Noman.

SPRINKLES: It's Rainbow Sprinkles, Miranda.

(He tosses confetti in Miranda's face and exits with dignity.)

MIRANDA: *(Picks up the phone.)* Jessy, I am afraid that this one didn't work out either.

(Pause.)

I can't imagine why he didn't want to do the party.
(Pause.)
Sure. Whichever is next in the phonebook.
(She hangs up the phone.)
(Miranda notices that Sprinkles has left the balloon animal behind. She picks it up and turns it in her hands. A sad nostalgic smile sweeps across her face.)
(Blackout.)

END OF PLAY

The Rental

MARK HARVEY LEVINE

The Rental had its first Equity production at The Phoenix Theatre, Indianapolis, Indiana, in May 2005 as part of Cabfare For The Common Man, an evening of plays by Mark Harvey Levine. Artistic Director: Bryan D. Fonseca. Director: Bryan D. Fonseca. Cast: Sonya — Sara Riemen; Harold — Michael Shelton.

CHARACTERS

SONYA, thirty, sweet, intelligent, low self-esteem

HAROLD, thirties, nice-looking, romantic

SETTING

The living room of Sonya's apartment. Not fancy, but nice and clean.

TIME

The present.

• • •

Sonya's apartment, early morning. There is a knock at the door. Sonya staggers out, half awake, tying on a robe. At her door is Harold, a thirtyish, normal-looking man in a nice coat. He carries a bouquet of flowers, a clipboard, and a picnic basket.

HAROLD: *(Through door.)* Hello, Sonya? It's Harold!

SONYA: . . . Who?

HAROLD: *(Through door.)* Harold! Valerie sent me. Valerie Persky?

SONYA: Valerie . . . ?

(She opens her door a little. She gapes at all the stuff he has.)

SONYA: Oh my God!!! What did she do?

HAROLD: *(Handing her the flowers.)* Happy Birthday from Valerie Persky. I'm Harold, your boyfriend.

(He kisses her in a familiar manner, and enters.)

SONYA: I . . . I . . . What?!

HAROLD: *(Quickly.)* Let me get this stuff in the fridge . . . Honey, did I wake you? I did. I'm so sorry. Sit down, relax, I'll be right back. Is this the kitchen? Great.

(He exits to kitchen. Sonya grabs a baseball bat she has by the door.)

SONYA: Excuse me! Excuse me! Hello? Who are you?

HAROLD: *(Off stage.)* I'm Harold! Harold, your boyfriend.

SONYA: My boyfriend?!

HAROLD: *(Off stage.)* Yeah . . . You know, for your birth — ?

(He reenters and sees her with the bat. He ducks behind the couch.)

HAROLD: *(Continued.)* Aaaah! Don't shoot!

SONYA: . . . It's a baseball bat.

HAROLD: Alright, don't hit.

SONYA: I'm pretty sure I'd remember having a boyfriend.

HAROLD: From Valerie! I'm from your friend Valerie! Wait, wait . . . I come with a card.

(He holds out a standard "enclosure card" which she grabs and opens.)

SONYA: Well, this IS her hand-writing. *(Reading.)* "Sonya . . . what do you get for the girl who deserves everything? Well, you deserve a really great boyfriend, so I got you one, for today at least. Don't wear him out, ha ha. Happy Thirtieth! Love, Valerie." *(Pause.)* You gotta be kidding.

HAROLD: You had no idea I was coming. OK, OK . . . this happens occasionally. Once they sent me to the wrong house; I thought I was gonna have to date an eighty-year-old guy named "Lou" . . .

SONYA: *(Waving bat.)* They?! Who's they? What is this?

HAROLD: Wait! I'm your birthday present! From Rent-a-Boyfriend, Ltd.! . . . Apparently, I'm a SURPRISE birthday present.

SONYA: Rent-a-Boyfriend, Ltd.?!

HAROLD: I can explain, if you promise not to shatter my skull.

(Still suspicious, she lowers the bat.)

HAROLD: *(Continued.)* Thank you. *(The company speech.)* "Rent-A-Boyfriend, Ltd., has been providing the finest in temporary romantic relationships to the discriminating woman since 1985." I've been rented to you for our sixteen hour "affaire de coeur" package. I'm sure you'll enjoy it, it's one of our most popular ones.

SONYA: I'm going to kill Valerie for this.

HAROLD: Listen, this is a generous gift. And I can promise you a relationship that, though brief, will create a burning, romantic memory that will shine in your heart to the end of your days. *(Pause, she snickers.)* They make me say that.

SONYA: So you're a . . . a gigolo?

HAROLD: No, no, no. A professional boyfriend. It's a specialized craft. There's six months of training, three months of supervised infatuation . . .

SONYA: Valerie rented me a boyfriend.

HAROLD: It's a very thoughtful present. She told me that . . . um, that you've had a lot of . . . disappointments in this area. Well, Sonya, you're about to have the most fantastically romantic day of your life.

SONYA: This is crazy . . .

HAROLD: *(Really selling it.)* Is it? Sonya, today you have someone who cherishes you the way you should be cherished. Who adores the way you curl your fingers in your hair, the way you move across a room. The way you hold a baseball bat. Someone who lives and breathes and dies upon the merest glance of your cobalt blue eyes . . .

(Sonya's starting to crack.)

HAROLD: *(Continued.)* . . . and all you have to say is yes, I deserve this. Yes, at long last. Yes.

SONYA: . . . Yes.

HAROLD: *(Whipping out a contract.)* Sign here.

SONYA: *(Signing.)* I don't believe I'm doing this. But you know what, I DO deserve it.

HAROLD: Of course you do. And initial here, and here.

SONYA: *(Initialing.)* After all the creeps, the bad dates, the blind dates, the personal ads, the — *(Harold kisses her full on the lips the moment she finishes signing.)* — mmmph!

HAROLD: Thank God we got that over with. Finally, I can hold you in my arms. Hello, sweetheart. Happy Birthday.

SONYA: Wh — OK. We've started, right?

HAROLD: Right. Your boyfriend has come to whisk you away on a fun-filled birthday celebration! I've got a picnic here I think you'll like. Salami and egg sandwiches! Chinese noodles in sesame oil! Chocolate Raspberry Mousse Cake!

SONYA: How do you know what my favorite foods are?!

HAROLD: Valerie told me. But remember, I'm your boyfriend. I know all about you. You like Louis Prima records and old Dick Van Dyke reruns. Your books are in strict alphabetical order. You never wear beige. You live in constant fear you've left your purse somewhere.

SONYA: My God.

HAROLD: But Valerie never told me you wake up first thing in the morning looking breathtakingly gorgeous. I thought that only happened in the movies.

SONYA: Wh-What? Oh God. I must look like hell.

HAROLD: You're stunning. Look at you. Your eyes are —

SONYA: Wait, wait . . . this is a little much for me right now, OK? I don't like to be cherished before my first cup of coffee.

(He takes out a "travel-cup" of coffee and hands it to her.)

HAROLD: Ah! I brought you some. Dark roast Kenyan. Your fav —

SONYA: *(Overlapping.)* — My favorite . . . of course. I don't believe this.

HAROLD: Sonya, my dear, this is just the beginning . . .

(She sits stunned on sofa, sipping coffee. Harold starts to massage her feet. Sonya protests, then with an "I give up" wave, lets him.)

HAROLD: First, I make you breakfast. Then it's off to Lavender Springs Spa, where you get a mud bath and a massage while I see how many sonnets I can compose about you. Then our picnic lunch in a secluded grove, —

SONYA: *(Stunned, softly overlapping.)* Uh-huh . . .

HAROLD: — a drive along the coast, sailing in the bay —

SONYA: *(Falling into his spell.)* Yeah sure . . .

HAROLD: — Our reservations at La Coupole are for seven-thirty, and afterwards a horse-drawn carriage takes us to —

(He produces two tickets from his pocket.)

SONYA: The Eric Clapton concert?!!! Oh my GOD!!! I love you!!!

(She throws her arms around him. Then realizes what she's doing.)

SONYA: *(Continued.)* I'm sorry! I mean . . . Wow. You ARE good. Are you sure you're just here for one day?

HAROLD: It'll be a day to remember.

SONYA: *(Makes a little noise of disbelief.)* I . . . gotta get dressed. Would you . . . excuse me for a minute? Don't go anywhere.

HAROLD: Of course.

SONYA: I'll be right back. *(As she leaves.)* Oh my God . . . Oh my God!

(She exits. He produces a dustbuster-type sweeper and begins to casually clean.)

SONYA: *(Off stage.) (Continued.)* So . . . um . . . Harold. Do you do this often? I mean . . . how many . . . uh, girlfriends do you — ?

HAROLD: Sonya . . . right now there are no other women for me. I've never met anyone like you.

SONYA: *(Off stage.)* Oh . . . my . . . GOD.

(She hops in, half-dressed, putting on shoes.)

Well, I've certainly never met anyone like — What the HELL are you doing?

HAROLD: Dusting.

SONYA: Don't! Don't . . . do that. Just . . . sit. Sit! Stay! You win. You are officially the best boyfriend I have ever had. Or ever will have.

(She exits. He appears a little concerned over this last remark.)

HAROLD: Really?

SONYA: *(Off stage.)* Are you kidding? Gold medal, Boyfriend Olympics, One Day Sprint.

HAROLD: I was a little worried. We got off to a kinda weird start there, what with you swinging a baseball bat at me.

(Sonya reenters, fully dressed.)

SONYA: *(Peeved.)* You've been my boyfriend ten minutes, already we're reminiscing? Anyway, I didn't SWING it, I brandished it.

HAROLD: . . . in a threatening manner.

SONYA: How do you "brandish" in a non-threatening manner?

HAROLD: All I'm saying, is, is, we started off on the wrong —

SONYA: What the hell did you expect, a strange man comes bursting through my door, kisses me . . . you kissed me! You're lucky I didn't bash your brains in!

HAROLD: *(Beaming.)* We're having our first fight! Oh honey!

(He hugs her.)

SONYA: I'm not sure I'm ready for this kind of relationship.

HAROLD: I'm sorry, sweetheart. Let's forget about it.

SONYA: Yeah . . . yeah . . . we let it go too long . . .

(He laughs. She leans back and relaxes into his arms.)

SONYA: *(Continued.)* I have to admit, this is nice. Y'know, this is all I wanted. Just to be in someone's embrace. Is this too much to ask?

HAROLD: Absolutely not.

SONYA: You know what? I want to walk down the street swinging our arms like we're fifteen.

HAROLD: OK.

SONYA: I want to sit at a restaurant and stare into each other's eyes and completely annoy everyone else.

HAROLD: You got it!

SONYA: I can't wait to show up at yoga tomorrow. You'll drop me off with a quick kiss, and then watch as I — you're not gonna be here tomorrow.

HAROLD: Forget about tomorrow.

SONYA: It's just . . . kinda hard. Here I am, in your arms. And then you just leave? It's not fair. This is all I get? One really romantic day? For the rest of my life?

(She starts to cry a little.)

HAROLD: The nice thing about this kind of relationship is you KNOW when — Sonya? Are you — ? No — don't cry! Oh God.

SONYA: I'm OK.

HAROLD: No, crying's bad. There's not supposed to be any crying.

SONYA: Oh, I cry all the time.

(He grabs a tissue and starts to dry her tears himself.)

SONYA: *(Continued.)* I'm OK . . .

(He hands her tissues — and then more tissues, until she has way too many. He places them on her, floats them at her, etc. She laughs.)

HAROLD: Much better. You know, I just discovered something. I can't stand to see you cry.

SONYA: Oh, Harold. You're very sweet, y'know.

HAROLD: Sonya . . . there's something else . . . I love you.

SONYA: What?!

HAROLD: I love you! Can't you see it in my eyes?

SONYA: *(Since she is wiping her eyes.)* Not at the moment, no . . .

(She continues to wipe her eyes. Jokingly glances at him for a split second.)

Yeah, now I can. Got it.

(Finishes wiping her eyes, then looks at him again.)

You can't be serious.

HAROLD: You don't believe in love at first sight?

SONYA: Do you mean it, or is this part of the package?

HAROLD: I'm your boyfriend. I really love you.

SONYA: How can you love me?

HAROLD: How could I not? You're warm, funny, smart —

SONYA: Stop, stop. Look, I don't know if you're crazy, or I am, but —

HAROLD: Don't you deserve to be loved?

SONYA: Of COURSE I do. EVERYONE does. But this — you just — I mean, you don't REALLY really love me. You're doing this because Valerie paid you.

HAROLD: We have today, because someone paid for it, sure. But I do "REALLY really" love you. I love you, Sonya.

(She stares at him. They move in closer . . . they almost kiss, but —)

SONYA: Wait a minute. As presents go, this beats a basket of bath gels. But don't come in here telling me you love me.

HAROLD: But I do.

SONYA: Well, that's just swell! Where were you when I needed you? Like when my car was stolen. Or when my Grandmother died? I could have used a boyfriend! You weren't there! I had to deal with that alone!

HAROLD: Sonya, I —

SONYA: And are you gonna be there tomorrow or the next day when something really good happens and I want to tell you about it? You gonna be there?

HAROLD: No, I'm not gonna be there.

SONYA: You love me. Ha! You're just like all the other men.

HAROLD: No, I'm not! I'm a trained professional!

SONYA: I mean, yes, I like romance. Yes, picnics are fun. But I want someone who . . . wants to do laundry with me. Or do absolutely nothing — with me.

HAROLD: We could do that too! I'm here to give you what you want!

SONYA: What I WANT is someone who not only knows my favorite coffee but also my soul. Love me? You haven't even MET me!

HAROLD: Listen, I thought I'd —

SONYA: You thought you'd give the girl a small thrill for once in her life?! I make my own thrills, darling. Hey, we're having our second fight!

HAROLD: I'm offering you love —

SONYA: No, thanks! Already got some! I've got my whole family! They drive me crazy, but they love me! And my friends — I have great friends! THEY love me! My God, look what Valerie did for my birthday. I have plenty of love, pal.

HAROLD: Do you.

SONYA: Yes I do. And I sure as hell don't need a Don Juan wanna-be. Guess what, Harold, we're breaking up! I'll remember the ten minutes we had with great fondness. But y'know what? This isn't half a couple standing over here. OK? I'm a whole couple all by myself. With a great family, incredible friends — I even kind of like my job! Y'know? So if I end up meeting someone, fine! If I don't, ALSO fine! Got it? I don't need you!

HAROLD: No, you don't.

SONYA: You better believe I don't! *(Still yelling.)* Did you just agree with me?!

HAROLD: Yeah, I did. Because you're right. You don't need me. But if you ever find someone . . . who deserves to love you . . . I will envy him. Goodbye Sonya.

(He exits. Pause. He returns, slightly embarrassed.)

HAROLD: *(Continued.) (Company speech.)* "This has been a date from Rent-A-Boyfriend, Ltd. If you've enjoyed our service, please . . . tell a friend."

(With a curt bow, he exits. Sonya stands stunned for a moment.)

SONYA: *(shouting after him.)* Hey! I enjoyed your service! Now get back here and MAKE ME BREAKFAST!

(Blackout.)

END OF PLAY

REvolutions

ELAINE ROMERO

Revolutions received its World Premiere in Manhattan Theatre Sources' 2009 Estrogenius Festival in New York City. Executive Producers (Manhattan Theatre Source): Fiona Jones and Jennifer Thatcher. Production Producer: Nichole Donje'. Director: Laura Tesman. Actors: Andrew Eisenman and Fulvia Vergel

For Irene

CHARACTERS

PILAR, a Latina in her late forties who is looking for her son. She assumes has disappeared because of the present military regime.

GENERAL, a Latino in his fifties. He is steeped in the present military regime. *General* is pronounced in Spanish.

NOTE

All names in the play are pronounced in Spanish.

TIME

A particularly dark day amidst political upheaval and revolution somewhere in Latin America.

PLACE

A military state. The morgue.

SETTING

A simple setting. A desk. A door. A dimly lit room.

• • •

Pilar wears a black dress and shawl. She is locked inside an office at the morgue. She pounds on the door.

PILAR: Let me out of here!

(Men march past the door, heavy boots on cement.)

Give me my son. I know you have him!

(The general, who is offstage, gently opens the door. He puts his finger on his lips, silencing her.)

GENERAL: You can leave anytime you want, but I'll be with you momentarily.

(Pilar quickly covers her face.)

GENERAL: *(To someone Off Stage.)* Ten-minutes I have to be out of here. My mother. She insists on tea every afternoon at two, like clockwork, or she threatens to die on the spot and leave me all alone.

(He laughs. Beat.)

Ninety-three, but she'll outlive me.

(He sits down, does not look Pilar in the face. He picks up a pad of paper.

Pilar looks disheveled and out of control in contrast to the general's calm demeanor. He wears military garb.)

GENERAL: You've got yourself all worked up, Señora.

(Pilar looks to the side door.)

GENERAL: Look, it's open. My assistant locked it accidentally. There was no plot to lock you in. This is not a police state as some people in this country have claimed. *(Beat.)* Would you like some tea?

(Pilar shakes her head "no.")

GENERAL: The party's name?

PILAR: Miguel Guerrero.

GENERAL: Husband?

PILAR: Son.

GENERAL: Your husband, Señora? Does he have a name?

PILAR: Miguel Guerrero is my son's name.

(The general looks up at her. She continues to hide her face.)

GENERAL: I know there have been many rumors since the guerrillas began their unprovoked attacks, but they're simply not true. We, in the government, have one motto: business as usual.

PILAR: This is a morgue, *General.* A place where they keep dead bodies. *(Beat.)* You seem surprised that I say that. The truth disturbs you —

GENERAL: We're amidst office renovations. I admit it's a bit awkward. I know how this appears to the outside world. It's distasteful to say the least. We'll be back at our headquarters at the *plaza* soon.

PILAR: *(Under her breath.)* It smells of death.

GENERAL: All I smell is the jasmine tree outside my window. Chinese emperors used jasmine to entice young women.

PILAR: *(Shaking.)* He calls every twelve hours. For safety. But he didn't call at ten o'clock and it's almost two.

(The general glances at his watch.)

GENERAL: Your son is a couple of hours late in calling, so you stomp in here accusing your government of kidnapping or worse? Your government is not in the business of kidnapping young children.

PILAR: He's twenty-eight.

GENERAL: Your government is not in the business of kidnapping anyone at all.

PILAR: He never misses the time. He plans his life around being by a phone. He waits to call me until that exact moment.

GENERAL: I understand your concerns as a mother, but your son is an adult and can take care of himself. Maybe he went home with a girl and didn't want to be caught checking in with his mother. *(Beat.)* I'll look into it for you as a favor. Then, I'll get back to you. I have your number somewhere.

(He shuffles through some papers, finds it.)

Here. When I call, you'll see this is an overreaction.

PILAR: What if you were to miss your appointment with your mother? Wouldn't she assume something terrible had happened? You're a grown man. What if you were home with a woman and you stayed in bed late into the afternoon —

(He looks at her. Again, she hides her face.)

GENERAL: Your voice. You remind me of someone. A woman from the last revolution. Almost thirty years ago. She's dead.

PILAR: You do honor to this uprising by calling it a revolution. Has it sparked something old in you?

GENERAL: I promised you I would look into your son's alleged disappearance and I will.

PILAR: You don't even know what he looks like.

GENERAL: I will ask for him by name, and I imagine he looks like his mother.

PILAR: No, actually, he looks like his father who wandered into the jungle one day and never came back.

GENERAL: Perhaps if you give me your son's photograph, I can keep my eye out for him.

PILAR: Not one single photograph. Can you imagine? Aren't mothers supposed to be the holders of all mementos and remembrances? I have failed in my task of charting his life for posterity. I may have no pictures, but I have an uncanny way with him, a kind of knowing when he wanders away. I sense him. I sense what moves him and doesn't, when he is discouraged or idealistic, how much he believes in this bloody revolt.

GENERAL: I really do need to leave to see my mother.

PILAR: Have you ever believed in a bloody revolt? For right? Why don't you tell me the truth then? A man who's devoted to his mother, I imagine, would be devoted to the truth.

GENERAL: My mother is scarier than any guerrilla I've ever faced in the jungle. That's my truth.

PILAR: Why don't you just look for my son over there?

(Pilar points down the hallway.)

GENERAL: You have it all wrong, Señora. That is not in use. There are no bodies in that morgue. We certainly wouldn't have the office here if there were. We are human beings.

PILAR: With all the people missing of late, I imagine that morgue is full of human bodies. Bodies of young men and women who believed in something. In the last revolution, they kept the bodies in the morgue, and then when there were too many of them, they turned to using mass graves. They'd dig a trench and throw the bodies in a hole. It's easier to commit mass murder if you don't count.

GENERAL: *(Remembering; simultaneously.)* — if you don't count.

(Breaking away from her, the General looks quickly away.)

PILAR: Everybody knows there was a murder on the *plaza* this morning. One young man shot down by five guards. Twenty gunshots. Five for each limb. That's what the woman who sells *elote* told me. Could you look into it and see if it was my son?

GENERAL: There have been no reports of a shooting and witnesses in the plaza tend to exaggerate the methods of our troops.

PILAR: You used to dream of something better when you took part in that last *revolución.*

GENERAL: Don't pretend to know my dreams.

PILAR: I imagine you fought because it moved your heart. And at that time, you were right. At that time, that was a horrid, horrid regime you were overthrowing. You saved our lives and we were thankful. We stood by you. *(Quick beat.)* I bet you never believed you would become — just like them.

GENERAL: I'll have you arrested.

PILAR: Go ahead, arrest me. Maybe my fellow prisoners will tell me the truth about my son.

(The general grabs her wrist. The general stops, looks her directly in the eye, realizing he knows her. He lets go of her wrist, stops all aggressive action.)

GENERAL: *Pilar*?

PILAR: You suddenly see me.

GENERAL: Forgive me.

PILAR: I imagine disposing of all those bodies can eat up one's day if not one's mind . . . if not one's heart.

GENERAL: *(Realizing.)* Your son.

PILAR: Miguel.

GENERAL: Almost thirty years old.

(Pilar looks down at the floor, regards her shoe.)

PILAR: *(Long beat.)* Yes, *Oscar,* he's yours. Don't act like you didn't know I was pregnant before you left to fight for your good, good cause.

GENERAL: It never felt real.

PILAR: You forgot. You were looking at your clipboard and you forgot.

GENERAL: I forgot.

PILAR: Funny, it took another revolution to bring you back home and not the birth of your — is he, was he — your only child?

GENERAL: Life's been short on love — the revolution — my time. The demands of my position.

PILAR: *(Short beat.)* Now, what's happened to Miguel? I would like for you to meet him. You would be very proud.

GENERAL: I would be very proud.

PILAR: What about that young man with twenty bullets in his back — five in each limb? Was he wearing a silver bandanna?

GENERAL: It was one bullet. One shot to the back of the head.

PILAR: I've felt his absence all morning.

(The General opens the door, taking precautions not to be seen.)

GENERAL: *(Whispering.)* Describe him to me once again.

PILAR: *(Realizing.)* You're not going to let me look?

GENERAL: If you look at him, nothing else will occupy your mind for the rest of your life.

PILAR: You don't think I will know my son's legs, nor his hands? Do you think something so gruesome would happen to my son that I would not want to look? Take me to him.

(The general takes her hand as they begin to take the slow walk to where the bodies are kept. The body has not been visible up until this point. It is, perhaps, hidden behind a scrim. Finally, the general slides out the body. Pilar looks down, grabs the hand of the body. Pilar's face confirms her worst fears.) *(A long, long pause.) Oscar,* meet your boy.

(The general looks down at the body, stunned.)

GENERAL: *(Long beat.)* He did move me. This young man. Charismatic. He knew how to win people — how to work up the troops. They believed in him so much that they'd die for him. Do you know how dangerous that is?

PILAR: Why do you think I fell in love with you — irresistible charisma?

GENERAL: We would have lost power, *Pilar.* I had no choice.

PILAR: *(Realizing.)* You shot him? How could you look at him and not know?

GENERAL: There are so many young men like him. How was I to know?

PILAR: His eyes, Oscar. You were supposed to know him by his eyes. They're yours. They had within them the fire for great change.

GENERAL: *(Realizing.)* You had my son.

PILAR: I had your son. Because I believed in you. I believed in you. *(Long beat.)* You would have liked him. Loved him, maybe.

GENERAL: I've longed for that — for a son.

PILAR: I know. Isn't that what men do? They long for sons? Long for sons who will carry the torch of the fire within them? Only some men who have killed that fire within themselves go out of their way to kill it in someone else. They extinguish it. Like you did. Today. Fathers and sons. Legacies. This one. This dream. Has come to an end. Goodbye, *Oscar.*

GENERAL: What would you have me do?

PILAR: Don't forget who you are. The men who oppress us are merely down that hall.

(Pilar starts to leave.)

GENERAL: I killed your boy.

PILAR: Our boy, *Oscar*. Ours.

GENERAL: Our boy.

(The General looks at his gun.)

PILAR: I'd like to think Miguel died for something. Like winning over your heart.

(The General looks up at her.)

PILAR: *(Long beat.)* Revolutions never cease, *Oscar*, they are merely inherited by the next generation.

GENERAL: I would have liked to have met him.

(Pilar points at his heart.)

PILAR: I say you know him very well.

(Pilar exits. The General takes his gun in hand and heads down the hall.)

(Blackout.)

END OF PLAY

Rightsized

Kate McCamy

Produced in the August 2009 Short Play Series at Arts Society of Kingston, New York (www.askforarts.org). Director: Richard Mover. Cast: Sheila — Julissa Roman; Lex — Sean Patrick Reilly.

Produced in February 2009 by The Drilling Company (www.thedrillingcompany.com) at the 78th Street Playhouse for their Freedom themed evening of one-act plays. Director: Hamilton Clancy. Cast: Sheila — Shawn B. Wilson; Lex — Michael Gnat.

CHARACTERS

SHEILA, a cleaning lady, any ethnicity, her age depends on how the director wants to go with the play.

LEX, a young, twenties to thirties, portfolio manager.

SETTING

An empty office down near Wall Street, NYC.

• • •

Lights up. There is a high end corporate desk, a trash can. Lex, dressed in casual, yet high end I just got off the golf course in Bermuda clothes, is looking through the desk. He finds a bottle of high end scotch. In the background there is a faint sound of a vacuum cleaner.

LEX: Johnny Walker Blue, Jack Bowman you o'l devil.

(His cell phone rings. He has to answer it.)

LEX: Fuck! Hi Mrs. Bowman, yeah I'm in Jack's office now. No, nothing so far. Hey no, don't worry about it, I got you covered. I will, I will, I know, I promise, it's gonna be OK. I'm going through all John's things, yes, yes. What time is it there in Tokyo anyway? Tomorrow night? Wow, well, have a great flight, I'll see you at the, ah, service. Yep. Bye bye.

(He answers the phone again.)

LEX: Cliff, what the fuck? Nah, his dragon lady wife Mika, she's in Japan. No, shopping. Hell no! I was in fucking Barbados! Nah, nobody, the office is empty. Yeah, looking through his desk now, nothing man, I can't believe Jack Bowman, Jack Bowman offed himself. Dude, you can't jump out these windows, they're hermetically sealed. In his kitchen, the maid found him. Yeah, nasty.

(The Vacuum cleaner gets louder.)

You sick motherfucker, no, a rope, or something. Yeah I'm OK. You kiddin'? I could guzzle six of them right now. See you over there.

LEX: Oh man . . .

(Sheila, the cleaning lady vacuums her way in.)

SHEILA: Oh, sorry sir. I thought the place was empty.

LEX: Tell me about it, place is a tomb.

SHEILA: I'll just be taking the trash . . .

LEX: Hey where's the shredder?

SHEILA: They took 'em all.

LEX: No way. They got here first, this is bad. Shit shit. Hey Selma, remember this? Last Christmas? We had a nip together?

SHEILA: I don' think that was me, sir.

LEX: I remember, we got hammered and stuck pencils in the ceiling. Here for old times sake.

SHEILA: Thank you sir, but I don't drink . . .

LEX: To Jack, may he be in a better place. And to better times, eh? Times is hard but they'll get better, right?

SHEILA: Well sir, it depends on what you mean by hard.

LEX: True, true. Prison sex, now that's hard.

(Pause.)

You think they'll send us to prison?

SHEILA: I don't think guys like you go to prison.

LEX: I heard white collar prison isn't so bad, there's a golf course. I'd prefer house arrest, the bracelet thing. Did you see anyone else come in here?

SHEILA: Oh I don't know anything, sir.

LEX: Please, call me Alexander, or just Lex is fine. I mean hey, right now, on paper, you're earning more money than me. Funny huh?

SHEILA: Oh I don't know about that . . .

LEX: Can't "downsize" you right? No you're recession proof. That's gotta feel pretty damn good about now. People always need someone to clean up after them. Shit right now a portfolio manager is about as useless as man breasts. You, probably got at least another week right here cleaning up after us.

SHEILA: Ain't a vacuum big enough to clean up Wall Street.

LEX: Funny lady. Where'd you put yesterday's trash?

SHEILA: They took it downstairs to wherever they take it.

LEX: Who?

SHEILA: The trashmen.

LEX: I just don't get it. Everything was all really really . . . sweet, that gravy train was cruising along. Chug chug chug. Like eating peanuts, you can't stop and then . . . I mean what the fuck? It just tanked, it went bad like dead fish, like some prick with a pin popped the balloon and it all went kaboom. And now they call it "rightsizing". Ain't nothing right about this development.

SHEILA: I'm sorry for your loss, sir.

LEX: It ain't just this company, they're all going down, I mean this shit's bad.

But not to, you know, end it all. That's just crazy, it's only money Jack. Wow, I can't believe I just said that. Well it's just a downturn, I was broke in college, I survived it.

SHEILA: I guess it was only a matter of time.

LEX: What?

SHEILA: Even a pyramid can get too big before it falls.

LEX: Hey Jack wasn't pulling a Ponzi?

SHEILA: What? No I was talking about the nature of things getting too big.

LEX: Whoa, sit down, let me school you here Selma, nature has nothing to do with the DOW or NASDAQ. Even top financial analysts don't understand how all this shit works. Actually in a way it is a Ponzi, isn't it? We all bought into the game, shuffling the money around assuming that the system was just going to keep on keepin' on. If you fool the whole financial world, then it has to be real because the system is based on the idea that it is real. Brilliant really. I wish I knew who thought that one up.

SHEILA: You think one person made this up?

LEX: It would be nice to blame some one, wouldn't it?

SHEILA: Why?

LEX: Because then it's not my fault.

SHEILA: Are you to blame?

LEX: No. No, it wasn't me. But I'm being punished like I was. Punished for doing my job. That's what really grinds me, I was just doing my job. Just doing like everyone else and what did I get? I got no job that's what. You know what the real bitch is? Yeah, there's more.

SHEILA: I couldn't possibly know . . .

LEX: You'da thought I'd a kept a nest egg, you know? Something to fall back on? A little rainy day fraud, I mean fund? But no, you know what this big money manager did? I did what I told everybody else to do.

SHEILA: What was that?

LEX: I invested! What an asshhole! Even worse, the loft I bought is way too . . . I way over . . . I'm screwed. I can't flip it because it's worth less than what I . . . I'm gonna be one of those foreclosure losers.

SHEILA: Maybe you should rent?

LEX: Shit I might have to move in with Cliff or worse, back home to my parents until this blows over.

SHEILA: You think this is gonna blow over?

LEX: Sure. Has to. The big crash of '29 blew over didn't it?

SHEILA: If the Great Depression and World War II is 'blowing over'.

LEX: Yeah, but it's the way it works, stuff like that helps reestablish the profit margin.

SHEILA: So where did the profit margin go?

LEX: What?

SHEILA: All that money, where is it?

LEX: Ah, well, that's the big question. It's hard to explain, actually. But suffice it to say . . .

SHEILA: You don't know do you?

LEX: Of course I do. I'm in finance. I know money. Say you give me a dollar to invest.

SHEILA: From what I read in the papers, you take my dollar and you go buy a Lexus.

LEX: Ah, Selma you crack me up. OK, I'll try to make this simple for you, the money, this, goes into a bigger pile from other investors and it is used to buy and sell options on funds, speculations and such which make money so the interest goes back into the big pile and everybody makes more dollars.

SHEILA: That's when things go good, but when things go bad, where did the money go?

LEX: Well when things go good there are more dollars and when they go bad . . . they just, well, go away.

SHEILA: Really, just away? Like that? Poof? My dollar goes into thin air? It can't do that, so where is it?

LEX: Well, this is why it's called speculation.

SHEILA: Who's pocket is it in?

LEX: It's not in any one's pocket, per se.

SHEILA: Uh huh. The way I see it Lex, is my dollar went somewhere other than my pocket. If I trust you to take care of my dollar then I think you would at least know where it is.

LEX: Ah, well its bundled in with other dollars.

SHEILA: Oh well that's nice I'm glad my dollar has friends to be with. Now where are they hanging out?

LEX: OK, ah, like on a plane, the air gets recycled, you breathe out and it goes up into the circulatory system and then you breathe in, but it's not your breath it's someone else's. From a previous flight. I know this is a little conceptual . . .

SHEILA: Uh huh. Yeah, I get it. My Grandpa once told me that the Earth is a bubble and all the water on the planet is recycled so your drink right there could be Cleopatra's tears from the Nile river.

LEX: Precisely. Your Grandpa was a smart man.

SHEILA: You're damn right he was, but what I want to know is how does this system of yours recycle my dollar back to me?

LEX: Look just forget about your dollar will ya? In the real world of finance your dollar doesn't exist. I mean come on, when the sum is really something that turns into nothing, well, you wouldn't get it, but trust me, nothing becomes something, big time.

SHEILA: Oh I understand something and nothing. You think I got nothing to lose? Let me school you Mr. Lex. I love my family and friends and I really want this whole damn crazy system to work. But you, all you think about is yourself and to think you're sitting here complaining to me. Recession proof? I take two trains and a bus to get here to do my job, and when you don't got a job I don't got a job. We're so knitted together, like one big sweater. Pull one lose string and it all comes undone. So just get over yourself for Godsakes. Be thankful for what you got. Oh and my name is Sheila, Sheila. You got that?

LEX: Yes ma'am. Sheila.

SHEILA: Yeah.

LEX: But Jack called you Selma.

SHEILA: Yeah? And where is he now? God bless his soul.

LEX: Right.

SHEILA: But you can call me Cleopatra.

LEX: Cleopatra?

SHEILA: That's right, I'm a queen and you, you're drinking my tears.

LEX: Tears? What am I gonna do?

SHEILA: Try to do something good.

LEX: I don't know how.

SHEILA: You need help, I mean like professional. You're so confused.

LEX: I know, I know. C'mon Sheila, I'm desperate. Cleopatra. Please.

(He kneels down in front of her.)

Please. Tell me how to be . . .

SHEILA: Honey the way I see it people do what they wanna do, nothing I can say is gonna stop that. But since you asked . . .

LEX: I did, I did, tell me, what . . .

SHEILA: Be there for your friend's family, they're gonna need you. Then . . . volunteer, help out strangers, some kids, play basketball with them, teach them how not to invest their money. Then go keep some old people company, read a book out loud, make soup, pick up trash along the highway, get rid of your Lexus, ride a bike, you got what, four phones, use one of them to call your mother. One day you'll be watching her die and wish you had spent more time with her. Then you'll be breathing your last breath and your life will flash before your eyes and what you gonna see?

LEX: Yeah.

SHEILA: So what are you gonna see when God takes you?

LEX: Ah, wow. Uh, let's see, schools, I went to a bunch of schools, then jobs, made money, I shopped, online a lot. I see computers, played games, downloaded porno. Went out to eat, a lot and . . . sports, watched some sports. Made money, and, well I hook up every now and then with some random babe . . .

SHEILA: Damn, that is pathetic. You're like that Pac Man thing munching everything in it's way. Is that what you wanna see?

LEX: No. I want, I need a better life to die with.

SHEILA: So live one.

(He kisses her gently, maybe, if the moment works.)

LEX: I'm sorry. You're married?

SHEILA: Yes.

LEX: Your husband is a very fortunate man.

SHEILA: Yes he is my king.

LEX: That's nice.

(He lays his head in her lap, she strokes his hair tenderly.)

(Black.)

END OF PLAY

Self Phone

BRENDON ETTER

Self Phone was originally produced at the Northfield Arts Guild Theater in Northfield, Minnesota, on January 11, 2008, as part of "Sex With Seven Women," an evening of short plays by Brendon Etter about women and sex. Cast: Lily — Lauren Hainley; Werner — Jamin O'Malley. Voice-over at the end: Shari Setchell. Director: Brendon Etter.

CHARACTERS

LILY, in her twenties.

WERNER, in his twenties.

SETTING

A busy public space, table, two chairs.

• • •

Werner is seated at a small table reading a book; he doesn't look up as Lily enters. Lily moves tentatively toward the table and the empty chair across from Werner.

LILY: Hi . . .

WERNER: Huh . . .

LILY: . . . Hi.

WERNER: Oh, uhhh . . . hi. *(Back to his book.)*

LILY: *(Holding an invisible cell phone, she speaks into the "cell" excitedly.)* He said "hi"!

WERNER: What?

LILY: *(Into cell.)* You were right! He's so cute! Yes! Oh, yeah, I'm standing near him right now . . . he's reading . . . like a book or something . . . I don't know! I'll ask him . . . *(To Werner.)* What are you reading?

WERNER: *(Confusedly.)* A . . . book.

LILY: *(To cell.)* Yep, it's a book! That's what you thought! Right, I remember you said that . . . yeah, he looks so smart . . . so smart and so cute . . . I know! That doesn't happen a lot . . . Isn't it weird that some people just look smart . . . yeah, I don't know . . . *(Sees Werner looking at her in disbelief.)* . . . hold on a moment . . . *(Turns her attention to Werner, he's surreptitiously trying to see her cell phone, then gives in to his curiosity.)*

WERNER: Who . . . who are you talking to?

LILY: Hannah.

WERNER: *(Looking around.)* Hannah?

LILY: Yeah, my friend, Hannah.

WERNER: Hannah?

LILY: *(To cell.)* I'm sure he remembers you . . . right . . . yes . . . yes . . . I know . . . yes . . . last Saturday . . . so what do I do now?

WERNER: *(Indicating her hand.)* This is Hannah?

LILY: *(To cell.)* Hold on, I think he wants to tell me something about you! I'll let you know!

WERNER: Do I know you?

LILY: Oh no, no, you don't, I'm so sorry . . . didn't I introduce myself? *(To cell.)* I forgot to introduce myself to him, ahhh, I know, so stupid! I can't believe I did that! He's going to think I'm such an idiot!

WERNER: No . . . I . . .

LILY: *(Continuing to cell.)* Yes . . . I know, I do things like this all the time . . . I know with Eric . . . remember . . . he just got so tired of me . . . yes . . . no, but he said, I just wasn't "there" when he wanted me . . . I don't even know what that means . . . "there"? . . . no, I don't think he was talking about 'that' . . . there was something else . . . I felt like such a moron, no . . . no . . . I loved him so much! I did! No, no, no, no, he wasn't . . . of course not, no . . . he wasn't perfect . . . but still . . . I really miss him . . . and now, you know, here I am . . . and I'm already forgetting to introduce myself . . . I know . . . so stupid . . . stupid and rude . . .

WERNER: I . . . really, it's not . . .

LILY: *(Shushing Werner with a raised finger, continuing to cell.)* What? No. I don't think so. I'd have to ask him . . . but I feel so dumb now . . . well, because . . . because he doesn't even know my name . . . yes . . . yes . . . a little awkward now . . . ummm . . . he's just kind of staring at me *(Werner makes an effort to return to his book.)* . . . yeah . . . OK . . . yeah . . . I will . . . Argh! He is SO cute! And I didn't even tell him my name. I mean how hard would it be for me to just say like "Hi! My name is Lily" or something like that . . . such an idiot . . . yes, I am! No . . . I . . . I . . . I . . . but . . . but . . . he'll hate me now! I know it! I can tell . . . well . . . he didn't even offer me the empty chair at his table . . . *(Werner gestures too emphatically for her to sit down, she ignores him.)* I saw that on Oprah, means he doesn't like you, doesn't want you to sit down or get comfortable around him, because, ultimately, he's not comfortable around me . . . but . . . no . . . I should go . . . he's totally not into me . . . I can tell . . . ohhh . . . like just little things, you know . . . yeah . . . he's kind of holding the book up to his chest. *(Werner becomes increasingly flustered as he attempts to "correct" each negative cue he is, apparently, sending.)* . . . and his legs are crossed . . . yeah, I saw it on Oprah . . . it's a bad date cue . . . right, oh . . . and his head is sort of tilted back and away from me at an odd angle . . . yeah, uh-huh, yeah . . . I saw it on Oprah . . . not ready to like really meet you, like he's looking to move away before he even knows my name . . . that kind of thing . . . now he's scratching his head and looking . . . yeah, I know, you saw that on Oprah? Me too! I don't remember, but I know Oprah said it's bad . . . What should I DO!? I am so flushed and, oh . . . he's totally going to reject me . . . what . . . just tell him my name? Just like that? "Hi! I'm Lily!" Like that? You sure? You sure? You're absolutely sure you're sure? All right . . . I'll do it . . . yeah . . . I'll let you know what happens, OK? *(To Werner, as she finally takes the seat.)* Hi, I'm Lily! *(Puts down the cell phone and offers her hand to Werner.)*

WERNER: Uhhh . . . yeah, I . . .

LILY: *(To cell.)* Hannah? Guess what!? I did it! Yes, totally . . . I said "Hi, my name is Lily" or something like that! Can you believe it?! I'm so excited! Yes! I know! I know! Where am I now? I'm sitting! I'm sitting in the other chair! I know! I don't know! I know! Yes . . . well, I just stepped up and sat in it! Yep, just sat right down! Ha-ha! I know! Ohh . . . I don't know? Should I be worried about that? Ahhh, too late, I'm worried about it now! Thanks a lot, Hannah! Why . . . why do you always do that? *(Starts getting huffy and a little teary.)* I meet someone, I introduce myself and you have to ask me a question like that! No . . . no . . . I'm really mad right now! Yes, at you . . . well . . . come on! I never said that! I NEVER said that! No . . . no . . . I did NOT! I can't believe . . . you . . . but . . . I never . . . no . . . no . . . that's not what I said . . . I said . . . I said . . . will you listen to me? I said . . . I said that I just sat down . . . in the chair . . . I don't know, and I don't appreciate you bringing it up all the time . . . yes . . . yes . . . well, I FEEL like you bring it up all the time . . . yes.. I do . . . you know how sensitive I am about that, and you bring it up all the time . . . and, yes, you do! You do! All the time, like you're trying to pick on me . . . you know, find the weakness like that one time on Oprah that girl said her best friend always knew her weaknesses, and she used them to control her like a puppet, like a puppet-friend, dancing on a string . . . and Oprah got really mad, and told her to stop it, and didn't she see that it was hurting her friend? And didn't she realize that it wasn't a real friendship if . . . if . . . one friend always held the strings . . . not real strings, but like fake strings that you can't really see but that the friend with the weaknesses CAN ALWAYS FEEL! And then Oprah told the friend with the fake strings that she needed to be her friend's friend in a real, no-strings, way . . . and then, do you remember what happened then . . . do you? Do you?! No?! Well, I do!

Oprah wept! She wept, Hannah! Real tears like I'm crying right now! I don't want to be a puppet-friend! No! Alright, then I'll answer your question, Hannah! No! OK!? No, I am not "smothering" him! No, it just started . . . our relationship . . . and it's very special, and I won't let you ruin it by making me worry if I'm smothering him! It's a beautiful relationship, Hannah! We are getting on just fine! Better than fine! So, stop the QUESTIONS!! Alright?! Alright!? Fine! Fine! GOOD-BYE! Yes! FOREVER!! GOOD-BYE INFINITY!! *(She hangs up, and sits staring at the table and weeping openly.)*

WERNER: Uhhhhh . . . I'm Werner.

LILY: *(Crying.)* I'd really like to take a moment here.

WERNER: Right . . . sure. *(Lily's cries slowly subside. Long pause. Werner looks at Lily, then at her "cell phone". He begins very cautiously.)* Hey . . . Lily? I'm . . . uh . . . Werner. I'm really sorry that Hannah did that to you . . . I have a friend like that too, and . . .

LILY: *(Looking up, wiping snot and tears away.)* Did you see that on Oprah that one time? That's how I feel! Hannah always makes me think that I'm smothering my boyfriends; so I pull away from them, and, guess what? They break up with me! Say I'm too distant, that I'm not really "there", and I always want to tell them that it's Hannah's fault . . . 'cause it is . . .

WERNER: *(Attempting lightheartedness.)* Maybe you should break up with Hannah!

LILY: *(Seriously.)* I'm not dating Hannah.

WERNER: *(Unsuccessfully stabbing at some humor in the situation.)* Right! Ha-ha! Good one . . .

LILY: Sorry, where are my manners? Usually pretty good at manners . . . what's your name?

WERNER: *(She didn't hear?)* Ummm . . . Werner . . .

LILY: Hi, I'm Lily.

WERNER: *(Relieved that something normal is happening.)* Right, yes, I remem . . . uhhh . . . Hi Li —

LILY: My friends call me Diamata . . . Werner?

WERNER: Right, Werner . . . umm . . . hi, Dia . . . mata . . .

LILY: That's a weird name, are you a Nazi?

WERNER: A Nazi?

LILY: Yeah, they we're really bad guys from Australia, or something, that killed a lot of people a couple hundred years ago . . .

WERNER: No . . . I mean, yes . . . no . . . I . . .

LILY: I think my Dad said one of them was called Werner, and Werner and his friends ran around South America, Australia, somewhere and beat up and killed a lot of people a couple hundred years ago . . .

WERNER: No . . . it's Germany . . . they . . .

LILY: *(To cell.)* Hannah? Listen . . . I'm really sorry . . . that wasn't nice of me . . . I know you were just trying to help . . . I know . . . I'm really sorry. I know. I shouldn't have used Oprah against you . . . that was a low blow . . . I'm sorry . . . ohh . . . that's soooo sweet! Don't worry, I'll never let some boy get between us! Yes! Sister power! Friends? Great! 'Cause, guess what? I know his name! Yes! It's Werner . . . no, I know . . . he's so cute and really smart! Yeah . . . and I shook his hand! Really nice . . . no he has really nice skin on his hand . . . on the one I shook anyway! No, I haven't checked out the other one yet! Ha! You're so racy, Hannah! I know what you're thinking. Oh, but guess what? He's probably a Nazi! *(Werner starts protesting silently, Lily doesn't notice.)* Yeah . . . remember them? They were on Oprah once, but she kicked them off . . . I know . . . "You go, girl!" That's what I say . . . Oprah totally kicked their Nazi butts. Anyway, my Dad knows the Nazi's first names, and he told me Werner was one of them . . . no . . . they killed all those people in Canada or something a few hundred years ago . . . I don't know. I might have to break it off. Well, 'cause I don't want to be connected to a Nazi guy! It's too bad too . . . 'cause he's really cute, and smart . . . Yeah? Oh, you're right . . . yes, just like that killer . . . he was all cute and smart and girls wanted him, so he'd pick them up in his nice car and kill them! I don't know . . . I suppose he could be both . . . yeah . . . a Nazi and a murderer . . . I don't know . . . no . . . I feel pretty safe . . . yeah, there are other people here . . . if he tries anything, I'll just call you and you can call 911, OK? I don't know . . . I'll ask him. OK. Hold on . . .

WERNER: *(Jumping at the chance.)* I'm not a Nazi!!

LILY: *(To cell.)* Whoa . . . He says he's not a Nazi. Yeah, super defensive about it . . . I know . . . that's one of Oprah's warning signs! That's exactly what I was thinking to myself! We are totally soul sisters! We think about the same Oprah shows at the same time and everything! Yeah, he says he's not a Nazi, but he didn't say anything about whether or not he kills girls that he picks up with his cuteness and smartness . . . I don't know . . . should I be worried? I'll check . . . yeah, right, he could have been in prison for a while and now he doesn't kill girls anymore . . .

WERNER: *(Jumping again, shouting, and obviously drawing concerned stares from those around their table.)* I DO NOT KILL GIRLS ANYMORE! *(Recoils.)*

LILY: *(To cell.)* Yeah, that was him, real defensive again . . . but, you know what, I believe him. I'll bet he doesn't kill girls anymore. Oprah always says "Ultimate love means ultimate forgiveness" . . . Yeah, I think it's going to work . . . I forgive him. We've all made mistakes, and I'm sure he's sorry that he killed all those girls, and beat up all those Australia people, but we have to move on in life. Plus, he's just so cute and so smart! No, the book he's reading is really big and thick! What?! *(Screeching in mock horror.)* What!? You are so dirty! I don't know, maybe I should ask him about that . . . *(Giddy laughter at her own dirty thoughts.)* . . . alright, yeah . . . I should get back to my date, here . . . OK . . . I love you too, you know that. I'll let you know what happens. *(Hangs up cell, focuses intently on Werner.)*

WERNER: *(Rather annoyed.)* I mean . . . I meant . . . I've never killed girls before. I'm not a Nazi. They were from Germany, not Australia, not South America, not Canada. They were in power in the 1930s and '40s, and they killed millions of people systematically . . . *(Beat.)* and we are not on a "date"!

LILY: *(To cell.)* Hannah, hi, it's me . . . no, don't call 911, they don't fix broken hearts. *(Breaking down.)* It's horrible! No! He's breaking up with me! I don't know; he's really sensitive about the Nazi thing, and he got all mad that I brought it up I guess, and I was trying to be understanding . . . no . . . I don't know . . . why can't it just go back to how it was when we started out? His name, my name, the book, the chair, girl killing and Nazis . . . those were the good times. Why is it all so complicated now? I guess we're just too different . . . exactly. . . I've never killed anyone, so I forget that other people might not want to talk about it so much. Right, it's just like on that one Oprah show where the wife of the murderer . . . *(At this point Werner grabs her cell phone hand and pins it down to the table.)* uhh . . . do you mind? . . . *(Dawning horror as she comes to the realization.)* Oh my God! You're not going to kill me, are you?! *(Obvious concerned stares from those around, Werner abruptly removes his hand from hers, Lily goes back to cell.)* Hi . . . no . . . that was him . . . he grabbed my arm and got really serious and scary . . . No . . . it felt good, just like his other hand! Anyway, I thought maybe he was going to kill me or something like that. *(Werner gets up, putting on coat and getting ready to leave.)* Hannah, I gotta go . . . yeah, I think I can patch things up . . . I gotta try, right? What other option do I have? *(To Werner, overly desperate.)* Don't go!

WERNER: *(Coming back toward the table.)* Listen, Lily . . .

LILY: Call me Diamata.

WERNER: No thanks . . . Listen . . . Alright, listen Diamata, I was reading my book, just sitting here and you came by and, somehow, you automatically considered yourself my girlfriend. I don't know how else to explain this to you — I don't even know you! Just because your friend Hannah seems to think she knows me, doesn't make me your girlfriend . . .

LILY: *(Angered.)* You were listening?

WERNER: What?!

LILY: You were eavesdropping on my cell phone conversation with my best and dearest friend in the whole world?

WERNER: What?! No, it can't be considered . . .

LILY: I am shocked by your behavior! Shocked! Oprah says that people who spy on the lives of others are compensating for the fact that they don't have their own life!

WERNER: I can't believe this! I can't believe you! Are you listening to yourself? Do you even realize how unbelievable this whole situation is?

LILY: It's perfectly believable, SPY! I never should have started dating you in the first place. Oprah says sometimes you have to look ugly in the face and get out of the way!

WERNER: We are not dating! We never have been dating! I was not spying on your . . .

LILY: You were! You're horrible! You have to accept your faults before you can really change, that's what Oprah says!

WERNER: I don't care what Oprah says!!

LILY: *(Taken aback by his ferocity, pausing while the dust settles, then quietly.)* Oprah says shouting is the first sign that you're losing an argument.

WERNER: *(Contemplates shouting again, but takes Oprah's advice, quietly intense.)* OK. Three things: one, I'm not nor have I ever been a Nazi or murderer; two, we are not dating; and three, it cannot be considered eavesdropping when you are speaking at a normal volume and I am three feet away from you.

LILY: That's four things. The Nazi and murder thing should be two different . . .

WERNER: *(Interrupting.)* AND a fourth thing, it can't be considered eavesdropping on a cell phone conversation when you're not even talking on a cell phone . . .

LILY: What?

WERNER: Where is it?

LILY: What?

WERNER: You don't have a cell phone! Please don't pretend that you do . . .

LILY: My cell phone?

WERNER: Is not here . . . you don't have a cell phone . . .

LILY: Are you jealous?

WERNER: What?

LILY: Jealous of my cell phone? Are you? That's sad . . .

WERNER: No! I am not jealous of your *(Makes air quotes.)* cell phone! How could I be jealous of something that doesn't even exist?

LILY: It does exist! And you're so obviously jealous of it . . .

WERNER: No! You have been talking into your right hand this whole time . . . pretending to push buttons . . . I've watched you do it, right here in front of me . . .

LILY: You're pathetic . . .

WERNER: *(He takes out his own cell phone.)* Look! I have a very real cell phone right here! While they are getting smaller and smaller each year, they have yet to reach the point of invisibility . . . You see, this is what they look like . . .

LILY: You're just jealous that I get so many calls!

WERNER: What! No, you were making all the calls, pretending to make them. I heard no phone ringing. BECAUSE THERE IS NONE!

LILY: It's right here! *(She holds out her bare right hand, he slaps at it.)* Don't! You'll break it!

WERNER: I'm sure . . . OK listen . . . give me your cell phone number, and I'll call you . . .

LILY: Why would I want to give a Nazi my cell phone number?

WERNER: Because this Nazi is also a murderer, and he will kill you if you keep pretending . . .

LILY: Big man! Big threats! Oprah says that people who make . . .

WERNER: SHUT UP ABOUT GODDAMN OPRAH!

LILY: Big mouth!

WERNER: Listen, you started all this: You come along and insist on having very loud conversations about me, right in front of me! You go on and on and on, making me very self-conscious. You don't even really try to speak to me. You make up a romantic relationship by talking loudly and, again, right in front of me, to a friend who may not even exist on a cell phone that definitely does not exist, you accuse me of being horrible things, a Nazi?! A murderer!? A boyfriend?! You accuse me of these things in public, with people around, pretending to be my girlfriend, and I don't even know you . . . So, come on, what's your number? Let's set this straight. Give me your number. *(Pause.)* I'll call the number, if you pick up and we have a conversation, then I'll stop.

LILY: You have to believe.

WERNER: To believe?

LILY: Yes.

WERNER: Believe in what?

LILY: My cell phone.

WERNER: I don't believe in your cell phone. You don't have a cell phone.

LILY: You HAVE to believe, or it won't work.

WERNER: It's a cell phone, not a deity. It either works or doesn't work.

LILY: Not my cell phone. I am my cell phone. It is me. No belief, no connection.

WERNER: OK. Listen . . . let's try this. *(Werner hands LILY his real cell phone.)* You dial your number into my cell phone, then we'll talk. If it works, I will go on a date with you. We can even talk about Oprah. If it doesn't work, then delete the number from my phone, so you don't have to worry about random Nazis or murderers calling you before they kill you.

LILY: *(Imploring.)* You must believe, Werner. You must.

WERNER: I'll try. Dial . . .

LILY: *(Dialing.)* OK . . . *(She hands the phone back to Werner.)*

WERNER: *(Listening.)* I'm not hearing anything . . .

LILY: *(Picking up her phone.)* See, it's ringing!

WERNER: What?! No, it's not!

LILY: It's ringing again!

WERNER: I'm hearing nothing, complete silence, no ringing, nothing . . .

LILY: It's still ringing . . .

WERNER: *(Angered, but also a bit intrigued.)* No! It's not! Nothing. *(Long pause.)* Well, if it's ringing, why don't you answer it? Go on! Answer it!

LILY: I'm scared.

WERNER: That you won't be able to talk to me?

LILY: Well . . .

WERNER: Because you know I'm right! I know you're faking it.

LILY: No. I'm not.

WERNER: Then answer it!

LILY: I am scared that you won't be able to connect with me.

WERNER: Answer it! Come on!

LILY: I'll answer, Werner, but it might be worse than you're expecting.

WERNER: Isn't your voice mail going to pick up soon?

LILY: My phone rings as long as I want it to. I am my voice mail.

WERNER: Answer it! Quite stalling! I'm getting no ring on my end, just a void.

LILY: *(She answers it.)* Hello, Werner?

WERNER: *(Triumphant.)* Nothing, nothing at all.

LILY: No. I can hear you just fine.

WERNER: Gee, maybe that's because I'm standing right next to you?

LILY: No, on my phone, I can hear you on my cell phone.

WERNER: Really? Let me listen. *(They exchange phones.)*

LILY: *(Getting a little ashamed.)* Hello, Werner . . .

WERNER: *(Mocking.)* Hmmm, strange . . . Getting nothing on this end . . . like I'm listening to air . . .

LILY: *(Holding out her hand for her phone, Werner plays along, hands her phone back.)* You are.

WERNER: Yeah. Here delete your number from my phone, then we can go our separate ways.

LILY: *(She looks at his phone, then hands it back.)* That's OK. I think your battery's dead.

WERNER: *(Looks at his phone.)* No, look it's almost fully charged. I just . . .

LILY: *(She looks at him sadly, shaking her head, reaches out to him, lays her hand flat and full over his heart.)* I said . . . "your" battery . . . *(She holds her hand there for a little bit, turns and starts leaving.)*

WERNER: *(Shocked, calling to her as she walks off.)* I . . . maybe we could try again . . . start over . . . you know, without Hannah and the Nazi stuff . . . *(He looks at his phone, hits redial, audible rings on stage, Werner is very surprised at this, rings continue for a while then we hear in the tone of a standard mechanical operator voice, but would be great if it could be Oprah's voice.)*

VOICE-OVER: "We're sorry, but the number you have dialed has been disconnected. *(Pause.)* Disconnected from you, Werner. Forever."

(Werner looks out in shock.)

END OF PLAY

Smile

Nina Mansfield

Smile premiered as part of Turtle Shell Productions' 8 Minute Madness Playwright Festival at the Shell Theatre, 300 West 43rd Street, Suite #403, New York, New York, on February 27, 2008. Director: David Letwin. Cast: Man — Bristol Pomeroy; Woman — Pia Ambardar. Producer/Artistic Director: John W. Cooper.

In addition, *Smile* was a winner in Longwood University's 1st Annual 10-Minute play competition. It also appeared as part of the 2008 Boston Theater Marathon.

CHARACTERS

MAN, a man. Mid to late thirties. A professional.

WOMAN, a woman. Twenties-thirties. A professional.

PLACE

Two separate interrogation rooms of the same police station.

TIME

The present.

• • •

On one side of the stage sits a man. He holds an ice pack to his eye. He is definitely a man, not a boy. He might be wearing a suit, his jacket slung on the back of the chair, his sleeves rolled up, tie loosened. On a table next to him, or perhaps on the corner of a desk, is a clip board with some forms, with a pen attached by a string.

On the other side of the stage sits a woman. They are sitting in separate interrogation rooms of the same police station, and speak to an unseen police officer. The woman might be anywhere from her early twenties to late thirties. She is conservatively dressed in a suit. She exudes confidence.

MAN: Look, I didn't touch her, if that's what you're asking. No way.

WOMAN: *(Rubbing her wrist.)* Yes, I understand my rights, and no, I don't need a lawyer.

MAN: And don't go telling me PMS is an excuse these days.

WOMAN: Have I ever been hospitalized? No, no . . . I mean, I'm sure if you just check, you'll see that I have no criminal record. I've never done anything remotely violent or illegal. I've never even gotten a parking ticket. Seriously.

MAN: My wife gets like hell on wheels. If any woman had an excuse to, uh, you know . . .

(He motions to his eye.)

. . . it would be her. Not that she ever would. She's not that kind of gal.

WOMAN: Don't I get a phone call or something? I need to call the office.

MAN: I should probably call her. She'll wonder why I'm not in my office.

(Man flips open his cell phone.)

WOMAN: No it can't wait. Look, I have an important meeting to get to. I'm the boss, I'm in charge, and if I am not there, the deal doesn't go through. There are large sums of money at stake. Can't you just take my card and we can deal with this at a more convenient time?

MAN: *(Closes cell phone.)* Whatever, she'll live. I'll call her later.

WOMAN: *(Under breath.)* This is ridiculous.

(Addressing officer.)

Of course I was provoked. It's not like I just walked up to a stranger and —

MAN: Hell yeah I wanna press charges.

WOMAN: What kind of person do you think I am?

MAN: *(Very matter-of-fact.)* It's not like I told her to suck my dick. I'm not that kind a guy. I respect women. Trust me, I've seen some of these guys with their suck my dick and their fuck me's — hanging out of windows, waving their arms. I'm not totally sure what they are trying to accomplish — like someone should explain to them, that won't get you laid. I could totally understand any woman wanting to lay one in on one of them. Not that I condone violence — but jeez. No, I'm not like that. For Pete's sake, I've got a daughter.

WOMAN: He said — she said. I get it. I'm telling you I was provoked.

MAN: But this chick — woman, sorry.

WOMAN: I'm not a violent person. Really. I mean, yes, I've had to . . . become more aggressive. My line of work is cut throat. It's still a man's world. But violence . . .

MAN: What kind of wacko feminist bullshit. I mean, I'm all about equal rights. Don't get me wrong. Equal pay for equal work — equal rights amendment, and all that. I've got nothing against women. I did mention, I'm married.

WOMAN: For God's sake, I'm a pacifist.

MAN: But some of these women. I mean — even you've got to agree. Some of them, some women — won't even let a guy open a door for them. Like it's some political statement. Like, that's the shit I don't get.

WOMAN: Why are you looking at me like you don't believe me?

MAN: Yeah, sorry. I'll stick to the facts. My point is, I was just on my way to work. Had the cab drop me off on Lexington, because of the traffic.

WOMAN: Do I consider myself a feminist? I am not sure how that's relevant. I mean, I've admitted what I did. I'm sorry. I told you, I've never done anything like this before. Can you just charge me, or whatever it is you do?

MAN: You want me to just write it down here. No problem. You think you could get me another ice pack? This one's not really that cold.

WOMAN: Am I a member of any groups? What, you think I am some sort of militant feminazi? That I go around looking for trouble? I'm a little too busy for that. Career minded. Probably like you. I suppose I'd call myself a feminist, whatever that means these days, and certainly not militant. In high school I wrote a paper entitled "Why Women's Lib Doesn't Work, and Why I'm Happy About It." Seriously. You can look it up. I'm sure I have a copy of it somewhere.

MAN: *(As he's filling out the forms.)* Must be tough — being a women on the force. Don't get me wrong — I think it's great. I used to argue with my mom about stuff like that. Her brother was on the job — thirty years. She'd be like, a woman should know her place. And I'm like, Ma — come on. You think you couldn't do a better job than Uncle Mike keeping the streets safe. My mom could be a pretty scary woman when she wanted to be. I mean, I used to be terrified of her.

WOMAN: I had, what you might call, a convoluted sense of womanhood — back in the day. The very thought of burning the bra was laughable — and insulting. Who were these flat chested ninnies telling me that I needed to go au natural. No offense, I mean — not that you're flat chested. But I was a little clueless then. You know — what's so wrong with a friendly whistle — just take it as a compliment, right? Clueless.

MAN: She was one hell of a lady. Raised me and my two brothers, pretty much on her own. I mean, my dad — he was great too. Worked a lot though.

WOMAN: I would have traded my right to vote for a man to drape his frock over a puddle for me. Clearly I've come to my senses since those days. Seemed like half the girls in college were just there for their M.R.S. Not me.

MAN: I'm sorry . . .

WOMAN: I'm good at what I do. I've had to work hard to get there. And I have to deal with men every day — so no, I don't hate them, if that's what you're asking. I've had to earn their respect in that board room. And I have.

MAN: Do I have to fill out this form too?

WOMAN: Which is why it's so infuriating — on the street. Every day. I know what these men want. These *guys.* They want a reaction — a remark. A fuck you. A go to hell.

(Man shakes his pen as if it's running out of ink.)

WOMAN: A smile.

MAN: Name and address here too?

WOMAN: I've learned to keep my head down. My eyes looking at the sidewalk in front of me. Eye contact — forget it. If you can pretend not to hear them — pretend not to see them — Turn back to look — you can forget it. Once, and I am totally serious, I caught a guy licking a subway window. Licking. But I've learned not to react — to just keep walking. They rarely go beyond that first comment. And believe you me, I have heard it all.

(Very matter-of-fact.)

They want to fuck me. Lick my clit. Suck my cunt. Marry me pretty girl. You know I'd really like to spank you. Oh baby. I'd like to get a piece of you. Come on over here and sit of my face. I don't react. I just keep walking. Really. I do. But this — this one.

MAN: You don't think this is going to show up in the blotter?

WOMAN: Here I am, just minding my own business, waiting for the light to change. I feel like I spend half my life waiting to cross Lexington.

MAN: I've got friends who read the blotter religiously. They'd get a kick out of this.

WOMAN: And suddenly, this guy is just in my face, with this shit-eating grin.

MAN: Yeah, this pen has definitely died. Could I get another one sweetheart?

WOMAN: No not aggressive and yes, I was scared, but not like that. I didn't think he was a rapist. It was a crowded street. And the city has gotten safer. I was mugged once, a while back. That freaked me out . . . started taking Tae-Bo . . . but this wasn't like that.

MAN: *(Smiles, half-joking.)* All this paper work, when I'm the victim here.

(He winks.).

WOMAN: You know, I try to look down, look away, but he's right there. Like there's twenty of him, and he's everywhere.

MAN: *(Man hands back the clipboard to the invisible officer.)* I think that's it. It's all right there.

WOMAN: Smile. He tells me to smile.

MAN: I told her to smile. Big deal. I've got a daughter. She's four. Sunshine of my life. Whenever she's crying, pouting, cranky, whatever, I say, give daddy a smile. Where's my sunshine? Where's my sunshine?

WOMAN: *(Woman stands, acting out what she says.)* Light changes, so I start to cross. But he's there, he's right there next to me.

MAN: *(Man stands and begins to cross to woman.)* Aw come on. Why the frown? It's a gorgeous day.

WOMAN: I turn around. He's in my face.

MAN: What's the matter? Smile—

WOMAN: What right does anyone . . . I'm running late. Just a couple of minutes. But still, this deal could put my company on the map.

MAN: She looked sad. Focused. On something unpleasant. Dog died, broke a heel. I don't pretend to understand women. What do I know, right? I mean, clearly she was deranged, but how was I supposed to know that.

WOMAN: I promised myself I'd start taking a car service if the deal goes through. Subway can take anywhere from ten to twenty-two minutes. You really never know, so I always leave time. Which means, door to door, on a good day, twenty-four minutes. Bad day — well, you can do the math. I'm never late, even when trains get stuck.

MAN: Hey there, smile

WOMAN: I know what it takes to make it in a man's world. We've got to work twice as hard. So I get there early, stay late. It's just the way it is.

MAN: I figure, a woman like that . . .

WOMAN: I was just crossing the street, trying to mind my own business.

MAN: . . . body boxed in by business suit. She could be pretty if she'd just . . .

WOMAN: Am I supposed to look happy at 8:07 in the morning? Is there some sort of law that says I need to —

MAN: . . . smile.

WOMAN: Who the hell walks around this city smiling, you'd look like some kind of psychopath.

MAN: Smile.

WOMAN: I'm not crazy. I'm just minding my own business. God, if I was a man, do you think anyone would ask me to —

MAN: Smile.

WOMAN: Does it really matter *what* he said?

MAN: Smile.

(Woman tries to move around the man but he blocks her way.)

MAN: Smile.

(He blocks her way again.)

MAN: Smile.

(Woman punches man. It is slow, dramatic, climactic. He turns to the audience, clutching his eye. She turns to the audience. She is smiling.)

MAN: I just don't get it. I'm a nice guy.
WOMAN: *(The smile fades.)* Can I get that phone call now?
(Blackout.)

END OF PLAY

Steve

Liz Bartucci

Steve premiered at Cultural Development Corporation's 2009 Source Festival in Washington, D.C. on June 23, 2009. Director: Gregg Henry. Cast: Ann — Julie Garner; Steve — Joseph Thornhill.

Characters

Ann, single urban woman, formerly hopeful. Thirties-forties.

Steve, Ann's formerly Mixed Labrador Mutt. Thirties-forties.

Setting

Single Mixer in the basement of a Synagogue.

• • •

Ann and Steve are standing face to face. Long pause. Then—

ANN: . . . STEVE.

STEVE: Yes!

ANN: Steve. As in. My . . . *dog* STEVE.

STEVE: Your former dog Steve, yes.

ANN: Well. You look great.

STEVE: You know what? I feel really great.

ANN: Oh yea? And what sort of sick motherfucker —

STEVE: — Hey!

ANN: — What sort of sick horrible —

STEVE: I'm not sick —

ANN: No, my dog's not sick anymore because I had to put my dog to sleep —

STEVE: I'm awake. I'm awake now.

ANN: Are you a friend of his?

STEVE: Who?

ANN: NO ONE was in my bedroom that night except me, him, and my dog. My dog who sat at the foot of my bed who looked at me while he let that guy do that to me —

STEVE: You wanted it. You looked at me! You looked at me and said with your eyes "*I want this —* " You looked at me and said "*Get out!*"

ANN: Oh yes, I forgot — you're Steve the Telepathic Dog.

STEVE: I use to be.

ANN: You know, it took me years to get here. My first time out of the house in . . . here in the basement of a Synagogue up against the living and the horribly dressed. I actually was going to let people touch me — actually hold hands with someone. Tonight I said I'll try. This time. I came back. I'm here among the Drakkar Noir and cinnamon Dentyne. And I go up to you. The one man in a sea of women and you're my dead dog.

It's not fair. I'm here aren't I?! That's got to count for something! I'm here. I'm back. I'm here — I'm here — I'm here — I'm here.

STEVE: But. You're not.

ANN: But I'm not am I? Oh God. I'm not — I'm not — I'm not — I'm not —

(Steve takes her, holds her.)

STEVE: . . . Is it OK that I hold you like this?

ANN: If you're going to hurt me too, at least hold me first.

STEVE: I would never hurt you. I'm Steve —

ANN: — I know I know because you're my dog STEVE. I'm drunk.

STEVE: Isn't that ginger-ale?

ANN: You drugged me.

STEVE: I would never — Listen — Listen — Listen. We dogs do not normally go ahead and reveal our identities to our former — it's a common courtesy not to. But OK, sometimes we just go back and take a look. Watch from across the street, from our cars . . . I wanted to just cut to the chase. Yes, I am STEVE. Your beloved dog. I'm back. This is my human life. I heard that some dogs go and have hearts — no — *romances* with their former — in their second lives, but I don't think that's entirely fair — rather *cat* — rather — *sneaky,* no? But that's just my opinion. I think one should always GO! FETCH! — *Go forward.* This? This *life* is an opportunity. That's what I came back to tell you. That . . . You know, I have to say it's very nice to hold you like this.

ANN: I have finally lost it — I had it — I had it up till what — like six minutes ago? And I lost it — It's really really scary how in one minute it's all one fist tight rubber band ball —

STEVE: — You lost a ball?

ANN: — so carefully crafted and thought out — shaped over the course of years but then in a minute — gone. It's not rubber at all — it's actually fine — like spider spit —

STEVE: Did it fall out of your pocket?

ANN: I LOST MY MIND! OKAY? I LOST MY MIND.

STEVE: Maybe we should sit.

ANN: Sit.

(Steve sits, pulls Ann down.)

STEVE: You are, as far as I can tell, perfectly fine.

ANN: Perfectly fine.

STEVE: This is just how it goes.

ANN: This is just how — what goes?

STEVE: I don't know all the laws and orders and solutions — I myself am still learning all the right words. The words are so . . . The cats — the cats — they know everything! And they don't tell anyone. They know about Stonehenge, Nazca Lines, Fatima, Machu Picchu, Atlantis, but they're so (*Growl.*) — because they only get the one shot, so they just keep it all to themselves. You see how Shadow is, right? But the treat — the *reward* of not knowing, the reward of being a dog is that you get a second life. We get a shot at being human. And not just any human, a human of our longing of our character and spirit, of whatever age we want to be. Whatever time. Whatever place. Whatever . . . Speak.

ANN: That was a lot to process.

STEVE: That was an enormous amount to process. I'm sorry.

ANN: So, what you're saying, what you've said . . . wait. I was once a dog??

STEVE: — Actually no. No, not anymore. I mean for a while everyone was, yes. Some guys are dogs, *true*. But not all guys are dogs. Not even all girls are all dogs for that matter. The dogs, the dogs decided that it was an option, not a mandate. A reward they did not actually have to receive. They decided not to . . . Well . . . They're not coming back. They're not taking a second human life. They're sticking.

ANN: Sticking.

STEVE: With what we had as dogs. The second life is nice and all. Wonderful to be able to say these words, to close your mouth and sweat and not smell EVERY. LITTLE. THING. ALL THE TIME. You cannot imagine what every thing smells like all at once and how hard you have to work at separating yourself from it — sometimes it was a relief when you pulled me away with the leash — It's nice to be limited. We, as a group, as a *country* are mainly sticking because this life, is just too tough. Don't you think?

ANN: Why did . . . Why did you —

STEVE: Me? Well. I for one. I came back, because I was worried.

ANN: About me.

STEVE: I got a sense. That you weren't . . .

ANN: What.

STEVE: Sticking.

ANN: . . . It's funny. They say that dogs can smell cancer, disease, weed — anything. You smelled my desperation.

STEVE: — I can smell your . . . apart. Your depart. Your Island. Kind of smells like the cancer with a little bit of weed. Actually everything kind of smells a little bit like weed. But I really got the sense, not the smell actually, but the sense that something was going to happen — like when the electricity shoots into the box on the wall, like when the plates shift under our — I got the sense that you were going to . . .

ANN: . . . Go ahead. Say it.

STEVE: That you were going to . . .

ANN: SAY IT! SAY IT!

STEVE: I don't know the word!

ANN: . . . Of course. Of course you don't know that word.

STEVE: I should not have left you that night.

ANN: No. I didn't want you there.

STEVE: Did he hurt you?

ANN: I hurt me. I hurt me more. Do you remember the pit bull? A pit bull attacked you in the dog run one day. And we didn't go back there for a long time. One day, I took you back, just to look — but you ran in, you ran in and ran around as if it didn't hurt you, as if you didn't remember and you let every dog come near you, lick and paw you as if they could never hurt you. I wanted to be like that. Like you. I wanted to go back to the dog run.

STEVE: . . . And here we are. Just like that. Memorize? I mean — *Remember?* You'd look at me, I'd look at you. Just the moment in the middle of the sky. Only I'd be here on the floor and you'd be there. And then you'd pet my belly with your foot.

ANN: How humiliating.

STEVE: No! Not at all. You should feel what that feels like.

ANN: Me and my book and you on the ground . . . You felt so safe that you'd sleep. You'd dream of chasing things.

STEVE: Actually I was practicing —

ANN: Practicing.

STEVE: Dancing. I thought if I'm going to come back . . . I really wanted to dance. But I'd have to practice. It takes a lot of balance, this standing here takes a lot of — no? I so looked forward to dancing. Isn't this a place for —

ANN: No. This is not a place for dancing. You should know that things are not always what they appear to be . . . This place isn't really about learning how to do anything. It's a place where once again fifty women and one man show up. It's an empty promise — you only learn one thing over and over that everyone's looking. Everyone's back at the dog park.

No matter what. Maybe they want to get bit. You were the only guy that showed up and I decided I'd be brave tonight. I would get to you before they all did. And I did. And you're my dead dog.

STEVE: . . . My possession — my *confession* is that I have been watching you. I've been following you down the steps — down the blocks, on the trains — one time I nudged you to see if you would look up, but you didn't. I'd offer you my seat, you'd take it, but you never look up. You go to work, you come out for lunch and sit in the park — chewing and reading, but not chewing and reading at all. I remember that bull but I don't memorize him. You have to look up, look around. Sometimes. C'mon. Look up. Look around. See? It's not so bad, is it?

(They look around.)

ANN: You just can't see what humans see.

STEVE: Now I can. Quite frankly seeing blue and yellow is not all what's it's cracked up to be. And yes, OK, it was softer before, and yes, there was always movement before. It's slower and harder now. Sometimes it helps to squint to make it softer —

ANN: You know, you use to be able to cheer me up.

STEVE: It was easier when you were my former . . . I could just —

ANN: — Wait. Former . . . former what. What did you call me?

STEVE: Well, we had different names for you.

ANN: Well what did *you* call *me*?

STEVE: Babe.

ANN: . . . Babe? Babe. I always wanted . . . I longed for the day for someone to call me Babe. And there you were all the time, calling me Babe. Say it. Please.

STEVE: Babe.

ANN: Use it in a sentence.

STEVE: Babe? Does Drakkar Noir *not* smell good?

ANN: I'm sorry. You're perfectly fine. STEVE?

STEVE: Yea, Babe?

ANN: How am I ever going to let someone rub my belly with their foot?

STEVE: I think you have to — *belly up to the sky* — no — tr — ust! Trust.

ANN: Trust what. Trust *who*?

STEVE: It's more of a feeling.

ANN: A feeling my foot had.

STEVE: Yes!

ANN: It's hard to trust feelings Steve.

STEVE: Quite frankly I don't know how you people don't. What do you trust? 'Cause the words? These words — they are *so tricky*. You know?

ANN: I know . . . What was I before? If I wasn't a dog.

STEVE: I don't know — ask Shadow.

ANN: Oh. Steve. Shadow's dead.

STEVE: Oh. God. Well. Good. Stupid bitch.

ANN: Hey! That cat loved you. She went looking for you for days.

STEVE: She knew exactly where I went.

ANN: She cried.

STEVE: You sure she was crying?

ANN: I'm not sure of anything anymore . . . Except that I'm sure I have wasted so much time with my first shot. My only shot and now it's almost over.

STEVE: Nothing is wasted. Let alone time. It's . . . *dig.* I mean *stored.* C'mon. Let's dance.

ANN: No. No. No. If you're going to come back as a human you cannot be another one of those humans who says things like that. Like "Well, she has a pretty face," or "At least it's not raining," or "Let's just face the music and dance," or "It could be worse." IT IS WORSE. Humans don't like humans who do that. Humans don't want to hear those things when they're in a basement of a stinky carpet Synagogue.

STEVE: — You're right — You're right — you're right. It's actually the other way.

ANN: Which way —

STEVE: — Dogs don't get second lives, cat's brains weigh only 30 grams. There are no mysteries in the world, but buildings and signs and mistakes that make you think there are. Some people will never have a great romance and lots of people live the rest of their lives eating Lean Cuisine over the sink. Like you. Maybe like you. Maybe not. No one knows. Not even the cats — Things that poop in a box of sand can't possibly *know.* And I'm just a guy that reeks of cologne and spicy gum that reminds you of your dead dog. Better?

ANN: . . . Better. I'm sorry. Sometimes it's better to be dragged away on a leash. Sometimes it's hard, it's . . . every little thing all the time. OK?

STEVE: OK.

ANN: You can actually put your hands here.

STEVE: Better?

ANN: Yes.

STEVE: Should I give the other ladies a shot?

ANN: Stay.

(They dance.)

STEVE: Hey. I think I know that feeling. It's coming, the word? . . . *Be-long.* Is that it? It's not beshort. Because it takes a long time. It lasts. It's belong. Foot on the belly; I belong.

ANN: To me.

STEVE: More. I belonged to the sweetgum, silver linden and smelly ginkgo leaves, to the dirt and plastic deli bags, to the bugaboo strollers, to the Retrievers, the Bulls, the Shepherds and the Pointers, to the pigeons, the starlings and the chickadees, to the mockingbirds that do not shut up, to the litter, the cumulous clouds, the homeless men, the sinews, even the other single women on benches pretending to read. Then through all that — cutting right through the wind — the foot — to the Babe. To the me. See? The words they're . . .

ANN: . . . they'll always be. But I think I know what you mean.

STEVE: Did Shadow really cry for me?

ANN: Cats don't cry. They just moan. Full of secrets with no one to tell them to. Moaning in a language we don't understand saying . . . what?

STEVE: Saying "This is how it goes."

ANN: "This is how it is . . . "

STEVE: "I know where he went."

ANN: "I know where he is." I know where he is. I know. I know . . .

END OF PLAY

Use Unknown

Ali Walton

Use Unknown was first produced by Journeymen Theater Ensemble as part of the production It's Not Easy Being Green in Washington, D.C. for the 2009 Capital Fringe Festival. Director: David E. Binet. Cast: Girl — Azania M. Dungee; Guy — Matt Dewberry.

"It seems cruel," she said, "that after a while nothing matters . . . any more than these little things, that used to be necessary and important to forgotten people, and now have to be guessed at under a magnifying glass and labeled: 'Use unknown.'"

— *The Age of Innocence, chapter thirty-one*

"The one thing that astonished him now was that he should have stood for five minutes arguing with her across the width of the room, when just touching her made everything so simple."

— *The Age of Innocence, chapter eighteen*

CHARACTERS

GUY, twenty-something, a low-level programmer.

GIRL, twenty-something, a well-educated museum worker.

SETTING

SCENE 1 takes place on a teleporture platform in a large city.

SCENE 2 takes place in the FirstGen wing of the Humana Museum.

• • •

The year is 2450. Both the Guy and Girl are NexGen humans. The Next Generation is a recovered species, which arose from the ashes of the First Generation, whose way of living led Earth to near-complete devastation in 2050, otherwise known as The Purge. It took 300 years for humanity to recover.

The Guy is dressed in modern day clothes of 2450: every inch of flesh covered in stretchy, shiny metallic material. He wears a solar-paneled hat, with wires that run from the hat to each of his fingertips. He also wears platform shoes or rain boots, whichever is more ridiculous. The Girl wears old, worn clothes, specific to 2009: a casual, miss-matched outfit of neutral colors.

Scene 1

The Guy is standing to the left, waiting. The Girl is standing to the right, waiting. The Girl is reading a book. The Guy is stealing glances at the Girl.

GIRL: Hey.

(Guy pretends not to have heard her.)

GIRL: Excuse me. Hi.

GUY: Oh, hi.

GIRL: You've been staring at me for like ten minutes, and all you can say is, "Oh, hi"?

GUY: Oh, hi. I mean, um . . . oh, hi, how are you?

GIRL: Fine, thanks.

GUY: I wasn't staring at you. I was looking at the traffic android over there. It must have short-circuited or something because I could swear it just changed the hoverlane to green at least 3.5 seconds earlier than normal, and that's really the only explanation for such . . . *(He trails off because even he doesn't believe what he's saying anymore.)*

GIRL: Hmmm.

(Girl returns to book.)

(Guy begins to steal glances at her again.)

GIRL: OK, seriously? What's up?

GUY: Nothing. It's just, um . . . it's just that you look absolutely ridiculous. Not you, I mean. Your clothes.

GIRL: Oh! You should have said something. I get that a lot. This is just my uniform. For work.

GUY: Uh-huh. Then what is that thing you're holding?

GIRL: Woah, somebody skipped out on FirstGen Studies.

GUY: Yeah . . . I'm only a Level 3 programmer, so I never took FirstGen Studies.

GIRL: Oh. *(Embarrassed pause.)* Well, this is called a book. It's like, a primitive dataPod from the 20th century.

GUY: It's massive. It's gotta hold at least, what, a billion gigabytes?

GIRL: No. No gigabytes. Just pages. Three hundred and sixty-two, to be exact.

(Guy mouths to himself, "pages?", not wanting her to see that he doesn't know what a "page" is.)

GIRL: This one is called *The Age of Innocence* by Edith Wharton.

GUY: What's its dataPurpose?

GIRL: It doesn't have a dataPurpose. It's just a story.

GUY: I don't understand.

GIRL: You know that line of virtual vacations that were advertised a few years ago as "Classic Adventures?"

GUY: Yeah, I definitely remember those.

GIRL: Well, all of them were based on these things. *(She indicates the book.)*

GUY: No kidding. I went on one with my dad called "Ithaca or Bust." We went to this crazy planet with tons of water and I was trying to find my dad and he was trying to find me, but he kept running into all kinds of monsters and stuff.

GIRL: How old were you?

GUY: I was pretty young, young enough to still believe in virtual vacations. Mostly I remember the water. No pollution, no chemicals, just tons and tons of water, as far as the eye could see . . . *(He trails off, lost in the vision of the water.)*

GIRL: Then what happened?

GUY: Oh. Right. Well it ended. Just like all virtual vacations end, I guess. I broke the rules. I tasted the water. Instead of tasting salt, I got a mouth full of metal and the illusion was instantly shattered.

GIRL: Let me guess, on this virtual vacation your name was Telemachus, and your father's name was Odysseus.

GUY: Yeah! How did you know that?

GIRL: I read it. In one of these. If you had followed the rules long enough, your father would have found you, but he would have disguised himself as an old man in order to test you.

GUY: Jeez, you're really into that FirstGen stuff.

GIRL: Yeah, well. I work at the Humana Museum. First Generation wing. Hence the uniform.

GUY: You work *there*?

GIRL: Yup.

GUY: Every day?

GIRL: Yessir.

GUY: How can you stand it?

(She laughs. She's heard this before.)

GUY: No, I mean really, how can you stand it?

GIRL: Well, I don't *hate* them, if that's what you mean.

GUY: How can you *not* hate them? The First Generation nearly wiped us off the planet. How can you be in the same building with all their *objects* and their *machines*? It's like, spending every day in the evidence room for a mass murder case.

GIRL: Woah, slow down, buddy. This is my job you're talking about. I spend almost every day inside that "evidence room," and I like it, so watch yourself.

GUY: I'm sorry. I just never understood the point of the Humana Museum. I mean, let's face it, the First Generation were a bunch of shortsighted, self-absorbed imbeciles. First-class freaks, if you ask me. I think that we should learn from their mistakes, but glorify their artifacts in a museum? It just feels . . . wrong. *(Pause.)* Sorry.

GIRL: *(She thumbs through her book to a specific place, and reads aloud.)* "I want somehow to get away with you into a world where we shall be simply two human beings who love each other, who are the whole of life to each other; and nothing else on earth will matter."

GUY: Um, wow, I mean you seem like a nice girl and everything, but I just met you. Maybe we could start with a cyber date?

GIRL: No, it's from the book. Newland Archer is desperately in love with the Countess Olenska, but they can't be together because of New York high society. Are they not the most beautiful words you've ever heard?

GUY: Um, I guess?

GIRL: This is why I can work at the Humana Museum without being consumed by hate for the First Generation. I actually admire them. Yes, they were self-absorbed to the extent that they almost wiped themselves off the planet, but they were focused on other things.

GUY: Other things?!? What could possibly be more important than preventing your own extinction?

GIRL: Love. Connection. Happiness.

GUY: I don't understand.

GIRL: When was the last time you saw your dad?

GUY: In real space?

GIRL: In real space. Not just a hologram.

GUY: Um . . . two, no . . . three years ago.

GIRL: My point exactly. Our NexGen way of life feels so empty sometimes. I didn't even realize it until I started reading these things. I always felt like something was missing, but I never knew what it was. I mean, I can't even remember the last time I touched someone. Or someone touched me.

(The Guy and Girl catch each other's gaze, and hold it, perhaps for the first time. She slowly reaches out to touch him, but at the last second, pulls her hand back.)

GIRL: Listen, I have to go. It's almost my teleporture time. Take this. *(She hands him the book.)* Read it. Maybe then you'll understand.

GUY: Wait. When will I give it back to you? When will I see you again?

GIRL: You know where you can find me.

GUY: But . . .

(Too late. She has vanished. The Guy looks down at the book as if it carries some awful disease. He carefully opens the cover and begins to read. Darkness.)

Scene 2

Lights up on the Girl, at the Humana Museum, standing guard next to a large metal trash can, which is roped off by velvet museum ropes. She is reading a different book. The Guy enters, dressed as before. He looks around the room and spots the Girl. He gathers his courage, then approaches her.

GUY: Hi.

GIRL: Oh, hi! It's you! I was starting to think I would never see you again.

GUY: Yeah, well. It took me a while to get through this. *(He pulls out* The Age of Innocence.*)* It's been years since I uploaded a dataset *manually.*

GIRL: What did you think?

GUY: What is it that Newland Archer said when he read the book that reminded him of the Countess? "It gave a new and haunting beauty to the most elementary of human passions."

(Pause.)

GIRL: Wait, did you just quote that from *memory*?

GUY: Yeah . . . well, I might have read it more than once. Or twice. Or, um . . . anyway, what is that thing?

GIRL: This? We're not exactly sure. It's one of the FirstGen artifacts that survived the Purge. We're pretty sure it's a container of some sort.

GUY: For what?

GIRL: Well, that's the mystery. One of the museum's top FirstGen researchers believes that they used it to store waste. Then they would compile all of the waste from these small containers into large containers, and then the large containers of waste would be dropped into large piles that grew bigger and bigger.

GUY: That's. Completely and utterly. Absurd.

GIRL: I know. That's why I'm standing guard here. As soon as the researcher went public with his theory, we had a fresh wave of vandalism from FirstGen hate groups. One group broke in overnight and programmed a hologram of a FirstGen human that continuously ripped its own head off and threw it into the container.

GUY: That's sick. Totally awesome. But sick.

GIRL: Yeah. Too bad it was some of the best programming I've ever seen. I wanted to take it home and save it as a Halloween decoration, but the police kept it for evidence.

GUY: What a waste of talent.

GIRL: It's good to hear you say that.

GUY: Why?

GIRL: After our conversation on the teleporture platform, I couldn't help but think that you might belong to one of those groups. *(Pause.)* I don't know what made me give you that book. I never do stuff like that.

GUY: I'm glad you did.

GIRL: Yeah?

GUY: Yeah. I still think that the First Generation was made up of a bunch of first-class freaks. I mean, stuff like this *(Indicates trash can.)* is just ridiculous. What were they thinking? On the other hand, I look at Newland Archer. He was completely, totally consumed by his love for the Countess, right? I mean even after he married someone else and the Countess moved away, all he could do was think about her. It ruined his life.

GIRL: Exactly!

GUY: I think I understand what you meant when you said that the First Generation had other things on their mind. I mean, why would someone waste his time saving humanity, when he can't even be with the person he loves?

GIRL: Most of the time, I just feel sorry for them. Sometimes I think that the Earth simply allowed it to happen. Time stood by and watched them self-destruct, just to get rid of them. It could have easily been us, you know.

GUY: But it wasn't. We're here. And we're here to stay, at least for a while.

(The Guy reaches out and grabs the Girl's hand. It's super awkward. He's never done this before. She is startled, but quickly recovers, and then looks up at him.)

GIRL: What's your name?

GUY: George. What's yours?

GIRL: Ellen.

(They both smile.)

END OF PLAY

Wish You Were Here

Claudia Haas

Wish You Were Here was produced by Eastbound Theatre in Milford, Connecticut, in June 2008. Original cast: Ashley — Shannon Bolcer; Jean-Louis — Michael Fortunato. Director: David F. Salvo

Characters

Ashley, early twenties, very American, meaning there is a zest and exuberance to her. She has completed her cooking certificate with the Cordon Bleu School and is in the park saying good-bye to Paris before she gets a taxi to the airport. She has on jeans and a sweater — very comfortable — very American.

Jean-Louis, mid-twenties with all the charm the French are noted for. Impeccably dressed, he is an incessant flirt who cannot let a charming woman slip by him. Please note: His English is impeccable — you do not need a French accent.

Setting

A Paris park. All you need is a bench. Lighting indicating the time the streetlamps come on is helpful.

Time

Dusk; today.

Synopsis

A possible pick-up in a Paris park leads to a lifetime of wishes and a bittersweet parting.

• • •

At Rise, we are in a small park in Paris. There is a park bench (of course) with a young Mademoiselle sitting and watching. It is evening. Just before the street lamps come on.

JEAN-LOUIS: Escusez-moi, c'est libre?

("Excuse-me, is this free?")

ASHLEY: What? Oh! Yes. Oui. There's an empty bench over there though. It's freer than over here. Ici. Go over there. La.

(Ici — pronounced "ee-see" means "here." La means "there.")

JEAN-LOUIS: Ahh! Vous-étes Americain?

(You are American?)

ASHLEY: Sure. Maybe. The empty bench? La? Do you see it? No one's sitting there. It looks quite comfortable. Wish you were there.

JEAN-LOUIS: No. I think here is much more comfortable.

ASHLEY: OK. I'll leave. You're creeping me out.

JEAN-LOUIS: Non! Mademoiselle! I am quite harmless.

ASHLEY: You speak English.

JEAN-LOUIS: After two years in the States, yes. Without an accent. I worked very hard.

ASHLEY: That's nice. So tell me, Mr. Frenchman "without-an-accent" — why can't a young woman in France just sit on a park bench without being hassled? What is it about you guys?

JEAN-LOUIS: I do not hassle. I find charming young women irresistible. It is natural.

ASHLEY: No! It's — yucky.

JEAN-LOUIS: Yucky? I do not know "yucky."

ASHLEY: Yeah, you do . . . you're — English is — as you say — very good.

JEAN-LOUIS: Thank-you.

ASHLEY: It's — nothing. I try to see the good in everyone — even perverts.

JEAN-LOUIS: Mademoiselle, I am merely a young man who has just returned to his native country and wishes to reacquaint himself with it and it's charming inhabitants.

ASHLEY: I no longer inhabit here. I am leaving. To go home. To the States. Je pense. I think.

JEAN-LOUIS: You're French — is not very good.

ASHLEY: I know — but every time I speak to someone in French — they answer me in English — so what's a girl to do?

JEAN-LOUIS: Speak to me in French.

ASHLEY: No.

JEAN-LOUIS: A little more nasal —

ASHLEY: That was an American "no." Can't you tell the difference?

JEAN-LOUIS: Non.

ASHLEY: It's been — well . . . it's been. You're welcome to the bench. I need to go.

JEAN-LOUIS: Wait! At least for the street lamps to come on. And then you may leave. If it's your last night in Paris, you don't want to miss the street lamps.

ASHLEY: I can't. I have a plane to catch. An international flight — must be there three hours ahead, you know. They don't hold planes for street lamps.

JEAN-LOUIS: It's funny what you miss when you are away. I thought — how can I go two years without a proper croissant — an exquisite petit pain?

But in the end — it was the street lamps I missed. And I will feel so lonely if they come on and I have no one to share it with.

ASHLEY: America has street lamps.

JEAN-LOUIS: But Paris street lamps have a rhythm. They come on in time with the song of the city. They invite you. They beguile. In the States, they just — turn on. They send you quickly into the night without any time to pause for twilight.

ASHLEY: That's what I miss — twilight. At home. The sky. I'm a Montana girl — there's lots of sky in Montana. Not as much here. There are no street lamps where I'm from — just stars.

JEAN-LOUIS: Paris — the City of Light — it hides the stars. It's amusing, no?

ASHLEY: Yes, amusing . . . as this has been . . . nice meeting you. Welcome home.

JEAN-LOUIS: Running away?

ASHLEY: No. To something actually.

JEAN-LOUIS: A lover?

ASHLEY: A fiancé. He's been waiting — for me to get my "squirrelies" out. I wanted to get my cooking certificate in Paris — see a bit of the world before I settle down.

JEAN-LOUIS: And did you — eliminate your "squirrelies?"

ASHLEY: Sort of. Trouble is that now that I've been here — I have itchy feet — to see more — to go to more places. I don't think you could possibly understand —

JEAN-LOUIS: I — scratched.

ASHLEY: What?

JEAN-LOUIS: My feet were also itchy. I scratched in New York, Boston, the Grand Tetons, the Grand Canyon — the States have many "grands." I wanted to see your "big sky." And yes, it is so different than here. And wonderful in its own way. And everywhere I went — my feet got itchier for more. I stayed away longer than I planned. But my lover — she wanted the inside of a church and a home close to her family and she got that — while I was busy scratching my feet.

ASHLEY: I'm — sorry. So, you can see why I need to go home and — stop scratching. For one year I have gotten these notes from him. "Wish you were here." And I thought — how nice. But I don't want to be there. Yet. I wanted to be here. And he's waited. Oh sorry. Not that he waited — but that your sweetheart didn't.

JEAN-LOUIS: We planned a large family. We would both work hard at our business in the beginning.

ASHLEY: That is our plan — to start our own business — a restaurant!

JEAN-LOUIS: Long-hard hours —

ASHLEY: Working side-by-side.

JEAN-LOUIS: Until the business takes off —

ASHLEY: And then hiring some help —

JEAN-LOUIS: Which will come in handy when the babies arrive.

ASHLEY: Babies?

JEAN-LOUIS: At least two.

ASHLEY: I was thinking the children would come much later. I am just in my early twenties.

JEAN-LOUIS: Chantal would be our skier.

ASHLEY: I was thinking a figure skater. For Chrissy. Chantal. I like that name. It would forever remind me of my time in France. It's wrong though — isn't it? To make your children live up to your dreams. Or your past. All the talk show psychiatrists say so.

JEAN-LOUIS: Well, if Chantal did not excel in skiing, Pierre might. You never know.

ASHLEY: Chantal. I like her a lot. Not so sure about Pierre.

JEAN-LOUIS: You don't like Pierre? But he's just a baby! How can you not like a baby?

ASHLEY: William. After my father. Definitely William. And I would love him very much.

JEAN-LOUIS: And what will he do?

ASHLEY: I don't know. I seem to have given him free reign, where I have made Chrissy a skater. Should I leave Chrissy alone? Or make plans for William?

JEAN-LOUIS: We will have to leave William alone. When his teacher calls to say he dreams instead of works —

ASHLEY: I will give the teacher a piece of my mind! Everything is not work. One must make space for dreams.

JEAN-LOUIS: But the teacher does not teach dreams —

ASHLEY: So I must.

JEAN-LOUIS: When Chantal grows up and does not like the cold —

ASHLEY: — She won't be able to ski or skate!

JEAN-LOUIS: What will we do with her?

ASHLEY: I could take her to work — at the restaurant —

JEAN-LOUIS: The restaurant? You will work?

ASHLEY: Of course I will work. I just got my certificate from the Cordon Bleu!

JEAN-LOUIS: A bistro!

ASHLEY: Organic natural foods.

JEAN-LOUIS: But William has a taste for fast food.

ASHLEY: I will not allow him to damage his body with junk! I am a natural foods chef!

JEAN-LOUIS: Young men can be stubborn.

ASHLEY: Then we will have to move to a remote island to cure him.

JEAN-LOUIS: But Chantal is now a teenager and will not leave her friends!

ASHLEY: Who is in charge? The parents? Or the children?

JEAN-LOUIS: With nothing to do, Chantal will sleep in the island sun and turn her skin to leather! She is in a delicate time in her life. You must be careful.

ASHLEY: Then we will need to compromise. You will need to stay home with Chantal while I whisk William away to a deserted island — that has a restaurant of course. With whole natural foods where I will work.

JEAN-LOUIS: Of course. Parenting is hard.

ASHLEY: I had no idea.

JEAN-LOUIS: But they do grow up! Look at us.

ASHLEY: Yes — look at — us? Us? There is no "us!" I need to get a taxi!

JEAN-LOUIS: But you cannot abandon Chantal and William!

ASHLEY: They do not exist!

JEAN-LOUIS: They are our dreams! If you leave — we have no dreams.

ASHLEY: I have other dreams! With a man who wishes I was there — in Montana — not here — in France.

JEAN-LOUIS: Christmas in the Loire Valley — New Years in Montana — on my ranch — Every other year — a compromise! A French Yule log one year and — American as apple pie the next year.

ASHLEY: I do not bake!

JEAN-LOUIS: But I do! Artisan breads, Croissants! Brioche! I have come home to open a patisserie!

ASHLEY: You're all about butter and eggs —

JEAN-LOUIS: I can go organic!

ASHLEY: You deceived me!

JEAN-LOUIS: It is our first test. If we can get past this — we will have a summer home near Nice — where we will retire and eat Charlotte Russe in our old age —

ASHLEY: But we will be too old to be gorging ourselves with butter and eggs —

JEAN-LOUIS: We will not gorge! We will pace. With organic products from our own garden. We will keep hens and churn our own butter —

ASHLEY: It's impossible —

JEAN-LOUIS: Everything is possible!

ASHLEY: People do not plan a life with someone they meet in a park.

JEAN-LOUIS: Ah — but they do. Especially if they meet waiting for the street lamps to come on.

ASHLEY: I have a plane ticket!

JEAN-LOUIS: And I have a passport!

ASHLEY: What are you saying?

JEAN-LOUIS: It is a small world these days. People commute.

ASHLEY: Not between Montana and Paris!

JEAN-LOUIS: We must. For Chantal and William.

ASHLEY: They have not been born!

JEAN-LOUIS: They are already — what do you Americans say — twinkles in our eyes?

ASHLEY: Suppose Chantal is a Pierre? Suppose there are no children.

JEAN-LOUIS: Then there will be us. Living the best of two worlds.

ASHLEY: You are confusing me.

JEAN-LOUIS: Relationships do that.

ASHLEY: I don't know you.

JEAN-LOUIS: It is better that way — we discover each other's bad habits over time. It makes for a long and eventful marriage.

ASHLEY: Marriage? To someone whose name I do not know?

JEAN-LOUIS: How unforgivable of me! Jean-Louis.

ASHLEY: Ashley. I — really have to go. With the traffic — I'll never get there in time.

JEAN-LOUIS: Then you must take my number. If you miss the plane.

ASHLEY: I'll stay over night in the airport.

JEAN-LOUIS: If you insist. Mademoiselle, it's been a pleasure sharing a lifetime with you.

ASHLEY: Yes . . . the same here. Excuse me.

(Ashley starts to exit and the street lamps come on. All you need is a light bathing the stage. Ashley stops still in her tracks. Jean-Louis does the same.)

JEAN-LOUIS: *(Softly.)* I have missed you.

ASHLEY: What was that?

JEAN-LOUIS: The lamps.

ASHLEY: They — are extraordinary. Why have I never noticed that?

JEAN-LOUIS: You have been busy. Too busy. To pause.

(They slowly come closer together looking at the lamps in the distance.)

ASHLEY: It's sad — to just discover something when you are leaving —

JEAN-LOUIS: Better to have discovered later —

ASHLEY: — than never? Maybe. And now maybe — I will forever wonder —

JEAN-LOUIS: Mademoiselle — here — my number. In case you find yourself wondering —

(He hastily writes a number down.)

ASHLEY: All right. Thank-you. For the street lamps. Thank-you very much. Good-bye.

JEAN-LOUIS: Until later —

(Ashley exits. Jean-Louis watches her go. He waits for a moment and then slowly goes off.)

The street lamps — at least they are still here to welcome me.

(The lights start to dim. Jean Louis's cell phone rings or vibrates. He looks at the phone and sees it is a text message. He fiddles with the buttons to find it. Ashley appears in the distance. She is texting him. He smiles.)

You have one message. One message to welcome me home.

ASHLEY: *(Talking as she is "texting.")* "Wish you were here."

JEAN-LOUIS: I'm here

(Lights fade to black as both smile at their phones.)

END OF PLAY

PLAYS FOR TWO WOMEN

Hedge

Jerrod Bogard

Originally produced at the Players Theatre Loft, New York, New York, January 22 to February 7, 2009. Presented by Shortened Attention Span and Wide Eyed Productions as part of "The Spin Cycle: an Evening of One-acts by Jerrod Bogard." Cast: Amber — Lauren Bahlman; Celine — Melissa Johnson. Director: Jake Witlen.

CHARACTERS

AMBER, mid-thirties; brash, aggressive. Her mind races. Would have been featured on *Girls Gone Wild* if they'd come to her spring break.

CELINE, mid-thirties; sweet, understated. She's the Mary-Anne to Amber's Ginger.

SETTING

A sunny day in the Hollywood Hills. 2:30 PM. A lawn.

• • •

Lights up. Two women, Celine and Amber sit in lawn chairs in the grass outside a million dollar home in the Hollywood hills. There is a cooler with beverages. They are taking some sun. No other scenery.

AMBER: Christ . . . That photographer.

CELINE: Again?

AMBER: Still. I swear, this guy drives around the block, grabs a taco supreme and then rolls back here for another four-hour stakeout.

CELINE: So that's what that is.

AMBER: Huh.

CELINE: At the corner of his mouth. Sour Cream.

AMBER: We only hope.

CELINE: Yuk.

AMBER: Yuck times uck to the square root of ewe. That guy is . . .

CELINE: Skeeezyyy. AMBER: Skeeezyyy.

CELINE: Shady.

AMBER: Do you think he gets any decent shots off from over there?

CELINE: Telephoto lens.

AMBER: Who's he work for you think?

CELINE: Does it matter? All the same. Rats and weasels.

AMBER: Oh, they're not all the same.

CELINE: They are all the same.

AMBER: Where would you rather see a picture of yourself taking out the garbage? The inquirer? Or the Weekly World News?

CELINE: *(Beat.)* OK . . . OK. But — but — let's don't give this sleaze our energy, alright? He's not getting anything from over there. Not with this hedge in the way.

AMBER: So now you like the hedge?

CELINE: I didn't say —

AMBER: No — no, that's fine. Now you like it.

CELINE: I'm saying yes, there's something to be said for privacy. Feeling safe. Really this should be a gated community.

AMBER: If they gate this community, the entire city economy suffers. No more orange salesmen at the traffic light at the bottom of the hill. No more paparazzi vying to snap nude sunbathing domestic spats. No more map salesmen to the celebrity homes. You know what pays for unemployment? We do. Taxes go up. Crime goes up. It's a can of worms. Soon as you start putting up walls — you create conflict.

CELINE: I don't think one of those jobs actually contributes to any part of the economy. Maybe the orange salesman.

AMBER: I could go for some juice about now.

CELINE: Hm.

AMBER: You can say what you like about the hedge though, it gives good shade come about five in the evening.

CELINE: Yes it does.

AMBER: Yes it does. And I told you that when it was first going in, didn't I?

CELINE: Yes you did.

AMBER: Yes I did. And you said it was going to obstruct our view.

CELINE: And it has.

AMBER: Yes, well, regardless, I still think it was the right thing to do. People need protection from this sort of thing. *(Calling to the man off stage.)* Hey!

CELINE: What are you doing? Don't do that.

AMBER: Hey buddy!

CELINE: Aim. Amber. Stop it. You're going to bring attention.

AMBER: *(To the man.)* You wanna take a picture?! *(To Amber.)* Attention? Watch this.

(Amber rips open her shirt exposing her push-up bra and cleavage.)

CELINE: Amber!

AMBER: WoooHooo! Can you picture that?! Can you picture *this?!* You pervert S.O.B!!

CELINE: Sit down.

AMBER: Ha.

CELINE: Please sit down. The neighbors'll call the cops.

AMBER: The neighbors — Since when are you caring about the neighbors?

CELINE: Since the hedge went in. Sit down.

AMBER: Relax please. God. *(Sits down, buttons her shirt.)* See what privacy has done? Made you paranoid. You never cared who saw you out here before that hedge. Now, skulking around — peeking like some trench-coat peeper, "Who's there? Can they see me? Can they not see me?"

CELINE: Peeking is the only way I get to see anything anymore, isn't it? Like prisoners.

AMBER: Prisoners? That's a little dramatic.

CELINE: Celebrity is like a . . . it's like a . . . —

AMBER: Prison?

CELINE: Prison! It absolutely is. That's why I'm out here, and that's why I'm thinking that if that hedge doesn't disappear, then maybe we should just . . . move on down the road. You know what I mean?

AMBER: What do you mean?

CELINE: You know that Jennifer Aniston just bought the little place at the top of the rise.

AMBER: The one with the dribbly fountains?

CELINE: Uhuh.

AMBER: That's a beautiful house.

CELINE: With that beautiful front walk-garden-type path. Lots of open space.

AMBER: That is a beautiful place. Perfect for this type of afternoon, sure, but are we Jennifer Aniston people? No. We're Penelope Cruise people.

CELINE: That's it. Right there. This lifestyle does that to you. It puts you in a box and as soon as you try to step outside that little box, whap! Somebody comes and smacks you on the nose with last week's *Variety.*

AMBER: Oh, please with the dramatics.

CELINE: What time is it? Is your phone on?

AMBER: Should I go ask that guy for his card? Do you think he's gonna put me up on a website or something?

CELINE: He didn't take any shots.

AMBER: What? . . . Are you serious?

CELINE: He didn't even lift up his camera.

AMBER: What?! That's — what? Well, screw that guy. So he's gay too. That's a great addendum to his already sparkling social status. *(To the guy.)* Hey!

CELINE: *(Defeated.)* Don't.

AMBER: *(Yelling at the guy.)* That's a great addendum to your already sparkling social status, creep!

(Amber sits. Pause.)

AMBER: *(Continued.)* I've got the alarm set for three. We won't miss it. You know how Thursdays goes.

CELINE: Any chance the spa changed its hours or something?

AMBER: Don't be a worrywart . . . Uh . . . Oh, . . . there he goes.

CELINE: What.

AMBER: Now he's taking pictures.

CELINE: Huh?

AMBER: Oh yeah, baby. Clicky clicky.

CELINE: He's not shooting you.

AMBER: Get my good side, butthead.

CELINE: He's not shooting you.

(Looking behind her.)

She's leaving early.

AMBER: *(Also turning around.)* Oh! Oh!

(Both facing upstage, they jump and wave and yell like crazy fans at a red carpet ceremony.)

AMBER: Penelope! . . .

CELINE: Penelope, we love you! . . .

AMBER: Penelope! Over here! . . .

CELINE: Are you having a good day?!

AMBER: You're so beautiful! We love you, Penelope! *(To Celine.)* Damn this hedge.

CELINE: Have a great spa!

AMBER: Over here! Hi! Hi! *(To Celine.)* She waved.

CELINE: We're like your sisters! We'll see you tonight!

AMBER: She waved.

CELINE: We love you! . . . *(To Amber.)* Do you want to run to the gate and throw flowers at her car?

AMBER: Why would she wave?

CELINE: Cuz she likes us, cuz we're gonna be friends, cuz we're the sisters she's never had. Come on come on come on come on come on.

AMBER: No wait.

CELINE: What!

AMBER: Did you see that?

CELINE: I think so. What?

AMBER: The wave. Did you see her wave?

CELINE: I think so. Do you have your sign?

AMBER: Hold on. Just wait.

CELINE: We're gonna miss her at the gate.

AMBER: Shhhh. Listen. Listen. She never waves.

CELINE: So?

AMBER: But now, with the hedge up, . . . she waves.

CELINE: So what?

AMBER: So I don't think that was a real wave.

CELINE: You said she waved.

AMBER: Right, but I think it was a backhand.

CELINE: *(Demonstrating the wave types.)* Well, you saw it. Was it a backhand, or was it a princess?

AMBER: No, it was definitely backhand. I knew this hedge was a bad sign!

CELINE: But you said —

AMBER: Sal, Penelope Cruise is not our friend.

CELINE: But —

AMBER: No! I think we've been made fools of us. She has — I mean — made fools of us.

CELINE: But —

AMBER: Sal, maybe it's time we really saw this for what it is. You know? Face reality?

CELINE: *(Beat.)* Really?

AMBER: The fact is that we're not Penelope Cruise people. Not anymore.

CELINE: Because of the hedge?

AMBER: Forget the hedge! That's just one more barrier to keep the real world out. I'm telling you. We have to tear down all these barriers. We have to get a fresh perspective.

CELINE: Damned hedge.

AMBER: So, . . . so let's go. Let's just go, OK?

CELINE: You don't want to wait for her to get back?

AMBER: Wait for who, Sal? Penelope Cruise? Who's she? Huh? Just another fame-brained girl with too much money. She's not special.

CELINE: So . . . where are we going.

AMBER: Let's go be with our real friends. Friends that don't need spa treatments and hedges to make them somebody.

CELINE: Maybe, yeah, you're right.

AMBER: That's right.

CELINE: So, . . . over to Jennifer Aniston's?

AMBER: Over to Jennifer's Aniston's. She'll be thrilled to see us. New place can be lonely. We'll give her a house warming.

CELINE: I'll get the vitamin water!

(Celine packs the cooler. Amber folds up the chairs. Amber's cell phone alarm sounds. It's "Every Step You Take" by The Police. She turns off the phone.)

AMBER: I'll be reprogramming that alarm now I guess.

CELINE: I guess you will.

AMBER: I guess I will.

CELINE: Aim?

AMBER: What's up?

CELINE: This doesn't feel right.

AMBER: *(Beat.)* One last one?

CELINE: Don't you think?

AMBER: I do think.

(Celine goes into the cooler and retrieves two one-oz. "airplane" bottles of vodka. She hands one to Amber.)

CELINE: Here we are. *(Lifting her bottle up.)* Oh.

AMBER: What.

CELINE: Well, what do we drink to now?

AMBER: Come on. We're big people. We don't have to be petty about this.

CELINE: Of course we don't.

AMBER: Of course not. We'll drink to what we always drink to.

(They unscrew the tops of their bottles and lift them up. They recite this old toast together.)

AMBER AND CELINE: *(Together.)* "That all her lovers have been true, and that her life keeps getting better and better."

(They drink.)

(Blackout.)

END OF PLAY

Parental Consent

S. D. Graubert

Parental Consent was chosen for HB Studios' Spring Writes festival, and in April, 2009 was a winner at Theatre Oxford. *Parental Consent* won a place in Penobscot Theatre Company's new play festival, Northern Writes, in Bangor, Maine, Scott RC Levy, Producing Artistic Director, February 2009. *Parental Consent* was a semi-finalist in Short & Sweet, Singapore, 2009, and was produced in Sydney's Short + Sweet Festival, February 2010. It is also a winner of the 6-Women Playwriting Festival, with a production, April 2010. Also produced in New York, as part of Love Creek's Brief Acts festival, 2009.

CHARACTERS

EDNA, forty, proud, confident, highly strung.

DANIELLA, seventeen, Edna's daughter, eager, patriotic.

SETTING

Edna's kitchen, in her house in Pittsburgh.

TIME

2002.

NOTE

A slash "/" indicates where dialogue should overlap.

• • •

Daniella helps Edna unpack groceries.

EDNA: So, I finally had to tell Mrs. Brody, I had to say it, and you know I don't like talking politics with the patients, but she kept on and on, 'til finally I said, and I didn't say it badly, but I had to say, I had to say it, I am proud of my country — no, that goes in a baggy — I am proud of how the Republicans are protecting my country, I wasn't angry, I mean I didn't say it angry, I was angry inside, she's clearly ignorant, does she want this country to be ruled by terrorists?

DANIELLA: They attacked us. So, we should —

EDNA: Exactly. They attacked us. She thinks it's all a conspiracy. About a, a, what'd she say? Pipeline. She thinks everything's a conspiracy. Oh, and the September attack was about oil. Oil? And I say to her, I say, there was no oil in the World Trade Towers. There was no oil in the Pentagon.

DANIELLA: They want to destroy America

EDNA: They want to destroy America. Don't put the tomatoes in the fridge, they lose their flavor. I mean I told her, and I said it nicely, I didn't say it badly, in her day women didn't get to be doctors, not without it being an issue, she knows this, but we fight, we inch forward and you, you get to be a doctor / you get to be the

DANIELLA: Yeah, hey, and you also —

EDNA: one calling the shots, you can't do that in those countries, in Saudi

Arabia, with the head scarves — because this is America. This is America.

DANIELLA: What'd she say to that?

EDNA: Well, she said . . . *(Dismissive exhalation.)* Phoo . . . but I said that's not racist, women don't have rights in Saudi Arabia, it's a fact, that's not racist, they don't have birth or death certificates, is it racist to comment, to observe that women don't have rights over there, no birth or death certificates? That's, that's like cattle. That's not racist.

DANIELLA: Women have rights in America.

EDNA: Everyone has rights in America. Our kids can be whatever, president, doctor — I'm so proud of you, Danny. Yeah. Her nephew signed up, Mrs. Brody, there's been a, a what do you call it, recruitment drive, at the mall, that's why she being so . . . she wishes he hadn't. We upped her meds.

DANIELLA: For the marines?

EDNA: I guess. I said where do you think our soldiers come from? Look! It's an odor-buster! Then she says the whole WMD thing is an excuse, and I say, do you honestly, honestly think the president would lie about a thing like that? I said it's a good thing your nephew signed up, / you should be proud. / Our rights have to be protected. Because there's a whole

DANIELLA: Yeah. *(Second interruption.)* Yeah, proud!

EDNA: big part of the world that would like to take that away.

DANIELLA: That is so right.

EDNA: I don't want to be forced to wear a head scarf. Do you?

DANIELLA: No way.

EDNA: She says it's not about head scarves, I say what's it about then? These potatoes, they had a demo in the store, they're purple inside. *(Cutting potato.)* You know how hard my job would be if I had to wear a head scarf? Look! That's pretty, right?

DANIELLA: Hey, Ma, can you sign this?

EDNA: Sure, ach, fingers. I thought we'd done all the paperwork.

DANIELLA: It's kinda like permission.

EDNA: You don't need my permission. You can do whatever you want.

DANIELLA: I'm not eighteen yet.

EDNA: Ten months.

DANIELLA: So, once you sign I'm good to go.

EDNA: Is this, like, for a society or something? Is that how it works now?

DANIELLA: I signed up.
EDNA: For extra credit? That's my girl.
DANIELLA: For the marines.
(Beat.)
EDNA: How hard is it to pack a bag?
DANIELLA: I told him you'd be so into me going.
EDNA: Lighter groceries on top. It's not rocket science.
DANIELLA: Hey, not like Mrs. Brody!
EDNA: She crushed the cheese. Look at that.
DANIELLA: I'm gonna show them who's boss. Isn't it great, Ma?
EDNA: Yes. What is?
DANIELLA: That I'm able to sign up. Same as Mrs. Brody's nephew.
EDNA: *(As if she is better.)* You are nothing like Mrs. Brody's nephew.
DANIELLA: Like, we're both marines.
EDNA: You're going to be doctor.
DANIELLA: See, it's cool. I get to be a doctor, and I get to be a marine. Right?
EDNA: But being a doctor is so much more impor —
DANIELLA: It's not an 'issue.' Like you said.
EDNA: People who join the marines have a propensity, they —
DANIELLA: He said I'm perfect marine material.
EDNA: And I'm sure they work very hard, but a doctor —
DANIELLA: They're an elite force. They're the vanguard of operations.
EDNA: Going to college is much —
DANIELLA: Yeah, and, like, the Taliban would stop me going to college. That's why we need to fight them.
EDNA: And there are people who do that. People who are trained.
DANIELLA: Oh, we get a full training.Twelve weeks / in Parris Island. Plus I get a $4000 sign up bonus. Then I get assigned. Afghanistan. Kosovo.
EDNA: Twelve weeks? *(After Kosovo.)* Kosovo? Is that even a country?
DANIELLA: It's, like, in Europe. Boring. Hey, can you sign? I need to get it back to him today.
EDNA: Today? But, but, doesn't this mean, aren't you, wouldn't this mean, you're going to be older, it'll put you at a disadvantage, if you, if your friends, aren't you going to be, if you —
DANIELLA: It'll make me a better doctor. That's what he said.
EDNA: *(Trying to stay calm.)* OK. It's a big decision. Why don't we think about this? For a couple of days. That's all. Just a couple of days.
DANIELLA: He says it's urgent.

EDNA: Nothing good is done in haste.

DANIELLA: But we got attacked.

EDNA: New York! Washington! Nobody attacked Pittsburgh!

DANIELLA: Close enough.

EDNA: Yes, well, they didn't mean to land in Shanksville.

DANIELLA: If Al-Qaeda hadn't attacked America, it wouldn't have landed there at all. Look, they started it.

EDNA: I am aware of that, Daniella.

DANIELLA: I so want to get Osama Bin Laden.

EDNA: We all do, honey.

DANIELLA: Can you imagine? Yeah, I'm a woman and I'm kicking your Taliban butt!

EDNA: You're too young.

DANIELLA: No, see, you just have to sign the release. It's easy.

EDNA: There must be more to it than that.

DANIELLA: I read the leaflets. And spoke to the guy. For ages.

EDNA: But, see, don't you want to be with your friends? At college?

DANIELLA: They stop women being doctors out there, midwives, everything. You couldn't even be a nurse out there.

EDNA: No-one's going to stop you being a —

DANIELLA: The Taliban would. If they invaded. It was on the news! You know, Ma, you don't seem to be supporting my choice.

EDNA: I have always supported your choices.

DANIELLA: Then will you sign the form?

EDNA: Look. At least start college, just start it, do it for me, then in a couple of years —

DANIELLA: We might not have two years!

EDNA: But the money. It's set up. Do you know how hard I worked to secure that?

DANIELLA: Yeah, I went through it all that with the recruiting officer.

EDNA: At the mall?

DANIELLA: Legally, they have to hold everything in place. 'Til I get back.

EDNA: What if you get injured? Have you even thought about that?

(She takes ice cream out of the bag.)

DANIELLA: I'll be fine.

EDNA: The ice cream! I can't discuss this now, I have to defrost the fridge.

DANIELLA: I'll be fine, Ma.

EDNA: It has to be done now, or the ice cream will be ruined.

(Edna, very aggressively, empties out and sorts the remaining groceries.)

EDNA: You could get raped. Sweet Jesus. They rape women out there.

DANIELLA: They rape women here.

EDNA: It's not the same! If you get caught by a, by a, a Taliban person, they'll —

DANIELLA: I won't get caught, Ma.

EDNA: It's war! You have no idea.

DANIELLA: I know about war, Ma, I am nearly eighteen.

EDNA: But what if you get. Danny, have you really thought? Or, or blinded, or you, or you, *(Her voice cracks.)* say, you don't come back? What's the point of holding a place, if you don't come back, Danny?

DANIELLA: God, why are you being so negative? Of course I'm gonna come back.

EDNA: You don't know!

DANIELLA: I thought I could count on you.

EDNA: Please, Danny, trust me, I know what's best for you.

DANIELLA: Doesn't look like it.

EDNA: Daniella. There are other people —

DANIELLA: Who do you think they are, Ma?

EDNA: It doesn't have to be —

DANIELLA: Mrs. Brody's nephew?

EDNA: What if she's right? I mean, it's, it's —

DANIELLA: So, now you think the president is lying?

EDNA: Of course not, I'm, I'm. I'm not saying it's. But what if?

DANIELLA: That my commander-in-chief is lying?

EDNA: Not your commander. He's not your commander.

DANIELLA: Only 'cause you won't sign the form.

EDNA: If, if, yes, what'd she say, the neo-con, the big event, like Pearl Harbor, that's what she said, then you'd have to wait, right? 'Til you knew for sure. About the pipeline. / Yes, she said that, I think, a pipeline. In Afghanistan.

DANIELLA: I can't believe you're — *(After "Afghanistan.")* I can't believe this. You said we had to fight, that we needed to protect —

EDNA: I know, I know, I know that. And I agree. But what if. Best to wait, couple of years, that's all. 'Til we know for sure.

DANIELLA: Our rights have to be protected, that's what you said. That's what you always say. You always say that!

EDNA: And Iraq. Well. That's a huge country.

DANIELLA: Ma! God. I can't believe — Anyway, we're not going into Iraq. That's what the guy said. He has it on official authority. I'm not supposed to tell you. Top secret.

EDNA: We're not going to get Saddam?

DANIELLA: Nope. And, hey, even if we did, he said it wouldn't take long. Didn't last time.

EDNA: Your allergies. Your hives. You'll be in Afghanistan with hives.

DANIELLA: He didn't say it would be a problem.

EDNA: *(Venom.)* Of course he didn't. He wouldn't.

DANIELLA: We've got to fight. / Inching forward. That's what you say.

EDNA: Absolutely. The army should. That's why we pay our taxes.

DANIELLA: Sign the form, Ma.

EDNA: There's a lot of small print.

DANIELLA: It's not a warranty.

EDNA: You know I always read the small / print —

DANIELLA: I want to get it back to him today.

EDNA: Can't find my glasses.

DANIELLA: On your head.

EDNA: Pen doesn't work.

(Danny grabs a jar of pens.)

DANIELLA: Here.

EDNA: I.

I can't.

I know it's.

I'm sorry.

I can't.

DANIELLA: I think you owe Mrs. Brody an apology.

EDNA: She's on strong medication.

DANIELLA: Then I give her more credit.

(Daniella storms out. Edna looks at the document, lost. She picks up the odor buster, pulls it apart. Granules pour out onto the floor.)

END OF PLAY

The Pickle Lady

Sharyn Rothstein

The Pickle Lady was first produced by Youngblood at The Ensemble Theatre in September of 2007. Director: Alexis Poledouris. Cast: Sarah — Erin Mallon; Bekah — Julie Fitzpatrick.

CHARACTERS

BEKAH, twenty-six.

SARAH, twenty two.

SETTING

A small one-bedroom apartment in the Lower East Side.

• • •

Bekah, 26, in a lacy top and underwear, comes out of the bedroom into the dark living room to get a glass of water. She picks up a candle and lights it, suddenly revealing — Sarah, 22, dressed up for a night out in 1912, looking for something.

BEKAH: Um, can I help you with something?

SARAH: I lost them. I can't find them anywhere.

BEKAH: How did you get in here?

SARAH: What do you mean, how did I get in here? How did you get in here?

BEKAH: This is my apartment.

SARAH: This is my apartment. See? I have a key.

(Sarah holds up her key. Bekah takes it.)

BEKAH: This key is like a million years old.

SARAH: What're you talking about? Pauly just had them made. I told him: You know, Pauly, we're five girls living alone in this apartment. What happens if one of those meshuginah Italians tries to break down our door?

BEKAH: You're . . . holy crap . . . what's your name?

SARAH: Sarah Leshovsky, although I don't know what business it is of yours. Now where did I leave them?

BEKAH: You lived in this apartment?

SARAH: No, I live in this apartment.

BEKAH: That's amazing.

SARAH: I don't see what's so amazing about it. We all have to live somewhere, don't we?

BEKAH: Yeah, but you're my great-grandmother. You're my mother's mother's mother.

SARAH: Don't be ridiculous. I'm not even married. I'm just a lonely old maid. *(Sigh.)* Can you believe I'll be 22 next month?

(Bekah laughs.)

SARAH: What's funny?

BEKAH: I'm 26.

SARAH: And you're single? Oy vey, if I'm single at 26, I'm throwing myself off a bridge.

BEKAH: So you lived — live — here in this shithole apartment with four other girls?

SARAH: Sometimes four, sometimes six.

BEKAH: Wow. That's like: *Girls Gone Wild, Depression Era Edition.*

SARAH: Girls Gone what?

BEKAH: Nevermind.

SARAH: You're 26 and you're not married. So what is it you do exactly?

BEKAH: I'm a designer. For clothes. I make stuff like T-shirts, onesies.

SARAH: Onesies?

BEKAH: For babies? They say things like: Free Poop. See Below.

SARAH: Poop?

BEKAH: Yeah, like . . . nevermind. What do you do?

SARAH: I sell pickles. I know, it's not exactly glamorous. My hands smell like half-sours every day. But I'm saving to take a typing course. In case tonight doesn't work out, and I'm single for the rest of my life.

BEKAH: What's tonight?

SARAH: Ugh, a friend set me up with her cousin's cousin. I'm meeting him at Stanton and Delancey. I said: Where at Stanton and Delancey? She said: Just at the corner. I said: You want I should meet a strange man on the corner? I mean, in the old country that'd be fine, because, let's face it, there was only one corner! But here? So many corners! So many strange men! How do I even know I'll find the right one?

BEKAH: What's his name?

SARAH: Leo something.

BEKAH: You'll find him.

SARAH: How do you know?

BEKAH: I just have a feeling about it.

SARAH: Well I won't find him if I don't find my gloves first. I am not leaving without those gloves. I know they're here somewhere . . . *(She notices Bekah's underwear.)* and what exactly do you call that outfit you're wearing?

BEKAH: Oh, um . . . it's a . . . I've kind of got company.

SARAH: Company where?

BEKAH: In the bedroom.

SARAH: *(Surprised.)* There's a bedroom?

BEKAH: Yeah, it's, I guess it's new . . . Listen, would you mind coming back in an hour or so, so I can ask my company to leave —

SARAH: You've got "company" in the bedroom?

BEKAH: Yeah . . .

SARAH: I thought you said you're not married.

BEKAH: I'm not.

SARAH: Are you engaged?

BEKAH: No.

SARAH: Are you a prostitute?

BEKAH: Um, no.

SARAH: Then you're a hussy!

BEKAH: I guess you could say that, yeah.

SARAH: What will this do for your prospects?

BEKAH: Things have changed since you lived here. It's not uncommon for women to take lovers.

SARAH: Lovers?

BEKAH: Yes.

SARAH: And how many "lovers" have you had?

BEKAH: Um, just a few . . . dozen . . .

SARAH: With all these lovers, how do you find a husband?

BEKAH: Actually, it's kind of hard. Most people go online.

SARAH: Online.

BEKAH: Yeah, it's like this . . . imaginary place where you meet strangers.

SARAH: That sounds lonely.

BEKAH: Sometimes it is.

SARAH: It's not easy living without your family, is it?

BEKAH: Easier than living with them.

SARAH: That's what I used to think. When I boarded the boat, I was seventeen years old. I came all by myself. I thought: Who needs a mother and a father when there's such a thing as opportunity? Little did I know, opportunity would mean selling pickles on Orchard Street.

BEKAH: You must have been brave.

SARAH: Eh, what's brave if you don't have a choice?

BEKAH: That's how I felt when I left Roslyn.

SARAH: That's in Poland?

BEKAH: Long Island. It's like the *shtetl*, with better amenities.

SARAH: I see. Your parents, they wanted you to stay?

BEKAH: They wanted me to be . . . happy.

SARAH: What's so bad about that?

BEKAH: I just . . . Don't know how.

SARAH: I thought about it once, happiness. But then they lowered the price of pickles and business really picked up, so that was the end of thinking about anything. My fingers shriveled up from reaching in the barrel all day. That's why I'm looking for the gloves. I never meet a man without them. My mother, she'd say: What kind of man wants to marry a woman with pickled fingers?

BEKAH: Do you miss her, your mother?

SARAH: Who doesn't miss their mother? It's been, four years?, since I saw her. She was crying. There were goats. Everywhere. *(Beat.)* Do you miss your mother?

BEKAH: I see her now and then, Thanksgiving, Christmas.

SARAH: Christmas?

BEKAH: We're kind of . . . Jewish Lite. *(Beat.)* She always buys me the wrong gift. Like last year, she gave me a gas card. I was like, Mom, I live in New York. I don't have a car. I don't think she can get over that I chose to live here. She's always clucking about it, like "Do you know how hard we worked so that you could have a backyard to play in?"

SARAH: *(Wistful.)* Ugh, a backyard. That sounds wonderful.

BEKAH: I find open spaces claustrophobic.

SARAH: More claustrophobic than a one room apartment with five roommates and no toilet?

BEKAH: You don't have a toilet?

SARAH: We have a jug.

BEKAH: Oh my god.

SARAH: But it's a big jug. Oh boy, look at the time. Ugh, forget it. I'm not gonna go.

BEKAH: You have to go.

SARAH: I can't find the gloves. I'm not going if I can't find the gloves, and I'm supposed to be there in five minutes. I'll never make it.

BEKAH: It's right down the street.

SARAH: I'm not going without the gloves.

BEKAH: I don't think the gloves are here anymore.

SARAH: It must be Lillian. She's always stealing my things. May she grow upside down like an onion with her face in the bowels of hell.

BEKAH: I think you should go anyway.

SARAH: No. I'll meet someone else. You miss one train —

BEKAH: — you catch the next. My grandmother used to say that all the time.

SARAH: Where did you meet your "company"? The one in the bedroom.

BEKAH: At a bar on Orchard Street.

SARAH: That's where I sell the pickles!

BEKAH: His name's "Claude". He has two Chinese tattoos. I asked him what they meant. He said the one on the right means "Bubonic." He wouldn't tell me what the other one meant. I thought, I bet if I sleep with him, he'll tell me . . . but that was three months ago. *(Beat.)* I bet the other one is Chinese for "this guy's a big jackass."

SARAH: Chinese tattoos on Orchard Street. *(She shakes her head.)* Amazing.

(Sarah sits down.)

BEKAH: What are you doing?

SARAH: I'm going to bed.

BEKAH: You can't! You've got a date.

SARAH: He'll smell me a mile away. It'll be humiliating.

BEKAH: Maybe he likes pickles.

SARAH: Very funny.

BEKAH: I mean it. Maybe he . . . loves half-sours more than anything in the whole world. Maybe, the moment he takes your hand, he'll never want to leave your side. Maybe a girl who sells pickles on Orchard Street is exactly who he's been looking for his whole life.

SARAH: I don't know . . .

(Bekah takes Sarah's hands and sniffs them.)

BEKAH: I think they smell lovely.

SARAH: Oh please.

BEKAH: Like home.

SARAH: Like home?

BEKAH: Yeah. Kind of like home.

(Beat.)

SARAH: I'm already late.

BEKAH: He'll wait for you.

(Sarah starts to leave.)

SARAH: You didn't tell me your name.

BEKAH: Bekah. It's short for Rebekah.

SARAH: That's my mother's name.

BEKAH: I know. It was my grandmother's name, too.

SARAH: Well it was nice to meet you Bekah.

BEKAH: You too, Sarah.

SARAH: I hope you get out of this rat hole sometime soon.

BEKAH: Actually . . . I just moved in.

SARAH: Huh. *(She gives Bekah a wink.)* Well then don't forget to empty the jug.

(Sarah leaves. Bekah watches her go. Beat. Then Bekah blows out the candle.)

BEKAH: Hey "Claude"? Get the fuck out of my apartment.

END OF PLAY

Rally

Bridgette A. Wimberly

Rally was produced September 9 to 26, 2009, under The River Crosses Rivers by the Ensemble Studio Theatre (William Carden, Artistic Director) and Going to the River (Elizabeth Van Dyke, Artistic Director). Director: Clinton Turner Davis. Cast: Granny — Venida Evans; Tameka — Erin Weems.

CHARACTERS

TAMEKA, a twenty year old African American college student.

GRANNY, a seventy+ year old African American woman.

SETTING

A large parking lot.

TIME

2008, early afternoon.

• • •

Tameka, carrying two folding chairs, walks slightly ahead of Granny, who is walking with a labored gait downstage to an unseen podium in a parking lot. Granny is dressed in her Sunday best. Tameka is dressed nicely, but more casually. Granny is carrying a small cloth bag with a bottle of water and the Bible in it. Tameka's backpack has magazines, bottled water, sunglasses, and her ipod. Lights and sound can be used to get the effect of an enlarging crowd.

TAMEKA: You OK, Granny?

GRANNY: I'm . . . OK.

TAMEKA: Sure?

GRANNY: *(Stops.)* Well how much further is it!

TAMEKA: I want to make sure no one sits in front of us.

GRANNY: Bird's eye view, right?

TAMEKA: No point of getting this far to stand in the back.

GRANNY: You right! No point.

TAMEKA: Here. This is going to be front row, center. Trust me.

GRANNY: I trust you.

TAMEKA: OK!

GRANNY: How long you think it's going to be, Tameka?

TAMEKA: What do you mean?

GRANNY: Before the people show up, before the show starts. Before we see him!

TAMEKA: Hour and a half.

GRANNY: That long!

TAMEKA: If you want to see and not have all those heads in front of you, we had to get here early.

GRANNY: The early bird . . .

TAMEKA: Gets the front row seat. They're expecting fifty thousand.

GRANNY: People!

TAMEKA: No, birds! Yes, Granny. Could be more.

GRANNY: Fifty thousand! That's more people then I can imagine. And I got a good imagination. What I picture is a good sermon like back in biblical times. Jesus standing on a high hill, like this platform here, preaching to a sea of sinners.

TAMEKA: Well don't expect a sermon. He's a lawyer, not a preacher. And there won't be any redemption, not in the biblical sense anyway. But it may come close. I'm excited already.

GRANNY: Yes. Well that's good. A little excitement is always good for the soul. Makes you feel alive. Praise, Jesus! Say a hour uh?

TAMEKA: And a half.

GRANNY : I've waited longer for a lot less.

(Beat.)

Don't get to see you hardly at all anymore.

TAMEKA: I know. But with classes, papers, exams, me living out of town . . .

GRANNY: Boys, freedom . . . Who is it now . . . ?

(Tameka blushes a little.)

Ah, to be young again. Before me and your granddad got married, peace be on his soul, we sat in a crowded, hot juke-joint a good two hours once, waiting to see Billy Eckstine do his thing. "Mr. B" was the heart-throb of my day. Your granddad had his sweaty, throbbing palm on my willing, tender thigh, squeezing it the whole time.

(Squeezing Tameka's thigh.)

TAMEKA: *(Amused.)* Oh yeah!

GRANNY: Oh yeah. That's all we'd dare do, in those days. Praise Jesus. We had to wait until Mr. B finished his gig downtown and drove forty minutes across town to the colored club, but we made good time of the wait. Man could he croon.

(She hums or sings a few bars or "Tenderly".)

Things were segregated back then.

(Looking about, she gets out of her seat.)

Your granddad never would have believed anything like this. Not sure I believe it now. Haven't seen lines likes this since the government's free cheese and peanut butter. Things don't feel right. Seems like they should be singing or holding hands.

(Singing.)

We shall overcome, someday.

(Wiping her brow.)

Hot. Hope they got some rest rooms out here. This ain't nothing but a parking lot.

TAMEKA: They've got rest rooms, Granny. Port-o-potties all around the periphery of the lot.

GRANNY: *(As she retrieves and opens her water bottle.)* No thank you, I don't use them. I just as well piss in a pot behind a tree or on myself before I use them nasty, stinky things.

TAMEKA: Well let's not drink anything then, OK. We want this to be a happy, memorable event.

GRANNY: *(Sits.)* With all this sun and crowd, ain't gonna be able to help but to drink. Hot as you know where out here. Concrete and asphalt make what I call a urban hell. All they need is some housing projects and a bunch of poor folks looking for salvation.

TAMEKA: *(Putting on her sunglasses.)* When I get back to school tomorrow, I want to tell all my friends about this whole thing and just how much I . . . *we* made a difference by coming here and putting our faces on the cause.

GRANNY: Sitting here ain't doing much.

TAMEKA: We're here. That's important, Granny! Skeptics don't believe he can do it. But look at us. We've got a front row seat to changing this world. I'm geeked!

(Turns around, amused.)

I think that police officer was right. We just might see fifty thousand.

(Taking magazines out of a bag along with an ipod.)

GRANNY: In the old days at rallies like this, we'd meet at a church first. Pray hard 'cause we knew we were gonna need it, second. Organizers would give us lessons on how to get our asses beat without fighting back. How to bend over and protect your head as you called on Jesus. They'd talk about when the teargas goes off what to do. When the dogs charge you, what to do. When the hoses drown you, what to do. When . . .

TAMEKA: Granny, please. This is not that kind of rally. Nobody is going to do that.

GRANNY: I know, praise Jesus. At least I'm praying nothing happens like that.

TAMEKA: *(Giving her a magazine.)* Here, read your magazine to help pass the time.

(Puts headphones in her ears, begins to read her magazine.)

GRANNY: *(Looking about.)* Some of these people don't look Christian you know. They look like throwbacks from the fifties, sixties.

TAMEKA: Most of these people are fed up with the way this country is going.

GRANNY: We were fed up too. The difference between rallies back then and those now is we knew who the enemy was. Now-a-days everybody pretending to be your friend. Got a big smile on they face. But they got the same face as the faces in the fifties when I was your age and your mama was a baby. Or the forties when I was a little child and your great grandma was young. Or the sixties when he was a youngster.

TAMEKA: These are not the same times. The laws have changed! People have change!

(Sound effect: Large crowd talking.)

ANNOUNCER: *(Voice over.)* ATTENTION PLEASE, ATTENTION PLEASE. PLEASE MOVE IN QUICKLY AND WALK FORWARD TO THE FRONT OF THE PODIUM.

GRANNY: They got snipers you know. Sharpshooters that could nail your behind from way across the way.

TAMEKA: *(Removing an earpiece.)* What!

GRANNY: Like they shot Dr. King.

TAMEKA: Nobody's shooting anybody, Granny!

GRANNY: Fifty thousand people, Tameka!

(Leaning into her granddaughter.)

Ten thousand of them FBI, CIA, underground police.

TAMEKA: You mean undercover police.

GRANNY: That's what I said!

TAMEKA: This is an historic event. You wanted to witness this, remember! There are no dogs, no hoses, mobs with sticks and bad words . . . no sharpshooters. They checked each and everyone of us for a weapon before they let us in here.

GRANNY: What about those skin heads?

TAMEKA: What about them?

GRANNY: *(Quieter.)* I read the papers. But I'm more afraid of those look like regular folks, got regular jobs, say they love everybody. Say we done moved past all of that. Say, some of my best friends are Black. Those that think it ain't time for him yet!

TAMEKA: *(Quieter.)* A lot of my friends are white. Most of them are working to make sure things get better. Believe it's time for him, time for change. These aren't the . . .

GRANNY: Same times. I know. But I must got some Missouri blood in me, 'cause you got to show me before I believe it. People we know and love ain't got no money, no jobs, healthcare, houses being foreclosed. The government just gave all the people who stole the money, all of the poor working people's last dime to save the country and we sitting in a parking lot used to be full of working people's cars, now full of desperate people's prayers. Who you think they blaming it on?

(Beat.)

Your mother keeps telling me your generation is colorblind. Evidenced, as she puts it, by the rainbow coalition of boyfriends you paraded in and out of her front door when you lived at home.

TAMEKA: *(Rolling her eyes, gasp.)* You see why I can't talk to her? I can't do anything right. Never could. Never will.

GRANNY: You know I'm a lot like your father, I don't judge.

TAMEKA: But do you trust? He doesn't. He still brings up every little mistake I've made since I was two. I'm not a little girl anymore.

GRANNY: No, you a woman with big dreams and big plans. And my baby. Young people should have that. But with arthritis comes wisdom. The more things change, the more they don't change at all. I understood the fifties. These modern times are crazy. And we crazy, sitting in the front row with fifty thousand people between us and the only way out of here, once the bullets start flying over our heads aimed at him.

TAMEKA: You were so happy when we left home. So optimistic. You wanted to see him with your own eyes. What happened to that woman? That's the Granny I thought I was sitting next to in the car on my way down here. The one I told my friends about when I said I had to go home and do something important with her. We were going to witness this together.

GRANNY: Yes. Yes. I remember her. Yes. OK. I do remember.

TAMEKA: Are you OK, Granny? We can go back home, if this is too much for you. It would be a shame, but we can go home.

(Sound effect: Someone whistles high and loud. Talking crowd sounds are bigger but lower than first heard.)

ANNOUNCER: *(Voice over.)* THERE ARE STILL SPACES ON THE RIGHT AND LEFT SIDES OF THE PODIUM. PLEASE MOVE QUICKLY TOWARD THE PODIUM.

TAMEKA: *(Looking at her watch, then around her at the crowd. She stands taking in the crowd.)*

Wow, it's really filling up fast. Feel the excitement in the air?

(Deep breath, she hugs Granny.)

GRANNY: *(Feeling Tameka's excitement.)* You think they gonna let him do it? As much as we need him to be, he ain't Jesus.

TAMEKA: Read your book. It won't be long now.

GRANNY: Blessed are they that hunger and thirst after justice, for they shall have their fill.

(Sound effect: Talking Crowd Sounds.)

(Granny reaches in her bag and takes out her Bible. Shows it with a nod to Tameka, who nods back with a 'whatever'.)

(Long pause as Tameka pages through her magazine and bops her head as she hums to popular music on her ipod. Granny pages through her partly humming and singing, "Ain't Going to Let Nobody Turn Me Around." We should get the feeling that people are all around them, i.e., Granny moves her feet to let someone by, or moves her chair closer to Tameka, looks up at someone passing, maybe someone briefly sings along with Granny. Periodically, Granny takes a drink of water. Every now and then, she turns and looks about. She has a worried look on her face.)

(Tameka is content looking at her magazine and listening to her ipod. Tameka begins to sing. Her singing gets louder. She is singing a popular rap with questionable lyrics. Granny becomes concerned AND sings "I Want Jesus to Walk with Me" louder trying to drown out Tameka who pays her no attention.)

(Sound effect: A high pitched sound from a mic is heard.)

GRANNY: *(Arousing Tameka, excited.)* Tameka, Tameka. I think he's coming out! He's coming out!

ANNOUNCER: *(Voice over.)* TESTING, ONE, TWO, THREE. TESTING.

(Sound effect: A pop sound of a system backfire.)

(Both Granny and Tameka react. A small crowd cheers and claps.)

TAMEKA: Goodness, Granny. You've got me ducking. It's just the PA system backfiring. He's not going to test his own mic. *(Chuckles.)*

(Sound effect: A brief blast of cheering.)

GRANNY: I have marched and rallied too, you know.

TAMEKA: I know.

GRANNY: *(Rubbing her sore leg.)* Had water hoses full force blow me half a block down the road.

TAMEKA: *(Serious.)* I know.

GRANNY: Change! I keep hearing it. Young people think they invented it like they think they invented love making, rap, and new uses for the word nigger . . . I want "change" just as much as anyone here. Fear it, 'cause I know others fear it worse. Know the lengths people will go to, when they fear your equality will change their way of life.

I was a young woman too. Wore a big Angela Davis fro, had my fist raised high, and I dreamt of a day when I could sit at a peaceful rally with my granddaughter. I can't tell you the number of times I prayed for change and watched people die trying to make it happen. I don't want to see another person die . . . not him . . . especially not you!

TAMEKA: I don't want that either. Didn't think how this may affect you. Thought . . .

GRANNY: Thought what, Tameka?

TAMEKA: Thought you'd be . . . proud

(Beat.)

Do you want to stay? I'll do whatever you want. We came! We're a part of the count. We don't have to stay.

GRANNY: Are you kidding! Waited a long time for this. Me and my grandbaby.

(Beat as she steadies herself.)

(Singing boldly, mainly trying to convince herself.)

We shall overcome . . . Today!

(The crowd begins to roar.)

TAMEKA: *(Startled.)* Granny! Here he comes. He's coming to the podium!

(They both look up and outward. We hear a large crowd shouting a cheering. Elation is on both of their faces. Granny takes Tameka's hand and they stand with the crowd, look at each other and then shout together as the lights fade.)

GRANNY, TAMEKA AND THE CROWD: Change, change, change, change!

(As lights fade to black we hear louder chants for Change.)

(Black out.)

END OF PLAY

Saguaro

Philip Dawkins

Saguaro was first produced as part of Estrogen Fest at the Prop Theatre in Chicago, Illinois, May 2007. Director: Katie Klemme. Cast: Wren — Ann Filmer; Kira — Michelle Courvais.

Saguaro received it's New York premier in the fall of 2007 at the Manhattan Theatre Source as part of Estrogenius Festival 2007. Director: Shannon Ward. Cast: Wren — Julie Fitzpatrick (AEA); Kira — Amelia Campbell.

Saguaro received it's European premier in March, 2009 as part Painted Filly's "100 Minutes 2009" in Dublin, Ireland, at the Samuel Beckett Theatre. Director: Gemma McGill. Cast: Wren — Hilary Cotter; Kira — Lorna Quinn; Fiancé — Mark McCabe.

Saguaro was performed again in Ireland the summer of 2009 as part of the Electric Picnic Festival, produced by Shining Eyes Co. Director — Gemma McGill. Cast: Wren — Hilary Cotter; Kira — Lorna Quinn; Fiancé — Mark McCabe.

CHARACTERS

WREN, a twenty-something, likeable girl, frustrated with being single. She's desperately seeking "the one."

KIRA, Wren's best friend. Same age. Spunky, can be blunt, but she means well. Currently consumed by her upcoming wedding.

VARIOUS OFFSTAGE VOICES.

SETTING

Multiple locations. Setting and props should "suggest" location and action, but actors must be able to move fluidly and quickly between time and space. Complete black-outs between vignettes are strongly discourages, just something to indicate transition and passage of time.

Feel free to play with the locations of some of the scenes in your production. For instance, in the Painted Filly production, the treadmill scene was changed to an aerobics class and the final scene was set in a yoga class. In the Estrogenius production, the scene with the stipple stick was set at a bus stop. Have fun!

• • •

SCENE I

Lights up on an engagement party. Wren stands next to a potted cactus. She is annoyed and tipsy. From off, we hear people singing.

VOICES: *"Happy Wedding to you. / Happy Wedding to you. / Happy Wedding, Angie and Rob. / Happy Wedding to you."*

WREN: *(To herself.)* "And many more."

(We hear people clapping, and the voices of the Bride and Groom from off.)

BRIDE: *Thank you, everyone.*

GROOM: *Let's open gifts!!*

WREN: Let's poke ourselves in the eye balls.

GROOM: *This one's from Craig.*

BRIDE: *Oh, it's a trifle dish. How adorable! Thank you, Craig!*

GROOM: *Thanks, Craig.*

(The sounds of clapping and picture taking. Wren loses her balance just a bit and pricks herself on the cactus.)

WREN: Ow. Oh, sorry, I — I didn't see you there. No, really, it's my fault. My fault. Sorry. You, uh — how do you know the bride and groom? They're both my bosses at work. Temp work. I'm just temping. I don't actually know anything about hedge funds. I don't even think I know what a hedge fund is. I just, um, I just temp.

GROOM: *This next one is from Wren.*

BRIDE: *Wren? Oh,* Wren. *Hi, Wren. Thanks for coming.*

WREN: *(Half-heartedly waves.)* Actually, I don't even really know the bride and groom. But they're my bosses, so . . . To tell you the truth, I have a hard time remembering his name. It's like, I know his name is Rob. I *know* that, but something in the back of my head always says, "Are you sure it's not Bob?" So, whenever I see him at the office, I second guess myself and end up saying something like "Hi, Brorb." It's pathetic. I had to check the invitation twice before I filled out the card.

BRIDE: *Oh, a gravy boat! (Mild clapping.) Thanks, Wren.*

GROOM: *Thanks, Wren.*

WREN: No problem, Brorb.

(To the cactus.) I didn't know what to get them. I thought I'd be the only one here without a date. You look a little dry, can I get you a drink?

SCENE 2

Later, Wren is totally drunk and sitting across a table from the cactus.

WREN: So he says, "Well, if you're looking for 'something more,' then maybe you should look for someone else." and that was it. The end of the relationship. *THE* relationship. The only relationship I've ever —

(She laughs into her drink.)

Oh, I'm not sober. I don't know why I'm telling you all this. I hate these things! What the hell is an engagement party, anyway? How many more fucking parties can we throw around one fucking marriage? How much more of my time are these people going to demand just to prove how much they love each other? Right? Right? I'm just — you know, as singles, we have to band together. We have to — you are single, aren't you? I find you so easy to talk to.

SCENE 3

At the gym on treadmills with best friend Kira.

WREN: No, the worst part was the cash bar. At a wedding reception. A *CASH* bar.

KIRA: Tacky. When the fiancé and I get married, we're going to have a champagne fountain. We've already priced it. It's not as bad as you might think. And then there's going to be a smaller one right next to it with fruit punch for the kids and alcoholics.

WREN: That sounds really cute.

KIRA: It is. Ooo, look, I just burned a hundred calories.

WREN: Already? No fair.

KIRA: Oh, that reminds me, I've been meaning to ask you: Our best man just broke up with his girlfriend of like eight years or something. He's really smart, very clean, a little on the heavy side, but he's studying to be a doctor. And, I was thinking, since you're my beautiful maid of honor, and the two of you are both single —

WREN: I'm bringing a date.

KIRA: What?

WREN: Don't sound so shocked.

KIRA: I'm not. I'm just surprised. Who is it? Who is it?

WREN: It's nothing yet. It's still early.

KIRA: Good for you finding a date. It's about time. What's he look like?

WREN: He's very healthy looking.

KIRA: OK, I'm sensing not a lot of excitement. Is it because of the guy or the treadmill?

WREN: It's just . . .

KIRA: Say it.

WREN: I don't know that we have all that much in common

KIRA: Un hunh.

WREN: And I don't know if I'm interested. I mean, I think I like him. He seems, you know, stable, and pretty firmly planted. But, he's not really my type.

KIRA: Listen, remember when I first started dating the fiancé? Remember, I thought he wasn't all that attractive and that maybe he was a little bit boring? Well, now look. We're getting married. Just give it time.

WREN: He's a cactus.
KIRA: Oh. Like a *cactus* cactus?
WREN: Yeah.
KIRA: Oh.
(Beat. Beat.)
WREN: You're judging me.
KIRA: No.
WREN: Yes you are. You think I'm stupid.
KIRA: I didn't say that.
WREN: You think I'm desperate.
KIRA: No. Well, a little.
WREN: Whatever happened to "Good for you. It's about time."?
KIRA: Well, Wren, good for you. But, it's about *species.*
WREN: I know how it sounds, but if you could have seen him . . . Kira, I took the cactus back to my place, and he just sat there. And listened. He didn't even try to touch me.
KIRA: He didn't try to make a move?
WREN: He didn't move *at all.*
KIRA: Wren, that sounds really great, and what you do at home is your business, but —
WREN: I knew you wouldn't understand.
KIRA: I do. Or I don't. Look, it's not about me. I just want you to think about the social consequences of this. I'm totally fine with whoever or *what*ever you want to date, but some people might not be. I mean, picture it, Wren. Picture ending up with this cactus. Are you really prepared to spend the rest of your life with that?
WREN: You didn't think you could be with a computer analyst forever, but your guy totally grew on you. Maybe the cactus will grow on me, too.
KIRA: You're my friend. I don't want to see you get hurt by a cactus.
WREN: I'll be careful. I promise.
KIRA: Does the cactus make you happy?
WREN: I think so. I think he might turn out to be exactly what I've always wanted.
KIRA: If he hurts you, I swear —
WREN: He won't.

Scene 4

Wren at home with the cactus which sits in its pot. She holds up a large sweater.

WREN: I bought you this sweater. Isn't it so cute? I know it's not really your style, but I think it's so cute. I don't mean that I don't like your style. No, god, I love your style. You're perfect. Don't ever change. I just thought that maybe, you know, if we ever needed to go out somewhere, you might want something nice. Something just a little — I don't know — softer. What do you think? You'll grow into it.

(Beat.)

Oh, by the way, Kira invited us to her place for brunch this Sunday. Don't worry, you can watch the game with her fiancé.

(Beat.)

You're not saying anything. Do you not want to go? But it'll be fun. And it would mean a lot to me. Kira's my best friend, and I really want you to like her a lot. You'll have fun. I promise. And you can wear your new sweater.

Scene 5

Sunday. Kira's kitchen.

WREN: *(Entering speaking to "the boys" offstage.)* Now, you two behave. No rough-housing. I don't want to come back and find potting soil all over the floor.

KIRA: They're sure getting along.

WREN: I know, isn't it great? I think your future husband and the cactus have very similar temperaments.

KIRA: Sure. So, now that the boys are glued to the television . . . how is it?

WREN: How is what?

KIRA: Oh come on, don't be such a prude. How's the cactus in the sacktus?

WREN: Kira!

KIRA: They can't hear us. They're watching "Sports Center." Spill!

WREN: Well, things were a little slow at first. You know. He was a little, um, limp?

KIRA: Oooo.

WREN: But, then I picked up some Miracle Grow. And now? Well, now it's kinda dirty.

KIRA: Yes?

WREN: And rough. But, he can be tender too. Not like that professor I was seeing. No, the cactus has a lot of layers. Once you get past that tough exterior, he's a real softy. . .

KIRA: And that turns you on?

WREN: Would that be wrong?

KIRA: Absolutely not. Look, I totally understand. The fiancé's the exact opposite. Totally passive on the outside, but a predator in the bedroom. I actually have blisters . . . *you know.* Are you two using protection?

WREN: Gardening gloves.

KIRA: Mm. So, what's the problem?

WREN: Nothing. For the first time, nothing. I've finally found someone who is absolutely everything I want. Or at least I can tell he's going to be.

KIRA: I'm so happy for you.

WREN: Thanks.

(There is a sudden loud cheer from "the fiancé" in the other room. Someone must have scored a point. We hear him yell: "HIGH FIVE!" followed by "OOOUUUCH!!")

SCENE 6

Wren at home with the cactus which sits in its pot on a stool.

WREN: Hey. Can we talk? Please? I think we should talk about what happened at Kira's. With the high five? No . . . I know it wasn't your fault. No, you're right. He should have been more careful. But, well, it is sort of a problem with you. . . and not just with other people. With me too. I'm not saying I can't handle you. Well, actually I am having trouble handling you. I'm just being honest. Don't look at me like that. Look, I don't know what your problem is. I shaved for *you!*

(Beat.)

Are you absorbing any of this?!

Scene 7

Wren at lunch with Kira.

WREN: Sometimes I wonder if I'm being stupid thinking I can jump right into dating a cactus. I mean, he's great, but it's a whole different landscape, you know? Like the other day, it was our three week anniversary, right? So, I got him flowers. Well, he gets all upset. How was I supposed to know he used to date a carnation? He never said anything about it. What, like, I'm just supposed to assume that, because he's a cactus, he's automatically been with every other form of plant life? And then the other day, I make a comment about wanting to meet more of his friends. And I called them cactuses.

KIRA: You actually said that? You actually used that word?

WREN: I thought that's what they were called.

KIRA: It's cacti.

WREN: Well I know that now.

KIRA: What did he say? Was he offended?

WREN: I could tell he was trying not to be.

KIRA: But, of course, he was. Wren, why did you say that? It makes you sound so ignorant.

WREN: I ran it through spell check. It came up fine.

KIRA: You can never trust spell check.

WREN: I thought it was OK for me to say it. And the rules go back and forth on this. Funk and Wagnall says cacti. Miriam Webster says cactuses.

KIRA: Shhh, stop saying that word.

WREN: I thought our relationship was bigger than words. I like to think that what the cactus and I have together goes far beyond some sort of grammatically correct jargon. I mean, cactuses/cacti. What difference does it make?

KIRA: A big difference to a cactus. Jesus, Wren, I bet some of his best friends are

(She looks over her shoulder, then whispers.)

cactuses.

WREN: I think I'm in over my head.

KIRA: You need to give it time. It's all part of getting to know each other.

WREN: I know, but I feel like our relationship isn't going anywhere, like it's sedentary. He says he feels like I'm drowning him, that he needs space to grow.

KIRA: He actually said that?

WREN: It was *implied.* I think I'm pushing him away. Whenever I try to get close to him, he puts up all his natural defenses. Kira, what if I lose him?

KIRA: Then you'll be single. So what?

WREN: So what? Easy for you to say. You have someone.

KIRA: I have the someone who's right for me.

WREN: Not everyone's boyfriend can be a "computer analyst," whatever the hell that is. At least I know what my boyfriend does.

KIRA: Oh? What does he do?

WREN: He survives.

Scene 8

The cactus sits in the center of the dance floor, disco lights flashing. Gloria Gaynor's "I Will Survive" blasts. We hear people all around the club clapping and chanting, "Go Cactus, go Cactus. Go go go, Cactus!" Wren sits off to the side at a small table by herself. She drinks. She looks bored. After a bit, she drunkenly yells to the dance floor, "He's with me!".

Scene 9

Wren and Kira at lunch. Wren has little red pin prick marks all over her face.

KIRA: Your face is bleeding.

WREN: Still? Hang on. I think I have a stipple stick in my purse. Do you have a compact?

KIRA: *(They both dig in their purses.)* I don't know why you stay with the cactus, Wren. It seems like, even when it's good, you still end up getting hurt.

WREN: He really loves me. I know he does.

KIRA: I think you need to take a good look at what you're getting out of your relationship. How well do you really know the cactus? Is it really worth it, or are you just telling yourself it is because the cactus is all you've got? *(Handing her a compact.)*
Take a really good look.

WREN: What's your problem? You're the one who told me to stick it out with the cactus, to give it time.
(Looking in the compact.)
Oh my god, I'm a mess.

KIRA: Do you want me to give you the number of our best man? He's still single.

SCENE 10

The cactus sits on a stool. Wren walks in with a suitcase.

WREN: I guess that's everything. I'm sorry, it's not you, I swear. I thought I could make this work, but I guess I'm not good enough for you. Aren't you going to say anything?
(Beat.)
Typical.

SCENE 11

Wren and Kira at lunch again.

KIRA: Oh, did you hear?

WREN: Hunh?

KIRA: Angie and Rob broke up?

WREN: Who?

KIRA: Angie. And Rob. Our old bosses. They broke up. As in divorced.

WREN: Angie and Bob?

KIRA: Rob.

WREN: Right.

KIRA: They broke up.

WREN: No way. When?

KIRA: Don't know. I heard it from Marci who heard it from Craig, and you know Craig still works for them. Apparently, things are really weird at the office.

WREN: Wow. Did he say why?

KIRA: Because the two bosses got divorced.

WREN: No, I mean did he say why they broke up?

KIRA: Irreconcilable differences. It just goes to show, you may think you know someone, but . . .

WREN: Who would have thought? Angie and Bob?

KIRA: Rob.

WREN: Right. Well, maybe they're happier now.

KIRA: How could they be happier now? They're single now.

WREN: I'm going to pretend you didn't say that.

KIRA: Why?

WREN: Because, Kira. There are worse things than being single.

KIRA: Like what?

WREN: Like making your best friend feel like a total loner.

KIRA: But you're not single. You're — oh, no. Oh, Wren, no. You and the cactus?

WREN: Yeah.

KIRA: When?

WREN: Last night.

KIRA: Honey, why didn't you say something?

WREN: I don't — I don't know that there's anything to say.

KIRA: What happened?

WREN: That's just it. Nothing. Nothing happened. Ever. I just — I needed more.

KIRA: I take it the break up was your idea?

WREN: I think so. I'm not sure. He didn't say much.

KIRA: That sucks. You OK?

WREN: I think so. We agreed to keep in touch, but . . . Well, I'm not holding my breath.

KIRA: So, it's over?

WREN: Yeah.

KIRA: Like good and totally over? You're for sure never getting back together?

WREN: Yeah, why?

KIRA: OK, so I didn't want to tell you this when you were dating, but remember when we had you and the cactus over for brunch?

WREN: Yeah?

KIRA: OK, well, while you were in the bathroom pulling needles out of the fiancé's hand, the cactus totally tried to poke me.

WREN: Prick!

KIRA: No, poke.

WREN: No, I mean, Prick. Like, he's a prick.

KIRA: Oh, yeah, Prick.
WREN: Poke?
KIRA: Poke.
WREN: Prick!
KIRA: Prick.
WREN: Well, good riddens.
KIRA: Here here.
WREN: I can't believe it.
KIRA: You just never really know someone, do you?
WREN: I know.
(Beat.)
WREN: Oh, and you want to hear the funniest part?
KIRA: Hunh?
WREN: This whole time, I've been pronouncing his name wrong.
KIRA: What?
WREN: It's "Saguaro." Like there's no 'g' in it.
KIRA: "Saguaro."
WREN: Yeah.
KIRA: Hunh.
WREN: How about that?
KIRA: You'd think he would have said something.

SCENE 12

The cactus alone onstage in a spotlight. "I Will Survive" plays. The cactus looks perfectly content. Lights out.

END OF PLAY

The Shore

Daniel Talbott

The Shore was originally produced as part of the Source Festival 2009 in Washington, D.C., June 22 to 28. Director: Jessica Lefkow. Cast: Woman 1 — Rena Cherry Brown; Woman 2 — Marilyn Bennett.

CHARACTERS

WOMAN 1, mid to late sixties, wealthy, classy, with mischief in her eyes. Head to toe Hermes.

WOMAN 2, mid to late sixties, much the same, a sad searching heart, maybe a tad more on the St. John side.

SETTING

A restaurant like Elaine's or the Four Seasons in New York City.

• • •

Two women, both in their sixties or older, sit eating dinner together.

WOMAN 1: I got on a train today.
WOMAN 2: A train?
WOMAN 1: The subway. And I found a note.
WOMAN 2: A note?
WOMAN 1: It popped out of some girl's back pocket. I saw her get up, get her backpack and try to stuff it in, but her jeans were too tight. It popped out, now it's mine.
WOMAN 2: Yours?
WOMAN 1: She dropped it, now it's mine.
WOMAN 2: Did you . . .
WOMAN 1: No. I wanted it. I was watching her read it. Her face. I wanted it and God gave it to me.
WOMAN 2: God gave you
WOMAN 1: He saw fit I should have it.
WOMAN 2: A sign.
WOMAN 1: A sign.
(Beat.)
She was licking her lips. Biting them and blushing. Smiling.
WOMAN 2: The
WOMAN 1: The girl, while she read it. She smiled and seemed to know.
WOMAN 2: What?
WOMAN 1: Things. Fun things. Happiness. Contentment.
WOMAN 2: Fun?
WOMAN 1: Flirtiness.
(Beat.)
I don't think it was hers. I think it was about her.

WOMAN 2: Who wrote it?

WOMAN 1: I think another girl. A friend of the boy's.

WOMAN 2: It was to a boy?

WOMAN 1: For a boy. The boy wrote first, then the girl.

WOMAN 2: The girl on the train?

WOMAN 1: Another girl. A friend of the boy's. The girl with the note's Sasheena. She had gum and a Sean John jacket.

WOMAN 2: So you think another girl gave Sasheena this note from her boyfriend.

WOMAN 1: I think this boy was struggling and he reached out. And this friend helped. She showed her support and made sure Sasheena got it. She intervened.

WOMAN 2: Act of fate.

WOMAN 1: Fate or kindness.

I took it like a penny.

WOMAN 2: A penny?

WOMAN 1: A heads penny from the ground. Then I read it.

WOMAN 2: Do you have it?

(Woman 1 nods.)

WOMAN 2: Can I see it?

(Woman 1 takes it out of her bag and hands it to Woman 2.)

WOMAN 1: He's first. She comes second. She's harder to read. Takes a couple passes.

(Woman 2 begins to read it. Woman 1 sips in silence.)

WOMAN 1: My son's porking a woman.

WOMAN 2: Dennis?

(Woman 1 nods.)

WOMAN 1: Like his father.

Proving something.

I saw him in Saks today buying her a purse.

Little hands, little heels. Smiles and laughs all the time. Bobbing her head around like a bird.

(Beat.)

Bob used to come to dinner without showering.

I could smell him across the table.

(Short pause.)

I'm sending it to Laura.

WOMAN 2: What? Dennis' Laura?

WOMAN 1: The note.

I'm not saying who from. I'm just going to drive by, slip it in the box with her name on it.

WOMAN 2: She knows . . .

WOMAN 1: Typed.

I'll type the envelope and use gloves so she can't smell me.

(Beat.)

I like her. I like Laura.

She worked.

She takes her load.

She's not a yoga and shake mom.

WOMAN 2: How are Katie and Dar?

WOMAN 1: Functioning. Smiling. Making it work.

Tom's a pig. Sam's weak in the wrists but they get by.

He's kind.

(Woman 1 sips a drink. Woman 2 continues reading.)

WOMAN 1: I went to the beach.

WOMAN 2: Today?

WOMAN 1: *(Nods.)* Today.

Got off the train. Ate a corn dog. Drank a slushy. Got my feet wet. Sat in the sand without a towel. Was late to lunch and didn't call.

(Beat.)

I have sand.

WOMAN 2: Sand?

WOMAN 1: In my . . .

WOMAN 2: Your ?!

WOMAN 1: My . . . Sand. I'm not taking a shower.

(Woman 1 sips her drink.)

WOMAN 1: *(Continued.)* I brought you something.

(Woman 1 brings a shell from her bag and puts it on Woman 2's plate.)

WOMAN 1: *(Continued.)* It's a snail. Excavated from the sand. Thought of you. You could make a necklace. Wear it to a luncheon. We could both wear one, be like that hat club. The little ladies with the red hats.

Go to the mall, shop together.

(Silence.)

I want to go away.

I want my life back. I want to travel.

(Short pause.)

I think Laura should leave Dennis and go to Greece with me.I think we should all go to Greece and spend lots of money. Play tennis and cook.

(Beat. Woman 2 finishes the note. She folds it and puts it on the table. Woman 1 sips her drink. Silence.)

WOMAN 2: When's the baby due?

WOMAN 1: Katie's? October.

WOMAN 2: A . . .

WOMAN 1: A boy.

WOMAN 2: Have you thought about Mexico?

WOMAN 1: Still waiting.

WOMAN 2: There's a cruise in May.

WOMAN 1: That's nice.

WOMAN 2: We thought we could take the kids. Maybe Laura and Dennis'd . . . ?

WOMAN 1: I'll ask them.

WOMAN 2: Might be nice.

WOMAN 1: Might.

(Woman 2 pours more hot water for her tea. Woman 1 watches the other diners. Short silence.)

WOMAN 2: I've been thinking about us. Summers at the beach with our families. We've become our mothers.

(Beat.)

I thought about that boy.

WOMAN 1: Huge hands.

WOMAN 2: Huge hands, chipped tooth, worked the rollercoaster. How big he was. How heavy his arms were on our shoulders. Free rides and walks. Ice cream.

WOMAN 1: Lemonade.

WOMAN 2: I remember how different our lives were going to be.

(Beat.)

WOMAN 1: The Village.

WOMAN 2: In winter. Writing. The snow. Two desks. Each facing a different window.

WOMAN 1: Fresh cut flowers . . .

WOMAN 2: Fresh cut and books. And music.

WOMAN 1: Stealing them.

WOMAN 2: If we had to. Meals and bread. Fans and bare feet in the summer. Walks and coffee. Pitchers of water with lemon in them.

WOMAN 1: Tea. And sex. And music.

(Silence.)

WOMAN 2: I feel like I've watched my life sift by me. I feel like I've never stood up and said no.

(Silence.)

Do you remember that game we played? When we were kids? The death game? In the water?

WOMAN 1: Bikes to the shore?

(Woman 2 nods.)

WOMAN 2: We'd ride to the sand. Undress.

WOMAN 1: Swim out.

WOMAN 2: Hold our breath.

WOMAN 1: Sink.

WOMAN 2: And disappear. Eyes open. Without light.

WOMAN 1: Holding hands.

WOMAN 2: Floating in darkness.

(Silence.)

END OF PLAY.

Worse Things

MONA MANSOUR

Worse Things was included in an evening of short plays called Infiltrage at the Flea Theater, New York City. It starred Colleen Werthmann and Jennifer Morris. Director: Sharon Lennon.

"Hell is other people" — *Sartre*

Characters

MAEVE and LIZ, two women, any ethnicity, a couple. Late twenties or thirties.

Setting

An apartment in a city.

• • •

Lights up: Maeve reads. Liz approaches her from behind, kisses her neck.

MAEVE: Oh my god that feels so good.
LIZ: Good.
MAEVE: So good.
LIZ: That's excellent.
MAEVE: Oh my god.
LIZ: Most excellent.
MAEVE: God that's great.
LIZ: Good, good.
MAEVE: I . . .
LIZ: Yeah?
MAEVE: I like it.
LIZ: I can see.
MAEVE: I . . . don't let myself relax enough.
LIZ: You don't.
MAEVE: I'm constantly somewhere else.
LIZ: You are. *(Beat.)*
MAEVE: Wait. I am? *(Trying to keep in sex mode:)*
LIZ: Sometimes.
MAEVE: You think I'm constantly somewhere else?
LIZ: You've said that.
MAEVE: Oh.
LIZ: Before. You go places.
MAEVE: Uh-huh.
LIZ: Your mind is always, going.
MAEVE: Yeah.
LIZ: *(Scrambling.)* You know, but then, when you're really here, it's like,

incredible. I've never seen anything like it. You're the passenger and the DRIVER all at once, I'm along for the, um. The RIDE.

MAEVE: Hm.

LIZ: You . . .

(Losing steam.)

take . . . me.

MAEVE: Huh.

LIZ: So.

MAEVE: What're you talking about, *driver, passenger*? What's that?

LIZ: I don't want to get into it.

MAEVE: It? What's "it"?

LIZ: Our sex life. Or lack of . . .

MAEVE: *(Hurt.)* So that's your solution: You just don't want to talk about it.

LIZ: I mean — no.

MAEVE: It's not the worst thing in the world to talk about . . . There's worse things.

LIZ: Yep.

MAEVE: A lot worse.

LIZ: Like what.

MAEVE: Huh?

LIZ: I mean . . . like, what?

(Maeve is thrown: Is she for real?)

MAEVE: *(Where to start?)* A million — problems, things. Iraq. Afghanistan. Soldiers coming home with no limbs, that's horrible.

LIZ: That is awful.

MAEVE: Darfur, no one wants to talk about that.

LIZ: I do.

MAEVE: What?

LIZ: I would. I mean, rather than, this stuff. *(Beat.)*

MAEVE: You'd rather talk about ethnic cleansing than our relationship? *(Beat.)*

Think about that. Before you respond. That is a big statement. *(Long beat.)*

LIZ: I just don't want to spend all our time talking about our sexual enjoyment. Every day, every WEEK we spend time talking about our shit, our SEXUAL shit, whether we can fully relax or not. Why, why not, what it means to completely GIVE IN, why we feel we can't, why we need to have time BEFORE, but not AFTER — before because we need the tonal change, the tonal shift, into sex. And it's hard, because this world is fucked up and you get pushed in this world, just to go out and buy soymilk or whatever can be a trial, and you have to wear sunglasses to protect, to see out but not let them see *in*, my god — and in fact this same protective covering is what we need to let go of when it's time to FUCK, be fucked, etc, and I gotta be careful not to use that word at the WRONG time with you because some days it just hits you as dirty, the whole thing, and fuck or be fucked sounds either A) crass or B) like I'm just this suburban person, this actually asexual person trying to BE sexual and therefore B1) that's even worse, because what's worse than an actual asexual, nonsexual, nonsexed person using words like fuck, and so on? Nothing. I'm made needy, I'm made dirty, by saying that word. God I'm sick of myself. *(Beat.)*

MAEVE: I had no idea.

LIZ: Well.

MAEVE: That all that was going on.

LIZ: Oh.

MAEVE: I'm the one who is never fully present?

LIZ: Sometimes.

MAEVE: Yet you've got this *Beowulf* / *Canterbury Tales* / epic struggle going on, informing every move. You're watching me, tallying it all up: IS IT WORKING? IS IT NOT?

LIZ: No . . .

MAEVE: Lips, now. Tongue, now. Fingers, now. Is it working? You're full of synapses. Doing, checking the doing, all at once. You must be nearly having a SEIZURE from all that brain activity. What a nightmare for you. But hey, you were being honest.

LIZ: Well I was, but you know . . . hyperbolic, a little.

MAEVE: Don't second-guess yourself. That's how you feel.

LIZ: I . . .

MAEVE: I didn't realize I was so demanding.

LIZ: I'm sorry I said anything. I, uh, I'm sorry I said it.

MAEVE: No. Don't be.

LIZ: OK.

MAEVE: It just might mean we aren't meant . . . to have sex. Again. *(Beat.)*

LIZ: Are you serious?

MAEVE: No-oh. *(Beat.)*

LIZ: Are you kind of serious?

MAEVE: Nooo . . .

(Liz watches Maeve intently to see where things stand. Maeve loves fucking with her, making her sweat it out . . .)

So It's OK

Lights up on Maeve and Liz at their breakfast table. It's late morning. They are finishing up what appears to have been a long conversation. Liz readies herself to leave for the day.

LIZ: So it's OK?
MAEVE: Yes.
LIZ: OK . . . You feel OK about things?
MAEVE: Yep.
LIZ: OK then. I do, too. I mean, I feel like we got it all out.
MAEVE: We did.
LIZ: I'm tired,
MAEVE: Yes.
LIZ: whatever, but — I just want you to feel, uh, heard. You, I know you haven't had that, felt that way in the past.
MAEVE: In my other relationships.
LIZ: Yeah.
MAEVE: No. I haven't.
LIZ: So it's important. I really get you. It's a completely reasonable request.
MAEVE: I know.
LIZ: I just don't want you to feel rushed or anything. It takes time . . .
MAEVE: Yes.
LIZ: Communication. Like eating. We have to sit down, and really, just, well, sit down, take time.
MAEVE: *(Sharply.)* I know.
LIZ: *(Hurt.)* OK.
MAEVE: Please don't get lecture-y with me.
LIZ: OK.
MAEVE: Thank you, you took the time, I appreciate it.
LIZ: We *really* took the time.
MAEVE: Yes.
LIZ: *(Impressed.)* TWO hours. We've been talking for TWO hours.

MAEVE: Have we?

LIZ: Yes! We started at seven, I don't know, seven-thirty — an hour and a half anyway. Like, just after we woke up.

MAEVE: I didn't think it had been two hours.

LIZ: It was right when we woke up, like right then.

MAEVE: I had no idea.

LIZ: That's — *movies* last that long. *(This is funny! a realization!)* We could've seen a movie in that time!

MAEVE: What?

LIZ: A short one.

MAEVE: You're measuring out our time?

LIZ: Not. While it happens.

MAEVE: Wow.

LIZ: Just . . . afterward. It's like . . . My friend Lora's therapist, she said to her, once, like way into her therapy, "There's plenty of ways you could be spending that 100 dollars other than sitting here with me every week."

MAEVE: The therapist said that?

LIZ: Yeah!

MAEVE: That's not right . . . Had Lora had some kind of breakthrough?

LIZ: It's just a funny story. It's — you know.

MAEVE: So the therapist decides that suddenly it's not worth anyone's time or money.

LIZ: No . . . I mean, I guess what the therapist was saying was, you know, we're *finished.* Your time can be spent elsewhere.

MAEVE: We're finished.

LIZ: Yeah. Like. Go spend your money on fun things! Like that.

MAEVE: You don't want to do the hard work of this relationship.

LIZ: That's not what she said.

MAEVE: That's what I'm saying.

LIZ: Oh my god . . .

MAEVE: What you really want is a couple of movie passes, you want me to say, we're done. You can GO now. You always look at me at the end of a conversation, after we've talked, like, parents putting a baby to bed. You tiptoe away. You want to make sure I'm really OUT.

LIZ: That you've been heard! That's all. I want to make sure you're happy.

MAEVE: So you can creep away to more fun things! Right! Because this is such TORTURE!

(A tense, pensive moment. A breath.)

LIZ: OK. Can I please — I'm sorry — just, go off topic, for one second? Are you with me? OK, now don't get angry. I just, I don't want to forget, and I'm afraid I'm going to forget.

MAEVE: What?

LIZ: Don't get angry. Did you get detergent last night, cause I have to do the laundry tonight. Don't get all — I'm not trying to change the subject, I just need to know, it's just a quick thing. *(Beat.)*
Otherwise I have to stop at an ATM on the way home. I'm just asking.
(Maeve stands up.)

LIZ: *(Continued.)* Are you mad?

MAEVE: *(Not mad at all.)* No. I just can't remember. I have to go check.
(She leaves. Liz is left alone for a minute. Or two. The silence is nice . . . And then Maeve returns.)

MAEVE: *(Continued.)* Yes.

LIZ: What?

MAEVE: Detergent.

LIZ: Oh. The unscented kind?

MAEVE: Yes.

LIZ: OK. Good. Thank you for checking.

MAEVE: You're welcome.
(Liz thinks she's off the hook. Maeve sits down, in her former position. Then:)

MAEVE: *(Continued.)* If you can't DIG in and do the HARD WORK of this relationship — you want the spoils, the fun stuff? This IS the fun stuff! This is it. Our process. Us communicating. I've tried to tell you that.
(Liz sighs.)

MAEVE: *(Continued.)* And yes, I do feel you hear me,

LIZ: OK then —

MAEVE: thank you for that,

LIZ: You're welcome.

MAEVE: more than I've been heard in other relationships,

LIZ: That's what I was gonna —

MAEVE: But it's not enough.
(Beat.)
(A lead weight has been dropped on Liz.)

LIZ: It's not.

MAEVE: No.

LIZ: O-K . . .

MAEVE: Someone in a state of flow, in a real state of ENGAGEMENT doesn't come out of it and say, "wow, that's the running time of a movie" —

LIZ: I didn't say that. When did I say that?

MAEVE: They don't TRACK it that way. They're just IN it. I thought we had a lot of great communication this morning, we covered a lot of things, that's great, I did feel heard, thank you, but you RUINED it by finishing and then clicking the stopwatch.

LIZ: I didn't click.

MAEVE: One hour, thirty minutes, fifteen seconds, click.

LIZ: Oh my god. I am totally late for work. Again. It's nine fifteen, I'm late. Again. We talk, we sit, like this three times a week, do you realize? And I'm sorry to be TRACKING it like that, but I do. I guess I do. I do that with everything. I spend, on average, we spend, OK, some days THREE hours, some days ONE hour, at bedtime, plus maybe four different fifteen-minute increments, so all together, times it times seven, it's FOURTEEN HOURS a week, unearthing, finding new connection points or understandings or whatever. It's a part time job! I'm working a part-time job with no benefits! Do you realize how hard it is for me to just sit for hours, facing you or whatever, and just TALK, incessantly TALK, and listen CLOSELY? I swear to god, I'm about to go out of my fuckin' mind. I can't stand it. But I do it, I sit here, and do it, because it's what you need, you've said you need, and really, I can provide it. I just have to play little word games or math puzzles or something in my head sometimes to keep me going. Keep me able to sit for this long. *(Beat.)*

MAEVE: How complicated of a math game or word game? Like, columns of numbers, times tables?

LIZ: I don't know.

MAEVE: We should know. We should find out. Maybe you're some kind of GENIUS. Being able to calculate an average while sitting here nodding, pretending you're listening to me.

LIZ: It's not like I do it all the time.

MAEVE: Are you doing it right now?

LIZ: OK, yes.

MAEVE: OK. So now I have a math question for you. How many fingers am I holding up?

(It's, you guessed it, the FINGER.)

Huh? What do you think of that? Look. I've brought it all together for you. *(Waves it around for emphasis.)* You can do your math problems AND pretend to listen to me. *(Drops the gesture. Ashamed.)* Look at me. *(Excruciatingly long pause. Sighs. Each in their own experience.)*

LIZ: *(Slowly, measured, this is bile.)* You . . . want to . . . talk about it?

(Maeve considers, nods head indignantly as if to say PROBABLY . . . PRETTY MUCH YES. Something dies inside of Liz . . . as Lights fade . . .)

SERENADE

Lights up. Maeve and Liz dance together. Liz starts to hum Glenn Miller's "Moonlight Serenade."

MAEVE: Awwww, that's nice.

LIZ: "Doo, do-do-do, do-do-do do doo doo."

MAEVE: Nice. That's one nice song.

BOTH: "Do doo-doo, do doo-doo."

LIZ: Our song.

MAEVE: It is. It's our song.

BOTH: "Do doo-doo, do doo doo."

MAEVE: Wait. It's not, "Do doo doo, do doo doo." It goes "do DOO doo, do DOO doo." It goes up.

(The dancing stops.)

LIZ: Hm.

MAEVE: That middle note. "Do DOO do, do DOO do . . . "

LIZ: OK. Got it.

(Maeve waits on Liz. Nothing happens.)

MAEVE: "Do DOO do, do DOO do."

LIZ: OK.

MAEVE: You want to try it?

LIZ: Uh, no.

MAEVE: You don't want to try it?

LIZ: Nah.

(They dance again, and sing that part of the song. There's an off note.)

MAEVE: That's that part —

LIZ: I just won't sing there. In that section. OK? You can carry us.

LIZ: *(Continued.)* You . . .

MAEVE: It's OK. I'm not . . .

LIZ: *(Overlap.)* . . . got it.

MAEVE: *(Overlap.)* . . . a singer. I just. I've always been able to hear pitch. My family, we all have that.

LIZ: You do.

(Liz hums again, gets to that part of the song, points to Maeve as if to say: You're up. Maeve hits it perfectly.)

LIZ: *(Continued.)* Beautiful.

MAEVE: Thank you. They dance again.

(Maeve stops.)

MAEVE: *(Continued.)* I would love it if somehow, maybe, you could at least try to hit it. I think you could.

LIZ: I know. I'm sure.

MAEVE: You're pretty on pitch.

LIZ: I don't want to.

MAEVE: Oh.

LIZ: OK?

MAEVE: Yeah.

LIZ: Yeah, I just don't feel like it. I want it to be — I think it's OK if it's flawed, a little.

MAEVE: But it's our song!

LIZ: Yes! Exactly.

MAEVE: Don't you care to get it right, knowing it's significant?

LIZ: No.

MAEVE: Now see that I don't understand. I just don't. I want to get it right, it's — I don't think it's compulsive. It's Glenn Miller. It's a classic. It has significance. This is one to get right.

LIZ: Yep.

MAEVE: OK. So?

LIZ: I got it. OK? I just don't want to overthink this, all right? I just don't.

MAEVE: Do you want to be with me?

LIZ: Huh? God. Yes.

MAEVE: Then just do it. Just jump through this hoop. I'm not asking you to crap on yourself and dance around the room, or do cartwheels. Just this.

LIZ: I know!

(Finally: Liz does the tricky part of the song. It's hardly inspired, but Maeve is thrilled.)

MAEVE: There you go! You got it. That's it. You got it perfectly.

LIZ: *(Deflated.)* OK.

MAEVE: I knew you could. That's all I wanted. *(Starts in again on the dance / hum.)* Isn't that nice?

(Liz nods. They keep dancing. Maeve keeps humming, energetically. After a bit, Maeve realizes that Liz has stopped humming. The dancing continues, but then Maeve's humming also starts to fade, until finally it goes away completely. Dancing gets slower; each has lost steam. Fade out.)

END OF PLAY

PLAYS FOR TWO MEN

Canadian Tuxedo

NICOLE PANDOLFO

Canadian Tuxedo premiered in April 2009 at the University of California-Irvine. It was produced regionally in June 2009 at The Seven New Works Fest at The Fusion Theatre in Albuquerque, New Mexico with stars Michael Finnegan and Demet Vialpando.

Internationally, it was produced in June, 2009, at the NAAA Annual Playreading Festival, Bridewell Theatre, London England; July 2009, it won the People's Choice Award, Short + Sweet Singapore, Singapore, starring Stuart Lightheart and Muza Fazal; November, 2009, as part of Short + Sweet Melbourne, in Melbourne, Australia, starring Andrew Belsten and Dylan Cole.

CHARACTERS

SAL, (twenties-thirties, any ethnicity) takes a job for the mafia to kill a man in order to get enough money to buy his pregnant girlfriend an engagement ring.

LOU, (thirties-forties, Irish) works for the mafia. This is his last job before he leaves the industry to go into the life of "New-Age Philosophy."

SETTING

The interior of a car parked outside of Forelli's Bar, somewhere in Jersey.

TIME

Present day, evening.

• • •

At Rise: Lights up on Salvatore (twenty-eight) and Lou (thirty-five) in a car. Both are dressed in all black and Lou has a silencer handgun in his lap while munching on turkey jerky.

LOU: Jerky?
SAL: I'm good.
LOU: It's turkey.
SAL: So?
LOU: So it's better for you than beef. And yet, still tasty.
SAL: No thanks.
LOU: You sure? It's low in cholesterol.
SAL: I don't want any fucking jerky!
LOU: Alright alright. So, how do you know Vinnie?
SAL: I used to work for him a lot, about 8 years ago. Then I got a legit job.
LOU: So why are you here now?
SAL: He's doing me a favor.
LOU: Oh yeah?
SAL: I need cash. I gotta buy an engagement ring for my girlfriend, Bernice.
LOU: She knocked up?

(Lou lets out a stupid laugh. Sal looks at him like he has a lot of nerve then,)

SAL: Yeah and she's the skinny Catholic type and I don't gotta lot of time before she starts showing, you know.
LOU: Well, this is my last job.

SAL: Why's that?

LOU: I'm going straight. I found inner peace.

SAL: What the fuck is that supposed to mean.

LOU: I done a lota bad things in my life. But this one day, about 3 months ago, I had to pop this guy for stealing business from Vinnie. I'm waiting for him to come outta the dry cleaners, I'm snacking on some jerky, when out of nowhere this unleashed dog lunges at me with his mouth open. He was going for the jerky, but without thinking, I shot him. *(Pause.)* I killed a dog, man.

SAL: Big deal.

LOU: Big deal? Dogs are like, sacred. Killing dogs . . . that's just not what I signed up for. I realized, this ain't right for me. I'm just the wrong guy in the wrong job. Ever since then, I've devoted my life to the Secret.

SAL: What the fuck is that?

LOU: It's this amazing philosophy that if you project positive energy and your desires to the universe, your dreams will come true. It's the power of positive thinking.

SAL: So then why the fuck are you still working for Vinnie?

LOU: Contractual obligations.

SAL: Whatever . . . Vinnie said you'd give me the pertinent details regarding tonight's hit.

LOU: Oh yeah, sure. The target goes by the name Michael "Macaroni." 5'8. Brown eyes and hair. Wears a Canadian Tuxedo.

SAL: What the fuck is a Canadian Tuxedo?

LOU: It's when you wear denim jeans with a matching denim jacket. Same wash.

SAL: Jesus Christ.

LOU: Some people really can pull it off though. Not me, I'm too tall.

SAL: OK, so we'll know who this jerk off is by the Canadian tux, you'll shoot him twice in the head from behind with the silencer, hop back in the car, and then we'll head into Philly to pick up our money from Vinnie.

LOU: Sure . . .

SAL: What?

LOU: No, nothing.

SAL: What?

(Lou looks concerned.)

LOU: He's a twin.

SAL: So?

LOU: An identical twin. Who happens to be best friends with his brother.

SAL: And this matters why?

LOU: According to my source on the inside, they just so happen to be in the bar together tonight. Both dressed in Canadian Tuxedos.

SAL: You're shitting me right?

LOU: I wish I was, Sal.

SAL: MOTHER FUCKER. How the hell did we end up on a hit, with a pair of identical twins dressed alike?

LOU: Apparently they had an electric keyboard rock band together in the early nineties called, "Ticklin' the Ivories." All denim was their signature style, a way to stand out in the electric keyboard crowd. They dress that way in an attempt to pick up chicks with stories of the glory days. Supposedly they opened for Milli Vanilli once in Atlantic City.

SAL: What are the fucking odds that this shit would happen?

LOU: Well, if you figure Vinnie sends out a hit on someone about every three months, and there's something like six billion people in the world, then that would mean that in a given year four out of six billion people have the potential to be on Vinnie's list and so —

SAL: Shut the fuck up. Let me think . . . Fuck.

LOU: You look concerned.

SAL: Did it occur to you that if we kill the wrong guy we won't get paid?

LOU: Well why would we kill the wrong guy?

SAL: Because Lou, he's at the bar, with his twin, dressed alike like it's a MOTHERFUCKING DOUBLE MINT COMMERCIAL!

LOU: I never thought about that.

SAL: No shit. And do you know why you never thought about it? Because you're a moron.

LOU: I wouldn't say I'm a moron . . .

SAL: We can't go back to Vinnie until we kill this guy.

LOU: I know.

SAL: Vinnie will skin us alive if we fuck this up. You do realize that don't you?

LOU: Of course.

SAL: Do you know if there's a way to tell them apart?

LOU: Ummm . . .

SAL: Fucking great.

LOU: Wait. The one we gotta pop. His name is Michael. They can't both be named Michael.

SAL: So now we have to fucking talk to them?

LOU: So?

SAL: So if it's not Michael that we ask first, say it's his brother. Later, when he finds out that Michael is fucking dead, he's gonna go "Oh shit, some Irish prick dressed in black with jerky breath asked me if I was Michael the same night my brother was murdered." Next thing you know there's a police sketch of you all over the evening news. Do you want to end up in jail because you are a fucking idiot? Because I don't.

LOU: I'll wear my ski mask.

SAL: That's discreet. Someone approaching you in a dark parking lot with a mask on.

LOU: In the trunk I have a woman's wig, trench coat, and heels. I could put those on.

SAL: I'm not even going to fucking ask . . . but that is clearly NOT going to deflect attention.

LOU: You're a real ball breaker, you know that?

SAL: That's because you're self-help New Age voodoo bullshit has potentially lost the ten grand I was supposed to be getting paid tonight to save my relationship with Bernice.

LOU: There's an entire force field of negative energy around you.

SAL: Lou, shut the fuck up.

(They're both quiet for a moment.)

SAL: Shit look.

LOU: What?

SAL: It's a guy in a Canadian Tuxedo.

LOU: Fuck that must be him.

SAL: Or his brother.

LOU: OK. OK. I'm gonna roll down the window and scream his name. If he responds we know it's him.

SAL: Don't fuckin' do that.

LOU: Why not?

SAL: I don't want anyone to notice us asshole.

LOU: Do you have a better idea?

SAL: How can someone leave the house wearing that? I mean, denim head to toe? Fuck it, just take him out.

LOU: What if it's his brother?

SAL: We have to kill them both.

LOU: Both?

SAL: Yeah.

LOU: But that's murder.

SAL: What do you think killing one of them is?

LOU: I know but one's an innocent.

SAL: Well, it's his own fucking fault for dressing like an asshole in the first place. That's reason enough.

LOU: I see your point.

SAL: Just do it.

LOU: Wait, I can't.

SAL: Yes you can.

LOU: No, I have to make sure he's Michael.

SAL: Then just go the fuck over there and ask what his name is.

LOU: Shit look. The brother.

SAL: Motherfucker, dressed completely the same.

LOU: Acid wash.

SAL: Fuck this. Go.

LOU: Alright. In ten seconds start the car.

(Lou exits off stage. Sal looks ready to roll. Moments later Lou runs back on.)

LOU: Let's go.

SAL: Did you do it?

(No response.)

SAL: Lou, did you do it?

LOU: No.

SAL: Why the fuck not?

LOU: I tried. I pulled the trigger. It didn't go off.

SAL: You're kidding right?

LOU: I secreted that I didn't want to kill the wrong man, and the gun didn't go off. It's the universe answering me.

(Sal looks at the gun. Flips a switch.)

SAL: You had the safety on.

LOU: I . . . oh.

SAL: Secret my ass. Fuck it, I'll do it myself.

LOU: No! Don't you see? The universe is telling us that we are not meant to kill Michael.

SAL: Fuck your Secret positive energy bullshit, I gotta ring to buy.

LOU: No. *(To Universe.) I'm* putting out there that Sal will not go and kill Michael Macaroni.

SAL: Give me the gun!

(Sal, overcome with anger, tries to grab the gun from Lou. Lou struggles to

hold onto it, we hear a gunshot and Sal jumps out of the car, exits off stage, a pause.)

LOU: FUCKKKKKKKKKKKKKKKKKKKK.

(Sal returns, despondent.)

SAL: They're fucking gone! What the hell are we gonna tell Vinnie?

LOU: You shot me!

SAL: I did?

LOU: Yes!

SAL: Oh my God, the Secret. I thought about how I wanted to shoot you in the head for fucking this up, and look, I shot you. It was in the thigh, but still — it was the universe!

LOU: Get me to a hospital!

SAL: This Secret thing aint no bullshit.

LOU: HOSPITAL!

SAL: Alright! Here, bite on this.

(Sal puts the jerky between Lou's teeth. Lou clenches in pain.)

SAL: Still tasty?

(Lights down.)

END OF PLAY

His Daddy

Cori Thomas

His Daddy was originally produced at Ensemble Studio Theatre September 14, 2009, as part of River Crosses Rivers Going To the River Festival 2009. Artistic Director (Ensemble Studio Theatre): William Carden. Artistic Director (Going To The River): Elizabeth Van Dyke. Director: Stephen Fried. Cast: John — Matthew Montelongo; David — Lindsay Smiling.

CHARACTERS

JOHN, thirties to forties. Caucasian. Works in construction.

DAVID, thirties to forties. Must be played by a person of color: African American, Latino, Asian etc. He is an attorney.

PLACE

The hallway of an institutional building — The morgue.

TIME

The present.

• • •

In the dark.

JOHN: Oh God! Shit! Shit!

(Lights up on a hallway of an institutional building. It is the morgue. John, dressed casually in jeans and work boots, sits on the floor, his hands covering his face. David, dressed in a suit and perhaps tie, emerges from a door.)

DAVID: You all right?

JOHN: No. Oh God. How could you be so calm in there? It felt like . . . it felt like . . .

DAVID: You got sucker punched.

JOHN: Yeah. Yeah, that's what it feels like.

DAVID: I can't even process . . . I've dreamt about that moment. I practiced /

JOHN: You practiced?

DAVID: You know what I mean.

JOHN: No. I don't. I didn't practice anything. I was hoping. I was wishing. I was praying. I was praying.

DAVID: Me too. But, I knew . . . Deep down I knew . . .

JOHN: Don't say that.

DAVID: I can't help what I felt.

(Beat.)

I was praying too.

JOHN: You just don't know, not until you see . . . and touch . . .

(Exhales.)

you don't know anything . . .

DAVID: I know.

JOHN: *(With deliberate and sudden ferocity.)* You. Don't. You cannot in a thousand years know what it feels like to be me at this particular moment. To have gotten that call and have to come here and identify our son's body.

DAVID: I do. I got that call too.

JOHN: No, David, you don't.

DAVID: OK I don't.

(Beat.)

Shit!

(Beat.)

Sorry.

JOHN: Yeah right. Sure. Sure.

DAVID: And now we know. OK. We know and it's over.

JOHN: Yes.

DAVID: *(Beat.)* I didn't think that you had . . . I mean, yes I blamed you. I blamed you and I thought you were responsible. I know it makes no sense but you can't help what you feel. I look at you and even now . . . knowing . . . even now . . .

(Dialogue overlaps.)

JOHN: God, David. Shit, David. This again? Damn it! Damn!

DAVID: I'm sorry. I can't . . . I can't help it.

JOHN: But still . . . ? Really? Still?

DAVID: Going in there and seeing . . . I know that you couldn't . . .

JOHN: *(Making move as if to hit him.)* Don't even go there. Don't you fucking even . . . if for one second that ever crossed your mind . . . You heard what Officer whatever the fuck his name in there just said; he waited, that fuckhead waited patiently till the moment when I let go of Billy's hand. I looked at him like this,

(Shows him.)

So he would know not to move. I took my hand from his to stick in my pocket to get the 3 pennies to make the exact buck fifty-eight for the Snickers bar. It was in that moment. That second, and if you know how many times I have gone over this, it was no more than 63 seconds. One minute and 3 seconds. That's the long count. I turned away from Billy for barely more than a minute to put the money on the fucking counter. To count out the 3 motherfucking pennies and then to return the extra 3 pennies and a dime and the nickel back into my pocket. It was then that I turned my head to look down for him, and noticed he was not there. He wasn't there so I looked around. It took maybe 3 or 4 seconds to begin to feel worried and to start asking the people standing on the line behind me waiting to pay if they had seen a little boy. Some of them looked around too. They shook their head. Not more than 5 seconds and I realized, Oh my God! They think he looks like me. I yelled. "I am looking for a five-year-old boy, he is biracial, he does NOT look like me." I don't have to tell you . . . I've told you so many times. You know.

DAVID: Yes. I know.

JOHN: I live it over and over again. In the past six weeks since he disappeared, maybe eight hundred or nine hundred times. I can't stay in here. I gotta get out of here. I'll call you about picking up the rest of my stuff.

DAVID: When do you want to have the funeral?

JOHN: Never. I don't ever want to finalize this /

DAVID: We have to.

JOHN: Why?

DAVID: Dr. Pearlman /

JOHN: *(Incredulous.)* The therapist!!??

DAVID: I think it helps me.

JOHN: Well, good for you.

DAVID: I'm not like you. You have your work to . . .

JOHN: What? What!

DAVID: Relax! I'm just saying you work with your hands. It's physical . . . construction . . . It's like going to the gym. Or I don't know . . . yelling.

JOHN: OK, I see what you mean /

DAVID: You didn't have to . . . you can . . . not speak to anyone if you don't want to. I have to speak to people all day. On the phone. "How are you?" "How are you?" If you say "Fine." They're like, "Really?" In the halls. In the elevator.

JOHN: I know.

DAVID: You don't! Jerry Johnson calls me in. He's sitting at his desk. He doesn't even get up. He looks at me and I can see in his eyes, I'm just a ______ you know. I don't know, maybe I'm reading into it, I've become so paranoid. Anyway, he doesn't even ask me to sit. I mean I'm a partner, he doesn't even say "David, please sit down." No. He says "I feel for you, but people take one look at you and they know something is wrong. We can't have that in our halls you know. Company morale. I say "I'll work on my demeanor, Sir." He says "Good, you should be over this by now anyway." And I want to say "Don't you tell me what to be feeling. You don't know what I feel. You don't know what I go through every morning to get to this stupid fucking office. How I stand and wait for the bus. You know how that was our thing? I'd drop him off at school and then get back on and go . . . Now, every morning, I see all the people, all the mothers all the kids every one we used to see. They look up and their eyes touch me, and they look down expecting to see Billy, and of course he's not there. Six weeks and they still forget every morning. But then I forget every morning that I'm going to see them too. I wouldn't even get on the bus if I remembered. I feel their pity reaching out to try to curl around me like a boa constrictor and squeeze me but I smile back when instead I feel like snarling and baring my teeth and attacking them for still having their children. These are people who mean me no harm. I know they loved Billy and they care about me but I hate them.

(Beat.)

I can't believe we're here. I can't believe what we saw in there just now /

(Beat.)

His body . . . cigarette burns . . .

JOHN: That fucker! That fucking asshole! /

DAVID: And you were the last person to see him. And I am furious that I let you take him shopping.

JOHN: Wait a minute, you LET me take him shopping?! He was my son. You didn't have to let me take him anywhere.

DAVID: He was my son and you could tell.

JOHN: What are you like two!???

(Beat.)

It's fucking terrible what I feel in my heart right now, David. And to know that you feel this . . . still?

(Dialogue overlaps.)

DAVID: I can't help . . .

JOHN: Fucking terrible. 'Cause he didn't just kill Billy. He killed everything. He killed us.

(Long beat encompasses the "us".)

I wanna kill Robert Pierce. I want to hurt him like he hurt Billy. Worse. I want to keep him alive long enough so he'll suffer. Every time he looks like he's going to succumb, I'll back off. Let him come down a little. Let him feel hope that I'll stop, let him catch a breath and that's when I'll come back twice as hard. I'll burn him once the first time, I'll burn him three times the second time. Then I'll start on his knuckles. I'll go at 'em, one at a time with my titanium drywall hammer. I want to hurt him worse than he hurt my little boy. Every single thing he did to Billy, I'm gonna do three or four more times back to him.

DAVID: God, John.

JOHN: This is what I'm thinking David, once the trial begins we figure out when they're moving him, how they're moving him. You got connections with the courthouse . . . so we get him for what he did to our little boy.

(Long beat.)

DAVID: You would do that?

JOHN: *(Beat.)* Yeah. I think so.

(Beat.)

I think I could.

DAVID: I feel numb. I just feel . . . numb.

(Beat.)

I don't believe you would. You're not that kind of person.

(Long beat.)

JOHN: Not before, but now I know what it feels like . . .

DAVID: I know, but still . . .

JOHN: *(Long beat.)* Yeah. But I mean you know . . . I don't think . . . I really could . . . No.

DAVID: No.

CHILD'S VOICE: Daddy!

(David and John simultaneously turn towards the door.)

DAVID AND JOHN: Billy!

(They both laugh: shocked, embarrassed, overwhelmed.)

JOHN: I guess . . . some kid . . . Oh my God!

DAVID: Oh my God!

JOHN: Every time I hear that . . . word . . .

DAVID: Yes.

(Long beat.)

JOHN: We didn't even know if he'd be mine or yours . . .

DAVID: I know /

JOHN: He was perfect though, right? He was perfect. He looked like you spit him out. Every time I saw the two of you walking down the street together. It took my breath away. It took my breath away /

DAVID: Whenever he got upset, he wanted you — his Daddy John.

(David turns towards John. John turns away from him and looks towards the door.)

JOHN: OK . . .

(Long beat; John goes to the doorway.)

JOHN: *(Continued.)* It's almost like you can feel him.

DAVID: Yes.

(Beat.)

I don't want to leave him in there.

JOHN: I don't even want him to be in there.

DAVID: I know.

(After a long beat, David makes a physical gesture towards John. Something simple and non-sexual but with ramifications of the possibility of something beyond this moment. Lights slowly fade to black.)

END OF PLAY

Ron Swoboda's Wish

Anna Ziegler

Ron Swoboda's Wish was performed at The Mile Square Theatre in Hoboken, New Jersey, on March 14, 2009. Director: Linsay Firman. Cast: Jason — Ross Cowan; Nate Whelden — Jacob.

CHARACTERS

JACOB is 25; he and Jason are twins. Jacob is autistic. Please note that although he sometimes does and says things that might be perceived as childish, he should not be played as though he's a child.

JASON is, of course, also 25. He's as aggressive as Jacob is passive and as unpredictable as Jacob is even keeled.

SETTING

A very simple space that suggests a middle class livingroom.

• • •

Jacob sits in a chair on one side of an otherwise dark stage. Somewhat mechanically, he recites the following:

JACOB: In the four seasons that Casey Stengel managed the New York Mets, from 1962–1965, they had records of .250, .315, .327, and .309. They didn't break fifty until 1969 when, under the management of Gil Hodges, they went 100-62 and defeated the Baltimore Orioles in a 4 games to 1 World Series title. Game 5 took place at Shea Stadium on October 16th. 57,397 fans were in attendance. The score was 5 to 3. Donn Clendenon was the series MVP and had a batting average of .357. His teammate Ron Swoboda had a higher batting average of .400 and even one more at bat but he didn't win MVP. Donn Clendenon did. Also, Donn Clendenon got 3 homeruns and Ron Swoboda got none. I bet Ron Swoboda wished he had hit just one homerun.

(The lights shift so that now the other side of the stage is visible. Here, Jason sits and addresses the audience.)

JASON: My boyfriend left me. Last night. Which also happened to be my birthday. He said he wished I was as nice a person as my brother, who at least has within him the milk of human kindness. That's what he said. Milk of human kindness. Only Freddy says shit like that. And to make everything that much worse, today my mother invited me for dinner for my and Jake's birthday, and weeks ago I said that was fine but I didn't know that today was going to be today and last night was going to be last night and sometimes I hate myself for making plans in advance.

(The lights shift. A few very simple set pieces that indicate the livingroom of a middle class suburban home are brought on. Jason and Jacob's chairs are

brought closer together. This is their mother's livingroom. Jacob is reading a book. After a long silence:)

JASON: What's that book?

(Jacob doesn't respond, doesn't even look up.)

Is it good?

(No response.)

It's nice talking to you, too.

(Jason stands and goes over to Jacob. He takes the book.)

JACOB: Hey!

(Jason flips through the book, which is barely holding together.)

JASON: How old is this book?

JACOB: 1969.

JASON: Yup. That's about right.

JACOB: Do you want to hear about Ron Swoboda?

JASON: Nope.

(He hands back the book. Jacob goes back to reading it. Jason sits down again. Another silence.)

Did you have a good birthday?

(No response.)

I had a great birthday.

(No response.)

When's our mother getting back?

(No response.)

It's just like her to invite me over and then go out. I doubt she really did forget to buy tomatoes. I'm gonna go check. I bet I'll find tomatoes in there and she's really out with that guy Lou who sells amusement park equipment. I mean, who sells amusement park equipment?

JACOB: Lou does.

JASON: Right. *(Beat.)* I'm going to look for tomatoes.

(A few moments pass. Jacob reads. Jason returns.)

JASON: Well, there aren't any tomatoes but that doesn't mean she isn't with Lou.

JACOB: Did you know that Nolan Ryan pitched nine games in the regular season in 1969? How many do you think he won?

JASON: Not tonight, Jacob.

JACOB: He went 6 and 3, and his ERA was 3.53. Nolan Ryan.

JASON: No one can be good all the time.

JACOB: Also, Jerry Koosman went 17-9 in the regular season and pitched two winning games in the World Series giving him an ERA of 2.04. Also, he was a lefty.

(Jason goes over to Jacob.)

JASON: Lemme see that book.

(Jacob hands it to him; Jason flips through it again.)

JASON: You're crazy, you know that?

(No response. Then, without looking at Jacob.)

Freddy thought it was so amazing, you know, like freakishly cool — what you could do. And I'd ask him if he thought what machines could do was amazing and he'd say "your brother isn't a machine" and I'd say "he is, basically" because ever since we were born that's how you've seemed to me, totally . . . impenetrable . . . and I've kind of had to face the world on my own, which isn't what you're supposed to have to do when you have a twin brother. And now I'm done with it. I don't want to play your games anymore.

(Jason looks up.)

Do you hear me?

(Jacob looks blank.)

JASON: I'm saying that I don't want to go to work. I don't want to wake up at six in the fucking morning. I don't want to come home to find we're out of beer. Freddy thought drinking beer was "uncouth" but fuck him. I'll keep drinking it and I'll get so fat that no one'll want to be with me ever again.

(Then, contemplative.)

I thought I had the luxury to get fat but I don't anymore.

(To Jacob.)

Mostly, though, I don't want to come over here to find you reading some book about baseball in the forties but spouting off stats from the sixties as though you were reading them. It freaks me out. I mean, if you can do that, you can get a job. There's probably some job where you need to memorize things and repeat them back. It's not fair that you don't have to work.

(Long beat.)

JACOB: Did Freddy die?

JASON: Did Freddy die. How do you like that.

JACOB: Let's go to a baseball game. Mets vs. Astros tomorrow night, 7 PM, at Shea Stadium. Undales Perez is pitching and he has an ERA of —

JASON: I don't care about his ERA.

JACOB: I do.

JASON: I know.

(Jacob goes back to reading.)

JASON: Did you hear anything I said? A word of it?

(Jacob looks up.)

JASON: Aren't we talking here?

(Beat.)

I asked you how your birthday was.

JACOB: It was great.

JASON: Awesome.

(Beat.)

What'd you do?

JACOB: The Mets played the Astros. 7 PM. At Shea Stadium. Johan Santana was pitching and he has an ERA of 2.39. The Mets lost 5 to 7 but David Wright hit a ground rule double and also walked twice. I ate two hot dogs with sauerkraut and drank a can of Coca Cola.

JASON: You went to the game?

JACOB: No. On TV.

JASON: Freddy dumped me.

JACOB: Freddy dumped me, too.

JASON: No he didn't.

JACOB: If he dumped you, he dumped me.

JASON: No, he dumped me, asshole. He was with me. In my apartment. He said "the last four years mean nothing if we can't get along right now" and I told him he was being a prime asshole to say that and he said I was embarrassed about . . . certain things and I'm not so I told him so and then he said I was embarrassed of you, which I'm not, and then he said if I continued to deny things he couldn't be with me and I said "you're an asshole" and then he left and took four fucking years with him, so . . .

JACOB: I'm sorry that you have to have me as your brother.

JASON: Shut up. Don't say a thing like that.

JACOB: I like Freddy.

JASON: He was nice to you.

JACOB: Can I invite him to the game tomorrow night?

JASON: No.

JACOB: Asshole.

JASON: What'd you say?

JACOB: Asshole.

JASON: Yeah, happy birthday to you too, dickhead.

JACOB: Dickhead.

JASON: Loser.

(Beat.)

JACOB: I'm sorry.

(Jacob puts the book down.)

I'm really sorry.

(Jacob begins to cry. It gets very loud, a little out of control.)

JASON: Stop that. Please stop.

(Jacob keeps crying.)

JASON: Jake. Jacob.

(Jacob stops, slowly, gathering himself.)

JACOB: Tomorrow night Johan Santana is pitching and he has an ERA of 2.53. He's an excellent pitcher. There are 304 fan sites on the Internet devoted just to him. I subscribe to eleven of them.

JASON: That's good, Jake.

JACOB: You never email me.

JASON: I do.

JACOB: No.

JASON: I will then.

JACOB: Sometimes I'm on the Internet all night long.

JASON: Sometimes I am, too.

JACOB: Mom says you watch porn. Which is disgusting and also denigrating to women.

JASON: That's not the kind of porn I watch.

JACOB: Do you think Johan Santana is gay?

JASON: I don't think so.

JACOB: One website devoted to Johan Santana is about what if he were gay. But I don't subscribe to that one.

JASON: There's a website for everything.

JACOB: I love you.

(Beat.)

JASON: I love you, too.

JACOB: So we'll go to the game tomorrow night at 7 PM.

JASON: Nope.

JACOB: For our birthday.

JASON: Nope.

JACOB: You're busy?

JASON: That's right.

JACOB: In 1969, on October 16th, the day the Mets won the World Series, it was unseasonably warm — 74 degrees Fahrenheit. 59,397 fans streamed into Shea Stadium. The anticipation was palpable. The pitchers were Dave McNally and Jerry Koosman. McNally had a season ERA of 3.22 compared to Koosman's 2.28. In the first inning, there are no runs scored. In the second inning there are no runs scored. But then, in the third inning, Baltimore's Dave McNally and Brooks Robinson hit home-runs, giving the Orioles a 3-nothing lead.

JASON: The pitcher hit a homerun?

JACOB: In the fourth inning, there are no runs. In the fifth inning, there are no runs.

(Jacob waits for Jason to say something.)

JASON: Tense.

JACOB: Yup. Then in the sixth inning, the New York Mets get two runs off a homerun hit by Donn Clendenon. Ron Swoboda flies out. Then in the seventh inning, the New York Mets get one more run. So . . .

JASON: *(Reluctantly, after a beat.)* The game is tied.

JACOB: Then, in the eighth inning, Ron Swoboda hits a ground rule double and two runs score. The score is 5-3 in favor of the New York Mets.

JASON: How do you think Dave McNally felt then?

JACOB: Dave McNally was replaced by Eddie Watt in the eighth inning.

JASON: But how do you think he felt?

JACOB: Then, Jerry Koosman didn't allow any runs in the top of the ninth inning and the game was over. The series was over. The excitement in the air was palpable. The fans flowed out of the stadium and into the night.

JASON: How did they feel?

JACOB: Most Valuable Player was awarded to Donn Clendenon, who had a batting average of .357. His teammate Ron Swoboda had a higher batting average of .400 in the series and even batted in the winning run but he didn't win MVP. Donn Clendenon did.

JASON: How do you think that made old Ron feel?

JACOB: Donn Clendenon got three homeruns in the series and Ron Swoboda got none.

JASON: How'd he feel, goddammit?!

JACOB: The fans flowed out of the stadium and into the night. The celebration lasted all night long.

JASON: Jacob!

JACOB: I think Ron Swoboda wished he had hit just one homerun. Then he would have won MVP. So, he felt . . . regret.

(Beat.)

JASON: Yeah, probably. He probably did feel some regret.

JACOB: But in the end, it was a 4-1 series. The New York Mets won for the first time. They were heroes. It was about the team. How much regret could he have felt?

JASON: You'd be surprised. Even if you're on a team . . . life is usually about . . . just you. You and your fuckups.

JACOB: Don't say that!

JASON: Why not?

JACOB: Because it was a glorious night. The celebration lasted all night long. The city was glowing, pulsing.

JASON: That's what the books say?

JACOB: No. It's how I imagine it.

(Long beat.)

JASON: It's how you imagine it?

JACOB: Yes.

JASON: Where are we, Jacob? Where are we now?

JACOB: We're there. We're at that game.

JASON: We're not.

JACOB: We are.

JASON: We are?

(Jacob puts the book down on the ground, pulls his chair closer to Jason.)

JACOB: We're there together. And the crowd is all around us and we're a part of it and we lose ourselves.

JASON: We're lost.

JACOB: Together.

JASON: Yeah . . . I guess we are.

(Lights down.)

END OF PLAY

PLAYS FOR THREE OR MORE ACTORS

The Attractive Women on the Train

P. Seth Bauer

The Attractive Women on the Train opened in New York on January 31, 2002 at Access Theatre as part of a festival of plays commissioned on the Heisenberg Uncertainty Principle entitled "The More You Look". Director: Holly Cate. Producers: Soo Kim and Margarett Perry. Cast: Bonnie — Heather Landry; Garreth — Brian C. Homer; Tyler — Paul Taviani; Young Girl — Shakai Shepard.

CHARACTERS

BONNIE, early thirties. Angular, attractive and sharp. Perhaps she is hard to hug.

GARRETH, late twenties, early thirties. Her boyfriend. A bit spineless, if well-meaning.

TYLER, thirties to forties. The man on the subway. Intense.

YOUNG GIRL, 18. Shy. Pretty.

SETTING

In and out of a New York City apartment and a subway car. The action should flow fluidly between the two locales.

TIME

Yesterday.

• • •

At Rise: An attractive woman Bonnie appears on the stage and addresses the audience. She is feisty and pretty if a bit angular. She speaks assertively.

BONNIE: Every morning, I get on the A train around nine-thirty, you know after the major commuters are gone. I got to do that otherwise, I'll burn right out on this city. Anyway, there's this guy who always seems to be on my car already. He's waiting for me. I thought maybe it's because he and I always choose the same car, the second from the front so it can be near the exit on the other end, but yesterday I changed my car to see what would happen. So I get on the car at the rear of the train and he's not there right. So we're riding along and this big guy sits next to me and his ass is so huge that when he sits down, his butt space kind of sneaks up under mine so I'm sort of popped up like a cork. And his legs are kind of stumpy and spread open wide and he's bulging over on top of me right, and I know he's enjoying it, because I'm wearing a skirt and something sleeveless so he gets to have all this contact with my body so I'm like fuck this I'm moving to the suburbs. Or at least to another seat. There were other seats too where you didn't have to sit on top of me, so you know what he was thinking.

(Lights fade and a young man Garreth is revealed. He has been listening to her story.)

So I get up and go across the car and sit down, but the fat bulging guy is looking at me now full on like he knows something about me, or like he caught me being disgusted by him and I'm like WHAT THE FUCK IT'S NOT MY FAULT YOU'RE BULGING ALL OVER ME. But he's smiling at me, and he looks down at my legs and he starts laughing like if you didn't want me to check you out then how come you're wearing that little skirt.

GARRETH: He said that?

BONNIE: He looked that. You could see it in his stupid face. So fuck if I'm going to stick around with bulgy boy, I haven't even had my coffee yet and I'm already posturing and feeling guilty like a rape victim who asked for it because it's hot out and I don't feel like wearing a snowsuit. That doesn't mean I want to get laid on the A train.

GARRETH: So you switch cars.

BONNIE: So I switch cars which is annoying enough cuz I feel like I'm letting him win, and I'm in heels so it's pretty shaky between cars and I can't get the door open cuz I've got one hand on my bag and I'm just trying to hold myself steady between the trains without breaking a heel and falling off the train when the door opens, and lo and behold.

(Tyler is sitting, looking up at her. Only she can see him.)

GARRETH: It's the first guy.

BONNIE: How'd you know that?

GARRETH: I don't know . . . it seemed like that's what you were gonna say.

BONNIE: Yeah but I didn't yet, did I.

GARRETH: Not yet —

BONNIE: So how did you know that the first guy would be on the second to last car of my train which you weren't even on.

GARRETH: It just seemed like that's how you were gonna tell the story, what?

BONNIE: What is it with you guys?

GARRETH: Are you gonna finish telling me or not? What? Sweetheart what are you looking at?

BONNIE: So the guy looks at me and he smiles —

(Tyler looks up at her and smiles.)

and I go, "WHAT?"

TYLER: Pardon?

BONNIE: What are you looking at?

TYLER: Nothing . . .

BONNIE: Why do you keep following me?

TYLER: I wasn't following you . . .

BONNIE: I've got eyes. You've been staring at me every day, don't think I don't notice.

TYLER: *(A little pleased.)* You noticed me.

BONNIE: Yes I noticed you. Are you a rapist?

TYLER: What?

BONNIE: Simple question.

TYLER: No! No . . .

BONNIE: Well then quit following me or I'll have you . . . killed.

TYLER: Look I didn't mean to scare you.

BONNIE: You didn't scare —

TYLER: I just like looking at you, that's all. Like a painting.

BONNIE: Well look at somebody else for a change.

TYLER: I tried that today, when you weren't on the second car. But looking at those other people didn't make me happy. See sometimes I get a little sad. Usually, if you want to know the truth. Especially on the A train. I'm usually all right on the F train I don't know why. But something about the A just makes me want to . . . but then I look over at you, and you're always there on the 9:30 train and you sit there with your coffee and your newspaper, I very much admire the way you fold your newspaper by the way. It's a beautiful thing and not many people are as good at it as you are, so you should be proud. And you sit there with your right leg crossed over your left sometimes with stockings on sometimes without depending on the day. And you sit there pleasantly reading the cover page before you switch to the Metro section. B1, B4 then B12. Because you care about the people in this city. And I appreciate that because I live in this city too. So I directly benefit from your dedication to the metro section as well.

BONNIE: Maybe I read the metro section so I can keep apprised of psychos like you.

TYLER: *(With a smile.)* Oh I don't think so. It's because you care about your fellow man. I see it in the way you tilt your neck to the left while you're reading. See, like this.

(He tilts his neck.)

BONNIE: You're looking at my neck.

TYLER: Yes and the way, your right hand holds the paper up like a vegetable or a banana maybe, and sometimes a little piece of your hair dangles down to the left and covers your eye, so it makes you wonder whether or not the girl under that hair has got two eyes or maybe just one. But I know how many you've got. Cuz I've seen them.

BONNIE: Listen guy, I don't know who you are —

TYLER: Tyler.

BONNIE: But you just — stay away from me alright.

TYLER: For real?

BONNIE: Yes for real.

TYLER: *(Disappointed.)* Alright.

BONNIE: You got me?

TYLER: Yes I have you.

(She exits the train and Tyler watches her go.)

GARRETH: You sure you don't know this guy?

BONNIE: Of course I'm sure and even if I did, it gives him no right to just go on gawking at me. I mean who the hell does he think he is.

GARRETH: Tyler.

BONNIE: What?!

GARRETH: You said — Tyler. He thinks he's a guy named Tyler.

BONNIE: Why are you taking his side?

GARRETH: I'm not, you said —

BONNIE: He's harassing me!

GARRETH: Did he touch you?

BONNIE: He's provoking me.

GARRETH: I thought you said he just liked looking at you. Like a painting.

BONNIE: That's the problem.

GARRETH: Seems harmless enough. He admires you.

BONNIE: So you approve of these guys.

GARRETH: I didn't say that it's just that . . . I just thought it wasn't that big . . . I mean he only . . .

(She looks pissed.)

GARRETH: But now I see your point.

BONNIE: You stare at attractive women on trains as well.

GARRETH: What —

BONNIE: Don't you.

GARRETH: No . . .

BONNIE: Come on.

GARRETH: This is ridiculous.

BONNIE: You never check out other women.

GARRETH: No I don't 'check them out'.

BONNIE: You don't even notice them.

GARRETH: Who?

BONNIE: The attractive women on the train.

GARRETH: I may notice them, but —

BONNIE: See?!

GARRETH: That doesn't mean that I DO anything about them. It. No them.

BONNIE: What tips you off that there's some sexy girl on the train?

GARRETH: I don't think I understand the — ?

BONNIE: Since you're so oblivious to the charms of the opposite sex —

GARRETH: I don't believe this.

BONNIE: How do you know for certain whether or not she's attractive? Hmm? Is it her ass? Her tits? Tell me.

GARRETH: I think this is a losing proposition.

BONNIE: I won't be mad.

GARRETH: What is the big deal, yes I have seen attractive women before but does that make me unfaithful? No. Does that make me a stalker? I don't think so, but maybe by your definition I shouldn't be attracted to anybody, maybe you would rather I were completely asexual. Perhaps it's my fault for having a penis, I should leave my penis at home locked up in a cupboard so it doesn't lead me down the road to temptation —

BONNIE: I never said that.

GARRETH: Maybe I just don't go around talking about it to everybody because it makes people uncomfortable.

BONNIE: Am I making you uncomfortable dear?

GARRETH: Yes to be frank. I mean no, but yes. I mean what is the big deal, men like to look at attractive women, what's so strange about that.

BONNIE: But you don't stare.

GARRETH: Just cuz I don't have the guts.

BONNIE: Excuse me.

GARRETH: You heard me. If I had the guts to just feast my eyes on some really good looking girl, I would. But I haven't, I know that, so I don't. I mean Christ what is the harm in looking.

BONNIE: So today I went back to my usual car at the front of the train. He was there. He glanced up at me.

(Tyler looks up at her. She puts him in his place, a hand on her hips. He looks away, chastised.)

So I sat down to read my paper.

(She sits down to read. She crosses her leg. He smiles at it. Then she deliber-

ately un-crosses it to prove a point. Her head tilts to one side. He smiles and nods. A lock of her hair dangles over her face and she severely tucks it back in, points to her eyes indicating that she's still got two of them.)

So I'm reading an article about police brutality and I'm all set to change to the Metro section when I remember —

(She shoots him a furious look. He cringes away, actively not looking at her.)

BONNIE: I can feel your look.

TYLER: I swear I wasn't looking at you.

BONNIE: Well don't.

TYLER: I'm not!

BONNIE: You better not be.

(She stares at him. He faces front, nervous.)

TYLER: Are you looking at me?

BONNIE: I've got my eye on you bucko.

TYLER: Well now see that just doesn't seem fair.

BONNIE: You've got a problem.

TYLER: Well yes as a matter of fact I do, it seems like a depressing solution to me that's all.

BONNIE: Learn to live with disappointment.

TYLER: Do you even find me attractive?

BONNIE: Don't make me slap you.

TYLER: You want to slap me?

BONNIE: Just — uhhh.

TYLER: Seriously, if you feel the need to slap me then I think . . .

BONNIE: Why can't you just leave me alone?

TYLER: *(Feelings a little hurt.)* Listen. I'm not the one who wants to slap other people. I said you looked like a painting and that was nice. But now you're all mean, I don't want to look at you anymore. So you just leave me alone alright.

(He exits.)

BONNIE: So then he leaves, like it's MY fault. And everybody's looking at me like I was a total bitch and it started freaking me out cuz they wouldn't stop looking at me and this mother started whispering to her kid who was pointing at me and these two gangster chicks started to laugh and shit and I was like, "WHAT THE FUCK ARE YOU LOOKING AT?! YOU DON'T KNOW ME. So stop looking at me." And the doors come open and all of a sudden the lady with the kid gets off and like a flood of Hasidic Jews and Muslims and like Hare Krishna dudes and Catholic schoolgirls all get on the train.

GARRETH: Only in New York.

BONNIE: I'm serious. It's like all the religions of the world are wedged up against my face, stepping on my feet, feeling my ass and they're all like praying and dancing and chanting in different languages and everything and they won't stop touching my ass.

GARRETH: Someone grabbed your ass?

BONNIE: Not an out and out grab, more like the only place they could hold their rosaries or their prayer shawls or whatever happened to be the dent between my butt cheeks. Like the only place they could hide their religion is up my butt!

GARRETH: So what did you do?

BONNIE: Switched cars. I couldn't take it. And I started heading down the car and it was like they were the Furies kinda grabbing at my legs and my breasts, sort of touching my hair and smelling my neck and I was like FUUUUUUUUUCK! I get to the new car which is practically empty of course and guess who's there.

(Tyler is sitting there, looking at a Young Girl in a miniskirt. She has a Walkman on and is maybe 17-years-old.)

GARRETH: Tyler!

BONNIE: Who?

GARRETH: Tyler, the first guy. The guy who thought you were a painting.

BONNIE: You know this guy?

GARRETH: No but you said —

BONNIE: I know what I said.

GARRETH: I'm just a good listener that's all. And I respect women.

BONNIE: Save it.

GARRETH: OK, but all I'm saying —

BONNIE: Anyway, there he is —

GARRETH: Tyler.

BONNIE: That's right, your buddy Tyler is sitting there and now he won't look up at me.

GARRETH: You're looking at him but he —

BONNIE: You're damn right I'm looking at him. You know what he's doing?

GARRETH: Looking at another girl?

BONNIE: What is it with you people?

GARRETH: What — you said he liked to look at women. You turned him down already, did you think he would give up on attractive women altogether?

BONNIE: What the hell do you think you're doing?

TYLER: Please stop staring at me. You're making me uncomfortable.

BONNIE: I'm making You uncomfortable.

GARRETH: Why couldn't you just leave him alone?

BONNIE: Because he's gonna go around — staring at people.

GARRETH: So . . .

BONNIE: Well he can't just do that.

GARRETH: Honey you're not in charge of monitoring the viewing habits of the men in this city.

TYLER: Listen Miss I don't mean to be rude, but will you please stop looking at me.

BONNIE: I don't think so.

GARRETH: I just don't understand your obsession with this guy.

TYLER: Well then what do you want?

BONNIE: I want you to stop staring.

TYLER: Stop staring at me!

BONNIE: You first!

TYLER: Alright. It's your turn.

GARRETH: Honey you're worse than he is!

TYLER: You haven't stopped.

BONNIE: How do you know?

TYLER: I can feel your eyes.

BONNIE: She's a bit young.

TYLER: For you or me?

(Pause.)

I don't discriminate against women. I believe they all deserve a fair shake.

BONNIE: Well, what are you waiting for?

(Pause.)

Hey kid, what do you think of this guy?

(The Young Girl cannot hear.)

I don't think she likes you.

TYLER: She will.

BONNIE: What are you going to do to her?

TYLER: I don't have to do anything to her. But watch.

(He stares at the Young Girl. Bonnie stares at Tyler. Tyler fixes a seductive, penetrating gaze on the girl, who finally looks up at him, and smiles nervously.)

YOUNG GIRL: *(With an embarrassed laugh.)* What? What are you looking at?

TYLER: Why you, dear.

(The Young Girl smiles back at him shyly. Bonnie watches as the Young Girl crosses her leg flirtatiously as Tyler leans in.)

(Blackout.)

END OF PLAY

The Bedmaker's Revenge

BEKAH BRUNSTETTER

The Bedmaker's Revenge was first produced by At Play Productions as part of the 24 Hour Plays festival (Celebrity Benefit) at the Atlantic Theater, New York, New York, Spring 2008. Director: Allie Maxwell. Cast: Julia Grob, Jamie Klassel and Matt Devin.

Characters

The Bedmaker, a lovely young woman who is extremely anal about making the bed. A go-getter. She folds her underwear. She sleeps just enough, always. Pretty recently she emerged from a coma after being hit by a car. She is just learning how to use her words again.

The Sleepyhead, the Bedmaker's lover. Works forty-five hours a week somewhere extremely important. He is anal about getting proper amounts of sleep at all times. Otherwise lazy in a justifiable, human sort of way. He is pretty articulate when only half-awake. All things are defined by sleep, or the frantic getting of it.

Disgruntled Sleep-fairy. This ageless cute thing is cursed with the never getting of sleep herself, though she can give it to others. She wears pajamas that strongly resemble a Sassy Skiing tight outfit thing. The whole play, she is fighting sleep. She fights it with bursts of cute sudden energy. There are lots of opportunities for tip-toe-ing and/or flitting about.

Setting

A bedroom.

• • •

Stage: A bed. The fairy floats nearby.

Lights up on the Disgruntled Sleep Fairy. She is awake, sort of, and optimistic. Nearby, in bed, The Bedmaker and the Sleephead Spoon and Sleep. The Sleep Fairy watches them sleep.

SLEEP FAIRY: Aren't they wonderful? They look just like babies. I put them to sleep.

(She might throw confetti here. They talk in their sleep as they spoon.)

BEDMAKER: The curtains should match the carpet. One teaspoon vanilla.

SLEEPYHEAD: I love sleeping.

BEDMAKER: Don't touch of me —

SLEEPYHEAD: I'm going to sleep you to death.

BEDMAKER: I have all of the crayons fixed by color and you give them to your cat. Ow — ow — ow —

SLEEPYHEAD: Mmm . . .

(He pulls her closer.)

SLEEP FAIRY: Adorable. They just got engaged. She celebrated with new sheets. He got drunk.

Incompatible, completely.

He's a journalist. She's just gotten out of a coma and can't use her words. That's how they met.

SLEEPYHEAD: You're my bitch — you're my —

SLEEP FAIRY: Shhh — they're sleeping. I put them to sleep. Later tonight, I'll put *you* to sleep, if you're good.

(She really looks at us, concerned.)

How are you? Tired? Oh — You'll have to excuse me, I'm already in my pajamas.

So are you tired? I'd like a count, please, how many of you are tired? Please don't really raise your hand. Awkward. You'll make the person next to you feel very uncomfortable, and that person is probably tired.

Speaking of tired, I'm tired, though I have never slept. Is it fun? It looks fun.

Would you like me to put you to sleep? Later.

There was something important I — I was —

(Pause. She thinks and dreams.)

I'm sorry, I had something important to say, but I was thinking of sleep. Ah.

So what time is it, anyways? How tired are you, if you could measure it? How many cups of tired?

You've had your coffee, I bet, this morning. And then more coffee, coffee part two, then wine with dinner — your bed is looking pretty good right now, isn't it? Well — your bed or the bed of your lover — the person you have chosen with which to bed.

By the time you get out of here, the 43 minute commute — by the time you've twice fed the whiney cat and taken out all recyclings — the getting of mail and the clipping of fingernails — you'll get five and half hours of sleep.

Not enough. Didn't your mother ever teach you?

You have to be at work by nine, which means you're up by seven, to allow for the hair-scrubbing and face scrubbing to give the ILLUSION of adequate sleep. Then there's the getting of the egg sandwich after the fiasco in which your metrocard expires and there you find yourself, tired, tired, cussing in front of small children.

And there's somewhere to be tomorrow night, too. Obligatory. You won't get a real night's sleep until Friday, and then if you sleep in Saturday, you'll have wasted half a free day, and I can tell you're not the type to waste anything.

Really, the only hope is that you've found a proper person to share your bedplace with — a person whose sleep sounds and sleep-moving lovingly juxtapose with your own. That they match.

That's the only hope, really.

But what if they don't?

(Lights shift, perhaps, to include the bed. The Bedmaker shoots up, wide awake. The sleepy head sleep-moans and reaches for her, but she is up.)

BEDMAKER: Get up, bunnyhon.

SLEEPYHEAD: No. NO. I love being asleep.

BEDMAKER: Come on, Sleepyhead! Get the fudge up, I need to make of the bed.

SLEEPYHEAD: It's too early. Blessed fucking sleep. It's warm, you're warm.

BEDMAKER: What are you doing?

SLEEPYHEAD: I'm SLEEPING.

BEDMAKER: I gotta make of the bed.

SLEEPYHEAD: It's too *early.* I, I can't get up now, if I get up now, I haven't gotten enough sleep, do you want me to die? Do you want me dead?

BEDMAKER: We lost of an hour last night, mommy, it's ten past two. Two past ten. Time for me to make the bed and you to get the fudge out of it. I'll make you a donut.

SLEEPYHEAD: *(Like a little boy.)* NO. Come back to bed.

BEDMAKER: It's LATE!

(She tries to pull the blankets off of him.)

SLEEP FAIRY: There was something important to say, somewhere — there something — I love beds, don't you? I was saying something.

Oh.

(She clears her throat, official, then loud: .)

ONE NIGHT EVERY YEAR, YOU ARE VIOLENTLY AND MALICIOUSLY AND VICIOUSLY ROBBED OF ONE HOUR OF SLEEP.

I'm sorry. It just really pisses me off. It's not my doing, I promise. It's got something very complicated to do with gravity or the growing of grass. Cruel and unusual. Maybe it's handed back to us months later, but by then, the tired has already happened, been dragged out over hundreds of days.

And for the following days, we find ourselves discombobulated. Picking fights, swinging our large bags into innocent strangers.

And by we — I mean you.

One day, I'd like to sleep. That'd be nice.

I think was saying something.

SLEEPYHEAD: You're crazy, come back to bed.

SLEEP FAIRY: I think I was saying something like — There is the first time you sleep with a person, and then the first time you Sleep with a person. One is more vulnerable than the other.

I think people are most lovely with their bed hair and broccoli breath. It is like — *this is me. This is how I look and smell when you're not looking.* Look at how lovely they are.

BEDMAKER: I am *not* — I am *not* cr- cr-

SLEEPYHEAD: You're crazy.

(The Bedmaker pulls a pillow out from underneath his head and fluffs it. Pissed, he is now awake.)

BEDMAKER: I just like the bad made. Bed. I just want to make the bed when I wake up. It needs doing.

SLEEPYHEAD: I need one more hour. Please. For the love of — I mean I love you and a lot but — If I sleep one more hour I'll have a full seven and a half. *Your* internal alarm is set for 3's every ten minutes, 6:13, 6:23, 6:33, baby, I love you, I love you stupid a lot, but I gotta sleep. Plus I only got five hours the night before last because SOMEBODY wanted to watch Dr. Schivago.

BEDMAKER: It's a love store, it's nice.

SLEEPYHEAD: And do you know how many serious ACCIDENTS occur because people are sleep deprived? Oil spills! And Car Accidents!

Like the person who hit you — maybe it was because they didn't get enough sleep. You want me to go out there, tired, and kill somebody?

BEDMAKER: You don't have a car.

SLEEPYHEAD: Just not this morning. This one morning, let's not get up. Let's spend the morning in our new bed. Last night, I asked you to marry me, you said yes. Come the fuck back to bed, let's be warm and asleep and love each other that way while we're sleeping.

BEDMAKER: You only love me when you're sleep.

SLEEPYHEAD: Whoa — that is *NOT* —

(And she begins to make the bed, around him, tucking the sheets in tight.)

SLEEP FAIRY: Never, *never* insinuate someone's sleep cycle is wrong or incorrect. It is the same as telling them that their God is fat or stupid.

(The Bedmaker tucks in sheets around him violently. As she attempts to do so, he messes her work up.)

SLEEPYHEAD: Hey!

BEDMAKER: If you will not out, I will do it anywhoo.

SLEEPYHEAD: This isn't working.

BEDMAKER: You laze, you laze around, I want a breakfast and a Day. Look at the day!

SLEEPYHEAD: It can wait, you're beautiful.

BEDMAKER: I — Just want — I just want — I like things to be did in a way that is good.

SLEEPYHEAD: Tell me about it.

BEDMAKER: I just *did.*

(Frantically, she keeps trying to make the bed.)

SLEEP FAIRY: I think I was saying — I was going to say something about compatibility, love, sleep numbers, mattress salesmen. Or wine glasses floating on mattresses while old men drop bowling balls to prove a point.

When you sleep, your body is paralyzed so you don't get up and do what you're dreaming.

Elephants sleep standing up, I was going to mention that.

If I had a lover, I would make him stare at me until I fell asleep. I would just pretend, though, and then he would fall asleep, and I would watch him do it.

SLEEPYHEAD: If you can't come back to bed, baby, I don't know if I believe in you, or us.

BEDMAKER: What?

SLEEPYHEAD: I mean, basically, you're saying — for the rest of our lives — the rest of *my* life — I can't sleep in. I can't sleep in for the rest of my *life.* You know how much I love it. There is nothing more wonderful and I just want to share it with you, and you're not listening to me, and you snore and say weird things about crayons and last night, you kicked me in the balls, so hard, like the Olympics, and I love you so much I didn't say anything I just went in the bathroom and cried because I didn't want to hurt your feelings.

BEDMAKER: I hate of you. I FAKE ALL OF MY ORGANISMS!

SLEEPYHEAD: Wait — What?

BEDMAKER: How can you said that to me when we are engorged to be married, forever?!

SLEEPYHEAD: I will UN-engorge! You! So.

(She gives up. She sits on the bed, pissed, tired, tears. Quiet.)

SLEEP FAIRY: People are babies who need bedtimes and naps.

Babies aren't allowed to fall in love with each other, and this is why.

(The Sleephead pokes the Bedmaker with his foot.)

SLEEPYHEAD: Hi.

BEDMAKER: Ha.

SLEEPYHEAD: You know what I think?

BEDMAKER: When I was little my Mom says make the bed, I think this is nice. I just like to — I just w-want — Bedthings are places of peace, they are a place where no bad happens. They are quiet and safe. They should stay nice.

SLEEPYHEAD: I agree. Also, they are for sleeping. You know what I think? I think you're tired. You're probably still tired.

BEDMAKER: Time to start the *day.*

(The Sleepyhead stands up, helps the Bedmaker to her feet. Together, on opposite sides of the bed, they lift the sheet high into the air. Together, they smooth it onto the bed. They get onto it. He lies down on top of it. He invites her into his warm arm nook. Reluctantly, she lies there. She closes her eyes. She likes it.)

SLEEPYHEAD: See, you're just still tired, is all. There you go.

BEDMAKER: It's late, the sun is — it is —

SLEEPYHEAD: Up, it's up.

BEDMAKER: Yar.

SLEEPYHEAD: It's OK.

BEDMAKER: I will try and — I will try and — for you. OK. OK, OK.

(They close their eyes.)

SLEEP FAIRY: If you oversleep you lie like a dog and pretend you didn't. Your forgot your keys or she forgot your keys or something exploded or someone died.

When you wake up, you are a like a baby, clenching your fists and kicking your feet.

I hear that sometimes, you're so tired, it's like you're drunk. You forget what it's like to not be tired and this becomes a constant feeling of average despair, which feels like life.

(She watches the two of them settle into each other.)

People are Babies and beasts. *Kiss me in the middle of my forehead,* they say, *stroke me like I fell off my bike.* Giant small people in need of soft goodnight songs.

(Quietly, in some cute way, she puts them to Sleep. They fall asleep, smiling.)

I was saying something, wasn't I? Something about sleep, the frantic getting of it, alarm clocks, some sort of injustice, some kind of —

(Pause.)

I'm tired, aren't you?

(She looks at the couple, proud of her work.)

Shhh. They're sleeping. And you're next.

(Lights.)

END OF PLAY

Bollywood Ending

R. D. Murphy

Bollywood Ending was first performed at Feverfest 09 produced by the Small Theatre Alliance of Boston at The Factory Theatre in Boston, August 6–16, 2009. This play was sponsored by Phoenix Theatre Artists. Artistic Director: Greg Maraio. Director: Thomas Martin. Choreography: Raina Lewis with assistance from Bo Richardson. Costume Design: Pasquelina. Cast: Gridley Riggs — Peter Brown; Pooja Chaturvedi (phone Id: Annette Kelly) — Rachael Hunt; Omkar Hati (phone ID: Cubby Bond) — Alex Castillo-Nunez; Annette — Kim Myatt.

Characters

Gridley Riggs, 52, owner of the now defunct Riggs Chevrolet.

Pooja Chaturvedi (phone ID: Annette Kelly), 24, brainy, considered the office specialist in debt collection. She is dressed in a flowing, hot pink Indian suit and wears jangly silver bangles. She wears a headphone and has a timer on a lariat around her neck.

Omkar Hati (phone ID: Cubby Bond), 20, neophyte debt collector at the Gurgaon Call Center, possessed by a singular passion for American movies.

Annette is the physical embodiment of Pooja's phone voice. A middle-aged woman, sympathetic, patient, supportive, she looks like she could be Gridley's wife, or favorite sister, or fellow parishioner. Annette is dressed Talbot's casual, but in hot pink and with a wristful of jangly bracelets.

Place

The deserted showroom of Riggs Chevrolet in Ipswich, MA, and a Call Center in Gurgaon, India.

Time

October 13, 2008. 4:15 pm in Ipswich; 2:45 am in Gurgaon.

Note

Whenever Pooja or Omkar conduct business over the phone as Annette or Cubby, they speak with flawless American accents. In the office, among themselves, Pooja and Cubby speak with Indian accents.

• • •

At opening, Omkar sits in a swivel chair in a spotlight stage right. He wears a telephone headset and holds a laptop on his lap. The screen that Omkar and Pooja consult is out in front, between them and the audience. Omakr is on the phone, as his American persona, Cubby Bond.

cubby: Your student loans were your decision — what did you major in PENURY? Are you trying to tell me this is not your AMEX Card? Yeah, a $17,000 balance! No, YOU listen to me, Miss American Excess. *(Ala*

Marlon Brando in "The Godfather".) How would you like to swim with the fishes? . . . Hello? Hello?

(Omkar, frustrated, spins in his chair. By this time, all of stage right is lit. Pooja has been standing alongside Cubby, evaluating his performance. She too wears a headset and a lariat with a timer.)

POOJA: *(She clicks the timer.)* . . . they are a proud people. Without the soothing sound of deference, they will hang up on you. *(Checks the timer.)* Eight minutes and —

OMKAR: Bitch.

POOJA: — no payment — What?

OMKAR: No, Miss, I mean Cassie Tupper. *(Blubbering imitation.)* "I am crucified by credit." —

POOJA: You think a fifty-year-old movie —

OMKAR: — Thirty-six-year-old movie. 1972. Known to every American. Know the movies; know the people.

POOJA: Delta is pulling their call center back to America —

OMKAR: The U. S. of A. and their fucking I. O. of U.'s. —

POOJA: Our cost is far cheaper. Our manner is causing complaints.

OMKAR: The world looks to them, yeah, to pay off their debts —

POOJA: You honored in enema analysis —

OMKAR: — Cinema analysis —

POOJA: — And you think you know Americans. You like threats? Then here's a threat. Close the next call or you're fired.

OMKAR: Be kind, Miss. You know I'm good

POOJA: I'm not telling you to be good. I'm telling you to get results. *(Looking over his shoulder to his computer screen.)* Take that next name on the screen: "Gridley Riggs."

OMKAR: *(ala Elliot Gould in* M*A*S*H.*)* Leave it to The Pros from Dover. We figger to crack this kid's chest and get out on the golf course before it gets dark. *(Phone rings.) M*A*S*H.* 1970.

(Lights come up stage left is the empty showroom of Riggs Chevrolet. It consists of a metal desk with two metal chairs. On the desk is a speaker phone, a black can of Raid wasp spray, and random personal effects, all of to be packed away. Clusters of balloons sit on the floor, still fully inflated, but the helium evaporated. During the following voiceover, Gridley, enters from stage left, carrying an empty cardboard box.)

VOICEOVER: *(As Gridley packs.)* Hello, this is Gridley Riggs. Welcome to the former home of Riggs Chevrolet. I'm sorry to inform you that the Columba-Rama Cavalcade of Chevy Savings has been cancelled.//

CUBBY: Pick up.

VOICEOVER: //After sixteen years of offering the best deals on the North Shore, we have closed our doors.//

POOJA: I'll take this one. Stand down. *(She looks over his shoulder at the screen.)*

CUBBY: *(ala Jack Nicholson in* Five Easy Pieces.*)* Tell him to hold his Columbarama between his knees.

VOICEOVER: //It has been our pleasure to serve the people of Ipswich and beyond.//

CUBBY: *FIVE EASY PIECES.* Same year as *M*A*S*H.* A Renaissance.

VOICEOVER/GRIDLEY: *(Gridley recites the last sentences along with the recording.)* //You have been like family. Goodbye and God Bless. — *(The phone beeps to record a message.)*

GRIDLEY: — Yeah, if your family is . . . a pack of howling coyotes . . .

(Gridley dodges a wasp flying by. He climbs onto the desk and stands on the downstage edge, carefully calibrating an attack on the wasp nest. The wasp nest is in the upper corner of the showroom window, which we come to realize is between him and us.)

(As Gridley reaches toward the nest. Annette appears upstage right. She is the embodiment of Pooja's phone voice. Annette walks diagonally downstage left to Gridley's desk. Note: when Pooja speaks simultaneously with Annette, she speaks with an American accent.)

ANNETTE AND POOJA: Hello Mr. Riggs. Gridley Riggs? Gridley, please pick up.

(Annette sits in the chair in front of the desk, just to the side of Gridley. Throughout this conversation, she is patient, solicitous, and occasionally confused. Although her eyesight is fine, she only responds to what Pooja can hear. No matter what happens, she wants to maintain the conversation.)

GRIDLEY: *(To the unseen wasp nest.)* Think you can hide in there? . . . shoulda flown south . . .

("Leaning" on the window, Gridley stretches forward with the can of Raid and furiously sprays the nest, dousing Annette sitting beneath him. She does not respond. He leaps to the floor behind the desk, expecting a fierce retaliation. There is none. He cautiously stands. Annette does not respond to this.)

ANNETTE AND POOJA: Mr. Riggs, I need your help.

GRIDLEY: Hello?

(He punches a button to turn on the speaker phone and talks while packing. It should look like he's conversing with Annette.)

ANNETTE: Yes, hello, Gridley. How are you today?

GRIDLEY: Other than standing in an empty showroom, packing up my life?

ANNETTE: I understand. I am sorry to hear of your circumstances —

GRIDLEY: *(He cautiously reclimbs the desk, approaching the wasp nest again with the can outstretched.)* I'd like to think it's water over the dam, but that's not pretty either. Beavers rerouted Jeffries Creek at the rear of the lot. Flooded the inspection bay.

ANNETTE: I'm sorry to hear that. Gridley I need your assistance —

GRIDLEY: You've said my name at least half a dozen times and I don't have the pleasure of —

(A large thump sounds as something strikes the showroom window. Standing on the desk, Gridley flinches and drops the can. Annette does not respond.)

GRIDLEY: What the — ??

ANNETTE: Are you alright?

GRIDLEY: *(Peering through the downstage window.)* Someone threw something. Dammit!

ANNETTE: I need your help.

GRIDLEY: *(Shouting to whomever might be outside.)* You'll be taken care of — read the sign on the door *(pointing stage left.)* —

(He scans the yard outside the window: there is no one out there. He looks down at the ground.) It's just a bird. Uh, a dead bird. A bird-i-cide. If I had a buck for every bird that took on this window . . .

ANNETTE: I need your help —

GRIDLEY: *(To the dead bird.)* Trying to eat the wasps? *(Looking up at the wasp nest.)* They're poisoned. Double bird-i-cide.

ANNETTE: Your American Express account —

GRIDLEY: *(To Annette.)* — Closed. Shut. Finito . . .

OMKAR: That's a wrap!

GRIDLEY: *(Note: Gridley remains standing on the desk from here on.)* . . . No cars. No service. Just some dead wasps, ramped up beavers, and a numb-skulled bird . . . Where are you calling from?

ANNETTE: American Express —

GRIDLEY: No. *Where* are you calling from?

ANNETTE: *(Slight pause, but not uncomfortable.)* I am asked not to say.

GRIDLEY: WHERE?

ANNETTE: *(Part of her routine.)* "Somewhere in the United States."

GRIDLEY: You don't tell who you are —

ANNETTE: Annette Kelley.

GRIDLEY: You don't tell where you are —

ANNETTE: I am asked not to.

GRIDLEY: *(Pause.)* What's a ta-ta?

(Annette looks to Pooja. Pooja looks to Omkar.)

ANNETTE AND POOJA: A Ta-Ta . . .

GRIDLEY: A ta-ta. As in — *(Omkar signaling — he knows!)*

GRIDLEY AND OMKAR: — "bodacious ta-ta."

POOJA: *(Looks to Annette.)* A car.

ANNETTE: *(Looks to Gridley.)* A car.

OMKAR: *OFFICER AND A GENTLEMAN.* 1998.

GRIDLEY: *In India,* it's a car. In my country, it's a breast . . .

OMKAR: A rack . . .

GRIDLEY: A boob.

OMKAR: A tit.

POOJA: *(To Omkar.)* Enough.

GRIDLEY: What day is it?

ANNETTE: October 13, 2008

GRIDLEY: *What* day is it? (*Omkar, on the case, checking his laptop.)*

ANNETTE: *(Pause.)* Monday

GRIDLEY AND OMJAR: *(Who has googled successfully.)* COLUMBUS DAY —

GRIDLEY: — The busiest weekend of the year, next to Presidents' Day. They cleared out the inventory Friday —

(Pooja and Omkar both checking his screen; Annette is now back on track.)

ANNETTE: I know Ipswich. You're located near the intersection of 133 and 1A on the way to the beaches —

OMKAR: *(To Pooja.)* — Hyannis *(Pronounce: Hy-ANUS.)*

POOJA: *(To Omkar, smugly.)* — Hyannis *(Pronounce: Hy-ANNIS.)*

GRIDLEY: Yeah, look for the empty building, next to the vacant motel. Pile of dead birds in front. Beavers and coyotes in the woods in back —

ANNETTE AND POOJA: I passed through on my way to Hyannis —

GRIDLEY: You go the long way? *(Pooja again glares at Omkar.)* — And deer. Lots of deer.

ANNETTE: On my way to the . . . beach.

GRIDLEY: Look, I'm just trying to close this place —

ANNETTE: I know. I would like to help you close this chapter honorably.

GRIDLEY: Do you have any idea what it's like to tell twenty-three people they don't have a job anymore? HONORABLY? Let me tell you about "HONORABLY."

ANNETTE: I know you want to do the right thing.

GRIDLEY: *(Increasingly irritated.)* GMAC shut down the financing pipeline. No one could qualify —

ANNETTE: You are a responsible man. Once the "funeral feeling" subsides and you settle back into life —

GRIDLEY: On those rare occasions, I could sell a car? GMAC wanted payment before the iron was over the curb. I ran out of money —

ANNETTE: — you will see that no door ever closes without — Let me work with you.

GRIDLEY: — I charged whatever I could on as many credit cards as I had — *(Another thump at the window. Gridley flinches again. Annette doesn't respond.)*

GRIDLEY: *(Looking at the ground outside the window, addressing another dead bird.)* What the fuck? Is it "Natural Selection Week" on Nature Channel?

ANNETTE: Gridley, you are a life-long car man. You'll find a way. You are the heart of your community —

GRIDLEY: It's time for a transplant. Look, skip the sympathy fuck. You'll get paid. I'm an adult. I clean up my own mess. A big-box pharmacy will pay top dollar to buy me and the motel next door. Assemble the site, scrape it clean, and build a 24/7 convenience store with two drive-thru lanes.

ANNETTE: Of course you will repay your vendors —

GRIDLEY: Two lanes: one for the drop-off window. The other a big ass vent, pointed toward downtown. *(Gridley faces stage left.)* Just suck all the life out. *(He makes a huge sucking sound.)*

ANNETTE: — Shame on them for doubting you.

GRIDLEY: *(Looking toward the downtown, addressing the people of Ipswich.)* You won't be left with two clam shells to rub together.

ANNETTE: That is why you are the boss, they work — clam shells?

POOJA: Sheckels?

OMKAR: *(On the case, googling.)* Clam shells . . .

ANNETTE: Send me that minimum payment so that you will remain our dependable, responsible business partner.

OMKAR: Oh God. They eat clam bellies. These people are barbarians.

(A thump, thump, thump is heard — three birds in a row. Gridley reacts to each, as if performing a continuous dance move. Note: This moment will be replayed by Gridley in the final dance number.)

GRIDLEY: *(Re: the birds.)* The empty showroom throws them off.

ANNETTE AND POOJA: When the market swings back, you will be poised to once again take charge.

GRIDLEY: You know how coyotes catch deer? I find the carcass in the woods —

POOJA: Will you agree to send me the minimum $100 payment?

GRIDLEY: — A pack singles out a deer and runs it ragged. The deer collapses. The they tear it to pieces.

POOJA: Gridley, I need your help. Will you mail me the minimum payment?

GRIDLEY: *(Pause.)* Yeah. *(He remains standing on the desk, looking out the window. Annette stands and takes the cardboard box off the table. She crosses stage right to the Call Center.)*

POOJA: Thank you and God bless. *(Hangs up. Pooja clicks her stopwatch, now speaking to Omkar in Indian accent.)* Four minutes thirty-nine seconds! One hundred dollars. That is how it must be done. How many times do I tell you that they are a sensitive race? You're fired. Clear out your desk. *(Annette is behind Omkar. He turns around and she hands him the cardboard box. Omkar takes the box and turns back to protest.)*

OMKAR: *(Ala Faye Dunaway in* MOMMIE DEAREST.*)* Don't fuck with me fellas, this ain't my first time at the rodeo.

POOJA: The movie about the clothes hangers? 1970-something? *(She is interrupted by:)*

LOUDSPEAKER: Congratulations! Congratulations to Pooja Chaturvedi! Once again she has surpassed this quarter's goal. Enjoy your new flatscreen TV, Pooja!

(Pooja squeals in delight; Annette and Omkar join her, singing and dancing in:)

SONG: "BOLLYWOOD ENDING"

The thump, thump, thump of birds hitting the window is heard. Gridley, still on the desk, reacts to each, performing the dance move we saw earlier.

POOJA, OMKAR AND ANNETTE: *Live within your means, but*
Love me to ex-tre-eemmes

Live within your means, but
Love me to ex-tre-eemes

POOJA: *(To Omkar.) Your interest in me is quarterly*
Ahh ahhh haaa

OMKAR: *(To Pooja.) My interest in you is interest free*
Haaa aahhh aahhh

POOJA: *(To Omkar.) So express all your success to excess*
Ahhh ahhhhh

OMKAR: *(To Pooja.) Courtesy of American Express*

POOJA: *Living the life of your fantasy*
You've had my chai and my sympathy
None of your wishes are left unfi-illed
Now it's time to pay the bi-ill
(Thump, thump, thump is heard. Gridley reacts to each, performing his dance move.)

ALL: *Live within your means, but*
Love me to ex-tre-eemmes
Live within your means, but
Love me to ex-tre-eemes

POOJA: *Reach beyond your reach,*

OMKAR: *Exceed your grasp*

ANNETTE: *Surpass your dreams*

ALL: *But pay in cash*
Love me to ex-tree-eemes.
(Gridley faces the window downstage left. Thump, thump, thump. He bangs his head against the window. He collapses. Pooja and Omkar embrace. The final tableau.)

END OF PLAY

Carwash; or In This Town, You Are What You Drive

STEPHANIE HUTCHINSON

Carwash; or In This Town, You Are What You Drive was originally produced at The Actor's Group in Universal City, California, in June 2008 by The All Original Playwright Workshop. Director: Wynn Marlow. Cast: Mr. Glendenning — Jordan T. Maxwell; Mitch — Joe Finfera; Cassie — Kate McDaniel; Woman/Silverr — Dylan Diehl.

Carwash; or In This Town, You Are What You Drive was also produced at Miles Memorial Playhouse, Santa Monica, California, October 17–19, 2008 by Fire Rose Productions, as a Finalist in ACTober Fest, Fire Rose Productions' 6th Annual Ten-Minute Play Festival. Director: Wynn Marlow. Cast: Mr. Glendenning — Jordan T. Maxwell; Mitch — Michael Uribes; Cassie — Kate McDaniel; Woman/Silverr — Christiann Castellanos.

CHARACTERS

MR. GLENDENNING, thirties, successful but down-to-earth movie producer, single.

MITCH, (any age) carwash cashier, a character.

CASSIE, twenties, small town girl, cute, naive but charming, single.

WOMAN/SILVERR, twenties, knockout starlet wannabe, a snob.

SETTING

An L.A. carwash, with a counter and a bench. [Note: three chairs may be used instead of a bench.]

TIME

The present.

• • •

At Rise: Mr. Glendenning stands talking to Mitch, who is behind the counter.

MR. GLENDENNING: *(Anxiously.)* You know, Mitch, I've never left my baby before.

MITCH: Yeah, it's hard when you're a new father.

MR. GLENDENNING: I'm pretty nervous.

MITCH: *(Comfortingly.)* Don't worry, Mr. Glendenning — we'll be very gentle.

(Hollers to Offstage.)

Jose! Be extra careful with Mr. Glendenning's Ferrari!

(Beat. To Mr. Glendening, softly.)

It'll just be a few minutes.

MR. GLENDENNING: OK.

(Mitch escorts Mr. Glendenning to the bench and hands him a copy of the Wall Street Journal *as he sits. Beat. Cassie enters, approaches the counter and looks around.)*

CASSIE: Uh, 'xcuse me, do I pay here?

(Mitch goes back to the counter.)

MITCH: Yeah. Are you getting the gold, the silver, or the platinum wash?

CASSIE: What's the cheapest?

MITCH: That would be the silver wash. Do you have a coupon?

CASSIE: Coupon?

MITCH: We send 'em out in the mail.
CASSIE: I just moved here. I haven't gotten any mail yet.
MITCH: That's OK.

(He slips her a coupon.)

We also have a frequent guest card. After ten washes, the eleventh is free. Here.

(He hands her a card as she pays.)

CASSIE: *(Surprised and tickled.)* Oh, wow, I'm a guest! Thanks!

(She approaches the bench.)

Uh, hullo.

(Mr. Glendenning grunts.)

CASSIE: Is anybody sitting here?
MR. GLENDENNING: Be my guest.

(He scoots over and buries his face in the Wall Street Journal. *Pause as Cassie looks around; she smiles.)*

CASSIE: Isn't this sunshine great? *(No response.)*

This is my first time at a carwash that's not do-it-yourself. I hope they do a good job.

MR. GLENDENNING: It's the top-rated carwash in L.A.
CASSIE: Truly?

(A Woman enters, wearing sunglasses, a sexy silver outfit, stiletto heels and carrying a large tote. Note: it is preferred that the entire outfit, including shoes and tote, is silver. Mitch approaches her.)

MITCH: *(Instantly infatuated.)* How can I help YOU today?

(She opens her wallet and holds out a $20 bill.)

WOMAN: Just make sure they do a good job on my Jag. The last place I went to scratched it.
MITCH: Oh, absolutely, miss. I'll personally make sure. What color is it?
WOMAN: *("Isn't it obvious?")* Silver.

(Mitch exits. Mr. Glendenning gets up to watch the cars going through the carwash. The Woman approaches the bench.)

CASSIE: Hullo!

(The Woman looks her up and down without replying. She pushes her sunglasses up on her head and stares imperiously at Cassie until she scoots over to make room for her. The Woman sits.)

CASSIE: *(Friendly.)* I guess it'll be a few minutes.
WOMAN: I hate waiting.
CASSIE: Well, I hear it's the best carwash in L.A.

WOMAN: *(Sarcastically.)* It's OK if you have nothing *better* to do.
CASSIE: I just moved here. My car is really dusty from the drive — it took me a week!
WOMAN: You *drove*?
CASSIE: Yeah. I'm from —
WOMAN: — Let me tell you Rule #1: in this town, you *are* what you drive.
CASSIE: *(Puzzled.)* What do you mean?

(Mr. Glendening is seen observing the cars going through the carwash. An old junker comes through. The Woman notices but Cassie doesn't.)

WOMAN: See that guy? *(She gestures towards Mr. Glendenning.)*
CASSIE: Yeah.
WOMAN: Total loser.
CASSIE: Why?
WOMAN: Did you see his ride? They haven't made cars like that since, since, I totally have no idea.
CASSIE: He seems nice.
WOMAN: *(Condescendingly.)* It's not about nice. It's about what you drive.
CASSIE: But that's so . . . superficial!
WOMAN: This town was built on superficial.

(Cassie digests this.)

CASSIE: Well, what kind of car do *you* drive?
WOMAN: A Jag. Silver.
CASSIE: Wow!

(Beat.)

My name's Cassie.

(She offers her hand; the Woman ignores it.)

WOMAN: I'm Silverr.

(Beat.)

With two r's at the end.

CASSIE: That's your NAME?
SILVERR: It's my stage name.

(Beat.)

Everybody in L.A. has one.

CASSIE: Truly?

(Beat.)

What's your real name?

(Long pause as Silverr struggles to admit it; finally.)

SILVERR: Doris. Shh!

CASSIE: OK, Doris —

SILVERR: — Silverr!

CASSIE: Oh, sorry, Silver . . . er.

(Beat.)

So you're a real, working actress? Wow! Where can I see you act?

SILVERR: *(Haughtily.)* I don't do theatre. There's no money in it. *(Proudly.)* I'm a film actress.

CASSIE: This is so exciting! What movies were you in?

(Beat as Silverr thinks of how to reply, as she has no resume.)

SILVERR: I'm up for the lead in the new Glendenning movie.

(Cassie knows she's heard that name before but can't quite place it.)

CASSIE: Glendenning . . . Glendenning.

SILVERR: He's one of the top producers in town.

CASSIE: I'm an actress too. That's why I came to L.A., to get my big break.

(Beat.)

Of course, I'm not nearly as experienced as you are.

(Mr. Glendenning comes back to the bench, notices Silverr and sits.)

MR. GLENDENNING: *(To Silverr; attracted.)* Good morning!

(Silverr turns away.)

MR. GLENDENNING: Beautiful day, isn't it?

SILVERR/CASSIE: *(Negatively/Pleasantly.)* Hmm.

MR. GLENDENNING: *(Trying to make conversation.)* I like this carwash. They do quality work.

(Silverr ignores him.)

MR. GLENDENNING: Do you come here often?

SILVERR:No.

(She rises to go watch the cars going through the carwash.)

MR. GLENDENNING: *(Under his breath.)* Women!

(Mitch enters and approaches Silverr.)

MITCH: *(To Silverr; flirtatiously.)* So, miss, is there anything else I *personally* can do to make your experience with us more pleasant?

SILVERR: *(Squashes him like a bug.)* No!

(Mitch retreats to offstage.)

CASSIE: *(To Mr. Glendenning, conversationally.)* I'm just glad my old car didn't break down. I drove cross-country.

MR. GLENDENNING: *(Excited.)* Is that your '62 Olds?

CASSIE: Yeah.

MR. GLENDENNING: Sweet! I'm a classic car buff. I love that model!

CASSIE: Truly?

MR. GLENDENNING: My friend and I love to restore old cars. They don't make 'em like that anymore! Where'd you get it?

CASSIE: It was my grandfather's. When I told my family I was moving here, they said, "Cassie, everybody in L.A. drives. You'll need a car. Take Gramp's."

MR. GLENDENNING: Cassie? I'm Bob.

(He extends his hand and they shake.)

CASSIE: Hi.

MR. GLENDENNING: So, are you looking to sell it?

CASSIE: No, sir —

MR. GLENDENNING: — Please, call me Bob —

CASSIE: — Bob. I need a car.

MR. GLENDENNING: Are you planning to restore it?

CASSIE: No. I'm just happy that it got me here all the way from Maryville.

(Beat. Mr. Glendenning does a double take.)

MR. GLENDENNING: Maryville? Did you say Maryville?

CASSIE: Uh huh.

MR. GLENDENNING: Not Maryville, Missouri?

CASSIE: Yeah.

MR. GLENDENNING: Are you from there originally?

CASSIE: Born and raised.

MR. GLENDENNING: What a small world! What's your last name?

CASSIE: Ellis.

MR. GLENDENNING: Do you know Jim Ellis?

CASSIE: He's my cousin!

MR. GLENDENNING: Jim's a good friend of mine! Does the name "Glendenning" mean anything to you?

CASSIE: *(An "aha" moment.)* Of course! You're not going to believe this, but — *(She rummages through her purse and pulls out a handwritten note.)* — Jim gave me your number, to contact you when I got to town! *(She hands the paper to Mr. Glendenning.)* He said, "Cassie, look up my buddy Bob. He lives in L.A. and will be a friendly face in the big city".

MR. GLENDENNING: It just shows that in L.A., you never know who you're going to meet at the carwash!

(They laugh; he hands the paper back to her; beat; thoughtfully.)

So, Cassie, there's an annual classic car show that my friend John and I enter. This year we don't have a car to work on. Maybe we could restore your Olds, free of charge, so we can enter the competition. What do you say?

CASSIE: *(Overwhelmed.)* Truly?

MR. GLENDENNING: Sure. I'll run the idea by John, but I'm sure he'll agree.

CASSIE: Bob, you are so sweet!

MR. GLENDENNING: *(Glancing over at Silverr.)* Not everybody thinks so.

(Mitch enters, holding keys.)

MITCH: Mr. Glendenning, sir! Your car's ready!

(Silverr overhears and rushes to the bench, knocking Mitch out of the way with her tote.)

SILVERR: *(Fawning.)* Oh, Mr. Glendenning! I didn't recognize you!

MR. GLENDENNING: Hmm.

SILVERR: I'm a huge fan! I'm auditioning for your movie on Tuesday!

(She scrambles in her tote for her headshot; while she is fumbling and throwing various items out, Mr. Glendenning and Cassie walk up to Mitch.)

MITCH: One red Ferrari, ready to go.

(He hands the keys to Mr. Glendenning.)

CASSIE: *(Gasps.)* Oh, it's gorgeous!

MR. GLENDENNING: *(Proudly.)* She's brand new.

(Beat.)

Say, Cassie, there's a coffee shop up the street. What do you say we stop in and get acquainted?

CASSIE: Sounds great!

(Silverr races up as fast as she can on her stilettos, waving her headshot.)

SILVERR: Mr. Glendenning! Wait!

(He ignores her; Cassie waves.)

CASSIE: Bye, Doris —

SILVERR: — Silverr —

CASSIE: — Oh, sorry, I mean, Silver —

SILVERR: *(Elongating the double "r".)* — ERR!!

(Mr. Glendenning offers Cassie his arm as they exit. Mitch produces another set of keys.)

MITCH: *(To Silverr.)* Here are the keys to your . . . *(He examines the key chain.)* . . . rental car. *(He flirtatiously dangles the keys out of her reach while making kissing noises; she tries to jump and grab them out of his hands.)* *(Lights fade.)*

END OF PLAY

The Cooking King

Sharon E. Cooper

The Cooking King was produced by the Milk Can Theatre Company's "Potluck Plays" in the Spring 2007. Artistic Director: Julie Fei-Fan Balzer. Each playwright brought in a recipe and then randomly selected a different recipe. *The Cooking King* was inspired by the recipe "Cold Asparagus Patina." The original director was Riv Massey. Cast: Susan — Marta Kuerston; The Cooking King — Chris Catalano; Paul — Matt Stapleton.

The play was remounted in the summer of 2008 by Rising Sun Theatre Company's "Perceptions" Festival.

In the summer of 2009, the play was one of forty plays (chosen from over 700 submissions.) produced as part of the Samuel French Off Off Broadway Short Play festival. Director: Kitt Lavoie; Associate Director: Jenny Kirlin; Costume Designer: Jamaal Hooker. Caste: Susan — Becky Sterling; The Cooking King — Chris Comfort, Paul — Josh Bywater.

CHARACTERS

THE COOKING KING, any age, host of a nationally syndicated cooking show, outrageous.

SUSAN, late twenties, married to Paul, a "stay at home mom" with a secret, attractive but looks like she hasn't slept well in a long time, never cooks.

PAUL, late twenties, a history teacher, tries to be even tempered, longs for the past.

SETTING

Susan and Paul's livingroom. The suburbs.

TIME

The present.

PLAYWRIGHT'S NOTE

It is important that Susan is the central focus in the play and that the surreal nature of the piece is addressed. In the production for the 2009 Samuel French Off Off Broadway Short Play Festival (directed by Kitt Lavoie) this was accomplished by placing Susan and the couch center stage and the Cooking King character behind her, so when she paused or changed the channel, she motioned in the direction of the audience but the Cooking King responded behind her.

• • •

Lights up on a woman sitting next to a bassinet. She selects her show, "The Cooking King" and hits play. We hear music from the show and the Cooking King appears.

COOKING KING: Welcome to the Cooking Corner. I'm your host, and your friend, The Cooking King.

SUSAN: That is my favorite part.

(She restarts the show. The Cooking King "rewinds" and —)

COOKING KING: Welcome to the Cooking Corner. I'm your host, and your friend, The Cooking King.

(She "pauses" him.)

SUSAN: Don't you think he's handsome?

(She hits "play.")

This is a new one —

COOKING KING: Today, we are going to make asparagus patina.

SUSAN: What's patina?

COOKING KING: You may be wondering what patina is.

SUSAN: How did you —

COOKING KING: *(Overlapping.)* In modern English, it means the film of green oxidation on copper or bronze.

SUSAN: Eeww.

COOKING KING: It's not as bad as it sounds. Now don't put away your cooking tray!

SUSAN: I won't.

COOKING KING: When we come back —

(She hits "fast forward" on her remote, and we see the Cooking King fast forward.)

SUSAN: Gone are the days of commercials.

COOKING KING: Welcome back to the king that cares. Don't forget to pre-heat the oven to 425. You can do it.

(She doesn't. She never cooks.)

SUSAN: *(To the baby.)* I had one of those easy-bake ovens, and on Saturday mornings, your mum-mum and pop-pop would watch cooking shows with me.

COOKING KING: Take cleaned asparagus, pound in the mortar —

SUSAN: Pop-pop was a chef. When he left for work, he'd wear a wide mustard tie; he wanted to enter the restaurant as a king.

COOKING KING: Add water, beat thoroughly.

SUSAN: He would say, "What is on the menu today?" And I would say, "Strawberry shortcake soup, banana seat delight"; I liked making up —

COOKING KING: Now do pay attention.

SUSAN: *(To the Cooking King.)* Oh. Sorry.

COOKING KING: Because now we need a sieve!

SUSAN: Sieve, do I own one of those?

(She "pauses" the show. The Cooking King freezes.)

SUSAN: Beginnings are so much more interesting than what's in the middle. Maybe we should have cupcakes for your first birthday! The Cooking King had a special once —

(She starts another show.)

COOKING KING/SUSAN: Welcome to the Cooking Corner. I'm your host, and your friend, The Cooking King.

COOKING KING: Today, we are going to make a delectable delight — creamy cupcakes with custard frosting. These are great for Christmas, birthday parties or just if you need a little treat.

SUSAN: I need a little treat.

COOKING KING: I know what you're thinking.

SUSAN: You do?

COOKING KING: You don't have time to cook cupcakes from scratch — well now, you don't have to! Just watch as I take these — How's it going out there kids?

SUSAN: It's going. I'm ready.

COOKING KING: Don't you wish they were already done?

SUSAN: Don't you wish we were married to the Cooking King? He would come home from work and —

COOKING KING: Boy do I have treats for you!

SUSAN: My Cooking King husband!

(The Cooking King, as her fantasy, comes out of the television. He is behind her.)

COOKING KING: A warm walnut apple strudel drizzled with caramel. If you want —

SUSAN: I want.

COOKING KING: — Wow — Can't you just taste them in your mouth?

SUSAN: Yes.

COOKING KING: How's the little apple strudel?

SUSAN: She missed you today.

COOKING KING: Are you ready?

SUSAN: Yes. Oh yes. I'm ready Cooking King!

(She turns to him, but he is already gone, back in the television.)

COOKING KING: Then make sure you have all the proper equipment. A cook without her pans is like a princess without her crown. You know what we say.

(Susan mouths the next line as the Cooking King speaks.)

Don't put away your cooking tray.

(The front door opens. It's Paul, Susan's husband.)

PAUL: Hi.

COOKING KING: Now let's get back to business and —

(Susan turns off the volume on the show. The Cooking King continues silently. She moves the bassinet out of Paul's sightline as he hangs up his coat.)

PAUL: Hi honey. How was your day? You know, you'd think students would learn to study by the time they got to high school. It's like, if sixty percent of the class fails the test, is it the students' fault or the teacher's fault?

SUSAN: I don't know.

PAUL: Right, right! You are right!

(He hands her a necklace.)

I know there are no set rules of what you give your wife when —

SUSAN: It's pretty.

(Paul notices the television is on with no volume.)

PAUL: Were you watching that all day?

SUSAN: No. I did — other things.

PAUL: I think we should go out.

SUSAN: I'd rather order in.

PAUL: Come on, it's been three months. I'll take you for white pizza. Remember, that's where we went on our first date. After the dance. Let's pretend it's our first date again.

SUSAN: I was so scared you were going to kiss me and so scared you weren't.

PAUL: Tonight I'm more of a sure bet. Come on —

(He tries to move her toward the door.)

SUSAN: One time, when I was five, both of my parents thought the other one was home. Mom touched my blueberry barrettes and left. I walked through the house, calling "Mom, Pop!"

PAUL: What does this have to do with —

SUSAN: *(Continuous.)* I was holding my little spatula and pretend eggs. I flipped the three channels on the television. If a good cooking show had been on, I would have been OK —

COOKING KING: *(Starting slowly.)* Nooowwww thiiis part is tricky —

SUSAN: What did you do to the television?

COOKING KING: *(Overlapping.)* Whhaatt hhaapppennnsss neexxxttt —

PAUL/SUSAN/COOKING KING: I didn't touch the television. / What is wrong with this? / I'm your welcome, And welcometothecooking — Cooking King, Cooking King —

(Paul grabs the remote and turns off the television. The Cooking King falls forward so that he disappears.)

SUSAN: No!

(She rushes downstage towards the television and tries to turn it back on. It doesn't work.)

PAUL: It's just a television program!

SUSAN: No it's not.

PAUL: Susan, for three months, I've wanted to come home to some sense of normalcy. You know, when you come home and say "How are you honey?" And we fall onto the couch laughing — I want to share a white pizza outside of this apartment.

SUSAN: What if you had been home that day?

PAUL: What if you hadn't been distracted by the Cooking King?

SUSAN: I can't believe you just said that.

(Paul approaches her. He stands behind her and holds her in a similar way as we just saw with the Cooking King.)

PAUL: This is about you and me. You and me on a Caribbean cruise where we could see each other's feet in the water. You and me and a bucket of baby blue paint because it reminded you of the sky. You and me.

(They face each other. He sees the bassinet.)

Not you and me and the Cooking King and this —

(He tips the bassinet; it falls.)

SUSAN: Don't!

(He lifts the blanket.)

PAUL: Susan, it's just a blanket.

(The blanket falls to the floor.)

SUSAN: No it's not.

(She folds the blanket, carefully.)

PAUL: I am trying. I went to the bereavement group alone. I cook alone. I live with you but I live alone. I can't do it anymore. Come out with me.

(Maybe he's getting through to her. He waits. She puts down the blanket. A moment. Susan steps towards the television.)

SUSAN: We have to get the television fixed.

(Paul looks back. Maybe he'll say something. He changes his mind. She doesn't seem to notice he's leaving as she taps the remote. It's working again. We hear and see the Cooking King doing his opening.)

COOKING KING: Welcome to the Cooking Corner. I'm your host and your friend, The Cooking King.

(Paul is gone. She laughs with relief at the TV. She straightens her hair. The Cooking King takes off his chef's hat.)

COOKING KING: Today we're going to try something different. I know, I know, you love the Cooking King. As you should. But we're going for a whole new whoppin' might o' delight.

(Susan looks towards the door.)

You can do it.

(She turns back to the Cooking King and picks up her necklace.)

Now let's get back to business and . . .

(Susan hits "mute" on the remote, puts on her coat and moves towards the door. The Cooking King is left alone in silence continuing the program as the lights fade.)

END OF PLAY

Driving Green

Martin Blank

Driving Green was first produced by Journeymen Theater Ensemble (Krista Cowan, Interim Artistic Director; Andrew Wassenich, Producing Director) in Washington, D.C., premiering on July 10, 2009. Director: David E. Binet. Lighting Design: Chris Holland. Stage Manager:Shanice L. Jones. Cast: Tom — Slice Hicks; Beth — Jill Levin; Dale — Matt Dewberry.

For my wife Penny

CHARACTERS

TOM, thirties.

BETH, thirties.

DALE, a man or woman, could be any age.

TIME

Now.

SETTING

Car suggested by two chairs and a steering wheel/dashboard.

• • •

Lights up on married couple in a car suggested by two chairs and a steering wheel/dashboard. Tom in driver's seat wipes sweat from his forehead. Beth is immersed in The Washington Post.

TOM: This car is an oven. I'm burning up.

BETH: The windows are open.

TOM: I want to roll up them up. Turn on the —

BETH: *(Taking out calculator.)* Do you know what turning on the air conditioning would do to our carbon footprint?

TOM: I'm late for work every day because you insist on this sado-masochistic ride-sharing. When I'm late to work — yet again — I'll have to park blocks from work. I hate this hybrid. It cramps my legs.

BETH: A small price for driving green.

TOM: If anyone at work sees me in this car —

BETH: So, resign.

TOM: Quit NAP?

BETH: The National Association of Petroleum is destroying our planet. How do you sleep at night?

TOM: We don't just sleep . . .

BETH: *(Smiles.)* No. We don't.

TOM: Come on, traffic, move! Move!

BETH: Face it. We're not going anywhere.

TOM: I'm burning up.

BETH: It's global warming.

TOM: *(Mocking.)* Global warming is a fact?

BETH: Even you must know the P.R. you put out is delusional.

TOM: Delusional? Yeah? Well the people in your office are insane.

BETH: My associates are liberals.

TOM: They're stoned.

BETH: The men at NAP drink and go around with hookers.

TOM: We don't all drink.

BETH: You go around with hookers, then?

TOM: Of course not. I love you. Even if your shoes are made from recycled tires.

BETH: At least my feet aren't covered in dead cow.

TOM: I see. Rethinking our marriage?

BETH: I'm sure it's not worth talking about.

TOM: Not worth talking about?

BETH: I guess I could say something about the mail.

TOM: The mail?

BETH: Yes, the mail. I've tried to get us paperless. What mail does come you never put it in the same place twice. It could be anywhere. It's like an Easter egg hunt. I hate it when you get the mail before me. I have a system. Three categories, read now, read later, recycle now. With you, the important stuff gets lost. The junk stays around until Earth Day. Also, you write people letters, thereby killing trees. As well as the fossil fuel to transport it. Thus emitting greenhouse gases, unless, fingers crossed, the mail truck runs on hydrogen.

And I've actually seen you drive three blocks to the mailbox. Would it kill you to walk?

TOM: No. The mail. Is that it? I mean, don't you disdain my job and everything it represents? I work for the sole purpose of accumulating material things. Your Freegan pals are right in that my job is stressful, boring, and monotonous; unless, of course, a guy comes to work with a really good hooker story.

BETH: You are right to say some Freegans oppose working more hours than necessary to survive.

TOM: Great. Rationalized laziness.

BETH: To save the planet you have to start somewhere. The mail was as good a place as any.

TOM: *(Disingenuous.)* Then there is global warming to consider.

BETH: Goes without saying.

TOM: What about you?

BETH: Me?

TOM: Yes, you and your limousine liberal vegan friends, who preach tolerance, but won't tolerate an opinion other than their own. Trust fund twits bragging about investing in socially conscience mutual funds when they own stock in Exxon Mobil, buying green houses and driving sport utility vehicles. Balding husbands in painted tans, with multiple face lifts. Their wives drinking spinach smoothies, sitting around solar heated swimming pools, with silicon breast implants, a non-biodegradable product, made by Dow Chemical, the company which brought you napalm. With vegetarian teenage children sneaking McDonalds cheeseburgers, collecting money for Greenpeace, secretly hoping it will get them into Vassar. The family sitting around the dinner table eating pumpernickel bread, carrots, and turnips they found while dumpster diving, droning on about T. Boone Pickens and his plan. I say screw 'em. I want my meat cooked on a charcoal grill, rare. I want to drive a '60s muscle car and, when I floor it I can see the needle on the fuel gauge go down, down, down. I say live and live now. Because there's a good chance some crazy we pissed off at Gitmo is going to get his hands on a biological weapon or a dirty nuke and use it.

BETH: OK, some of the people we know are hypocrites, but many, many, let me finish, are not. What happened to doing the right thing? I know I can't control some fanatical group waving a giant mushroom cloud flag. I'm one person. So are you. And we can hope to make a difference. Do something everyday. Even if it's sharing a ride in a hybrid car. Or paying bills on line. If you've lost all hope, who are you and what have you done with the beautiful man I met in Ameri-Corps?

TOM: You really want to try to stop so-called global warming?

BETH: It's real. And I do.

TOM: Then we both know —

BETH: Don't you dare say it.

TOM: Wind, solar, bio, are a start . . .

BETH: You'll regret it!

TOM: If you can't stomach the truth . . .

BETH: The truth? The truth is I'm hot! I wish you could turn on the air conditioning.

TOM: Maybe I will.

BETH: Shut up. Fine. You win, turn on the A.C. Just don't say —

TOM: No, I'm gonna leave the windows open. So the entire world can hear.

BETH: Don't do it.

TOM: If global warming is real, and if it can be stopped . . .

BETH: I'll put on the radio really, really loud.

TOM: The radio uses power. What about our carbon footprint?

BETH: Drat!

TOM: If you want to save Mother Earth . . .

BETH: Please.

TOM: The only way to fully drive green is . . .

BETH: Don't say it!

TOM: . . . nuclear power.

(Beth pounds Tom's head on dash/steering wheel — with next five words.)

BETH: Never. Say. Those. Words. Again.

(Pause, Tom tries to recover.)

TOM: I think you cracked the GPS.

(Dale, in a blue blazer, enters.)

DALE: Excuse me. There were several loud, violent noises. Is everything OK?

TOM: Fine.

BETH: Fine, thank you.

DALE: Perhaps you'd like to take the Prius off the showroom floor for a test drive?

TOM: Oh no. We're doing our test now.

BETH: To see if it stands up to our morning routine.

DALE: Well, when you get the car on the road . . .

TOM: Look, can you give us a moment?

DALE: *(Sensing a sale, quickly leaves.)* Certainly. I'll be at my desk when you need me.

(Tom and Beth are now alone.)

BETH: Energy waster!

TOM: You know what you can do with your carbon calculator?

BETH: I want a divorce! TOM: I want a divorce!

(Pause. Stony silence. Then, both smile.)

BETH: I don't really. TOM: I don't really.

BETH: Shall we buy the car?

(They kiss. Blackout.)

END OF PLAY

The End of a Perfect Game

Jay Rehak

The End of a Perfect Game was first performed at the Mile Square Theatre in Hoboken, New Jersey, on March 14, 2009. Director: Sturgis Warner. Cast: Al "Trainwreck" Sexton — Thom Rivera; Willy Morris — Jon Levinson; Lou Pascal — Gilbert Cruz; Umpire — Sturgis Warner.

CHARACTERS

AL "TRAINWRECK" SEXTON, major league pitcher.
WILLY MORRIS, major league catcher.
LOU PASCAL, the manager.
UMPIRE.
TWO OFF-STAGE ANNOUNCERS.

SETTING

The pitcher's mound during the final pitch of the World Series.

• • •

Scene: In darkness, two radio announcers set the scene.

ANNOUNCER #1: So it all comes down to this: The final game of the World Series, in the final inning of a 1-0 ballgame. After eight and two-thirds innings in which he hasn't allowed anyone to reach base, the veteran Al "Trainwreck" Sexton, after throwing two quick strikes to pinch hitter Jake "The Pounder" Johnson, has suddenly thrown three consecutive pitches nowhere near the strike zone. So close he can taste it, and yet . . .

ANNOUNCER #2: Looks like the pressure's getting to him. Marv. This close to history, it looks like "Trainwreck" is sliding off the rails.

ANNOUNCER #1: Certainly looks like it. One more wild one, and the Braves will have their first base runner and the you-know-what will be destroyed. Worse yet, if Sexton grooves one, it's a tie ball game. And over the years, The Pounder has had Sexton's number, hitting a hefty .521 lifetime against him. Time out has been called, and the catcher, Willy Morris, is strolling out to the mound. What do you think he's going to say to him, Monty?

ANNOUNCER #2: He'll probably go out and make small talk with him, because in the great baseball tradition, Marv, he's not going to talk about the fact that Al's pitching a . . .

ANNOUNCER #1: Don't say it, Monty, you'll jinx it.

ANNOUNCER #2: I'm not saying anything about the you-know-what, Marv, and I'm sure Morris won't talk about it either; he's just going to go out there and talk about the weather and do whatever it takes to try and calm down his pitcher.

Scene: Lights up as Al "Freight Train" Sexton stands on a pitcher's mound, center, as Willy Morris, in catcher's gear, strolls to the mound, mask up.

WILLY: How you doin', Al?

AL: I'm so tired, it's hard to think straight.

WILLY: Yeah, I'm tired, too.

AL: Really? You're not just saying that to make me feel better?

WILLY: No, man, I'm telling you. It's been a long season, plus there's a lot going on in the world right now. Wars in the Middle East, global warming, a broken health care system . . . there's a lot of stuff to keep you up at night.

AL: Exactly! Damn, Willy, I'm glad you're my catcher. Something I got to talk to you about.

WILLY: Really? You and Carmen doin' all right?

AL: Oh, yeah. We're all right. I mean, we have our ups and downs like everyone. Here's the thing, though. Last night, we're laying there, about three in the morning, and she turns to me and says, "Hey, Willy, do you think God exists?"

WILLY: And you said?

AL: "Yeah, sure, now go to sleep."

WILLY: OK.

AL: She says, "How do you know?" And I mumble back surely there's a God because look at all the flowers and sunsets and smiling little kids, all that sweet shit. Then I roll over and try to get back to sleep.

WILLY: Understandable. You're pitching a big game today.

AL: That's what I'm thinking, right? And then she says, "Well, if you believe God exists, don't you think you should be leading a purposeful life?"

WILLY: What's that supposed to mean?

AL: I asked her the same thing and two and a half hours later we were still stuck in this deep philosophical argument about doing something with our lives.

WILLY: Meaning?

AL: Meaning, according to her, maybe we should all be working towards a cure for cancer or teaching inner city kids how to read or working to end homelessness.

WILLY: Aw, come on. She ambushes you with that in the middle of the friggin' night, right before the biggest game of your life?

AL: That's what I said. I said, "Carmen, can't this wait?" And she said,

"Pitching in the World Series doesn't give you license to blow off the big questions."

WILLY: Wow.

AL: And I'm standing up here now, realizing she was right.

(Enter Umpire.)

UMPIRE: OK, you guys want to break it up here?

WILLY: Give us a minute, would you?

UMPIRE: Yeah, that's all you got. You've been standing around here for two minutes already. The only reason I've given you this long is because he's pitching a . . .

WILLY: Don't say it.

UMPIRE: *(Walks off.)* I'm not going to say it. What do you think, I was born yesterday?

WILLY: Hence the last three wild pitches.

AL: Hence the last three wild pitches. I mean, what am I doing with my life, here, Willy, standing on a hill trying to get grown men to hit a ball into someone else's leather. What kind of a life is that?

WILLY: I don't know. It's a damn good living.

AL: But is that enough?

WILLY: It's pretty close . . .

AL: Look, Willy, if I strike this guy out right now, you know what it means. For the rest of my life where ever I go I'll be known as the guy who pitched a __________ game in the seventh game of the World Series.

WILLY: That's true.

AL: Big deal! So what? Is that who I am? Is this really the defining moment of my life?

When I meet my maker is he going to reach out, pat me on the ass and say "Great game?" or is he going to say, "I gave you all this talent and all you could do was throw a ball around."

WILLY: You're right, Al. That's a lot to consider. But how about this: you strike this guy out; we win the World Series, and you go off and do something good with your fame.

AL: Too late! The question's been asked. I've got to answer it now. It's a cop out for me to get purposeless fame first and then use it for good. Got to do it now, Willy. This is my moment of decision. I say I walk this guy and prove to God that I'm serious about leading a purposeful life. Am I right or am I right?

WILLY: I don't know, Al. That seems kind of extreme.

AL: Remember, this is my soul we're talking about here.
WILLY: I understand. It's a big decision.
UMPIRE: *(Returning.)* What do you think, fellas?
WILLY: What do you think, Al?
AL: No, I already told you what I think. Tell me what you think.
WILLY: OK, Al, but I think he was asking us if we wanted to make a pitching change.
AL: Forget that for a second. This is important. Answer me.
WILLY: I don't think God wants you to walk the guy.
AL: You're not just saying that to make me feel better?
WILLY: No, straight up. That's what I feel.
UMPIRE: Fascinating. But what's it going to be, fellas?
WILLY: On the other hand, this is your soul we're talking about, so I'm not going to make the call. *(Willy waves to the dugout.)* Maybe I'm wrong and we should make a pitching change.
UMPIRE: You guys are stalling.
WILLY: We should probably ask Lou what he thinks.
AL: Oh, come on, don't get him involved. He's no help. He's just going to come out here and tell me it's my call.

(Enter Lou.)

LOU: What the hell's going on?
UMPIRE: What do you want to do, Lou? Take him out?
LOU: *(To Ump.)* Give me a minute, would you?
UMPIRE: Yeah, and then I want an answer. We've got to get this game going.
LOU: I know, I know. But you do understand what the magnitude of what this guy's about to accomplish?
UMPIRE: Yeah, yeah. I understand. Just make a decision. We haven't got all day.
LOU: Don't worry about it. It gives the TV stations a chance to run a couple more commercials.
UMPIRE: Hurry it up, Lou.
LOU: OK, Bill.

(Umpire walks off.)

Is this son of a bitch deliberately throwing wild pitches?

WILLY: He's in crisis, Lou. Not sure he's leading a purposeful life.
LOU: Oh, come on. With one more pitch to go? Now?
AL: Why not now?
LOU: Oh, for Christ's sake . . . Of all the times . . .

AL: If not now, when?

LOU: Oh, I don't know. How about immediately after the game?

AL: This is important, Lou. A defining moment in my life.

LOU: One more pitch, Al, one more pitch.

AL: What if he fouls it off?

LOU: Well, I'd say stick around and throw another pitch but that's just me.

AL: I'm tired, Lou.

LOU: Oh, hell, Al. Who isn't? I went out last night and I must have swallowed a quart of scotch. I woke up this morning with two heavy metal bands playing inside of my head. Neither one of them any good.

AL: Yeah, Lou. I hear you. But I'm a different kind of tired. It's not one that comes from drinking too much scotch. It's something deeper. I'm standing here, in front of fifty thousand people, and I can't figure out if I give a shit or not. I mean, if I strike this guy out, or if he hits a home run off of me, what difference does it make? Does it really change the world? I mean, in the end, who cares?

LOU: Well, right now, I'm going to say about fifty thousand people in the immediate proximity, and probably a couple million more in the TV viewing area. But that's just a rough estimate.

WILLY: I think what's he's saying here, Lou, is he's lost his purpose, his raison d'être, if you will.

LOU: Look. You think I don't wake up night after night staring at my hands, trying to figure out what it's all about? You think you're the only guy on the planet who questions his existence?

AL: No.

LOU: Well, then, snap out of it, man. You're not the only one. We're all just a bunch of scared microbes making shit up as we go along so it'll all make some kind of sense. Now forget all that and focus. We've got a game to win here and you've got a chance to do something special.

AL: Special? What's so special about winning a baseball game?

LOU: Oh, for God's sake. OK, in the grand scheme of things, it's not so special. It's not healing the sick, it's not teaching inner city school kids to read, but it is something special in its own way.

AL: Do you hear yourself, Lou? Putting throwing a . . .

WILLY AND LOU: *(Coughing loudly.)* Don't say it!!!

AL: . . . with doing something great! *(To Willy.)* Listen to this guy.

WILLY: Evidently, baseball is very important to him.

LOU: Well, pardon me, if that makes me some kind of a freak.

WILLY: Cool down, Lou.

LOU: What, because I care about this team, and winning the World Series for this city makes me some kind of a whack job, is that what you're saying, Al? Because if it is, I swear to God, I'll take you out right now and have the GM put you on waivers.

UMPIRE: Gentlemen, it's time.

AL: Here, take the ball.

LOU: He's kidding me, right?

WILLY: He wants out, Lou.

UMPIRE: You calling for the righty or the lefty?

LOU: Help me out here, Willy.

WILLY: OK, Al. How about this? You throw one last pitch. Groove it to him. Let God decide. If he hits a home run, so what?

LOU: They tie the game.

WILLY: If you strike him out . . .

AL: So what?

LOU: We win the game.

AL: I don't know. I think I'll hate myself if I throw the pitch. If I had any moral fiber, I'd walk off the field right now. What would you do, if you were me, Willy?

WILLY: Oh, hell. I'd throw the pitch as hard and fast as I could and hope to God the guy strikes out. I'm not saying it's right. Maybe I'm a soulless, moral coward. But that's just me.

AL: Well, I'm stuck. I need you to tell me what you think *I* should do.

WILLY: It's not my call, it's up to Lou.

AL: Fine, it's up to Lou. Am I out or in, Lou?

LOU: I like everything you guys are saying, except the part about grooving it to him.

WILLY: That's his last best offer, Lou. So what do you think?

LOU: You know what, I'm leaving it up to Al.

AL: See? What'd I tell you?

WILLY: You were right.

UMPIRE: It's time.

AL: Give me the ball.

LOU: All right!

UMPIRE: Play ball!

(Umpire, Lou and Willy leave the stage.)

ANNOUNCER #1: All right, Monty. This is it. Discussion's over. Looks like Lou's finally calmed Trainwreck down.

ANNOUNCER #2: I'm not so sure, Marv. Sexton still looks agitated to me. It's as if he can't believe he's on the precipice of greatness. One more successful pitch and he goes down in history.

ANNOUNCER #1: Right. But one bad pitch and he's a guy no one will remember. We all know he wants it. The question is, does he have it in him?

ANNOUNCER #2: I'm sure that's what he's asking himself right now.

AL: *(Yelling in the direction of the off-stage batter.)* I'm throwing it right down the middle. You hear me, Johnson. It's going straight down the middle.

ANNOUNCER #1: Did you hear that, Monty?

ANNOUNCER #2: I sure did, Marv. Crazy as it sounds, Trainwreck's taunting The Pounder with what he's going to do. Now that's confidence!

ANNOUNCER #1: He must be trying to add to his legend.

ANNOUNCER #2: Well, if he gets this one by The Pounder, Trainwreck'll be talked about forever. But I've got to tell you, Monty, Johnson sure looks locked in.

(Al winds up and throws the ball off stage.)

ANNOUNCER #1: Here's the windup, and the pitch . . . And The Pounder just looks at strike three! The fans are going wild.

ANNOUNCER #2: The man's a legend! The man's a legend!

ANNOUNCER #1: Al "Trainwreck" Sexton drops to his knees, overcome with joy. Willy Morris rushes out to be the first to congratulate him.

(Despite the announcer's interpretation, Al looks stricken and Willy seems to the audience to be consoling him.)

ANNOUNCER #2: It's a perfect game! A perfect game! The man's a legend!

ANNOUNCER #1 & #2: The man's a legend! The man's a legend! The man's a legend!

(Al is on his knees bawling like a baby as lights fade.)

(Curtain.)

END OF PLAY

For Our Mothers and Fathers

Crystal Skillman

For Our Mothers and Fathers was commissioned by Stella Adler Studio and developed in part with the support of Voice & Vision Theater at the 2009 Envision Retreat for Women Theatre Artists at Bard College. It was produced August 6–7, 2009 by the Teenage Conservatory, Stella Adler Studio (31 West 27th Street, New York, New York). Director: Melissa Ross. Cast: Max — Alice Oshima; Lil — Naomi Boyce; Donya — Liz Lukasiewicz. Special thanks to Megan E. Carter, Julie Crosby, Allison Prouty and the Women's Project Playwrights Lab for their support.

For Mom and Pop Skillman

Characters

Max, sharp, a natural kind of anxiously putting down everything. Bass. Sixteen.

Lil, whimsical, all over the place, hates conflict, loves rhyming. Drums. Seventeen.

Donya, seemingly confident and cool, but has her own fears for sure. Guitar. Fifteen.

Time

Now.

Setting

All Girls Rock Camp in the wilderness — Hocking Hills of Ohio.

Punctuation & Beats

-. = character cutting themselves off

— = character being cut off

. . . = trail off

Beats are small, never pauses you can drive a truck through.

Note about Song

Actors are encouraged to come up with their own melody for the song at the end. It should sound raw and new, full of potential, but doesn't need to sound polished. If instruments are unavailable to use as props, Max can be listing to her ipod and writing down song lyrics. When Donya meets them, she can take out a piece of paper with what she's worked on so far. At the end they could sing a cappella, and the final moment could be them writing down the lyrics they've just come up with.

• • •

Sound of strumming. Lights up on the woods. Max is strumming an electric guitar with headphones plugged into a teeny amp. She might be muttering lyrics she's working out. Her T-shirt says: It's Not Me, It's You *and with her American Apparel knee highs and army shorts, bent over, intense, she's a sight sitting on a log.*

LIL: Max? Max . . . Max!

(Lil appears on a path. Max still doesn't see or hear her. Lil jumps in front of her.)

Hey!

MAX: *(Jumping.)* Lil — what the hell. I'm writing.

(Lil starts laughing.)

What?

LIL: Just looking at you — and those knee highs. Don't move.

(Saying Jesus out of habit, but stopping herself trying not to use the "Lord's name in vain":)

Jesu- . Seriously this is.

(Lil takes out her phone.)

MAX: What?

LIL: *(Taking her picture.)* I'm totally putting this on Facebook.

MAX: What's the caption? Yeah, I know.

(Lil laughs harder.)

"Girls Rock Camp out in the Hocking Hills of Ohio turns just turned sixteen-year-old Maxine Singer into a lunatic." Funny. I'm working. And we're supposed to embrace the big outdoors — inspiration.

LIL: But we're supposed to be inspired by what's around us. The birds and shit. That's why we're here right? I mean what if a bear came up behind you or something?

MAX: The bears are on the other side.

LIL: Well you wouldn't hear them and — You've seen *Grizzly Man.*

(Looking around.)

There are really bears?

MAX: Oh yeah, Lil — tons.

LIL: No shit. They like stay over there right? I mean they're slow, or tired from hibernating.

MAX: Just like when we go into town and order something.

LIL: What do you mean?

MAX: How everyone seems a little "touched." Takes forever on line. Like that woman ringing us at the Mart when we got a ride into town. That slow down-home timing. Even upstate New York, this whole year, it's been like hell.

LIL: It can't be that bad.

MAX: You weren't dragged out of Brooklyn. You're still a Park Sloper while in my world it's *(Imitating how long it takes to ring something up.)* One potato, two potato.

LIL: Max.

MAX: I can't help it — my bass heart is always ticking. And there are two types of people in this world — those that move and those who don't. Who just —

LIL: Jesu-.

(Beat. Lil just stands there, looking down.)

MAX: Do you want something *Lilith?*

LIL: Yes, *Maxine,* we're supposed to sign up with what we're going to play tonight.

MAX: That stupid like end of camp variety show at the pavilion for all the parents who have nothing better than to do than to drag their asses to Ohio?

LIL: Hey — my mom gets enough jokes about her fat ass. But seriously — what are we-?

MAX: No way. Forget it.

LIL: I thought you had a new song.

MAX: I might if I was left alone to be inspired.

LIL: We didn't form Dolphin and Porpoise to leave each other alone.

MAX: Shark. Dolphin and Shark. And it's gonna change because it's stupid.

LIL: We've had it forever. And we should keep it — animal names for bands are hot right now.

The Unicorns, Grizzly Bear, Wolf Parade —

MAX: I came up with it when I was like ten.

LIL: *We* did. *We* came up with it.

MAX: We did.

LIL: Band members don't keep secrets, Maxie. So if you're having trouble —

MAX: I'm not having trouble. I don't need help. And I'm not a cat, so don't call me —

LIL: Maxie — what's wrong with you? All day you've been like *(Imitates her.)*

MAX: I just need to be alone for a sec, OK?

LIL: OK. Jesu-.

MAX: And what is that, you keep doing that.

LIL: My dad came back. You know that. Was just trying to watch my language that's all.

MAX: Great, you were always a nut but now you're a religious nut like him.

LIL: I'm not a nut! I just don't want to make baby Jesus cry.

MAX: *(Genuine outburst.)* Christ.

(Lil stares at her.)

Sorry. Really. I just want to work thru this thing. OK?

LIL: OK.

(Beat.)

Did you see the skunks? They're like everywhere, on the sidewalk, like nibbling at the grass.

(Max puts her music back on, her headphones to drown Lil out. Lil doesn't notice, keeps talking, drumming on stuff while she does.)

Did you hear Bobby today when we were going over progressions? Going on and on about them. The skunks. Man Bobby, he's . . .

(Laughs.)

He's totally freaked out about them, when he sees them walks around. Like they're going to spray him. Ohhh, I'm scared. I'm scared of a little fuzzy black and white fuzzy lolloping towards a firefly. Stupid. Skunks. I think it's mating season. They're so cute. I love them! We should write a song about them for tonight! Yeah, *Skunky Skunk. Ska-ska-skunky skunk.* Or maybe that's what we should call our band! The Skunks. Nasty, awesome. Yeah, right?

What if I liked Bobby, do you think that's stupid? Right. It's stupid. Yeah.

(Sees Max has put her headphones on.)

Hey. HEY!

MAX: What?

LIL: Whatever.

(Turns to go, then turns back.)

Just because you made me eat worms when I was six doesn't mean you can make me feel like shit now.

MAX: Look, I didn't mean to —

LIL: It's just — just —

MAX: Just?

LIL: Since you moved upstate, we don't have much time to —

MAX: A few years and we'll be together at Oberlin anyway. I mean we have a plan.

LIL: I'm just saying we're lucky we have the summer.

MAXINE: What do you mean? Lil.

LIL: Just tell me what we're playing — I'll leave you alone, put us on the list. OK?

(Sound of something in the woods. They both jump.).

MAXINE: Holy fuck.

LIL: You heard it too!

MAXINE: Yeah.

LIL: Do you think it's a bear?

MAXINE: It's probably just a chipmunk.

(Another louder sound.)

A big ass chipmunk.

LIL: You said the bears were on the other side.

MAXINE: Shut up!

LIL: *(Whimpering.)* My mom was right. Nature does want you dead.

(Rustling. Maxine lifts up her guitar. Donya enters, carrying her guitar case. Lil and Max both stare at her.)

DONYA: Sorry. Didn't know anyone was —

(Lil and Max crack up.)

I should play this swamp more often.

MAX: Sorry we just thought —

LIL: You were a "Big Ass Chipmunk"

(Then as if inspired.)

Hey — that could be our new name!

DONYA: I see you guys are working hard.

MAX: Donya, right?

DONYA: Yeah.

MAX: I remember your nametag that first day where we had to write our obsessions below our names. The one who likes Hendrix?

DONYA: Is there anyone who doesn't like Hendrix?

(To Lil:)

You're the one that listens to like forties show tunes in the closet.

LIL: Lil. Seriously, don't tell anyone about the show tunes, OK. I have a rep.

DONYA: *(Saying hi to Max.)* And you're —

LIL: Oh this? This thing here is Max, King of the Beasts.

MAX: And I didn't write shit on my nametag because those exercises are stupid.

(Awkward moment — Lil jumps in.)

LIL: You playing for the show tonight?

DONYA: I don't know. I don't have anything yet lyric wise, just a little . . . Can I . . . ?

(Max gives her guitar.)

DONYA: *(Does a quick melody line.)* Da Da, Da Da

LIL: Nice. Nice. Maybe there you —

(Adds to it a bit.)

De De De Do

DONYA: *(Thinking.)* Maybe.

(Liking it.)

Yeah, maybe.

MAX: Yeah, if you want it to sound like everything else around.

(Lil looks a bit upset, Donya looks at Max.)

What?

DONYA: So what are you working on?

MAX: A masterpiece.

DONYA: No pressure there. What's it called?

MAX: "Alone, all alone, how I enjoy writing Alone."

DONYA: I get it. I'm just going back to the cabin anyway.

LIL: Donya, don't. She's just being — wait. Wait. I got something in town. Wait.

(Takes a Jack Daniels bottle out of her bag.)

DONYA: Woooahhh. Nice.

MAX: You can't use the Lord's name in vain but you can get bombed.

LIL: It's how the best sermons get written. My dad told me.

(Lil swigs right out of the bottle. Max and Donya are saying things like "Whoahh" and "that's crazy".)

LIL: Oh god — I think my throat's on fire.

(Offers to Donya who swigs. Donya offers to Max. Max shakes her head no — looks at Lil who looks a little sheepish, then just turns to Donya.).

LIL: *(Continued.)* You're from around here?

DONYA: Just a little town. Chagrin Falls. It's like a retarded Bedford Falls. You know — *It's a Wonderful Life*? That movie about angels and bars or something?

LIL: *(Clearly not getting it but still saying:)* Right.

DONYA: Anyway, where I am is all like old timey shops and — and I'm just glad not to be to be wearing some dumb ass catholic school uniform or stuck home or working at Wendys. You guys from New York?

LIL: Brooklyn.

MAX: Used to be Brooklyn. Now — glorious Woodstock.

DONYA: Right. That was your mom who talked to us today.

MAX: Right.

(Max grabs the bottle and drinks — faster and more than the others.)

DONYA: My mom loved all her shit. Tanya Singer this, Tanya Singer that. Had like all her records.

MAX: *(Trying to hold it in.)* Cool.

DONYA: It must be weird having her being our guest artist.

MAX: Why would that be weird? Why would it be weird that my old rocker mom and her one hit wonder ass is so cheap she gets me into this camp by saying she'll spend one of our lovely two weeks here with us lovely children learning ye old rock and totally humiliate me with her absolute revolting breath of Absolut Vodka.

LIL: She did seem a little loopy.

MAX: Ya think? What was the hint — when she couldn't remember the cords to "Yesterday" or when she put her head down on the table and was like lying there snoring for an hour.

DONYA: It was really just like a minute.

MAX: If an eternity is sixty seconds, then you would be correct.

DONYA: Look, I'm sorry —

MAX: You should be because you don't know shit.

DONYA: Look, maybe I should —

MAX: No really. Do you know it's the one person like your mom who buys all my mom's stupid fucking songs that fucks her up. Because she's got it in her head that people still want to listen to her has-been stuff, but they don't — not really. Most of them don't anymore. So — you, the only child accidental result of haziness after some gig, wakes her up at noon, and tries to make something of it. Use it. And you write and write in the middle of nowhere on some stupid log but nothing's coming and even though you don't care what your mom thinks you care and she's going to be there tonight and expecting — actually — thinking — . Like you have talent or something. But you don't. You don't have shit.

LIL: Max. Jesu-.

MAX: Just say it. Say what you want to say. Lil.

LIL: What do you care if I'm trying —

MAX: To what? Find God? Suck up to the so called father who leaves you and your mom to find himself every October and comes back every July and you act like nothing's happened. You keep that up when we get to Oberlin and I'm not even going to —

LIL: I'm not going to Oberlin. I'm graduating early and going to Berkeley next year. I got the letter today. My mom sent it up here.

MAX: But we decided.

LIL: You decided. You always decide. Write the songs, freak out with your bullshit. And I'm over it Max. Because it's not us — it's you. It's your shit you have to work through. But you can't because you try to hole yourself up, block everything out. And the only *we* there is is me trying to tell you but you never listen. You never . . . I want something that's mine. Max. We can visit each other. Max.

MAX: I just want to sit here. I want to write. Finish something. And I just want something to fucking — to fucking last.

(Beat.)

DONYA: They used to call me Rabbit because I used to try to run away all the time. Like since I was five. Just get the fuck out of my shit town where everyone looks like me and no one, no one is like me. When we applied here I was like — this is it. Just turned fifteen. Practically half my life if I died at forty like my cancer-ridden dad so I thought this would be it. Pack for two weeks? I packed *everything*. And when I was like zipping up my bag I couldn't stop crying. My mom, saw me like that, and we barely talked, she was so soft or something and would just do what he said and then when he was gone, she wouldn't do anything really. If I was a rabbit, she was a mouse. Small to me. The morning I woke up to get the bus to come here — I saw it there on my empty dresser — this old black and white photo — a girl about fifteen in this skimpy outfit in front of some tent — and there's like animals in the background and people juggling pins and it's like clear it's some kind of circus. And I know those eyes. It's my mom. My mom. On the back, in this script — her name and the year. She came in the doorway and told me that's when she started to run away. And I was like why didn't you stay and she smiled this weird smile and I liked that it was soft, quiet and she said because she met my dad and wanted to have me.

And all that I felt in me made sense. And I knew what it was like to want to stay. Because I do feel like that when I write songs — like a part of me is running away and I want to catch her. If it's good I do.

(Beat. Then Lil starts to hum the melody line she did with Donya before. Donya joins in [could use her guitar if she has one] Max looks at them, then joins in on her bass. Lil softly drums on whatever is around.)

MAX: *So much I want to say to you*
Can't stop crying
Little rabbit, little mouse

DONYA: *In our tent, our little house*

LIL: *Why do you stay?*

MAX: *When a part of me is always running away . . .*

MAX WITH DONYA AND LIL: *(Joining in.) When a part of me is always running away . . .*

DONYA: *So much I want to be for you*
Stead of drinking
stead of crying, being brave

LIL: *In our house, our little cave*

MAX: *If I can stay*
When a part of you is always running away . . .

MAX WITH DONYA AND LIL: *(Joining in.) When a part of you is always running away . . .*

(They softly end. All look at each other.)

DONYA: That was . . .

MAX: Lil . . . Will you sign the three of us up?

LIL: Yeah, yeah. Name?

MAX: I don't why but I think something like . . . "For Our Mothers and Fathers" I mean only if you all think it's —

(Donya nods. Lil does too. Then gets up, as she's going:)

LIL: Be right back!

(Donya and Max look at each other.)

MAX: Ready?

(They strum.)

(Blackout.)

END OF PLAY

The Godot Variations

MERON LANGSNER

The complete version of *The Godot Variations* by Meron Langsner was presented at Christian Herter Park in Brighton, Massachusetts, as part of Orfeo Group's *Preludes* to their production of *The Complete Works of William Shakespeare (abridged)* in the summer of 2009. Director: David Gram. Cast for *Waiters for Godot*: Becky — Liza Burns; Sammy — Paul Cereghino. Cast for *Call Waiting for Godot*: Rags — Jon Bass; Vlad — Paul Cereghino. Cast for *Whining for Godot*: Didi — Liza Burns; Gogo — Andrew Gruen; Bozo/Lackey — Mark Villanueva.

Each section had previously been produced independently at the following venues. *Whining for Godot*: Harold Clurman Theatre, 42nd St., New York, New York; 1998 Samuel French Short Play Festival, City Theater, Wilmington, Delaware; SLAMBoston, Another Country Productions, Devanaughn Theatre, Boston, Massachusetts; Last Frontier Fringe Festival, Valdez, AK; Polaris North, W. 29th St., NYC; Imagined Reality One Act Festival, Space@24, New York, New York; Jewish Theatrical Project at New York University. *Waiters for Godot*: *Gone in 60 Seconds*, Harrogate Theatre, North Yorkshire, England; LamiaInk! One Page Play Festival, New York, New York. *Call Waiting for Godot*: *Gone in 60 Seconds*, Brooklyn College, Brooklyn, New York.

CHARACTERS

Variation #1 — Waiters for Godot:

SAMMY, a waiter.

BECKY, another waiter.

MANAGER

Variation #2 — Call Waiting for Godot:

VLAD

RAGS

Variation #3 — Whining for Godot:

DIDI, one of a pair of relentless whiners.

GOGO, the other one.

BOZO/LACKEY, played by one actor. Bozo does not whine, Lackey does not speak.

GODOT, does not keep appointments very well. To be played either by the same actor playing Bozo/Lackey or by a child.

• • •

VARIATION #1 — WAITERS FOR GODOT

Sammy and Becky are standing near an elegantly set table near a large potted plant.

SAMMY: Any word on when he'll get here?

BECKY: Who?

SAMMY: The VIP. Mr. Godot.

BECKY: No, but he still has a reservation.

SAMMY: He had one yesterday too. And the day before. He's five hours late.

BECKY: Maybe we can get another section till he gets here. Work before closing.

SAMMY: We're waiters for Godot. We'll watch his table till he gets here.

BECKY: Do you think everything is right for him?

SAMMY: We moved the tree to his table, just like he wanted.

BECKY: What do you think the tree is for?

SAMMY: Who knows. We just do whatever Mr. Godot says.

BECKY: Do you think it will get us anywhere?

SAMMY: What will?
BECKY: Being waiters for Godot?
SAMMY: Who knows. Who knows anything?
MANAGER: *(Entering.)* — You two can close up. Mr. Godot isn't coming today. Maybe tomorrow.
SAMMY: But he said today!
BECKY: We're his waiters!
SAMMY: Waiters for Godot! He said he'd come!
MANAGER: Come back tomorrow. He reserved his table for tomorrow.
BECKY: Let's go.
SAMMY: Yes.
(They do not move.)

VARIATION #2 — CALL WAITING FOR GODOT

Vlad is on the phone. Rags is watching him. Silence.

RAGS: Any answer yet.
VLAD: Nothing yet.
RAGS: What are you listening to?
VLAD: A recording. Muzak.
RAGS: Let me listen.
VLAD: Why?
RAGS: It will pass the time.
VLAD: Very well. *(He passes the receiver over.)*
RAGS: The muzak is nice.
VLAD: It is.
RAGS: There is a recording.
VLAD: There is.
RAGS: With a message.
VLAD: Yes.
RAGS: It says that our call is very important to them.
VLAD: I should hope so.
RAGS: The Godot Corporation believes in the highest standard of customer service.
VLAD: That's reassuring.
RAGS: Operators are standing by! We are saved!
VLAD: Excellent!

RAGS: Our call will be answered in the order it was received! Surely we were among the first.

VLAD: There must be many calls.

RAGS: Yes, many.

VLAD: Let me listen! *(He grabs the receiver and listens.)* No!

RAGS: What has happened?

VLAD: Due to high volume of calls, we will not be answered. We should try again tomorrow.

RAGS: We should hang up.

VLAD: We should.

(They do not move.)

VARIATION #3 — WHINING FOR GODOT

The scene is familiar; a road, a tree.

GOGO: I caan't get this booot offf!

DIDI: Then how come you always put it back ooon?

GOGO: Help me with this. Pull haaarder.

(At some point during the pulling of the boot Didi stops, notices that the laces are still tied, and makes a point of untying them before continuing to pull.)

DIDI: There it's off. Owwww. I think I hurt myself. Your feet smell, put it baaack ooon.

GOGO: Shuut uup, so does your breath.
WHENNN IS HE GONNNA COOOOME?

DIDI: I don't know. He said he'd be here already. WHHYY DO WE HAVE TO WAAAIT?

GOGO: Let's go then.

DIDI: Noooo. We have to waait, remember?

GOGO: I don't wannna beee heeeere. Why do we have to waaait?

DIDI: He should be here.

GOGO: Wait! There's someone coming!

(Bozo enters.)

DIDI: We're saved! Is it him ?

BOZO: Yes! It is I.

DIDI: Ohh noo, it's not him.

BOZO: I am the great Bozo!

GOGO: Why do we have this conversation every daaay?

BOZO: Because masochists are easy to please. What happened to your friend's foot?

DIDI: We're not sure but it was in the original script.

BOZO: I see. No telling what it is then. Interesting though, very interesting. Now then, what brings the two of you here?

(The following sequence is delivered mostly in quick deadpan until it finally degenerates into a whinefest.)

GOGO: We're waiting.

DIDI: Patiently.

GOGO: For our salvation.

DIDI: With neither complaint.

GOGO: Nor question.

DIDI: Nor common sense.

GOGO: Not even a linear plotline.

DIDI: Knowing he'll be here any second.

GOGO: Minute.

DIDI: Hour.

GOGO: To save us.

DIDI: To deliver us.

GOGO: To tell us what the deal is with the boots.

DIDI: And the tree.

GOGO: And why Irish people would choose to write in French.

DIDI: Yeah, if you really want to make a statement Gaelic is the way to go.

GOGO: So we stay by this tree and wait.

(The whining begins.)

DIDI: Whhhy do we haave to waaait?

GOGO: He said he'd bee heeere.

DIDI & GOGO TOGETHER: WHEN IS HE GONNNA COOOME?

(Beat.)

BOZO: Sorry I asked.

DIDI: Do you know when he's gonna come?

BOZO: Can't say I do. Listen, I'm sure I have something much more important to do.

DIDI: Are you going to go look for Lackey? We're going to have a hard time destroying this script without him.

BOZO: No. Lucy. She's new. I'm hoping to get lucky.

DIDI: We'll believe that when you get it on tape.

GOGO: Yeah, sounds like Krapp to me.

(Didi and Gogo high five.)

BOZO: First of all, you're starting to butcher the wrong script, second of all, that's a pretty pretentious and obscure comment from a couple slobs who wait around by a tree every day just to get stood up. Now if you'll excuse me, I'm going to go look for Lucy.
Farewell.

DIDI: Goodbye.

GOGO: Bye bye. That certainly passed the time.

DIDI: As if it wouldn't pass anyway.

GOGO: Stooop, you know what I meean. Why do we always have to get philosophical?

DIDI: Whhy can't you just pretend this is all very profound like everyone else?

GOGO: 'Cause nothing ever reaaally happens.

(Lackey walks quickly into the space. He is nervous and very twitchy, he should have completely different physical mannerisims than Bozo. He stops in front of Gogo, looks around, kicks him in the shins and exits.)

DIDI: And you say nothing ever happens.

GOGO: Owwwww! Why'd he doo thaat? I thought Bozo liked me.

DIDI: That wasn't Bozo that was Lackey.

GOGO: If I had any luck at all it would have been Lucy.

DIDI: No, it would have been Godot.

GOGO: I'mmmm sick of this. It's so aaabsurd. Why are we stilll waaiting?

DIDI: You're right. I think we should go.

GOGO: Are you suuure? What if he coooomes and weee're not heeere?

DIDI: He never coomes. Sometimes I think that's the point. It's all some sick joke!

GOGO: Let's go then!

DIDI: Yes!

GOGO: Are you sure?

DIDI: I think so.

GOGO: Lets go.

DIDI: Yes.

(Beat.)

(They go.)

(Beat.)

(Godot enters, he is a little bashful.)

GODOT: Hello? Didi? Gogo? It's me . . . Godot.

(He looks around.)

(Beat.)

Why didn't they waaaait?

END OF PLAY

Hands of Horror

A DISTINCTLY AMERICAN TALE

Ann Marie Healy

Originally produced through Theatre Masters at The Rattlestick Theater in New York, New York, in May of 2009. Artistic Director: Julia Hansen. Director: Andrew Volkoff.

CHARACTERS

TINNY MCGEE, a dame who has lived and learned some.

ROGER DAPPER, runs a small import/export piano supply super store. Or does he?

MAN IN A GROUCHO MARX MASK, Yes, as you might imagine, a Man in a Groucho Marx Mask.

SETTING AND TIME

The play is set in our memories of an older, darker and much more entertaining version of New York City.

• • •

Tinny stands alone in a pool of light. Does a saxophone play?

OLDER TINNY: Back then, I was as new to the city as the talcum powder cheeks of a fresh born babe. I was all wide eyes and wet ears. I was all open smiles and chapped lips. I was all good morning m'ams and howdoya do sirs.

You know where this is going, kid.

Back then?

I was fucked.

(We hear the sound of a bus pulling away — a puff of exhaust and fumes — and then, perhaps, we see an image of a Younger Tinny standing before us, carrying one hard suitcase and guarding a straw hat on her head from the wind.)

I left Dakota Farms and headed to New York. Took the 9:18 bus straight from obscurity to the center of the universe: a hot little vortex of concrete and steam built to deliver the special of the day: Fame . . . with a little fortune on the side. Hold the pickles please, Sam.

I wanted to be a singer. (But not just a singer, not just some ho-hum two-bit broad with a few clanking pipes.) *I wanted to sing my little heart out!* And I was determined to make this big ole city of New York sit down and weep for the sound of it.

After getting turned away at every open singing call in town, I wasn't about to give up. I may have been at the end of my rope but that rope was still made of ten thousand tiny shards of hope and faith and I was planning to use every one of 'em.

Maybe that's why I didn't see where I was going. Maybe that's how I ended up lost on that dark, lonely night so long ago. The street signs showed me where I had landed — the intersection of Tough Breaks Lane and Hard Knock Alley — but *he* showed me where I would end up. . . . *Him.* Roger Dapper: Not your every day friendly piano supply superstore salesman.

(We see Younger Tinny heading, dejected, down the street. Suddenly she sees a large, hand-painted sign that reads: ROGER DAPPER: PIANO SUPPLY SUPER STORE . . . SINGER/SWEEPER WANTED. *She looks down at the sign in disbelief and then looks around at the dangerous neighborhood surrounding her.)*

That's right, folks. That was the moment my whole world changed. The moment that led me to do the deed. Both deeds. Both times. Done by both of my very own . . . My very own —

(Perhaps she hides her face in a stylized pose of horror and shame.)

(The music breaks into full, melancholy cries. We see the following words in neon light up the night: HANDS OF HORROR.)

(Harsh fluorescent lights and some brushstroke of a grim film noir office. Younger Tinny stands facing Roger Dapper. Tap tap tapping of a tinny Underwood typewriter down the hall.)

TINNY: Um hello sir. I am here to apply for the singing position.

ROGER DAPPER: The what?

TINNY: The singing position, sir. I saw the sign on the —

(Suddenly an odd, ogre-like creature wanders through wearing a Groucho Marx mask. He sweeps and sweeps as he passes through. Tinny cannot help but stare.)

ROGER DAPPER: It's taken.

TINNY: What?

ROGER DAPPER: The gig, the singing and sweeping gig; it's taken so — *(Gesture for "go away.")*

TINNY: Is it taken by . . . *(Gesturing towards the ogre creature.) him?*

ROGER DAPPER: Geez, you sure is a nosy broad. Yeah, he's some washed up academic philosopher-type from across the pond. He came in to apply as a sweeper and he made me an offer I couldn't refuse.

TINNY: But sir, don't you still need a singer?

ROGER DAPPER: Don't mind me saying so but there's something about you that gives me the *(Distasteful lip smack.)* heevie jeevies. All that sunshine, bright eyes, white teeth kinda crap. Me, I like my workers broken a bit, in the heart, in the soul. (*In the body.*)

TINNY: Well. I can be. Broken.

(Tinny takes a tiny keyboard and tries to lounge on top of it. This is probably next to impossible. She sings a blowsy little number.)

I know that sound:
My broken heart

I know his cry:
My broken man

I know his key
My broken lock

I know how all of it
All of it
All of it
Comes breaking apart
My heart
Comes breaking apart
(A vampy little whisper.)
My heart

(A pause as Roger Dapper assesses and then speaks.)

ROGER DAPPER: That the best you can do? A broken heart? Been there. Done that. Call me when you got something worthwhile to break. *(He is about to slam the door in her face but she stops it with her foot or her hand.)*

TINNY: My eyes. My eyes are breaking. Broke, in fact. So that makes me. Blind. Did I mention that I'm blind?

ROGER DAPPER: Blind eh? How do you spell Piano Supply Super Store in Braille? Huh?

TINNY: I-I

ROGER DAPPER: *(Buzzer noise.)* BUZZ! Too slow. Now get yer mug outta my grill and go.

TINNY: I also have a hard time hearing.

ROGER DAPPER: GET OUT! DON'T MAKE ME SAY IT AGAIN!

TINNY: So I'm sure you won't care that I also *(Sliding an arm in her coat.)* lost my arm?

ROGER DAPPER: *(Taking this is with clear delight.)* Lost your arm! Well why didn't you tell me that before, doll?! Poor thing lost her arm! *(Suddenly very serious.)* Did you keep all your fingers?

TINNY: Yes! Wait. What?

ROGER DAPPER: Well even if you actually *could* bring your body parts in — and I'm not saying you could — but even if you could, it still wouldn't . . .

TINNY: *(Cut quickly to Tinny thinking to herself.)* Wait a minute! Did he just say . . . ?

(Cut back to Tinny and Roger Dapper in a pool of light.)

TINNY: Did you just say: *Bring your body parts in?*

ROGER DAPPER: No no. No no no. NOOOOOooooooOOOOOO! What kind of a man do you I am here? What kind of a business do you think this is? *(Nervous laughter.)* HAHAHAHAHA No no no. Not *your* body parts.

TINNY: Ohhhhhh.

ROGER DAPPER: *(Suddenly very serious.)* Other people's. Body. Parts.

(Cut back to Tinny alone in a pool of light.)

TINNY: And so began my days working for Roger Dapper's Piano Supply Super Store. In the front, the same six or seven Steinways would sit silent in the dust, while in the back . . . *(She shudders as she says it.)* In the back

(Cut back to Tinny opening up a pillowcase and dumping it on the ground. All sorts of body parts fall out. Roger is very immersed in his cell phone conversations. He looks at a ridiculous map of the world and punches in little tabs for his latest organ trade ventures.)

ROGER DAPPER: Yep yep Wayne. Getting in early on a hot global kidney trade. *(Inspecting the bag of body parts.)* These babies are born in the U-S-A! *(In a hushed tone to Tinny.)* Sit and wait for instructions. *(Tinny sits down, singing something as she goes.)* But Tinny. Doll.

TINNY: Yes Roger Dapper?

ROGER DAPPER: Don't sing *please.* You sound like a bagpipe giving birth.

(Roger Dapper carries ten cell phones on a string and they all go off suddenly with different ring tones. While Roger Dapper is talking on the phone, the ogre-like philosopher wanders through several times, just sweeping, sweeping and staring at Tinny and taking odd, furtive notes.)

ROGER DAPPER: HELLO! YES! Livers in El Salvador don't go across the border Wayne. They don't Wayne. Have you ever met the guerrillas they got down there Wayne? *(Another cell phone rings.)* Don't listen to Falun Gong Frank. We are not MADE IN CHINA you pathetic glass of urine-stained Yuppie vitamin water Frank. *(To Tinny.)* WHERE ARE THESE BOAOAOYSAHS PAPASTASITS FROM?

TINNY: The body parts?

ROGER DAPPER: SHHHHHHHHHHHHHHHHHHHHHHHHHHHHHH. The Feds. Are always nearby. (They still think I'm the one who shot Nixon.)

TINNY: Nixon? Ohhhh . . . Huh. *(She looks at him in confusion but lets it pass.)* Those body parts are from Sunny Lanes retirement home in Connecticut.

ROGER: *(Back to the phone.)* PURE WASPS! These things are gunna sell like hotcakes in the UK, Frank.

TINNY: Is this how you make money?

ROGER DAPPER: Are you *actually* retarded or do you just play one on TV? OF COURSE this is how we make money. Do you think we could pull a profit on PIANOS when they're producing them with toothpicks and Shoo-Glue in Shenzhen? *(He hands her a first paycheck.)* Smell the dough! Taste it! It's as easy as taking in air isn't it? *(He is on another cell as his voice fades.)*

TINNY: *(Staring at her paycheck.)* This is no way to make a living. I feel dirty and sick and wrong. What about my singing career? What about my hope and faith? What about my *(She is about to tear up her check in a dramatic gesture but instead she finds herself putting on a new mink coat and eating a steak tartar with her bare hands.) My heart.*

(Cut back to Older Tinny in the pool of light.)

TINNY: It's amazing how fast the object of a dame's desire can transform from a repertoire of tunes to tidy sum of cash. One minute, you're like the dirt in the ridge of the city's shoe and the next minute you're the bubble in the champagne of the missing glass slipper. *(She finishes off the near-raw steak.)* I told Roger that I couldn't do the trade; I told him I would hold down the fort with the pianos up front but, one day, it became surprisingly clear that there might be a little cut for me on the side.

(Younger Tinny walks in on the ogre-like sweeper but, to her surprise, he is not looking like an ogre. He is inspecting the bag of body parts using a cartoon anatomy chart. He wears dark sunglasses OVER his Groucho Mark mask.)

TINNY: Excuse me! I didn't realize you were in here —

SWEEPER: *(Speaking with thick German accent.)* Shhhh. Put these on first. We don't want anyone to see us. *[-He hands her some sunglasses to wear as well so they can speak completely "shaded.")*

TINNY: You-you can talk?

SWEEPER: People see my face and they expect me to be very funny. They expect me to make them laugh. All HA HA HA. Oh, Mister Good Time Man With A Moustache. Mister Big Laughs. I feel like no one is seeing the real me. The real me has much more serious aspirations for —

TINNY: Please don't tell me any more. I've heard enough dirty secrets for one lifetime.

SWEEPER: Sweet Tinny. You have to hear more; you're in far too deep to turn back now.

TINNY: *(She whips off her sunglasses and then takes his sunglasses off as well.)* Who-who are you?

SWEEPER: *Shhhh. People might see us!* I, too, am in the global organ trade. Word on the street has it that Roger Dapper is price fixing. We want to join together, join forces, so we can overpower him. Roger Dapper must. Poof! Disappear.

TINNY: Disappear? What does tha — Oh! Oh no! . . . *Murder?*

SWEEPER: Call it an investment in the future: Roger Dapper happens to have a most valuable liver, lined with Ertetetetgdshsjsks. A very rare fluid. Mongolians drink it with cornstarch. Do you know what this goes for in the 'Stans (as in *Paki, baby*).

TINNY: But how would we get it? And why?

SWEEPER: Why? *(He laughs a manic little laugh.)* In philosophy and politics, we only ask, *Why not?* Why not take over the world? I could take you for a tour in a Mongolian yurt, say, or a wild donkey ride down the ridges of Machu Picchu . . . I could take you. *(A seductive caress of a her cheek.)* So many places, Tinny.

TINNY: Not to do this. Not to commit a *murder.*

SWEEPER: I have one more thing to reveal then —

TINNY: No more! *(She holds her ears.)* I said I don't want to hear anymore!

SWEEPER: Oh Tinny: A revelation for your eyes! *(He opens up his outfit for a final "revelation": it turns out, he is also a flasher.)*

TINNY: That's quite some newsflash there, Mister. *(She swoons slightly.)* . . . I think I'm in over my head.

(The sweeper and Tinny begin to kiss as silhouettes behind the door of Roger Dapper's office. Tinny walks away back to the pool of light on stage.)

TINNY: You guessed it kid: I fell for that mask-wearing German philosopher flasher and I fell hard. I mixed two cups of goo-goo with a quarter cup of ga-ga and the recipe made me a goner. Little Miss Tinny McGee was in love. A letter sent straight from the heart.

Before I knew it, he had talked me into performing a full-on dissection while Roger Dapper was asleep. We were gunna get the liver, chop it up into ten million little pieces and give everyone in the global trade a cut of the goods. Then we would live out our days singing and yurt-hopping in a Mongolian paradise.

That was the plan at least . . .

(The sound of Roger Dapper snoring at his desk. We see a silhouette of Tinny coming around the corner with a searing, silver butter knife. Roger Dapper wakes up and sees her knife in his face.)

ROGER DAPPER: Tinny . . .

TINNY: The time has come to get my greedy little hands on that luscious liver of yours. Seems your vitals are the gift to give in the 'Stans.

ROGER DAPPER: That *sweeper* set you up to this, didn't he?

TINNY: He's not just a sweeper. He also happens to be a very well-respected flasher.

ROGER DAPPER: Oh Tinny. Did he seduce you?

TINNY: Seduce me? SEDUCE ME? *(She laughs a brittle little laugh and then stops suddenly.)* He loved me. And he still loves me. He thinks we can all *make work* together, we can all *make love* together. Do you know what love is Roger Dapper? Love is a wild donkey ride down the ridges of Machu Picchu.

ROGER DAPPER: Did he offer you your very own yurt?

TINNY: *(Oh no.)* . . . Yes.

ROGER DAPPER: Tinny. He's just spouting off some old world crap from a windbag camp. Did I tell you I caught him stealing pennies from petty cash the other day? I fired him right there on the spot and I shoved him back out on the streets. He's a retired nobody on the express train to nowhere.

(Back to Tinny in the pool of light.)

TINNY: Roger Dapper's news hit my heart hard. That's right folks: me — a righteous dame with legs the length of the Costa Rica coastline and I let a card-carrying member of AARP pop my cherry. Not even a flasher. Just a bargain basement bag of hot air.

Well I cried, kid. I cried so many tears so wet and salty, they made the

Dead Sea look like a goldfish bowl. I cried and I cried and then I did the thing that every dame does when her desire makes her feel like a fool. I got revenge.

(Tinny approaches the Sweeper on the designated corner. She carries a bloody bag.)

SWEEPER: Excellent, my little Tinny. You know, I wasn't sure if you had the stomach for this line of — Work.

TINNY: Roger didn't suffer much. And once I got a look at his books . . . Do you know he's sitting on over ten million in assets right now.

SWEEPER: Doesn't surprise me in the least. And what did you ever get out of it? Besides a possible twenty-count murder charge for those innocents up at Sunny Lanes.

TINNY: *(She shudders bitterly.)* Well, I've grown up a bit. Instead of singing about life; I've lived it. And then some.

SWEEPER: Think about the communal investment the two of us will contribute when — *(The sweeper dips his hand in the bag and pulls out a rotisserie chicken.)* What the! . . . This isn't a liver! This is rotisserie chicken from . . .

TINNY AND SWEEPER: Boston Market.

TINNY: *(She pulls out a tiny lady's revolver and aims it at him.)* Why didn't you tell me the truth about filching Roger's pennies?

SWEEPER: Tinny . . . Roger Dapper must have lied to you. I'm not a thief. I am still quite active in my field. I would even go so far as to say — prominent.

TINNY: What field? The field of DREAMS!

SWEEPER: Oh God Tinny. *(An anguished touch of her face.)* Even a revolutionary slash political philosopher can find himself getting a little *too* involved . . . I'm not Groucho Marx. I'm . . . I'm . . . *(He whips off his mask. Underneath the Groucho Mark mask, he still has an UNUSUAL amount of hair.) KARL MARX.*

TINNY: Karl Marx!

SWEEPER: That's right Tinny . . . Your first roll in the hay was with the author behind *The Communist Manifesto.* I never wanted our labors of love to be exploited.

TINNY: *(Genuinely confused.)* Is that why you left me a twenty by the bed?

SWEEPER: Tin Tin: There are so many things you Americans will never understand about the world. I had a vision for the global organ trade: One Liver, One Life! People's Republic of Quivering Lungs! The Proletariat's

Right to a Well Functioning Bladder. And then blasted Roger Dapper, *Roger Dapper* had to keep the whole honey pot for himself. *Greedy little prick! (He kisses her head.)* But all that is a *man's* business. As for you, my little lady, I never should have gotten you involved. I'm a much better man when I'm making sweet love to a woman.

TINNY: How many women have you *labored* with *(She can barely speak the words.)* . . . Hundreds?

SWEEPER: There weren't hundreds. Oh no.

TINNY: *(A spot of hope.)* No?

SWEEPER: There were hundreds of thousands. I loved young, beautiful exploited labor all over the globe. *I had to.* But none of that changes the fact that I think you're cute as a bug, Tinny McGee. Keep in touch and no hard feelings, eh?

TINNY: *No hard feelings?!*

(He starts walking and she shoots him in the back. He falls.)

TINNY: *(In shock, looking at Sweeper's dead body and then looking at the revolver, shaking in her hand in disbelief.)* My feelings aren't hard. My feelings are *broken.* And that, that is a *woman's* business, Karl.

(Back in a pool of light alone.)

TINNY: From that moment, it was a long, cold slide to the dark side. I walked straight to Roger Dapper's and I shot him in mid-snore.

(We see the shadow of Tinny McGee raising her lady's revolver to shoot Roger Dapper in the middle of sleep apnea. He opens his eyes for one terrified moment.)

ROGER DAPPER: Tinnnny! Why me?

TINNY: Why you? *(She laughs and laughs: brittle and harsh and then stops.)* In philosophy and politics, we only ask, *Why not?*

(Roger Dapper falls over dead, in some kind of film noir silhouette.)

TINNY: I coulda packed my bags for the next donkey ride outta town but fact is I'm good and dirty like the rest of 'em. I could take a hundred showers and they still wouldn't let me set foot back on Dakota Farms. I belong to this city now, for better or for worse.

(We see Tinny create a new sign: TINNY MCGEE: PURVEYOR OF BROKE DOWN, DAMAGED GOODS.*)*

I rolled up both Karl AND Roger and sold 'em off to the 'Stans for a tidy sum. I was gunna use my new dough to get myself a Steinway big as St. Louis and maybe a few singing lessons but . . .

Who was I kidding?

I was a businesswoman. Always would be. I knew exactly what the markets wanted from me: broken goods, baby. It's all about broke down, damaged goods.

(She opens up her shirt and there is a bandage where her heart should be. She picks up her cell phone and speaks as she walks away.) A beautiful pulsing red heart and it's ready for sale, Wendell. Yes it's American, Wendell. I can prove it Wendell. It's in 100 percent perfect condition except for one little break along the side. *(She exits on the cell and her voice fades with her.)* Damaged, sure, a bit broken on the side, Wendell, but other than that this baby is impenetrable, Wendell. That's the way we make 'em on these hard knock streets, Wendell. That's the way the market likes 'em.

(Big bold music and titles.)

END OF PLAY

His Last Fight

JACQUELINE GOLDFINGER

His Last Fight was produced at the New Perspectives Festival in San Diego, California, June 19-28, 2009; Festival Director — Kelly Lapczynski. Director: Brendon Slater. The Palooka — Terence J. Burke; The Kid — Sara Moneymaker; Male Boxer — Reed Willard.

His Last Fight had a workshop production in the Resilience of the Spirit Festival at Compass Theater in San Diego, California, June 26–August 3, 2008; Artistic Director: Matt Thompson. Director: Chelsea Whitmore. The Palooka — Don Pugh. The Kid — Olivia Espinosa. Male Boxer — Fernando Huerto.

CHARACTERS

THE PALOOKA, forties to fifties. Ancient in boxing years. Scarred

THE KID, 19, an upstart

MALE BOXER, 19, another upstart

MALE VOICE, unseen Male Voice, unseen Fight Announcer (Actor usually doubles with Male Boxer.)

SETTING

1985, Miami, Florida. A concrete warm-up room in the basement of a stifling boxing arena.

• • •

A concrete warm-up room in the basement of a stifling boxing arena. We hear the crowd above, chanting for blood. An old worn out boxer, The Palooka, cleans, keeps to the deep shadows of the room. He watches The Kid tape her hands for her first professional match. The Kid sweats rivers. She wraps her hand in tape. The tape twists.

KID: Need more tape.

(In frustration, she rips the tape off her hands.)

More tape here!

(The Palooka hands her a new role of tape.)

KID: You slow, that why they got you cleanin'?

(Palooka enters the light, she sees his face.)

KID: Shit, sorry.

PALOOKA: Ever'body needs to eat.

(Palooka continues cleaning.)

(She sweats some more.)

KID: Got any advice?

(He ignores her.)

KID: Hey, Palooka, cain't you remember anythin'? Tips, nothin'?

(He keeps cleaning.)

KID: What good all those gold belts do if you cain't remember nothin'?

PALOOKA: Go home.

KID: Fuck you.

(She wraps her hands.)

(Her watches her, gauges her nervousness, shakes his head.)

PALOOKA: Show s'more leg.

KID: Huh?

PALOOKA: You know.

(He pulls up his pants leg, lets out a low appreciative whistle.)

(The Kid lunges at him, knocks him down. They wrestle. He puts her in a headlock.)

PALOOKA: 'Cause that's all they wanna see of you.

(Palooka shoves her away, slaps her ass hard and quick.)

PALOOKA: You're outta your class, sweetheart.

KID: Fuck you, you ain't the Mighty Palooka any more anyways.

(Under breath.)

Gone to seed piece a' shit.

(The crowd roars upstairs.)

PALOOKA: They're ready for the titty show, kid.

KID: They come to see me fight.

PALOOKA: They come to see you jiggle.

(She gives him a mean stare.)

PALOOKA: Eye fuck me all you want, sweetheart. You're still the sideshow before the main event. Lady Boxers, Bearded Ladies, One-eyed dogs — all the same, good for staring at, not much else.

(The Kid stands toe to toe with the Palooka. She spits in his face. He wipes it off slow.)

PALOOKA: There you go. Grab your balls, babycakes. That's real good. It gives the suckers a better show.

(The Kid moves away from him, warms up, jabs, ducks, slides.)

(The Palooka watches; shit, she's gonna go through with this . . .)

PALOOKA: You takin' that She-Bear to dinner? Gonna let her eat your pussy after, too?

(He lifts his open palm to her. She hesitates, then punches into it.)

PALOOKA: Weak.

(The Palooka reaches out, adjusts her wrist.)

PALOOKA: Again.

(She punches. He absorbs.)

(They circle each other in a mock match. The Palooka, palms up and open, adjusts her wrists and arms between punches; the sounds of flesh slamming into flesh and heavy breathing.)

(The Palooka shakes his head.)

PALOOKA: Harder. Harder! HARDER! Why in the holy hell are you here, sweetheart? Cain't move worth shit, cain't punch worth shit, you'll end up on your ass 'n all they'll gotta do is set on you. You like that? You get into this for bush in the face, angel? Let some big honkin' bitch from De-troit or Birmingham set on you, shit on you? Huh, babycakes?

(The Kid finally gets the punch right — and almost breaks his fingers.)

PALOOKA: Good! Stay mad. It keeps you alive.

(The Kid stops moving, puts down her arms.)

THE KID: I'm stronger than them.

(The Palooka hits her square in the chest. She falls.)

PALOOKA: You cain't ever be stronger than all of 'em.

KID: I been so far. I got outta Texas with 19 wins, 1 loss, and that was rigged 'cause she was ova' the weight rules, even if I was the only one to know it.

PALOOKA: Upstairs, that girl trained for real, for years. She got coaches, she got corporate sponsorships —

KID: Fifteen, I'm workin' for cash at a titty bar in Odessa, men always layin' hands on me. After work one mornin', one of 'em stays after, an' I laid him flat. Laid him out good. Didn't need no bouncer. Didn't need nobody. Ain't nobody touched me without my say-so since.

(The Palooka is not impressed.)

KID: I get in that ring an' I see his fuckin' face, an' we back in that dirt parkin' lot, an' he come up from behind this doublewide, an' he grabs a hold of my hair, an' I head butt him good. His nose is the first to run with blood. Then his mouth, an' after some more — not even his kids know his looks to call him daddy.

(Silence.)

(The Palooka takes cash out of his pocket.)

PALOOKA: The 9:15 bus leaves in twen'y minutes.

(He stuffs the cash in her elastic waistband.)

KID: I kin take 'em all down, Mister.

PALOOKA: You already won, Kid. Go home.

MALE VOICE: *(Off stage.)* 'Ur next, Kid.

KID: *(Calls off stage.)* Yeah.

(She takes the money out of her waistband, fingers it, looks at it.)

PALOOKA: Any other way, you'll be punched out by twenty-five.

(The Kid looks up at the Palooka, accusing him shakily.)

KID: You just jealous you ain't out there tonight.

PALOOKA: I been dropped on my head 'nough.

(Crowd roars upstairs.)

KID: You cain't even remember the last time they called your name.

PALOOKA: I still hear 'em.

(Silence.)

(The Kid hands him the money. He won't take it. She lays it on the table.)

(The Kid jerks on her gloves.)

KID: Don't trouble over me, old man. I got plans. Gonna make a name in the pros, then get an announcin' gig, set back an' make the calls, not even get a sweat.

(Kid smiles, self-satisfied.)

PALOOKA: You got a plan.

KID: A good one, too. I looked it up. All them announcers made names someways. I'm gonna, too.

(The Palooka shakes his head, pulls out a cigarette, smokes slow.)

KID: Why not? I'm just as pretty as any a' those girls on the TV. An' I ach'ually know what's goin' on, how to give fans more 'n some paint-by-the-damn-numbers idea a' what's hittin' the mat. I could really tell 'em the guts a' it, blow for blow; who's missin' a chance at the title 'cause they hit too hard one way or not 'nough the other. They listen to my broadcast an' it changes boxin' all together, changes the world.

MALE VOICE: *(Off stage.)* Come on, girl.

(The Kid air-punches a couple of more times.)

(The Palooka, grabs her arms, stops her, pulls her close, growls orders:)

PALOOKA: Keep your fists up, protect your face. All them announcers got mugs like Budweiser commercials. And don't forget, that MacTruck out there got feet like wings, fuckin' trick a' nature.

(The Palooka releases her.)

(The Kid begins to exit.)

PALOOKA: An' don't leave your side open. She knock the wind outta you, she's not givin' you any time to get back on your feet.

(The Kid stops, nods to him.)

(He nods back.)

(The Kid exits.)

(A couple of beats as The Palooka finishes his cigarette.)

(The Palooka flips a speaker button on the wall.)

ANNOUNCER: *(Off stage.)* The Kid looks sharp. She was top of her weight class in amateur, but this ain't the back of somebody's garage in Odessa, Texas, is it folks?

(The Palooka cleans. Lays towels on the rubbing table, carefully prepares for her return. We hear the sharp bell that signals the start of the match.)

ANNOUNCER: *(Off stage.)* The Kid looks good. She ducks right, turns . . .

(We hear a smack and the crowd screams.)

ANNOUNCER: *(Off stage.)* . . . Oh, lands a solid left hook. The crowd goes wild. She turns, waves at her fans.

(Another smack.)

ANNOUNCER: *(Off stage.)* And The Kid tags Delta again. Delta is moving slower than we saw in Mobile and La-fay-ette. The Kid is cocky. Smiles.

(A sickening smack and the crunch of bones. The Palooka freezes, recognizes that sound, bows his head. It's the same sound that took him out of the ring years ago.)

ANNOUNCER: *(Off stage.)* The Kid is falling! The Kid is on her knees!

(Another crunch. In his mind, the Palooka is on the mat again, forty years ago, reliving the horror with the Kid. The bell signals the end of the fight. The crowd is going fucking nuts.)

ANNOUNCER: *(Off stage.) (Gleefully.)* Oh, Jesus! The Kid is down. Her face took the brunt of it. She's spitting one, two, three, folks, half her teeth are on the mat. Delta must have made a deal as same as Robert Johnson. She moves like nothing we've seen in professional boxing today.

(The Palooka grimaces, we see that he has three gold teeth. He reaches up, touches his gold teeth.)

ANNOUNCER: *(Off stage.)* The Kid's jaw is completely unhinged. Jesus. The Kid'll be lucky to ever speak again. Let's hope someone can put her face back together. What a ride we're taking you on tonight folks. And we'll be back with the title bout after a word from our sponsors . . .

(The Palooka pulls the Kid's towels off the table. Throws them in a laundry basket, slams the lid.)

(A Young Male Boxer enters.)

YOUNG MALE BOXER: Hey, this room free?

(The Palooka nods, prepares the room as the Young Male Boxer warms up. The Palooka stops to watch the Young Male Boxer.)

PALOOKA: The pussy I got in here before had a better swing. You gonna go faggot out there and make sweet sweet love to' him or do you wanna win?

(The Palooka opens his palm, holds it up to the Boxer. The Young Male Boxer swings, connects.)

PALOOKA: Weak.

(The Palooka grabs the Boxer's wrist, turns it.)

PALOOKA: Again.

(The Boxer hits again. The Palooka shakes his head, adjusts the Boxer's wrist again.)

PALOOKA: Go home, boy.

The Young Male Boxer punches again. Lights fade as the Boxer and the Palooka spar.)

(The crowd roars from above, ready for a fresh kill.)

END OF PLAY

L.A. 8 AM

Mark Harvey Levine

L.A. 8 AM was first produced in May 2007 by Collaboraction as part of Sketchbook 7 at The Steppenwolf Garage, Chicago, Illinois. Director: Michael Patrick Thornton. Cast: AAA — Haruna Tsuchiya; GGG — Ray Baker; Kevin — Bob Turton; Paige — Kelly O'Sullivan.

CHARACTERS

AAA, otherworldy creature.
GGG, otherworldy creature.
KEVIN, twenties-thirties, vaguely disatisfied.
PAIGE, twenties-thirties, harried.

SETTING

The dining/living room of Kevin and Paige's apartment.

TIME

The present.

• • •

A small but clean apartment in Los Angeles. Two otherworldly figures, AAA and GGG are present. Neither Kevin nor Paige ever see or hear them.

AAA: It's 8 AM.
GGG: In Los Angeles, California.
AAA: On a bright and sunny Saturday morning.
(Kevin enters, in his robe. During the following, he gets out a bowl, spoon, cereal and milk.)
GGG: This is Kevin Kirkwood.
AAA: Who believes everything can be reduced to numbers.
GGG: Even himself.
AAA: He's Five feet eleven.
GGG: One hundred and eighty pounds.
AAA: He contains 4 billion, 423 million, 521 thousand cells.
GGG: He is about to eat a bowl of Froot Loops.
AAA: "Froot Loops" is a registered trademark of the Kellogg's Company, Inc.
GGG: And are fortified with eleven essential vitamins and minerals.
AAA: This is the 127th bowl of Froot Loops he has eaten in his lifetime.
GGG: It has 10% of his daily requirement of zinc.
AAA: 15% if milk is added.
GGG: And he plans to add milk.
AAA: He finds numbers comfortable.
GGG: Ordered.
AAA: Neat.

GGG: With numbers, life is not messy or chaotic.

(He opens the box to pour the cereal in the bowl and it all comes flying out, chaotically and messily spilling everywhere.)

KEVIN: Paige!

(Paige enters. She is completely dressed. During the following she gets her keys and puts her coat on.)

AAA: This is Paige Kirkwood.

GGG: She does not believe life can be reduced to numbers.

AAA: She does not believe life should be neat and ordered.

GGG: She does not believe in keeping the cereal in the little cellophane bag provided by the Kellogg's Company, Inc.

PAIGE: Yes?

KEVIN: Did you take the cereal out of the little cellophane bag?

PAIGE: I cannot tell a lie. I did take the cereal out of the little cellophane bag.

KEVIN: Why would you do that?

PAIGE: It makes it too slow to pour.

KEVIN: It all came right out!

PAIGE: See?

KEVIN: How many times have I asked you not to do that?

AAA: Three.

KEVIN: Now I've got Froot Loops all over the place.

PAIGE: It's a crisis.

KEVIN: I just wanted a bowl of cereal. That's all I wanted. Is that too much to ask?

PAIGE: I guess so.

(Kevin begins to clean up the cereal.)

AAA: There are other numbers in the world, he believes.

GGG: Numbers that are unavailable to him.

AAA: The count-down numbers.

GGG: For instance:

AAA: When Kevin woke up this morning, the song playing on his clock radio —

GGG: — was "Pictures Of Matchstick Men."

AAA: A Top 40 hit by The Status Quo.

GGG: There is a certain specific number of times he will hear "Pictures Of Matchstick Men" again.

AAA: Every time he hears it, that number goes down one.

GGG: Until finally —

AAA: Though he will not know it when it happens —
GGG: — one day he will hear that song for the last time.
AAA: And never hear it again.
GGG: Every time he hears a song, its number ticks down one.
AAA: And one day, the numbers of all songs will hit zero, and then —
GGG: The numbers of everything he will ever do will hit zero.
AAA: The number of spoons he will pick up.
GGG: The number of shoes he will tie.
AAA: The number of times he will say the word "Look."
GGG: The number of breaths he will take.
AAA: The number of beats of his heart, and then —
GGG: All counters will align at zero, and he will die.
AAA: But that day is far off. And the numbers are not known to him.
KEVIN: Look, I don't want to fight about Froot Loops.
GGG: They know it is not about Froot Loops.
PAIGE: Good, I don't want to fight about Froot Loops either.
AAA: But they do not know what they are really fighting about.
GGG: Kevin wonders how many fights they have had.
AAA: And how many more they will have.
GGG: And whether the frequency of fights has increased, over time.
AAA: And how you might go about calculating that number.
GGG: Paige wonders if this is the person she wants to spend the rest of her life with.
PAIGE: Look, I have to go meet with the graphic designers.
KEVIN: OK. Let's just let it drop.
PAIGE: Fair enough.
KEVIN: See you when you get back.
PAIGE: OK.

(He picks up the spoon.)

GGG: Number of spoons Kevin has left to pick up:
AAA: Forty nine thousand, three hundred and nine.
GGG: Think of that!
AAA: All those spoons.
GGG: Number of spoons Paige has left to pick up:
AAA: Zero.
GGG: She picked up her final spoon last night at 9:27 PM.
AAA: Distracted by the Froot Loop fight —
GGG: She will fail to see a car turning left in front of her —

AAA: And will be killed in seventeen minutes.

KEVIN: See ya.

PAIGE: OK.

GGG: Number of kisses between Paige and Kevin left:

AAA: One.

(Kevin and Paige kiss perfunctorily.)

GGG: If he had known that was the last time he would kiss her . . .

AAA: . . . he would not have used it as an opportunity to express his unhappiness.

GGG: But he did.

(She exits out their front door.)

AAA: He does not know that he will never have another fight with her.

GGG: She does not know that he was, in fact, the man she spent the rest of her life with.

AAA: He has thirty-six minutes left before he gets the phone call.

GGG: He will forever associate the taste of Froot Loops in his mouth with that phone call.

AAA: Number of bowls of Froot Loops he will eat after today:

GGG: Zero.

AAA: But this number is not known to him now.

GGG: Right now, he is just having a bowl of cereal.

AAA: And thinking about numbers.

GGG: On a bright and sunny Saturday morning.

AAA: In Los Angeles, California.

GGG: At 8:07 AM.

(Kevin crunches his cereal.)

(Lights fade.)

END OF PLAY

Let's Not Talk About Men

Carla Cantrelle

Let's Not Talk About Men premiered at the 15th Annual 15 Minute Play Festival presented by Turnip Theatre Company and American Globe Theatre, New York, New York, May 6, 2009. Cast (in order of appearance): Kristy — Jill Balch*; Gwen — Carol Jacobanis*; Melanie — Sheri Graubert*; Jake — H. Dan Harkins*; Susan — Melinda Wade*; Janice — Sharon Eisman*; Wendy — Margot Avery*; Waiter — Aaron T. Hinds.
*(*member of Actors Equity Association)*

CHARACTERS

KRISTY
GWEN
MELANIE
JAKE
SUSAN
JANICE
WENDY
WAITER

The cast can be any ages from mid-twenties to mid-forties as long as it is believable that they would be interested in having brunch together. The only character with any physical "type" is the Waiter, who should be handsome enough to flummox the characters on sight.

The very last line of the play may be a voice over announcement or may be delivered onstage by the actor playing the Waiter.

SETTING

A restaurant. Present-day. Brunch.

• • •

Kristy sits at a large table perusing menu. Gwen enters.

KRISTY: Hey. Hi.
GWEN: Hi.
KRISTY: You look great.
GWEN: Oh ugh.
KRISTY: Stop.
GWEN: Please.
KRISTY: Really.
GWEN: Bleh blah bleh yeah.
KRISTY: So hi.
GWEN: Is Susan coming?
KRISTY: Yes.
GWEN: Oh.

KRISTY: I thought, you know, it was —

GWEN: Oh no fine fine I just . . . she . . . we . . . I have to — well. Maybe not today. You know . . .

KRISTY: I'm sorry I thought she didn't —

GWEN: It's just — no, fine. Fine.

(Pause.)

KRISTY: Is Janice coming?

GWEN: Yeah.

KRISTY: Good. I don't think I've seen her since she moved in with John.

GWEN: Nobody has seen her since she moved in with John.

KRISTY: Has John seen her since she moved in with John?

(Pause.)

GWEN: I hate John.

KRISTY: Thank God! I hate John too! Does she know you hate John?

GWEN: Everybody knows I hate John.

KRISTY: John is so . . . so . . .

GWEN: Yeah. How's Peter?

KRISTY: I hate Peter too.

GWEN: You always hate Peter. Or is that only since you guys got married?

KRISTY: Who do you hate? Besides John.

GWEN: All of them. Today I hate all of them.

KRISTY: Even the ones you don't know?

GWEN: Especially the ones I don't know. Them most of all. Because soon I'll know them and they'll do something to make me hate them. But since I don't know them, I don't know what that horrible thing will be. I won't be prepared. And because I'm an idiot, I'll think that everything will be different with them. Because they're new.

KRISTY: And you don't know them.

GWEN: And I don't know them. Exactly. Exactly right.

KRISTY: I don't know which are worse. The ones you know or the ones you don't.

GWEN: At least if you know them, you kind of know where the land mines are.

KRISTY: Not always.

GWEN: Well, yeah, but you're married. That's a whole different mine field. Dating. Gack. You think you're blithely strolling through the park but its really the de-militarized zone and poorly defined at that. Then POW!

one misplaced reference to some movie that reminds him of his last girlfriend! No warning. Kaplooey! Or one too many "Does this make me look fat?" Wham!

KRISTY: I can't believe you think you're fat. You are so sick.

GWEN: You sound like —

KRISTY: Don't say it.

GWEN: I just hate them. In fact, I don't even want to think about them. Just once, I'd like to get through a day without even mentioning them.

KRISTY: I know what you mean.

GWEN: Let's make a pact. For this brunch, let's not talk about men!

KRISTY: Deal!

(Pause.)

(Pause.)

(Pause.)

KRISTY: I like your dress.

GWEN: Thanks.

(Pause.)

(Pause.)

GWEN: So, what's good here?

(Melanie enters.)

MELANIE: Hiya!

KRISTY: Hi Melanie.

GWEN: Mel.

MELANIE: Listen. I have to ask you guys something. I cannot figure this out. OK. I met this guy. And the thing is —

KRISTY: Stop right there.

MELANIE: What?

KRISTY: Don't say another word.

MELANIE: Is something wrong?

GWEN: We have a pact.

KRISTY: Right.

GWEN: For this entire brunch we are not allowed to talk about men.

MELANIE: Huh?

KRISTY: Not one word.

MELANIE: Oh. OK. Nothing?

(Gwen and Kristy shake their heads.)

MELANIE: Oh. OK. Well, that shouldn't be too hard.

KRISTY: Right!

MELANIE: I mean, God, there is so much else to talk about besides men.

GWEN: Exactly.

(Pause.)

(Pause.)

(Pause.)

MELANIE: But I really need to know what you think about what this guy did! Can't we start after that?

KRISTY: No.

GWEN: Nope.

MELANIE: OK.

(Pause.)

(Pause.)

MELANIE: Can I ask you tomorrow?

KRISTY: Sure.

GWEN: Maybe. I may never talk about men again. I'm thinking maybe this will be the start of an entirely new way of life for me.

MELANIE: It shouldn't be so hard. I mean, there is so much else to talk about.

KRISTY: Right.

GWEN: Exactly.

(Pause.)

(Pause.)

(Pause.)

(Pause.)

(Jake enters.)

JAKE: Hello ladies!

KRISTY: Hi sweetie.

GWEN: Hi.

MELANIE: Hi.

JAKE: I have to tell you what Billy did yesterday.

KRISTY: You can't.

JAKE: *(Ignoring her.)* It was so sweet. I am so in love.

GWEN: Listen, Jake, we aren't going to —

JAKE: *(Ignoring her.)* This is it, I swear. This time its for real. I know I always say that —

MELANIE: Hey! That's not fair! If he can talk about men so can I! So this guy I met —

GWEN: Stop! No one is allowed to talk about men. Not at this table. There's a table over there. If you can't take the pressure.

(Pause.)

(Pause.)

JAKE: Is this some new kind of therapy?

GWEN: It's a pact. To see if we can get through brunch without talking about men!

(Susan enters.)

SUSAN: Hello.

JAKE: Stop! While you still can! Turn back.

SUSAN: What are you talking about?

JAKE: It's dangerous over here. They've lost their minds.

SUSAN: What is he talking about? Hello Gwen.

GWEN: Susan.

KRISTY: I'm hungry.

SUSAN: Kristy. How's Peter?

KRISTY: I'm not allowed to tell you.

SUSAN: What?

JAKE: She's serious. They've made some rule that men are not to be discussed.

SUSAN: What a good idea. Men can cause such trouble. Right Gwen?

(Gwen doesn't respond.)

KRISTY: Right. And there's so much else in our lives besides men!

JAKE: There is? Oh, of course there is.

KRISTY: Politics, for example.

SUSAN: Good choice. Important topics and the men are outside our dating pool.

GWEN: Speak for yourself.

(Janice enters.)

JANICE: Sorry I'm late. That John. He just wouldn't let me leave the house. If you know what I mean.

SUSAN: Spare us, please

GWEN: *(Mumbling to Kristy.)* She's lucky men are off-limits. Otherwise I'd have plenty to say about John.

JANICE: Excuse me?

KRISTY: Uhm, we have a pact. For this entire brunch we are not allowed to talk about men.

JANICE: That's dumb. Why?

GWEN: It's not dumb.

KRISTY: Work. How's work Susan?

SUSAN: I'm filing four sexual harassment and sexual discrimination suits.

GWEN: I'd be willing to bet that men are involved, right?
SUSAN: So? This is work, not men.
GWEN: If you want to have brunch with us you have to follow the rules.
(Wendy enters.)
WENDY: I'm sorry I'm late. Have you been waiting long? David knew exactly when I had to leave but did he get home on time? Nooooo. Of course not!
SUSAN: Stop.
WENDY: Excuse me?
GWEN: We've made a rule. We're not talking about men.
JANICE: I didn't make the rule. I think it's dumb.
WENDY: No, it's great! But can I add to that? Can we also not talk about kids?
GWEN: Deal.
KRISTY: Deal.
SUSAN: Deal.
(Pause.)
(Pause.)
(Pause.)
(Waiter approaches.)
WAITER: What can I get for you?
MELANIE: A different waiter.
WAITER: I'm sorry. Is there a problem?
MELANIE: Yes. You are very cute. The second you leave the table we'll have to talk about you.
JAKE: Compelled. We'll be compelled.
MELANIE: And we don't want to talk about men.
WAITER: Uhm . . .
KRISTY: Yes. Please send over that waitress.
JANICE: And tell her to bring us all large mimosas.
WAITER: OK.
WENDY: Go. Now.
WAITER: OK!
(Waiter exits.)
GWEN: Phew! That was close.
(Pause.)
KRISTY: So, uh . . .
(Pause.)
GWEN: I went to . . . oh . . . uhm . . . hm.

(Pause.)

MELANIE: *(Opens mouth. Shuts it.)*

SUSAN: Well. Well. Well.

JANICE: Did I mention — oh. Never mind.

(Pause.)

JAKE: Does this mean I'm not allowed to talk about myself?

(Pause.)

(Pause.)

(Pause.)

JANICE: This is really stupid.

(Pause.)

(Pause.)

(Pause.)

(Pause.)

ANNOUNCER: Please join us next time when the men perform LET'S NOT TALK ABOUT SPORTS!

END OF PLAY

Meatball Hero

Richard Vetere

Meatball Hero was first presented at the Cherry Lane Theater in New York City on January 15, 2009 as part of the New York Playwright's Lab's festival of one-act plays. Cast: Holly — Antoinette LaVecchia; Raymond — Jim Iorio; Waiter — Michael Bakkensen. Director: Richard Vetere.

CHARACTERS

HOLLY

RAYMOND

FRENCH WAITER

TIME

Now.

PLACE

French Restaurant in Meat Packing district, New York City. It is the Les Etoiles De Mougins Gala Dinner.

• • •

Set: Holly and Raymond, both attractive New Yorkers in their early thirties, are sitting at a table. Holly is talkative, educated and urbane but tries too hard to be sophisticated while Raymond is rough around the edges, successful self-made businessman. She is overdressed wearing a bright skirt and bright colored blouse that is trying to be way too French chic. She speaks French pronouncing every word with such exaggeration it sounds as if she is speaking another language entirely and until Raymond's last speech, he speaks with a world-weary tone. He wears a suit and tie. The Waiter is over-the-top French. Holly is exhilarated whispers asides to Raymond who is on his cell phone.

HOLLY: Is this not unbelievable that they picked me, *me*, to introduce the chefs?

RAYMOND: *(Into cell.)* Yeah, Holly, great. Hold on. *(Into cell.)* I told you the meeting would be a waste of time and I never got to eat a thing. *(He hangs up.) (To Holly.)* Hey, I am starving. Where's the food?

HOLLY: *(Ignoring him.)* Raymond, here I am from, what, Nutley, New Jersey and I am introducing the biggest French chef's event of the year! How do I look? *(Gestures to her blouse.)* The last thing I want to do is come off *(Whispers.)* American.

(Raymond gives her one slow look and wisecracks.)

RAYMOND: Don't worry about it. In that outfit, nobody will know *where* you're from.

HOLLY: Look at all the cameras! Look at the TV screen! They are filming everyone. We can see ourselves on TV!

(Holly fixes her blouse, her hair and smiles looking a little silly. She sees someone is pointing to her.)

HOLLY: It's time? *(Turns to Raymond.)* Why did I ever write the piece on French Cuisine? Why did I have to send it to the Op-Ed page? Why did I ever go to Paris when I was a eighteen?

RAYMOND: Waiter! I'm starvin' here!

(Holly stands. Light bulbs go off. A bright spot on her. She is suddenly very professional. Her voice drops an octave and is completely composed though sounding totally pretentious.)

HOLLY: Hello everyone, I'm Holly Belvedere and on behalf of *New York Magazine,* Chef International, Fig and The Olive Restaurant and Paris Lights, I'd like to invite you to the 2008 Les Etoiles De Mougins Gala Dinner, better known as the French Chef-off.

RAYMOND: Waiter! A beer! Anything to pick on!

HOLLY: *(Makes a face at him.)* We are so excited tonight. Why, you ask? Pourquoi? *(Big smile that she is mixing English with French.)* Because tonight we will be served a five course meal each served by a different rising young chef. Our first course, the soup, will be an Heirloom Carrot Soup and tomato Concasse de Mougins *(Stops to flash a big smile that she spoke in what she thinks is perfect French and it is not.)* with Wild Bay Scallops marinated in Lemon *(Pronounces it 'Lemuun'.),* Castelas Olive Oil and eighteen-year-old Balsamic Vinegar. It has been prepared by Pascal Lorange of the Fig and The Olive.

(Then.)

We are now being served so bon appétit!

(The Waiter brings them their soup with an exaggerated flare. He is in his thirties and well-dressed in black slacks and white shirt. Holly sits.)

WAITER: Concasse de Mougins.

HOLLY: *(To the Waiter.)* Merci beaucoup. It is so ele*gant.* That's a French word.

(The Waiter smirks at her accent while Raymond stares at his soup.)

RAYMOND: What *is* this?

HOLLY: It's soup.

RAYMOND: In a glass? Who eats soup in a glass? What, they can't eat it out of a bowl?

(The Waiter overhears and responds.)

WAITER: You eat your Cheerios out of a bowl, Monsieur. You *dine* on soup in a glass.

(Waiter exits. Raymond turns to him but the Waiter is gone. Back to Holly.)

RAYMOND: Did you hear what the waiter said to me?

(He looks into bowl.)

Oh! And what is *that*? In the bowl? Is it a wanton?

HOLLY: That's the scallop, silly. You pour it into the glass.

(Holly shows him how to do it. She sips her soup and is thrilled.)

RAYMOND: Come on, they have to have some real food here. Some rice? Some bread? Something with surface composition. How about a burger and fries? Fries are French.

(The Waiter quickly re-enters then brings a new plate and quickly takes the soup glass and plate from Raymond first, who is watching him and is not happy on how quickly he swiped his plate. Holly watches as the Waiter seductively places the new plate in front of her, pours her wine. She nearly swoons.)

(The Waiter exits.)

HOLLY: Did you notice his eyes? Both of them. So, so, French.

RAYMOND: Do you think I can order something else?

(Holly shoots him a look, then stands, reading from a menu.)

HOLLY: Our next dish is Roasted Lobster Tail with Osetra Caviar Taggiasca Olives, Tomato Rosemary Emulsion. It is prepared by chef, Serge Gouloumes . . . *(She hears a reaction from the Crowd.)* Oh, I'm sorry. Serge Gou . . . lo . . . umes. *(Big smile from her which quickly turns into a frown.)* He's from Le Mas Candille.

(Holly quickly sits. The Waiter re-enters and pours their wine.)

HOLLY: People are looking at me. *(Checks menu.)* I said it all correctly, no?

WAITER: Ah, *no*. His name is Serge Gouloumes.

HOLLY: I thought that's what I said.

RAYMOND: Is this our dinner? There's nothing here. Half my plate is empty.

WAITER: Exactly, monsieur. It gives more room to *see* your food.

RAYMOND: Hey, pal, I don't care if I see it, I just want to *eat* it. And the menu says lobster. Where's my lobster?

WAITER: It's right *there*.

(Raymond looks at his plate.)

RAYMOND: That's not a lobster? It's a *claw*. And what's this?

WAITER: Caviar.

RAYMOND: I hate caviar. What is caviar? I hear it's eggs from a fish. A fish never seen in this country. A fish that may not be a fish and it's definitely not named a 'caviar'! So, please, get rid of the caviar and get me a nice big lobster. One I can actually see. You know, big, brick red.

WAITER: *(Poking fun at him.)* And, with it, a beb?

RAYMOND: A beb? *(Gets it.)* No, a bib.

WAITER: A bavoir.

RAYMOND: Who cares? Just smother it in butter.

(The Waiter disappears and exits as Raymond looks back at him.)

RAYMOND: That jackass is making fun of me.

(Holly looks around with a growing sense of paranoia. She slugs down her wine and lifts her glass for more.)

HOLLY: In my sleep, when I dream, I am a perfect French woman.

(The Waiter appears and pours more wine into Holly's glass as she holds it out towards him.)

RAYMOND: Just the guy I want to see.

(The Waiter ignores him and exits.)

RAYMOND: Did you see that? He ignored me.

HOLLY: I'm exquisite, posh, refined. I'm so impeccable I don't want to wake up.

(Raymond looks at her and is about to say something when The Waiter returns and places two plates down in front of them both.)

RAYMOND: Great. What's this?

(Raymond examines the plate as the Waiter pours Holly more wine and she downs it. She is now getting really tipsy. She smiles at him, he makes a big moment of smiling at her.)

(She fixes her blouse, purses her lips, flirts the best that she can. The Waiter places a flower on the table in front of her and exits.)

(Raymond frowns and is about to say something to Holly when Holly turns quickly to him.)

HOLLY: Raymond, I was going to tell you this later, but in my dream, where I am so perfect, you're a slug. Yes, a slug. A ruffian. A hoodlum. A criminal.

(Raymond is distracted looking for the waiter, hungry.)

RAYMOND: You know, I came right from work, didn't even stop for lunch.

HOLLY: Now, we've been together six months now. I like you. I do. I think you're really, you know, intriguing. A little rough around the edges but I'm game. But in our relationship, we're way passed that *exciting* time, that long *anticipation*, between appetizer and entre.

RAYMOND: *(Looks around.)* Am I going to get anything to eat tonight?

HOLLY: I know your texture, its surface is something like a jagged piece of broken glass. You know mine. It's smooth like soft velvet, original. *(Pronounced really badly.)* You taste my flavor, I taste yours and we muddle through. But we have pronounced differences. I see myself as marinated in Lemuon . . . *(Pronounced wrongly.)* and I see you grilled with spices.

(The Waiter appears, and Raymond eyes him suspiciously. Holly can't take her eyes off of him. Raymond raises his hand for the Waiter's attention.)

RAYMOND: Can you get me *something* to eat? Please. Bread, anything?

(Holly looks at the Waiter with her eyes ablaze.)

HOLLY: I love you.

WAITER: Of course you do.

(The Waiter exits.)

RAYMOND: Did you just tell the waiter you loved him?

(Holly sees that people off stage are waving to her. Drunk, jumps up.)

HOLLY: *(Big smile.)* Oh, yes, ladies and gentleman, our next course is the Wild Striped Bass with Grilled Eggplant, Floral Essence prepared by Alain Liorca, from Le Moulin de Moughns. That will be quickly followed by Saddle of Lamb with Porcini Mushrooms, Petit Farcies Provencal, Jus de Garrigue.

(Drunk, Holly has completely destroyed the language.)

(The Waiter quickly places their plates down and quickly removes the others. He looks at Raymond as if waiting for something.)

RAYMOND: Did I hear *Saddle* of Lamb? A fly couldn't ride a seahorse with this saddle.

(The Waiter shrugs and Raymond looks at his plate.)

RAYMOND: You know what, no more sissy food. This is a restaurant, I'm hungry. Go back into the kitchen and tell one of those French chefs back there to make me a meatball hero.

WAITER: A meat bowl?

RAYMOND: A meat*ball* hero, Jack.

WAITER: My name is not Jack, it's Jacques.

(The Waiter ignores him and steps over to Holly.)

WAITER: Mss Holly Belvedere.

HOLLY: Yes, my dear, handsome, extraordinary Jacques.

WAITER: May I speak to you in private?

HOLLY: *(Thrilled.)* Speak to me in private? Yes, please do. Where would you like to do this? Out in the backyard? *Your* place?

WAITER: The owner said he wants you to stop introducing the food. Your accent is like having his teeth removed. He says, please, for the sake of an entire people, halt trying to speak French, or whatever language you think it is. Do you understand me?

HOLLY: *(Stunned.)* Oh, frig. It's that bad? I can't be. So sorry.

WAITER: Excellent. Now, if you'd like to have sex with me, please leave your email address with me. Be discreet. This cretin you are dinning is a madman.

HOLLY: We are not dinning *together.* But yes, he's . . . Of course. He is. You are. I was. I hope you'll call.

WAITER: I do not call. I *appear.* When I am in the *mood.*

HOLLY: Oh, I can't bear to wait.

WAITER: You will.

(She sits and slugs down her wine as the Waiter exits.)

RAYMOND: I want a meatball hero!

(Holly is humiliated but is so drunk now and confused, she can't react. Raymond stands.)

RAYMOND: I want a meatball hero now! Or I will take action. Get it, people?

(The Waiter rushes out.)

WAITER: Sit.

RAYMOND: Shut up.

(The Waiter takes a deep breath.)

WAITER: This is not Olive Garden. We have no meat*bowl* heroes.

RAYMODN: *(Big grin.)* He has no meatball heroes? None? No meat balls? Amazing. This is America and not one meatball to be had. Interesting. Jack, do you have any idea *why* I want a meatball hero?

WAITER: Jacques.

RAYMOND: A meatball hero is an essential to *everything*! It is round, like the earth. Like the sun and moon. Like the wheel, like a baseball, like your head, like your eye, like your balls, like a great pair of tits! Juicy, tender, round, got it? Like Buddha's belly and Saturn's rings. And in a meatball is *meat.* Real meat. Beef, pork or veal. And you know what? You put things in the meat. Good, tasty things. Like Ricotta and mozzarella cheese and pignola nuts. You don't want a spongy meatball. You want to drown it in flavor with a good meat sauce and a hero roll from an Italian bakery. And you don't want your meatball made by a machine. No, it has to be hand made. And it can't be weighed down with bread crumbs and leaden with the wrong cheese. It's food a man can sink his teeth into. It's masculine, virile. That's what a man needs to eat to fill his belly, not this sissy food! And more than that, a meatball is a hero. Yes, a hero, Jack. Do you people have any idea what a hero is? `

(Then.)

Holly!

(Holly lifts her head.)

HOLLY: Yes?

RAYMOND: We are leaving this establishment. They don't have any meatball heroes.

HOLLY: Oh, pity.

(Then.)

Raymond, I'm staying. I love Jacques. I want to kiss him.

WAITER: Of course you do.

RAYMOND: Frankly, Holly, I don't give a damn. All I want right now, is a tender, juicy, tasty, meatball hero.

(Holly and The Waiter eye one another.)

WAITER: All he wants is a meat*bowl* hero.

HOLLY: Yes, a meat*bowl* hero. Au revoir, Raymond!

(Waiter and Holly kiss. Raymond throws his jacket over his shoulders and steps away from them both.)

RAYMOND: Ah, Bon Chance, yourself. I learned a thing tonight. I learned first hand that a man can live without love, but he can't live without real, *man* food. *(Throws his jacket over his shoulder.)* You might get the girl, Jack.

WAITER: *Jacques.*

RAYMOND: But I get the meatball, *meatball.*

(Lights out.)

END OF PLAY

Odysseus Swims For It

JOSHUA H. COHEN

Odysseus Swims For It was produced by Turtle Shell Productions as part of their 2009 "Summer Shorties, Summ . . . ar Not" series. First preview was August 14, 2009; official opening was August 22, 2009; closed August 30, 2009. Director: Stasi Schaeffer. Producer: John W. Cooper. Set Design: Matt Brogan. Sound Design: Josh Liebert. Lighting/Projection Design: Rocco D'Santi. Costume Design: A. Christina Giannini. Props Design: Paulina Zima. Stage Manager: T. "Pope" Jackson. Cast: Young John — Artie Brennan; Aggie — Jenny Moon; Thel — Amanda Shy.

CHARACTERS

YOUNG JOHN, a shipwrecked sailor, twenties.

AGLAPHEME (AGGIE), a siren, mid-3000's, but looks about twenty-five.

THELXIEPEIA (THEL), also a siren, Aggie's twin sister.

SETTING

A large rock that passes for an island.

• • •

The lights come up on a desolate scene: a large rock that passes for an island. We hear the sound of waves, the occasional seagull. Not a place you'd like to build a vacation resort.

The inert body of Young John lays sprawled on the ground. His clothes are torn, his hair is full of seaweed.

Aggie enters, attempting simultaneously to tiptoe and run, and not doing either particularly well. She throws herself down next to Young John and begins, ineptly, to look for a pulse. She is ravishingly beautiful, in a green dress that appears to be made of seaweed. In fact, there is a blue-green tint to everything about her, her hair, her skin. Not enough to make her look like a Smurf, but enough to tip us off that she is not quite human.

Thel enters. Like Aggie, she is absolutely gorgeous, and has the same kind of blue-green tint to her hair, skin and clothes.

THEL: Don't touch it!

AGGIE: Shhh.

THEL: You don't know where it's been.

AGGIE: *(Whispering.)* He's just been in the water. He's clean.

THEL: And don't whisper. You'll get a sore throat.

AGGIE: So?

THEL: So, we have to sing soon. There's another ship headed this way.

AGGIE: We don't have to sing anymore. We got what we've been singing for.

THEL: *(Pointing to Young John.)* What, that?

AGGIE: Come on, Thel. Isn't three thousand years long enough? Luring sailors to our island. And they came, they always did. At least, they tried.

THEL: You have such a beautiful voice, they can't help themselves.

AGGIE: You're just saying that.

THEL: No man can resist a soprano. All that resonance. It makes their pricks vibrate.

AGGIE: *(Giggles.)* Thel!

THEL: Look at you blush. You'd think you'd never met one before.

AGGIE: I haven't. *(Pause.)* Neither have you. But you still go on like you know all about them.

THEL: Deduction, Aggie. You've seen the way they jump off their ships to get to us. Brutes who haven't bathed in a week, whose only idea of music is a drinking song, swan diving off the deck to try to reach us. It's not appreciation of our harmonic technique, I can tell you that.

AGGIE: Oh. Well . . . they weren't worthy of us. Yes, they had no love for music, so the sharks got them. But they missed him because his heart was pure and he only wanted to listen to us sing, and any minute now he'll wake up, and . . . Ohmigod! Any minute now, he'll wake up! He can't see me like this, I'm a mess! My hair is all tangled. Look at this dress. It looks like it's made out of seaweed.

THEL: It is made out of seaweed.

AGGIE: Don't start with me, Thel! I can still dunk you.

(Young John picks this inopportune moment to groan.)

Ohmigod. I'm gonna go get cleaned up. Don't let him wake up without me!

(She runs off.)

THEL: *(Calling after her.)* Aggie!

(There is no answer. She looks at Young John, checks over her shoulder to see if Aggie is in sightline, then turns back to Young John.)

All right. Time to feed the sharks.

(Attempts to lift him from under his arms.)

Oof. You're heavier than the last one.

(Tries again.)

YOUNG JOHN: *(He turns over, pulling out of Thel's grasp.)* Just another two minutes. Wake me when the coffee's ready.

(Now determined, Thel attempts to lift him from his waist. She succeeds in getting him a little ways off the ground, but she is obviously straining. Finally, with a gasp, she drops him hard on the rock.)

YOUNG JOHN: *(Continued.)* Ow! What the . . .

(He is now awake. He attempts to sit up.)

Oh . . . spinning . . .

(He lies back down again.)

THEL: You're just a little waterlogged. It'll pass in a minute. You have to swim back to your ship.

YOUNG JOHN: My ship? What . . . All I remember is suddenly needing to leave my ship, like, like it was my last chance . . . and voices . . . the voices were my last chance not to be alone, can that be right? And then water, nothing in my ears but water . . . Hang on. I'm going to try this again. *(He sits up, very very slowly.)*

THEL: Well, you're all better now, so off you go.

YOUNG JOHN: I don't think I am. You still look . . . I don't know, bluish green. Where am I, anyway? Who are you? Was that your voice I heard? Were you . . . singing?

THEL: I'm really sorry. But you have to get out of here before my sister gets back.

YOUNG JOHN: Why, what's the matter with your sister?

THEL: I think she's in love with you.

YOUNG JOHN: . . . Do I know her?

THEL: No. I think she's just very glad to see you.

YOUNG JOHN: That isn't likely. Women aren't glad to see me. Unless I've just been paid.

. . . And you?

THEL: *(As if she were telling him the time.)* I think we ought to kill you.

YOUNG JOHN: I'm serious.

THEL: You think I'm not serious? Let me show you.

(Aggie scampers in, wearing a pink ball gown. It is rather the worse for wear, looking as if it has been washed ashore and mended clumsily with makeshift materials, which it has.)

AGGIE: OK, Thel, I'm ready. Let's . . .

(She stops short.)

I told you not to wake him till I got back.

THEL: He woke up himself. What is that thing?

AGGIE: It washed ashore thirty, forty years ago. I've been fixing it up.

THEL: It looks ridiculous.

YOUNG JOHN: What is going on here? Why do you both look green?

AGGIE: I ask you to be the judge, sir. Don't you think my gown is pretty?

YOUNG JOHN: *(Not sure which one he most wants to avoid pissing off.)* Oh . . . yes, it's . . . nice.

THEL: Aggie, don't make a fool of yourself.

AGGIE: And you don't want my silly old sister, do you?

YOUNG JOHN: Hell no. She wants to kill me.

AGGIE: *(A stunned pause. To Thel.)* Is that true?

YOUNG JOHN: She said so.

AGGIE: Thel?

YOUNG JOHN: She . . . she also said you were in love with me. But you're not . . . are you?

(A pause.)

AGGIE: How could you?

THEL: Oh, come on. There's nothing special about him. He just got lucky.

AGGIE: You can't have him! He's my dream come true, not yours! Why do you want him to die?

THEL: Well, what do you think we've been singing for all these years?

AGGIE: . . . That's not a very nice thing to say.

YOUNG JOHN: Hear hear.

THEL: DON'T GET FRESH WITH ME! I CAN STILL FEED YOU TO THE SHARKS!!!!

(Young John scuttles to the other side of the stage, well away from both of them, but with Aggie between him and Thel.)

AGGIE: Don't you touch him!

THEL: Think about it, Aggie. We're on a giant rock, thousands of miles from land. No boat can approach because of the breakers. Sharks live here. The water itself is deadly, barely above freezing in the middle of the summer. And here we are, singing so sweetly that men, experienced sailors, who see women as a sex organ and a pair of tits to be used and discarded at their pleasure . . .

YOUNG JOHN: *(Overlapping.)* Now wait a minute . . .

THEL: *(Continuing on through the above, ignoring Young John.)*

. . . these men dive into the water by the boatful, abandoning their ships to wash up as driftwood, succumbing to an icy death, so enraptured by our singing they even forget to swim, sailor by sailor, ship by ship, fleet by fleet, forever . . . Do you honestly think we're doing it to get laid?

AGGIE: I . . . but he . . .

THEL: Cause there's a lot easier ways to go about it.

AGGIE: But I can't spend eternity alone!

YOUNG JOHN: Hey. Maybe I have a girlfriend, huh? Maybe I have a wife.

AGGIE: *(It's not a question. It's a fact.)* But you don't.

YOUNG JOHN: . . . No.

AGGIE: *(To Thel.)* See? I mean, OK. So you want to kill them. That's your problem. But me, I need somebody! And I haven't had that many options!

THEL: Look at him, Aggie. Look!

(She does so, reluctantly, still keeping an eye on Thel.)

Does he look like a knight in shining armor? He's filthy. He's in rags. He's got a pot belly.

YOUNG JOHN: I do not . . .

THEL: He's coarse, vain, and ugly, no more or less than any of them. Does it make sense that he is the one, the only one to make it in three thousand years?

AGGIE: What . . . what are you saying?

THEL: There have been others.

AGGIE: Who? When?

THEL: Men. Sailors. Just like him. Over the years. Not so frequently at first, but as the centuries passed, they got in better shape. There were more ships. We started getting one every few months.

AGGIE: That's . . . that's impossible.

THEL: Not at all. I just found them all before you did.

AGGIE: And what did you do? No, don't tell me, I don't want to know.

YOUNG JOHN: You didn't expect to get away with it, did you?

THEL: *(With a chilly smile.)* It speaks.

YOUNG JOHN: This is a small island. You couldn't hide it from her forever, you had to know that.

AGGIE: But . . . but they were coming for me . . .

THEL: No, Aggie. They were coming to die. They knew it even as they dove in. That is the power we have, the power we were created to wield.

AGGIE: All of them . . . the thousands . . . dead . . . for us . . . Why didn't you tell me?

THEL: You would have stopped singing.

AGGIE: Of course I would have stopped singing! How could we? How could we have done it?

THEL: THEY DESERVED IT!!!

(Aggie and Young John stare at her.)

Oh, they look big and strong. That's their weapon. But inside, they're just tiny, sniveling cowards. They spend their whole lives running away. First, they run away from their families. They run off to sea, to god-knows-where, where nobody hears from them for weeks, months on end, until it suits their fancy to drop a line, or until they die. Just to get away. To find something new. It never occurs to them to think about what they leave behind.

AGGIE: It's not true!

YOUNG JOHN: *(Troubled.)* It is. I never thought of it like that, but it is.

THEL: But once they're at sea, they aren't far away enough. They keep running. They run from the women they have in each port. They run from the children they father but never know. They run from each other, making dick jokes and bragging about all the girls they've laid so nobody will know how they really feel about dressing and showering in a cramped space with a dozen other men. Aggie, they run from themselves, never stopping to ask what it is that they're giving their whole lives to run from.

YOUNG JOHN: It's true! It's all true!

THEL: And then, at long last, they run from their ships, that haven they've been always running *to,* they run from it, into the water, to find us . . . Do you believe that once they'd had us, they wouldn't run from us too? Run, back into the waves, sniggering about the goddesses on the rock island, and how great we were in the sack?

YOUNG JOHN: THOSE BASTARDS!!!!

THEL: But it doesn't have to be that way. Not for us. We have power. Picture them. Running, headfirst, into the water. The salt stinging their eyes, the cold penetrating their bones, but our voices in their ears, resonating in their brains, flooding out all their other senses. Their pricks hard despite the freezing ocean, their lungs filling with seawater . . . and they swim. Against the current, against their will, against the odds, they swim. Just for the chance to see us, to touch us, to encounter, just once in their lives, true beauty. And then the cold grabs their muscles, the sharks smell their pounding blood, the rocks themselves seem to reach up and pull them down. And down they go, never to run away again, the sea caught up with them at last.

YOUNG JOHN: Yes! Let them see how it feels to be swallowed whole by the sea, to drown in their own desire!

AGGIE: But . . . but I'm so alone . . .

THEL: They want to drown. How can you save them?

AGGIE: I . . . I . . .

THEL: And what if you could? Would you still want him if you knew that tomorrow he'd be in some hole-in-the-wall on the nearest shore, describing to whoever will listen what you look like naked?

YOUNG JOHN: *(Forgetting that Thel is referring to himself.)* I'd see him dead first.

THEL: Aggie?

(There is a long pause.)

AGGIE: Let them drown. If they truly want to drown, let them.

(Very softly, in the distance, the sound of a boat cutting through the waves.)

YOUNG JOHN: That sound . . .

THEL: *(Hugs Aggie.)* You'll never regret it.

YOUNG JOHN: I know that sound.

(He turns to scan the horizon.)

AGGIE: I'm scared.

YOUNG JOHN: Look!

(They do.)

A ship! A proud, wind-walled ship, cutting through the waves like it owns them. Like it owns the men aboard it. How little have they guessed, those men.

(The sound fades out. Young John turns to the sirens.)

Well? What are you going to do?

(Aggie and Thel look at each other.)

AGGIE: *(Very small.)* Thel . . . ?

(Thel smiles reassuringly, takes a deep breath, and begins to sing. She holds a single note, low, clear, and true. Aggie lowers her head in a moment of quiet resignation; then lifts it up again, and joins in, a perfect fourth above Thel. They hold their note, looking at each other. Young John looks from Aggie to Thel, then out to sea, then at the Sirens again. He throws his head back and begins to sing, in falsetto, a tritone above Aggie. The dissonance crescendos to an unbearable intensity, then cuts off abruptly as the lights black out. In the darkness, we hear the sound of men shouting in awe and lust, and diving into the water.)

END OF PLAY

Off the Map

Rich Orloff

CHARACTERS

A GUY (SCOTT).
A GAL (JEAN).
A LOCAL RESIDENT, (male).

TIME

The recent past.

PLACE

Someplace very cold.

• • •

A fairly barren terrain, except for some rocks of all sizes, from boulders to pebbles. Jean and Scott, a young married couple, enter, carrying knapsacks. They've both been hiking long enough to become very tired and very, very irritable.

SCOTT: I can't go any further.
JEAN: We can't stop here.
SCOTT: Why not?
(Scott takes off his pack.)
JEAN: It's too bleak.
SCOTT: I don't care.
JEAN: It's freezing here.
SCOTT: Any place else we go might just be worse.
JEAN: Does this place look familiar?
SCOTT: This place looks even less familiar than every other unfamiliar place we've been.
(Jean opens a map.)
JEAN: We must be someplace, Scott.
SCOTT: We've been to 14,000 someplaces, Jean. I think we've finally arrived at No Place.
JEAN: I've never felt so lost.
SCOTT: Maybe we're in South No Place or No Place Heights.
JEAN: You're not helping.
SCOTT: So? Even when I try, you don't appreciate it.
JEAN: Maybe if you tried harder, we wouldn't be lost.

SCOTT: Jean, we've been lost since we got married.

(Jean looks at the map.)

JEAN: I, I think we took a wrong turn after our honeymoon.

SCOTT: That's because you refused to linger in Newlywed Bliss.

JEAN: I think if we had headed straight towards Parenthood —

SCOTT: Jean —

JEAN: It would've been so easy to get to.

SCOTT: But impossible to get out of.

JEAN: Scott.

SCOTT: I just want to visit some other places first.

JEAN: You keep wanting to steer us back to Partyland.

SCOTT: And we would've gotten there if you didn't turn us off at Biological Clock World.

JEAN: I just found it more real than Extended Adolescenceville.

SCOTT: I would've been glad to settle down at the intersection of Love and Lust, but, no, you had to drag us to Responsibility Gulch.

JEAN: It was a nice gulch.

SCOTT: It was a ravine! With a dead end!

JEAN: Having children is not a dead end.

SCOTT: I'm just not there yet.

JEAN: Well, I can't stay here. It's too cold.

SCOTT: Maybe, maybe we should just admit we'll never find a place we both like.

JEAN: Do you think that's true?

SCOTT: All I know for sure is — I'm tired.

JEAN: Well, I'm going to look around and see if there's a way out.

SCOTT: I'm just going to sit here, and see if there's a way in.

JEAN: Good luck.

(Jean exits. Scott thinks, perhaps kicks a pebble or two. Someone from the area — A Local Resident — who happens to be a Penguin — enters. Noticing Scott, the penguin approaches cautiously. Scott, in his own world, doesn't see the penguin. Scott moves, and the penguin scoots away. Working up courage, the penguin moves closer, and closer, and closer, till —)

SCOTT: What the —

(The penguin scoots far away. The penguin and Scott study each other.)

PENGUIN: You — you're not a penguin.

SCOTT: No, I'm a person.

PENGUIN: A person? . . . Oh, yeah, I've heard about your kind. You'll eat anything, won't you?

SCOTT: I don't eat penguins.

PENGUIN: Prove it. Show me your teeth.

(Peering into Scott's smile:)

No feathers. OK, I'll trust you.

SCOTT: Thanks.

PENGUIN: You go near my wife or kids, I'll peck your balls out.

SCOTT: OK.

PENGUIN: People. Whoever heard of creating a species whose genitals make such easy targets?

SCOTT: We have opposable thumbs.

PENGUIN: *(Sarcastic.)* Ooo, I'm impressed. So what are you doing in Antarctica?

SCOTT: I'm in Antarctica?

PENGUIN: Didn't you notice how cold it is?

SCOTT: I thought it was a chill in the marriage.

PENGUIN: Problems with the little hen?

SCOTT: Yeah. Are you married?

PENGUIN: Of course. Most penguins mate for life.

SCOTT: And the others?

PENGUIN: They just stand around and occasionally scream at the sky.

SCOTT: Oh.

PENGUIN: And humans?

SCOTT: Well, we're *supposed* to mate for life —

PENGUIN: But?

SCOTT: Some of us get married too early.

PENGUIN: I'm glad I waited till I was eight.

SCOTT: You got married at eight?

PENGUIN: I know, I know. My dad used to say, "You're 7½, when are you going to settle down?"

I wasn't ready; I was still having too much fun sliding down icy hills on my belly.

SCOTT: I remember days like that.

PENGUIN: And then one day I waddled past her, and suddenly there was more to life than belly-sliding.

SCOTT: I walked past my wife, and I thought, what a fox.

PENGUIN: Oh, you have an inter-species relationship?

SCOTT: No, no, it's — She just has some of the qualities of a fox.
PENGUIN: Is she furry?
SCOTT: No.
PENGUIN: I'm confused. I've never looked at a penguin and thought, "What a sea lion!"
SCOTT: I —
PENGUIN: This may sound odd to you, but what I look for in a penguin — is a penguin. Tight feathers, webbed feet. And when I met her, well, I grabbed the first stone I could find and placed it at her feet.
SCOTT: Why?
PENGUIN: How else can I show her I'm capable of building a good stone nest for our chicks? I gave her lots of stones.
SCOTT: Really?
PENGUIN: Well, how did you impress *your* hen?
SCOTT: I gave her *one* stone.
PENGUIN: Like a boulder?
SCOTT: It was smaller than a pebble.
PENGUIN: You must live in a very barren terrain.
SCOTT: Only since we got married. You two fight?
PENGUIN: We have the occasional squawk.
SCOTT: We squawk constantly. Constantly.

(Scott sighs. The penguin moves closer and puts his flipper around Scott.)

PENGUIN: Friendly flipper . . . What's there to squawk about so often?
SCOTT: Well, sex for one thing.
PENGUIN: Oh, yeah.
SCOTT: In the beginning, it was so adventurous. And frequent. Now it's, well, you know how it gets.
PENGUIN: Well, not to brag, but sex with my wife is as good as ever.
SCOTT: And frequency?
PENGUIN: Every single year.
SCOTT: You have sex once a year?
PENGUIN: All penguins do.
SCOTT: You have sex with your wife once a year?
PENGUIN: And she's *always* in the mood.
SCOTT: I'm glad.
PENGUIN: Once it lasted forty seconds.
SCOTT: More power to you.

PENGUIN: I remember one year. We were going at it, feather-to-feather — I hope I'm not being too graphic —

SCOTT: I can handle it.

PENGUIN: And when we finished, I bowed to her, and she bowed to me, and we just stood next to each other. It was dusk, and some of the clouds had soft pink edges. And we just stood next to each other, for hours. Nothing needed to be said. Nothing needed to be done. It was a moment that didn't need to be filled with anything beyond . . . existing.

SCOTT: Really.

PENGUIN: And a few months later, we had our first pair of chicks. You have chicks?

SCOTT: Not yet. How many do you have?

PENGUIN: Ten.

SCOTT: Ten?! That's quite a responsibility.

PENGUIN: That's why we're not having twelve.

SCOTT: Ten kids, wow.

PENGUIN: I love coming home after swimming for food all day, hopping on the beach with a belly full of krill, and having the youngest pair chase after me. "Feed me, feed me," they yell, and I keep running from them yelling, "Go away, go way." "Feed me, feed me." "Go away, go away." "Feed me, feed me." "Go away, go away." And finally I stop and let them catch me, and I tilt my head up and go gg-gg-gg-gg-gg* *(*the sound of someone about to vomit)* and I open my beak wide, and they stick their little beaks in my mouth and eat regurgitated krill. And I keep vomiting and vomiting, until they waddle away happy and full . . . It's great.

SCOTT: I never knew regurgitating could be so satisfying.

PENGUIN: Every day my wife and I, we swim for krill, come home, and throw up for the kids.

SCOTT: And you like doing this?

PENGUIN: Of course.

SCOTT: Why?

PENGUIN: Because I'm a penguin. And this is what penguins do.

SCOTT: Oh.

PENGUIN: And what do people do?

SCOTT: Well . . . Depends on the person.

PENGUIN: Sounds complicated.

SCOTT: You see, people, we don't just live by instinct like you guys. Our brains are more developed. We can determine what we do with our lives by thinking things through and deciding what we want.

PENGUIN: Ohhh . . . Are people happy?

SCOTT: Not in the least.

PENGUIN: Well, don't feel too bad. You're only human.

SCOTT: *(A verbal shrug.)* I have opposable thumbs.

PENGUIN: Well, I better not keep the family waiting. I got a belly full of krill, and I'm sure babies want papa. Friendly flipper?

SCOTT: Friendly flipper.

(They hug. The penguin begins to waddle away. He notices a stone, and brings it to Scott.)

PENGUIN: Here. I know it's not fancy, but it's solid. Give it to your wife.

SCOTT: Thanks.

PENGUIN: And make sure you always leave time for belly-sliding.

(The penguin exits, waddling. Scott looks at the stone. Jean enters.)

JEAN: Hi.

SCOTT: Any luck?

JEAN: Every place I looked was cold and bleak.

SCOTT: Yeah, well.

JEAN: But I realized something.

SCOTT: What?

JEAN: If I'm going to be someplace cold and bleak, I'd rather be there with you.

SCOTT: I feel the same way.

JEAN: Scott . . . Remember a couple of months ago, when we landed on an island of calm —

SCOTT: And we felt a warm gust of faith —

JEAN: And so we threw caution to the wind?

SCOTT: Yeah.

JEAN: I'm pregnant.

(Scott feels an upchucking feeling in his neck.)

SCOTT: gg-gg-gg-gg-gg

JEAN: Scott?

SCOTT: I feel like throwing up.

JEAN: Oh, God, I knew you'd be upset.

SCOTT: No, no, it's a good thing.

JEAN: You know, usually it's the woman who gets nauseated.

SCOTT: Depends on the species.

JEAN: Sometimes I have no idea what you're talking about.

SCOTT: Here.

(Scott hands Jean the stone the penguin gave him.)

JEAN: *(A bit bewildered.)* Well, gee, thanks, Scott.

(Scott begins to find more stones and puts them at her feet one at a time.)

SCOTT: Oh, this one looks good.

JEAN: Scott?

SCOTT: This is a great one.

JEAN: What are you doing?

SCOTT: I love you, Jean.

JEAN: I love you, too, but —

SCOTT: Ooo, this one's great, too. Have a seat . . . Comfy?

(From a surprising place, perhaps the back of the theater, the penguin watches them through binoculars.)

PENGUIN: What strange birds they are.

(The penguin resumes watching Scott and Jean.)

(The lights fade.)

END OF PLAY

Parachute Silk

Carson Kreitzer

Parachute Silk opened May 23, 2009, at the Minnesota History Center, St. Paul, Minnesota. It was produced by the Minnesota Historical Society for their exhibit *Minnesota's Greatest Generation.* Director: Craig Johnson. Cast: Katharine — Laurel Armstrong; Betty — Summer Hagen; Mr. Anderson — Kerry Foerster.

Characters

Betty, twenties to thirties, high spirited.

Katherine, twenties to thirties, a little more subdued.

Mr. Anderson, forties to fifties, taciturn.

Setting

A sewing room, the Home Front, World War II. Space should be spare and theatrical, with as little "set" as possible. This is a world of black floor and white silk. If possible, a real parachute. If not, smaller amounts will do. Sewing apparatus can be real or mimed, but get as much silk as you can.

• • •

Two girls, sewing. One at a machine, one by hand. If possible, there is a real parachute, and the girls appear only as torsos, popping out of a mountain of billowing white.

BETTY: It's just —

KATHERINE: it's so —

BOTH: beautiful —

BETTY: I've never touched —

KATHERINE: nothing this soft —

BETTY: like it could fly

KATHERINE: it did.

BETTY: Like a cloud. Gonna be like gettin' married in a cloud.

KATHERINE: Parachute silk. It even *sounds* beautiful.

BETTY: You're gonna look like Carole Lombard. Betty Grable. An' Ginger Rogers all put together.

KATHERINE: You're gonna look like Rita Hayworth.

(The girls squeal quietly together at the thought, lofting the silk slightly so it catches the air. They watch its movement in wonder.)

KATHERINE: I was scared to touch it. Seems so delicate.

(Betty nods.)

Washed my hands fifteen times. Scared I'd still have engine grease from the plant. Scrubbed under my nails till that brush was about fuzz.

BETTY: You get used to it.

KATHERINE: I still have to pinch myself. Imagine —

Both our boys comin' home.

(Betty exhales, nodding. They take a minute. sober.)

And we get to be brides in white.

BETTY: *(Laughing.)* I thought sure I was gonna get married in my navy blue suit. Which woulda been just fine, of course . . .

KATHERINE: But this is better!

BETTY: I was at the machine, sewing. The fabric flying under my fingers. Nylon now, the army changed over from the silk. And I'm talking to Jeannie at the next machine, asking her if she knows anywhere, anywhere at all that's got fabric. I'd been saving up, and my Momma and my sisters were gonna help, but you know how it is —

KATHERINE: uh-huh

BETTY: There's just *nothing*. And the boss comes by, right up behind me. Never said more'n two words to me, just Good Morning or Break's Over.

(Mr. Anderson appears.)

An' he says —

MR. ANDERSON: What kind of fabric were you looking for, Miss Rawls?

BETTY: Oh, anything, Mr. Anderson — taffeta, satin, poplin, whatever I can get my hands on as long as it's white.

MR. ANDERSON: So your Bobby is coming home?

BETTY: *(Blushing.)* Yes, sir. He got home last week. We're getting married next month.

MR. ANDERSON: That's good, Miss Rawls. Suppose we're going to lose you, then?

BETTY: Oh no, sir, not while the war is on!

MR. ANDERSON: *(Nodding.)* Good girl. You're a good worker, Miss Rawls.

BETTY: And he disappears, back into his office. End of the day hands me this.

(Gaily lofts the silk.)

Wrapped up in brown paper. I knew right away — you get to know the weight of 'em. Knew what it was. My mouth was open, but no sound coming out. And you know — this is not usual for me.

He just smiles. And says "I'll see you on the line tomorrow, Miss Rawls."

(The two women sigh at the perfectness of this story. The silk moves with them — a little sigh.)

Just goes to show. You think you know people. But you never know.

(They freeze — light on Mr. Anderson.)

MR. ANDERSON: The army said destroy 'em.

Switched over from silk to nylon. Nylon parachutes, stronger, more predictable in weather, longer lifespan. And they said any extras we had of the silk ones, I was to destroy 'em.
Just had a half-dozen left. The end of the bolts of silk, before they sent the nylon. Took 'em down to the furnace room.
Destroy 'em.
Threw one in. It burned.
Didn't feel right, though. That kinda waste. The silk. And the work. The girls running them through and through and through the machines, sewing the pieces. Everything perfect, no mistakes, no place where the ripcord tunnel gets too close, everything sewed perfect like it was a bomber. Like it was a battleship. Cos boys' lives depending on us. I've seen girls right outta high school get so serious. Grow right up, the minute they sat down at those machines.
I thought I'd burn the other ones later.
Then I hear Betty Rawls, near to crying at her machine. Gettin' married and no fabric to be found. Not anywhere.
Now the Army said destroy 'em.
It didn't say how.
I think gettin' cut up in pieces, made into a dress to welcome that brave young man home, start his new life . . .
It sure ain't a parachute no more. I'd call that destroyed.
One for Betty Rawls. Bring one home to my wife, a christening dress for our granddaughter, and any others come along.
Three left for the next three girls on the line I hear crying cos they can't find no fabric.
Let 'em get married in silk.
My boy may not be coming home, but theirs are. Got to welcome them back.
(Focus shifts back to the girls.)

KATHERINE: Betty —

BETTY: What kind of sleeves are you doing? First I wanted muttonchop sleeves, with twelve buttons . . . but now I don't know.

KATHERINE: Oh, pretty simple, I guess. Just something off the shoulder.

BETTY: Oooh.

KATHERINE: Saw it in the window, and I thought, something like that — simple, off the shoulder, to balance the full skirt . . .

BETTY: Like *Gone With The Winds*?

KATHERINE: Yes, like — Betty.

BETTY: *(Occupied with a detail.) Mmm?*

KATHERINE: You ever think . . . we're not gonna know 'em, anymore?

(Betty looks at her.)

It was so long ago they went away.

I sometimes . . . I don't know. Clyde and I were steady before he left, but that was . . . I look back at that now, and I . . . I've changed so much over these years, you know, Betty. åou have, too —

BETTY: *(Gentle.)* Well, sure.

KATHERINE: And when he came back, I was just so glad he was alive, so glad. And when he proposed, it just seemed as though . . . Of course. This is what we were waiting for, this is what we'd meant, back then. But what if it's not. What if he was just missing home, and I'm just that girl from home, he doesn't know me, and I don't —

(She looks at Betty, helpless, then stares miserably at the silk in her hands.)

BETTY: Shhhh, now. All brides get cold feet sometime.

KATHERINE: They do?

BETTY: Sure. You're just gettin' 'em outta the way early.

(She smiles. Then Katherine does. Both girls laugh. A little, then a lot.)

KATHERINE: Well, Maximum Efficiency. That's what they teach us at the Plant.

BETTY: Good planning!

KATHERINE: Keep it moving!

BETTY: No slowdowns on the line!

KATHERINE: Keep your hair away from the conveyor belt at all times!

BETTY: If yer gonna get the jitters, get 'em on your lunch break! Watch, I'm gonna get mine when I'm standing there in the dress and they start to play that music. I'll just be frozen to the spot!

(The girls laugh.)

I wish my Dad could be there to give me away.

(Katherine nods.)

But we're the lucky ones, Katie. We're the lucky ones who get to have the jitters.

KATHERINE: *(A breath.)* I know. I know.

BETTY: I think I'm ready to slip this on. Check the hem for me?

KATHERINE: *(Soft.)* Of course.

(Betty turns upstage, freezes. Katherine continues.)

I didn't want to cut it much. That's why the skirt is gonna be so full. I want to keep it, just as it is. Just pull the cords up, so it's shorter in front, and then let the back flow out behind me. We took out one panel for the bodice and sleeves, but all the rest is just as it was. When it saved his life.

Clyde was out on a bombing run, over Yowata. Coming home, the engine caught fire. They had to bail out. He —

(She breaks off, continues.)

landed on some rocks, he was hurt. It was dark, and — not knowing where he was, or — he found some shelter. Used this parachute as a blanket for the cold, as a pillow to lay his head on. When it was daylight, they found each other, somehow, were taken in by some friendly Chinese. Made it . . . made it back home.

And when he got down on one knee, he brought me this. The parachute that kept him alive. That brought him back down to the earth. That brought him . . . back to me.

I didn't want to cut it, much.

Just took out the one panel.

The rest of it . . . I'm gonna leave just like it is.

I can't imagine anything . . . more beautiful.

I don't think there is anything more beautiful. Than what brought him back to me.

(Over last, Betty has very quietly removed her sewing smock, revealing the wedding gown beneath. She turns, showing Katherine the dress, still pinned in places.)

BETTY: What do you think?

KATHERINE: Oh, Betty. It's perfect.

(Mr. Anderson enters.)

MR. ANDERSON: You look just wonderful, Miss Rawls.

BETTY: Oh, Mr. Anderson. Thank you. Thank you so much for the —

MR. ANDERSON: Don't mention it.

BETTY: I was also . . . you've done so much already, Mr. Anderson, but I was wondering. My Dad won't be with us, I'm sure he'll be watching over, but won't be able to give me away. I was wondering if you could do it, sir. If you could walk me down the aisle.

MR. ANDERSON: I'd be very honored, Miss Rawls.

KATHERINE: You'll be the prettiest bride ever.

BETTY: Till you get your dress finished!

Beats a navy blue suit, huh kid?

KATHERINE: *(Stroking the fabric of her dress.)* I can't imagine anything more beautiful. I can't, Betty. I can't.

(Katherine and Mr. Anderson freeze. Betty, alone, a moment out of time:)

BETTY: *(To herself, holding herself, soft:)* he came home he came home he came home he came home he came home he came home he came home

END OF PLAY

Post Wave Spectacular

Diana Grisanti

Originally produced in the Apprentice Tens, January 2010, at Actors Theatre of Louisville, Kentucky. Cast: Jordan — Brett Ashley Robinson; Allie — Alexis Bronkovic; Vivian — Erin Adams; Jessica — Jessica Rice. Director: Amy Attaway.

Subsequently produced at the Humana Festival of New American Plays, March 2010, at Actors Theatre of Louisville, Kentucky. Cast: Jordan — Brett Ashley Robinson; Allie — Alexis Bronkovic; Vivian — Suli Holum; Jessica — Liza Fernandez. Director: Amy Attaway.

CHARACTERS

ALLIE, 25, they were together briefly.

JORDAN, 22, had a couple months of bliss.

VIVIAN, 30, still can't get over him.

JESSICA, 28, the outsider, currently wrapped around his little finger.

SETTING

A tea parlor that's not exactly a tea parlor. Cave-like. Spooky.

NOTE

A slash "/" indicates where dialogue should overlap.

• • •

Jordan, Allie and Vivian, three spectacular women with fabulous accessories, drink tea. They're a little larger than life.

JORDAN: In this post-post-post era of post-post-post feminism, my girls and I call a meeting of the minds.

A chat. An afternoon tea. A little confab about this thing we've been thinking about. About this *guy* who's been weighing us down.

ALLIE: And like, we're cool. We get it. We know we're not supposed to sterotypify all the men on the planet. Because where does polarization get us?

JORDAN: Somewhere polar.

ALLIE: Sub-zero. Glacial. Cold.

JORDAN: Totally.

ALLIE: And we don't want that.

JORDAN: So we won't polarize. We won't typify.

ALLIE: We'll be very, very specific.

JORDAN: 'Cause this boy?

ALLIE: This one particular Y chromosome?

VIVIAN: Is totally under our skin.

ALLIE: And he thinks he can get away with it because he's all charming and unassuming and he has a really sweet grin and this mysterious limp — no really, nobody knows why he limps, it's a total mystery — but we're wise to his shit.

Cuz we've been there.

We've been witness.

VIVIAN: Many times.
JORDAN: A few dozen for me.
ALLIE: And eight and a half times for me.
JORDAN: And a half?
ALLIE: Blowjob. Without reciprocity.
VIVIAN: If I had a nickellll . . .
JORDAN: Viv was with him for a year.
VIVIAN: A long year.
ALLIE: And like, duh, we know we're tiptoeing on thin ice here. We're bordering on some neo-essentialist self-victimization toxic trash but like —
JORDAN: Whatever.
VIVIAN: Dude's a dick.
ALLIE: You see? See how he drives us to betray our undergraduate foremothers? Gendering our words, codifying our vocabulary, dragging us down the slippery slope of linguistic stratification?
But like we said.
JORDAN: He's a douche bag.
(A knock.)
ALLIE: She's here!
JORDAN: I'll get it!
VIVIAN: Is everything ready?
ALLIE: Yes. Oh wait. Eyelash.
VIVIAN: Thanks.
ALLIE: Make a wish.
VIVIAN: *(Blows.)*
ALLIE: Wish for something good?
VIVIAN: Mmhmm.
JORDAN: OK. Ready?
VIVIAN AND ALLIE: Ready.
(In walks Jessica. The door slams, startling her.)
JESSICA: Ah!
VIVIAN: Sorry about that. It's an old house. Heavy doors. Hard to open, but very weather resistant.
JORDAN: Jessica! Come in! Come in! You look fabulous!
ALLIE: You did your eyebrows. Plucking? Waxing?
JESSICA: Threading.
JORDAN: Amazing.
ALLIE: They complement the hell out of your cheekbones.

JORDAN: Totally.

JESSICA: Thank you.

ALLIE: Did you have trouble finding us?

JESSICA: No, not at all.

ALLIE: So the directions were helpful?

JESSICA: They were great.

ALLIE: Excellent.

JORDAN: And thank you for RSVPing. You know, replying really has become a lost art.

ALLIE: So true.

JORDAN: Would you like some tea? We have loose leaf, fair trade, decaf, caf, green, black, brown, red, full-bodied, slender, docile, affable, churlish, and mint.

JESSICA: I'll have the mint, I guess.

JORDAN: That's my favorite too.

JESSICA: I'm sorry but. Do I know you?

JORDAN: I am so sorry. I'm a social disaster sometimes. I'm Jordan. You were my TA for Postmodern Feminisms in Contemporary Architecture. I wrote the paper about Pansexual Desire in Midwestern Outlet Malls?

JESSICA: Oh, right. You're Jordan. That was a great paper.

JORDAN: Thank you.

ALLIE: And I'm Allie. We volunteer at the clinic together. Opposite shifts though. You never see me.

JESSICA: Allie? The Allie who introduced the flavored dental dams?

ALLIE: Guilty.

JESSICA: You're a legend. And the pineapple is to die for.

ALLIE: I know, right?

VIVIAN: And we've never met. I'm / Viv

JESSICA: Vivian.

VIVIAN: Viv.

JESSICA: Viv. Hi. I just, I know you 'cause —

VIVIAN: I used to date — .

JESSICA: You used to date — .

VIVIAN: Right.

JESSICA: He talks about you is all.

VIVIAN: Don't tell me that.

JESSICA: I mean, he doesn't say anything bad, / it's just —

VIVIAN: No. I know. But if I know he's talking about me, then I'll speculate, then I'll get all preoccupied and nostalgic and maybe a little obsessive, so. No. I'll just pretend you didn't say anything at all.

JESSICA: OK.

VIVIAN: Because I really don't want to know.

ALLIE: Neither do I. I mean, unless he said something I should really know about —

JORDAN: Or like, if he mentioned me in passing or something —

ALLIE: Or wondered what I was up to —

VIVIAN: Ladies. This isn't about us. It's about Jessica, right? It's about you.

JESSICA: Me?

ALLIE: Jessica, how long have you been dating him?

JESSICA: Oh, we're not dating.

JORDAN: Right. But how long have you seeing each other?

JESSICA: We're not seeing each other.

VIVIAN: OK, sure, but how long have you been together?

JESSICA: We're not / together —

ALLIE: Jessica! Jessie.

VIVIAN: Honestly.

JESSICA: Really. We're not together anymore. We spend a lot of *time* together, if that's what you mean.

VIVIAN: I see. And what do you do when you're together?

JESSICA: I don't know. We watch movies or talk or have a beer or. And we have the same taste in books and we both like poetry and. Our politics are really similar, so there's that and.

VIVIAN: But when he's having a bad day —

ALLIE: When he's just too tired or upset or bedraggled to talk about books or movies or politics —

JORDAN: And all he needs is a woman in his arms —

VIVIAN: When that happens?

JESSICA: We. I mean, yes, sometimes, but it's not. We have an understanding.

VIVIAN: I thought so.

JESSICA: He struggles with intimacy.

VIVIAN: Intimacy! ALLIE: Oh, the struggle! JORDAN: Mmmm.

ALLIE: So you're just friends.

JESSICA: Right.

ALLIE: Friends who sleep together.

JESSICA: Right.

ALLIE: And who take care of each other.

JESSICA: I don't need to be taken care of.

ALLIE: We know that. But he does. Right? He needs to be taken care of.

VIVIAN: . . . Right?

JORDAN: Your tea's ready. Do you take sugar? Cream?

JESSICA: Do you have soy milk?

JORDAN: We sure do.

(They sip their tea.)

ALLIE: You know what I miss? The neck kissing. He was really good at that.

EVERYBODY ELSE: Yeeahh.

ALLIE: The way he'd move in with a lust of a thousand soldiers coming home from war. The hunger in his eyes. The steadiness of his breath. That furtive limp smacking of countless romantic possibilities.

JORDAN: Maybe it was an accident. Some near death episode resulting in shattered knee caps and broken dreams.

ALLIE: Maybe it was congenital. A family secret. An evolutionary glitch.

JORDAN: Maybe it was a knife fight. Knives are unbearably sexy.

VIVIAN: Or maybe it's something horribly prosaic. But I really hope not.

ALLIE: His enthusiasm was uncanny, wasn't it? You can't find that kind of enthusiasm in most men. The sheer passion for contact.

VIVIAN: It was like adolescence. It was like living out a sex scene from the Judy Blume novels you'd pass around your sixth grade classroom. Everything about it — the breath, the smell, the touch . . . everything was so . . . fictional.

EVERYBODY ELSE: Yeeaahhh.

VIVIAN: And of course you assume it's different with you. That somehow *you*'re the cause of his staggering enthusiasm.

ALLIE: But no.

JORDAN: Turns out he's just an enthusiastic sort of guy.

ALLIE: With an intimacy problem.

JORDAN: And a penchant for blowjobs.

VIVIAN: And the sad truth of it is, we fell for it. He swaggered up to us, smiled, and we fell for it.

JESSICA: I should get going.

VIVIAN: You're meeting him. Aren't you.

JESSICA: We had plans.

VIVIAN: Dollar fifty Busch Light night?

JESSICA: How'd you know?

VIVIAN: It's so endearing, right? His love of cheap beer? The way he discusses it like a fine wine, affecting that agile combination of irony and reverence?

JORDAN: And his three dollar tips?

ALLIE: The waitresses would swoon over those tips.

VIVIAN: You know, Jessica, we thought about going straight to him. Directly to the source. But what good would that do? Female attention? A veritable buffet of scolding and coddling and armchair psychology. No. He'd love that. He loves to be scolded and coddled and psychologized.
And in the end, let's face it, he'd probably convince us all to sleep with him anyway.

JORDAN: He's very good at that.

ALLIE: Isn't he?

VIVIAN: So we came to you, Jessica. Or rather, we brought you to us.

JESSICA: So what do I do?

ALLIE: Break it off.

JESSICA: But he's just a friend. I can't break up with someone I'm not dating.

VIVIAN: Exactly. You see how he operates?

JORDAN: You'll have to start dating someone else.

JESSICA: But everyone thinks I'm dating him.

ALLIE: You could always move. Leave the city? The state? That's a proven method of detachment.

JORDAN: No, moving doesn't work. He sends emails. He writes dazzling emails.

JESSICA: He does. He really does.

JORDAN: You see?

JESSICA: But what if I don't want to leave him? What if we're meant to be?

ALLIE: Oh Jessica. *We* were meant to be.

JORDAN: We were meant to be.

VIVIAN: We were meant to be.

JESSICA: I can't just stand him up, you know.
I mean, we'd planned to meet before this, this —

ALLIE: Chat?

JORDAN: Confab?

ALLIE: Afternoon tea?

(Jessica tries to open the door. It's locked.)

JESSICA: It's locked.

JORDAN: It sticks sometimes. Old house. Very old. Ancient.

VIVIAN: Actually, Jessica, I'd like you to think of our time here as a retreat. A detox period. A little respite from the outside world.

ALLIE: Have another cup of tea, won't you?

JORDAN: We have plenty. *(Jordan reveals a year's supply of tea.)* A year's supply.

JESSICA: A year?

JORDAN: It'll be over before you know it.

ALLIE: And we'll have so much to talk about in the meantime!

JORDAN: We do have a lot in common after all.

JESSICA: A year, you said?

VIVIAN: Time flies when you're in the company of friends.

JESSICA: But what will we do? For a year?

JORDAN: We could have sex with each other. It'll be just like the seventies.

ALLIE: Too old school. We should bake things and learn how to knit. Ironic domesticity is the new bra-burning.

VIVIAN: Wait!

Eyelash.

Make a wish.

JESSICA: *(Blows.)*

VIVIAN: Wish for something good?

JORDAN: I hope so.

ALLIE: So what do you think, Jess? About our little plan?

JESSICA: I think.

I think.

You don't happen to have Earl Grey, do you?

ALLIE: As a matter of fact, he's the only boy allowed.

(The ladies drink their tea.)

END OF PLAY

Pussy

Laura Jacqmin

Pussy was originally produced at The Public Theater on May 1, 2009, in the US/UK Cabaret: Mis/perceptions (presented by The Public and The Old Vic). Director: Colette Robert. Cast: Margot — Mary Quick; Alistair — Hal Fickett; Hood — Federico Trigo.

CHARACTERS

MARGOT, American. Doing a semester-long study abroad in the UK. Twenties.

ALISTAIR, British. A student. Probably a very proper, aristocratic accent (the one with the slight lisp). Twenties.

HOOD, British. Be-sweatshirted. Dangerous. Fucking sexy. Twenties or thirties.

SETTING

A small apartment in Cambridge, UK. The first days of spring.

• • •

Margot and Alistair are here. Alistair is bleeding profusely from the nose. He clutches it with a handkerchief.

ALISTAIR: It hurts.
It *hurts.*

MARGOT: Tilt your head back. Keep it tilted back!

ALISTAIR: I'll drown that way. It'll slip back down my throat, to my lungs. I'll drown in my own blood!

MARGOT: Haven't you ever had a nosebleed before? You tilt *back.* Back and *up.*
Stop putting your fucking face down.

ALISTAIR: This is not a nosebleed, Margot, I was *punched* in the *face* by a *stranger.*

MARGOT: I know you were punched.

ALISTAIR: You're not very sympathetic.
It *hurts.*

MARGOT: You're not bleeding very much anymore.
It's stopping. It'll have stopped in a minute.
You're fine. Everything's going to be fine.

ALISTAIR: It's throbbing.

MARGOT: Do you have ice?

ALISTAIR: Yes.

MARGOT: Put ice on it.

ALISTAIR: *(Pathetic:)* Can you get it for me?

MARGOT: I have to get back to the dorm. We have curfew. All the study-abroads have to be back by midnight, and it's almost midnight.

ALISTAIR: There's peas, in the freezer.

(Beat.)

I can feel my face swelling up.

(Margot gets the peas, reluctantly.)

Thanks.

Thanks for doing this. You didn't have to. I was sort of hoping — sort of planning — because we were hitting it off so well in the pub, you know, talking about Iraq and whatever, having a real meat-and-potatoes sort of discussion, that I would be asking you back here, to my place. Inviting you. If you'd wanted to. To — you know — get to know each other a little bit better.

Which is not a euphemism.

If you'd wanted to.

(Beat.)

Had you wanted to?

MARGOT: Yes.

ALISTAIR: *(Relieved:)* Oh. Right. Great.

MARGOT: But —

ALISTAIR: But?

MARGOT: But then when we went outside and I was smoking a cigarette and you were keeping me company, you — you know? — got punched in the face.

And the situation changed.

ALISTAIR: The neighborhood used to be better. Mildly. Then these guys with sweatshirts and wallet chains and working class accents started swarming all over the place and now you can't stand outside even for a second on a warm evening or this'll happen.

MARGOT: How did you know what sort of accent he had? He didn't say anything.

ALISTAIR: I know the type.

MARGOT: He smelled like a Fry-o-lator. Like hot vegetable oil.

ALISTAIR: How'd you smell him?

MARGOT: The air off his arm. As it connected. With your head.

(Hood enters. Margot sees him; Alistair doesn't. Hood looks mean, but not in a comical, cartoonish way: just regular mean and tough and thick and dense and dead fucking sexy.)

Do you think he wanted money? He didn't ask for your wallet. He just —
Boom.
Pow.
He knew what he was doing. He knew how to cause pain, and he knew because he liked doing it. Likes doing it. He knew just where to hit to get the maximum / amount of hurt —

ALISTAIR: Wanna know what I think? Do you? Do you wanna know?

MARGOT: Fine.

ALISTAIR: It was because he overheard our conversation.

(Hood flexes his arms, trying them out.)

MARGOT: About Iraq?

ALISTAIR: About bloodthirsty Americans. About all the wee precious little boy soldiers going abroad to play war and shooting and raping.
Wild animals.
Hungry for the unknown and desperate to prove themselves brave and adventurous and independent.
Thought we were maybe being too intellectual for our own good, is my guess.

(Margot approaches Hood. He watches her closely, but allows her to pull back the corner of his sweatshirt to investigate his neck.)

MARGOT: I told you. We're not bloodthirsty.
He had a tattoo, the guy. On his neck. Like a bar code.
For what? What does that mean?
A *bar* code.
For what sort of product? Groceries? An Xbox? Something else?

ALISTAIR: It's shameful, your country's behavior. And our following suit, I'm not denying that was bad as well, but we never would've if you hadn't in the first place.

MARGOT: You're ripping off the *Telegraph*, you know.

ALISTAIR: What? Am not.

MARGOT: 2002. Harold Pinter opinion piece. You are.

ALISTAIR: Well — I've absorbed it for my thesis, then. I've quoted it before. And he's right.

(Margot continues to circle Hood, examining him.)

MARGOT: Was right, maybe.
New politics. New people in charge. New everything. It's not the same way anymore.

ALISTAIR: You so sure about that?

MARGOT: Probably.

Yes.

Definitely.

He said *nothing*? Not a whisper, not a breath? Before he came at you. Before he rushed us both.

ALISTAIR: Probably coming off seeing something at the Cineplex a block over. *Resident Evil: Everyone Fucks Off And Bleeds Everywhere With Their Brains Hanging Out? Rambo Part One Million?* In an American state of mind, perhaps.

Fascinated with action movies, you are, all of you. High-speed chases and guns blazing and good versus evil, and you're always the good guys. And the military men get the satellite football hooked up at base — did you know that? Over in Afghanistan? They hook up the television before connecting the telephones when they move base, because why would you want to ring someone back home when you can watch your team slaughter the other team in hi-def?

MARGOT: Maybe he just didn't like your face.

(Hood opens his mouth, stretching his jaw.)

ALISTAIR: I have a nice face.

I have a classically handsome face.

MARGOT: Or your accent.

Or the way you were behaving.

The way you are, generally.

ALISTAIR: Oh, very funny. Very nice. I'm in pain here, right?

(Beat.)

Do you like the way I am?

You must, right? Because — you were going to come back, if I'd asked, weren't you? To get to know each other better. Which could or could not be a euphemism, depending on what you'd wanted and were comfortable with.

So you like me. Is the assumption I can make.

You could be persuaded to think of me in *that way.*

MARGOT: I get all these emails from my friends, you know? Also doing study abroad? In Spain and Italy and France?

I get these emails and they're like, *Met a dark, handsome man. A dangerous man with a dicey past. This man is trouble.*

And I believe them, because why wouldn't I?

And the sex they have is epic.

They need lube where they've never needed lube before. They miss class. They blow off trips to museums because they're so busy fucking in the broken-down, romantic, rust-stained flats of these dangerous men who smoke European cigarettes and have scarred knuckles and the whites of their eyes are enormous and the pupils are dark pits.
They fuck like they've never fucked before and the fact that they're fucking strangers makes it better because it's crazy. It's crazy to sleep with an unknown person who radiates something . . . worrisome.
It is violent and unwholesome and half-terrifying.
You're fucking someone who might murder you and it's fantastic and amazing and something to blog home about.
In France and Italy and Spain.
(Beat.)
And I came to England.
There is tea in England. And a certain breed of cow which is pleasing to the eye when it dots the hillsides. And the bottoms of the pint glasses say they were certified to hold a mathematically perfect pint by the Queen herself.
I am not sure I am having the adventure I was meant to have.

ALISTAIR: Look, I'd like to see you again. Under better circumstances. Once I've healed up. And you're here for the semester and all, so we have time. I'm working on my thesis, of course, but even if there's no time for a proper date during a certain week, we could at least get a coffee and talk. Discuss things in a rousing manner. I know you like to discuss things. You liked it, earlier tonight.
(Margot looks at Hood's fingers and hands.)

MARGOT: *(Not out of control or getting excited or anything stupid like that. Just matter of fact:)* If you throw a punch the wrong way, you can break a thumb.
He knew how to do it the right way.
I bet he knows how to do a lot of things the right way.
I bet he goes on adventures.
I bet he knows how to command a room, and fire a rifle, and tie off a wound.

ALISTAIR: Look, at the end of the day, that was a violent person.
A degenerate.
A reprobate.
Probably on the dole. Probably no prospects.

Who gets his rocks off punching strangers in the face. Making them bleed. His way or the highway.

(Margot kisses Hood. Hood doesn't kiss her back, but doesn't pull back, either. Kiss ends.)

There's no reasoning with people like that.

They're interested in one thing and one thing only: causing other people pain.

You wouldn't want to be around violent people, would you? You've just spent an evening in a pub convincing me of the fact that Americans are good and kind and don't join up just for the blood sport or to learn how to shoot enormous guns or fifteen ways to kill a man in under fifteen seconds, right?

Americans are like you.

Doing something when it has to get done?

Look both ways before crossing the street?

Good and strong and brave and true and smiles and nodding in agreement and above all, uncurious.

Let's be uncurious together.

(Alistair examines the handkerchief.)

The bleeding's stopped.

The blood's drying.

But thin, not thick.

Look: you can still see the floral border.

The floral border of the handkerchief. The blood didn't touch that.

(Hood slowly reaches up and — ever so slightly — ever so subtly — pulls Margot's hair so that her head is forced back, just a little. She is held in place. Hood puts his lips to her neck. She closes her eyes, in terrified ecstasy. Alistair still holds out the handkerchief. Lights out.)

END OF PLAY

Small Portions

Quinn D. Eli

The final draft of *Small Portions* was produced at the Shell Theater, 300 West 43rd Street, 4th Floor, New York, New York, by Turtle Shell Productions as part of its 2009 "Best of Eight Minute Madness" Play Festival. Artistic Director: John Cooper. Director: John Cooper. Cast: David — Ras McCurdie; Helen — Elena Chang; Kevin — Nathan Atkinson.

SYNOPSIS

In this fable of race and writing, an African-American playwright, an Asian-American hostess, and an oversexed bartender come together over daiquiris at a ghost-filled Chinese restaurant.

CHARACTERS

DAVID, African-American, thirties.
HELEN, Asian-American, late twenties.
KEVIN, Asian-American, early twenties.

TIME AND SETTING

Late morning in the Philadelphia suburbs.

• • •

The bar of an upscale Chinese restaurant. Kevin is taking David's order. Helen is nearby, at the hostess stand, talking on the phone.

KEVIN: *(To David.)* That's all you want, just the two appetizers?
DAVID: Sure. Sure. What the hell. That'll be enough, right?
KEVIN: Dumplings and egg rolls. The best in town. You want anything else, though, like an entree?
DAVID: No. Just another daiquiri.
KEVIN: Coming right up.
(Kevin exits through swinging doors, and a rush of noise comes from the other side.)
(David, startled by the noise, looks up.)
(In a moment, Kevin returns, carrying the daiquiri, and again there's a rush of noise.)
KEVIN: *(Continued.)* Your daiquiri, sir, number three. Enjoy.
DAVID: You all must be pretty busy.
KEVIN: Nah, it's too early. You're the first customer of the day.
DAVID: Oh. I thought — it's just, when I heard all that noise coming from the kitchen, it just sounded like you must be very busy.
KEVIN: The noise? I don't hear anything.
DAVID: When you went through the doors, I heard a lot of commotion. Activity. From the kitchen.
KEVIN: There is no kitchen.

DAVID: Wait. How can you not have a —

KEVIN: Behind *those* doors, you mean? Oh, sure: That's the tech shop. Technical director, master carpenter, you know, like that. I guess they *do* make a lot of noise, now that you mention it.

I must be immune. You get used to it after a while.

DAVID: OK. Now I'm confused. If there's no kitchen, then how —

KEVIN: Your food will be out soon.

(Kevin gathers two empty glasses from David and hurries through the doors. The noise of hammering is clear.)

DAVID: *(To no one.)* Um. OK. Thanks.

(David begins reading a book. Helen hangs up the phone, but it rings immediately.)

HELEN: Lotus Blossom Oriental Dragon and Haiku Restaurant. May I take your order? OK. Sure. OK. Yeah, he's here —

(Helen turns to David.)

It's for you.

DAVID: Pardon?

HELEN: The phone, David, it's for you.

DAVID: How in the world did you know my name?

HELEN: It's on the cast list: David, Helen, Kevin. You're David.

The black guy. The only one here.

DAVID: What in the — what cast list?

HELEN: You gonna take this call or what?

DAVID: Who is it?

HELEN: *(Into the phone.)* Who may I say is calling?

(Turns back to David.)

The forgotten voices of your ancestors, a proud and mighty African people, dragged in chains four hundred years ago into the bitter confines of slavery. They're calling collect.

DAVID: . . . Is this a joke?

HELEN: Well, the business about them calling collect was meant to be funny. Otherwise, though, no, it's not a joke. It's very, very serious. Art, David, is always serious.

DAVID: I have no idea what you're talking about.

HELEN: *(Into the phone.)* Oh, mighty ancestors, David is declining your call, turning his back on your legacy, refusing to acknowledge all that you suffered and sacrificed so that he might live with dignity. Huh? Oh, because he's having lunch — .

(Helen hangs up. Turns to David.)

HELEN: *(Continued.)* They said they'll call back.

DAVID: Is this the — I mean, is there entertainment here? Is that it? Are you the entertainment?

HELEN: David, David, David. Dear, sweet David. Painfully naïve.

DAVID: I don't understand how you know my name.

HELEN: *(As though explaining to a child.)* I already told you: it's on the —

DAVID: I know, I know. The cast list. But I don't get it. What cast list are you talking about?

Didn't you even bother to read the program? You're not one of those people are you, the ones who sit down and don't read the program? I hate those people. What's so important you can't take *two* minutes to find out the names of the cast? What are you doing that's so important? Huh? I wanna know.

'Cause I can tell you what you're NOT doing: you're NOT turning off your cell phones, for one thing. You're NOT unwrapping your candy wrappers in advance, like you were told. No, you'll probably do that bit of business *now,* right in the middle of the show, while the mysterious, exotic, former supporting cast member of the traveling company of *Miss Saigon* is giving her long-awaited monologue. THAT'S when you'll choose to unwrap your fucking candy.

(Beat.)

DAVID: You were in *Miss Saigon*? I love that show! That stuff with the helicopter was just so —

HELEN: Shut up.

DAVID: Hey, what the hell is that? "Shut up"? I'm a customer here, I'm paying money. You can't tell me to shut up.

HELEN: This is not *Snow Falling on Cedars,* David, OK? I don't do docile. It's the reason I'm still in regional theater. If I could do docile, I'd be making zillions in Hollywood. Or if I could, like, handle a sword while flying through the air on wires. That would help, too.

DAVID: OK, I'm going back to my book now, OK? I don't mean to be rude, but I just want to have my lunch and read my book.

HELEN: Some lunch. Daiquiris. What's that, number four?

DAVID: Three. So what?

HELEN: And it's not even noon.

DAVID: I have ordered food, too, in case you didn't notice.

HELEN: Dumplings and egg rolls do not qualify as a meal. Unless you're white and live in a frat.

DAVID: Like I said: I'm getting back to my book.

HELEN: What are you reading?

(David opens his mouth to answer, but just then the phone rings. Helen picks it up.)

HELEN: *(Continued.)* House of the Rising Sun's Raw Sushi and Geisha Emporium, may I take your order? What? How is that racist? But it's true! I'm telling you, they ARE all like that. 'Cause I used to date them exclusively, that's how I know. OK. Fine.

(Turns to the audience.)

If anyone in the audience is white and lives in a fraternity, I apologize for any comments I made that you may have found offensive.

(Returns to the phone call.)

Satisfied? Sheesh. The things I put up with to work.

(Helen hangs up the phone.)

DAVID: Who was that?

HELEN: Actors' Equity. Anyway. What are you reading?

(David holds up his book.)

HELEN: *(Continued.) How to Write a Ten Minute Play*?

DAVID: I'm a writer. A playwright.

HELEN: Like I couldn't have guessed *that* from the five daiquiris.

DAVID: Three! It's only been three.

HELEN: Whatever. What the hell do you care about ten minute plays for anyway, if you're a real playwright. Write a real play.

DAVID: It's tough to explain.

HELEN: *(Looks at her watch.)* I've got about four minutes left. Try me.

DAVID: It's really difficult to get, like, full-length plays produced these days, you know, because of the cost and all, and because nobody goes to plays anymore anyway, on account of they're all home watching "Desperate Housewives," so a lot of places put on these, like, ten-minute play festivals or whatever.

You know, short-attention span theater. It's not exactly Eugene O'Neill, but what the hell.

HELEN: What the hell?

DAVID: Yeah. What the hell.

HELEN: And you don't feel like it's a compromise, writing a ten-minute play?

I mean, I assume that's why you're reading that book there, right? To teach yourself how to write one.

DAVID: I don't know. I guess maybe I did feel . . . compromised for a while, like it was cut-rate playwriting or something. But now that I've actually read a few, I mean, a lot of them are quite good. It's not easy trying to create entire characters and a setting and conflict and everything in just ten minutes. It could be sort of a challenge, I guess. So I figure —

HELEN: "What the hell."

DAVID: Exactly.

HELEN: And this doesn't seem to you to have *racial* implications?

DAVID: What do you mean?

(The phone rings. Helen answers.)

HELEN: Flying Dagger/Hidden Dragon International House of Mushu Pancakes. May I take your order? OK. Well, it's not me. It's not me! It's him. OK. Sure.

(Turns to David.)

The director says we're about seven minutes into this thing, so you'd better pick up the pace. David.

Anyway, about the racial implications.

DAVID: The racial implications? Of a ten-minute play?

HELEN: Exactly.

DAVID: Sorry. I don't see it.

HELEN: Of course you don't. You're willfully blind. Listen: a lot of these theaters, they are primarily run by — I mean to say, they're not run by people who look like you and me, right?

DAVID: Sure. Yeah. Right.

HELEN: So people who *do* look like you and me are at something of a disadvantage, yes, because we're not the ones making the big decisions about what gets produced and what doesn't?

DAVID: Well, sure, but it's tough for everybody.

HELEN: I *know* that. I'm an actress. You don't have to tell me. But let's say I play the Dragon Lady one time on a cop show or something, and it's no big deal, right? I get a nice residual, I pay my rent, and then I'm free to do some less humiliating stuff, on the stage or whatever. The problem, though, is now there's a precedent. Now I've sort of made it known that for the right price and for the chance at a little exposure, I'm willing to occasionally play the Dragon Lady or the Geisha or whatever. And if that's the case, then why should anybody offer me anything else? I mean, why should anyone offer me a full course meal if they know I'll settle for appetizers?

DAVID: I'm not sure I — I mean, the analogy's kind of wobbly.

HELEN: Lots of good writers writing these ten-minute plays, yes?

DAVID: Yes. Absolutely. And I don't want to — disparage their hard work and their talent by saying, well, it doesn't count. Every time a writer puts pen to paper, it counts.

HELEN: You understand you're sucking up, right? Even as we speak.

DAVID: What? No I'm not! Who the hell am I sucking up to?

HELEN: I don't know. Other playwrights who might be in the audience. The white people running the theaters. You're sucking up. Letting them know you're a team-player. You're not a difficult Negro. You're not angry or militant or a threat. You want them to relax around you. Feel good around you. So they'll produce your plays and accept you and love you. *(David stands up and screams toward the double doors:)*

DAVID: CAN I HAVE A CHECK, PLEASE? A CHECK? NOW!

(Kevin comes running out.)

KEVIN: I apologize. Was there a cue? I didn't hear my cue — .

HELEN: Sorry, Kevin, my fault. You got any tips for homeboy here on how to write a ten-minute play?

KEVIN: Make the Asian guy, like, a stud for once. OK? Not geeky.

HELEN: That's kind of a tall order for just ten minutes.

KEVIN: Then take more time, shit! How come it's only ten minutes anyway? Is that because you're black?

DAVID: No, Christ, of course not! It has nothing to do with race — .

HELEN: Everything's about race. And as long as there's still more white folks than colored folks getting their full-length plays produced, then I don't think you can just happily write a ten-minute play anytime anyone asks. If you get too satisfied with small things, David, then after a while it won't occur to anybody to offer you anything big.

KEVIN: *(To David.)* Oh, that's another thing: You should have somebody in the play who is like "the moral center," you know, the voice of reason and clarity who stands apart from the others and says really cool, really profound things. But don't make it the Asian guy, OK? He should be the stud.

DAVID: *(To Helen.)* Bet you never get to say really cool, really profound things when you're playing the Dragon Lady or the Geisha.

HELEN: Sure I do. But it always sounds like I'm reciting from a fortune cookie.

DAVID: So maybe here's the virtue of the ten-minute play: You got to play a character with a little substance for a change, a little depth. And that's a good thing, isn't it?

HELEN: It's great. And I appreciate it, I truly do. Gimme another, oh, seventy minutes, and I'll feel like I'm Uta Hagen.

DAVID: Anyway. I guess this means I won't be getting lunch.

HELEN: Sorry. No lunch. And you might as well get rid of that book, too. You don't need it.

DAVID: I don't know. Maybe I should keep reading, just so I'm clear about how to write one of these things.

HELEN: You've already done it. And it's not half bad. Got a little racial politics in there, a little Afro-Asian solidarity, and a critique of contemporary theater to boot. Not bad at all.

KEVIN: Oh, this is turning into some serious cutting-edge shit! *(To Helen.)* Now you and me should have sex! Right on stage! Naked!

HELEN: *(To David.)* Except, in the re-write, you should get rid of Kevin.

KEVIN: Y'all want me wearing thick glasses and playing the violin, is that it? Is that why I gotta go? 'Cause that shit ain't fair, David, it ain't right. Don't hate the playa, hate the game.

(David and Helen stare blankly at Kevin before turning to one another.)

DAVID: Yeah, he's definitely out —

HELEN: — the whole hip-hop slang thing, it's gotta go.

KEVIN: Bitches. I'm rolling. Peace out.

(Kevin exits.)

DAVID: *(Packs up to leave.)* Tell me something. That wasn't really my ancestors on the phone before, was it?

HELEN: Dude, please, pay attention. This is the *point,* OK? This is the reason you can't let anybody tell you what to write or how long it should be or anything else. It offends the ancestors.

DAVID: It . . . offends them?

HELEN: Don't you get it — ?

(Lights rise brightly.)

HELEN: *(Continued.) (Looking upward.)* — They're watching.

(Blackout.)

END OF PLAY

Spirit Sex
A PARANORMAL ROMANCE

DESI MORENO-PENSON

Spirit Sex: A Paranormal Romance was first produced as part of the 2009 Going to the River Festival (The River Crosses Rivers): A Festival of 13 Short Plays by Women Playwrights of Color (Producing Artistic Director: Elizabeth Van Dyke; Executive Producer: Jamie Richards) at Ensemble Studio Theatre, New York, New York, on September 9, 2009. Artistic Director: William Carden. Executive Director: Paul Alexander Slee. Director: Adam Immerwahr. Designer: Maiko Chii. Sound Designer: Bill Toles. Cast: Martin — Jeb Kreager; Avy — Chris Wight; The Satyr — Fulvia Vergel.

CHARACTERS

MARTIN, late twenties to early thirties, paranormal investigator, a little uptight and autocratic, but not without compassion.

AVY, late twenties to early thirties, good-looking and easy-going, but can get upset at a moment's notice. Insecure and rather boyish.

THE SATYR, late twenties to early thirties, a beautiful Hispanic woman who's half-goat and half-human.

TIME AND PLACE

The action takes place in a nondescript room (possibly a bedroom, or a sitting-room) during the evening hours. It's best to keep the staging as simple as possible since the focus should be on the characters.

• • •

As the play begins, the room is more or less in darkness. That is, until we hear Avy's voice off-stage.

AVY: *(Off stage.) Martin!*

MARTIN: *(Off stage.)* Right behind you! And watch it . . . !

(We hear the lock of a door being opened. Martin turns to face the audience and begins to mime the action of carrying heavy equipment. As he 'sets something down' we will hear the sounds of the equipment being placed on the ground, turned on, switched off, etc. and Avy mimes the action of helping him to lug objects in as well. Lights are coming up slowly; the darkness is abating.)

AVY: *(Holding an 'object' out for him.)* Martin — come on; will you take this already?

MARTIN: What's the problem?

AVY: I don't know what it is. I'm afraid it's going to blow up in my hands or something.

MARTIN: Trust me, you're safe. Where's the light?

AVY: Just a second. I don't come in this room. I keep the door locked and I don't come in here by myself anymore — I told you.

MARTIN: *(Abrupt.)* Well, we're not going to be able to do anything if I can't see.

AVY: OK — *OK!* Jesus — Relax. Here . . . Here we go . . .

(He mimes the action of switching on a light. A small glow comes up on the

two men. One is casually dressed and very handsome; the other is considerably less so and rather nattily dressed. He is carrying a large, black doctor's bag. Printed on the bag, in large white letters, we see the words: GHOST SEEKERS. *Both Martin and Avy look around nervously.)*

MARTIN: OK . . . That's a little more like it —

AVY: *(Loud deafening yell.)* AAAAAAAAAHHHHHHHHH!!!!!!!!!!!!

MARTIN: *(Shocked.) FUCK*! What are you doing?

AVY: I just want to startle her and make sure she knows we're not scared —

MARTIN: What?

AVY: You know, so she doesn't try any funny stuff, you know?

MARTIN: What kind of stuff?

AVY: Ah, man — I don't know; *stuff* . . . You know? Making things shoot across the room and bash me on the side of my fucking head, *that* sort of thing . . . I mean, she knows we're here. She knows. And she's waiting. *(A beat.) Waiting. (Another beat.)* What the hell are you doing?

MARTIN: I'm placing random number generators in some of the corners.

(The sounds of Martin's equipment are heard; crude whirring, beep-beep, tooting sounds.)

AVY: Oh.

MARTIN: If positioned in the right spots, the rapidity of electric indicators will pick up on any psychic activity in the room.

AVY: Oh. *(Beat.)* You're going to electrocute her.

MARTIN: Of course not.

AVY: I don't think it's a good idea to piss her off . . .

MARTIN: A spirit can't be harmed by the physical.

AVY: Who told you that?

MARTIN: *(Irritated; abrupt again.)* It's simply *understood.* Spirits are no longer part of this physical realm; ipso facto WE CAN'T HARM THEM.

AVY: You take your job seriously.

MARTIN: I do. *(A beat.)* Anyway . . . on the phone, you said it spoke to you. Here. In this room.

AVY: Yeah.

MARTIN: You heard it speak to you.

AVY: Yeah.

MARTIN: And it's a woman . . .

AVY: Yeah. Well . . . I think it's a woman . . . I hope it's a woman.

MARTIN: Why?

AVY: Because of what she's saying.

MARTIN: What's she saying?

AVY: It's like . . . At first, I hear her from far, far away, right? And then slowly . . . slowly . . . she starts getting closer to me. Like a train whistle. It's like she's a train . . . a magnificent arriving train . . . and it's coming into my station. And she only says two words to me.

MARTIN: And those words are . . . ?

AVY: *(Intense; whisper.) . . . Screw me!*

MARTIN: *(A beat.)* OK.

AVY: You don't believe me, do you?

MARTIN: It just seems to be unusual behavior for a spiritual entity. Now, are you sure of what the voice says to you?

AVY: Of course, I'm sure. She says, "Screw me . . . Screw me, *Papi*!"

MARTIN: *Papi*?

AVY: She's Hispanic.

MARTIN: Oh. It's a Latina.

AVY: *(A little excited.)* Oh, yeah . . . !

MARTIN: Have you seen her?

AVY: No, but I . . . I *feel* her. I know that's not the same thing. I'm probably not doing a good job explaining all this . . . I'm . . . I'm sorry . . . I'm all mixed up here.

MARTIN: A haunting is always a difficult thing to get used to . . . What do you imagine she looks like?

(Sounds of Spanish music are heard. Lights change. Behind them we see a beautiful Latin woman dressed in a flowing, white dress with a long, full skirt. There is a languid sensuality to her movements that goes with the beat of the music. She begins to move provocatively towards Avy with a slight smile around her lips. Avy watches her intensely. Martin does not see her.)

AVY: *(Lost in reverie; he sees her.)* I can't be sure, you know, but I'd like to think she's . . . *stunning*. Oh man, I know there's something about her that when you see her, everything stops. All thinking, all breath, all movement . . . It all just comes to a *halt*. And all you can do is *feel* . . . the blood pumping through your veins, as you take in this vision, this dream, this need to almost reach out beyond your fingertips and lay a warm hand upon this *perfection*. The *definitive* woman. The ultimate. What red-blooded, full-balled American male doesn't dream of that, right? And as soon as you touch . . . feel skin upon skin . . . casing upon wits . . . it's that cool blue shiver that makes you aware of what is meant by the word *transcendence*.

MARTIN: *(Moved by his words.)* . . . I see . . . that's beautiful, Avy. She sounds lovely.

AVY: Yeah. *(A beat.)* Plus, I think I'm getting kind of a Brazilian vibe from her, too, you know?

(Lights go out on Woman and music ends. The mood's broken.)

MARTIN: Have you ever spoken to her?

AVY: No.

MARTIN: Why not?

AVY: *(Shrugs.)* I don't know.

MARTIN: Perhaps that's the problem.

AVY: *(Defensive.)* Are you saying this is my fault?

MARTIN: I'm saying that perhaps what's needed here is not so much a paranormal extraction, but merely some simple honest communication.

AVY: *(Rising anger.)* Why does she deserve special treatment? *I'm* the one being haunted here . . . !

MARTIN: This isn't about special —

AVY: Why, 'cause she's hot? It's 'cause she's hot, right? *(A beat.)* Yeah. I bet if this chick was some drooling, chains rattling, old man you couldn't wait to electrocute the son-of-a-bitch right into the next realm of existence!

MARTIN: *You can't electrocute them!*

AVY: I don't know how to talk to her. I don't know how to talk to girls . . . well, girl ghosts.

MARTIN: Do you know how to speak to live women?

AVY: *(Sheepish.)* Not really.

MARTIN: Maybe you should try.

AVY: I don't think so.

MARTIN: Try.

(A long beat. Avy takes a deep breath.)

AVY: OK. *(A beat; he turns towards where the Woman appeared before.)* Hello? *(Nothing happens. A beat. Avy turns towards Martin who smiles at him in a reassuring manner.)*

MARTIN: It's OK. Try again.

AVY: *(After another beat.)* Hello? Can you come back again and talk to me? *(A beat.)* Please?

(Suddenly, the sounds of Martin's equipment are heard. Again, these are crude whirring, beep-beep, tooting sounds.)

MARTIN: It's working.

AVY: It is?

MARTIN: Yeah. Oh yeah! Now, stay the course . . . just talk to her.

(Avy sighs, resignedly, and looks again towards the corner where the Woman appeared before. Lights change; music starts up again. The Woman appears; she is no longer swaying to the music. She only stands and looks towards Avy.)

AVY: Hi.

(She smiles at him, but says nothing.)

AVY: My name is Avy. What's yours?

(She says nothing, but continues to stare at him.)

AVY: How long have you been dead?

MARTIN: *(Sharply.)* Don't ask her that!

AVY: Wait a minute, wait . . . I'm sorry . . . that probably didn't sound right. Um . . . how long have you been here?

(She says nothing, but continues to stare.)

MARTIN: *(Nodding.)* That's better.

AVY: Yeah, but she's still not saying anything —

MARTIN: *(A little annoyed.)* Why can't you have a little more patience?

AVY: But she's not doing anything, OK? She's just standing there, standing there and staring at me with those big . . . beautiful . . . gorgeous brown eyes . . . God, she's got great eyes, you know?

MARTIN: Good; tell her that.

AVY: No, man, I can't tell her that shit. It's corny . . . !

MARTIN: It's honest!

AVY: What do you want from me? Huh? You want me to Mack on this ghost? You want me to Sarge on a dead chick? Huh? Is that what you want?

MARTIN: I'm only asking that you try to relate to her in some way —

AVY: What do you think I'm doing here?

MARTIN: You're acting stupid. *(A little frantic now.)* Sometimes when an entity has passed on, they're not always aware that they've actually 'gone,' you know? That's why it's necessary for you to be gentle, and to kindly relate to her present circumstances.

AVY: OK. You want me to relate? Fine. I'll relate . . . how about this . . . ? *(Draws himself up; in a confident, swaggering manner.)* Hey baby, you got a mirror in your back pocket? 'Cause I think I can see myself in that sweet, juicy ass.

(The woman, as though offended by what Avy has said, abruptly and almost angrily pulls her skirt all the way up to her chin. We see that she is in fact,

a Satyr . . . a half-human, half-goat creature. The tone of the music changes abruptly to something far more vigorous and dynamic.)

AVY: *(Horrified.) Holy shit!*

MARTIN: Its OK, Avy . . .

AVY: Tell her to get out of here, man!

MARTIN: *(Looking around; he can't see her.)* Calm down! Is she here with us right now? Can you see her? Avy?

(The Satyr is now playfully taunting Avy; wiggling her goat's rump at him and making faces. Avy is at a loss.)

AVY: Aw shit! Look at that! Look at it! She's wiggling her tail at me, bro! How messed up is that?

MARTIN: Her tail? Did you say *tail?*

(The Satyr is now dancing vigorously; she is enjoying herself.)

Avy? Does this being have a tail?

AVY: That's what I said, dude! Up here, you know — she's fine; she's *really* fine, all right . . . But, down here, it's . . . it's . . . It's *so fucked up* . . . ! I can't mess around with shit like this, you know? *(To the Satyr.) Go away, you freaky trick bitch!*

(The Satyr is suddenly startled by Avy's ferocity; she slowly begins to retreat.)

MARTIN: *(Excited.)* Avy, wait a minute. Wait! This could be a unique opportunity. You have to brazen out the spirit, you have to ask her why she's haunting you . . . we need to know why she's unable to 'cross over' . . . !

AVY: *(Not hearing him — to the Satyr; aggressive.)* I'm not afraid of you, Devil pony; I speak a little Spanish, you know! *Tu eres uno cabballito Del Diablo*! *(You are a devil pony.)*

(The Satyr is now visibly upset. She opens her mouth and screams, a long, drawn-out plaintive howl; similar to Avy's scream at the start of the play but there is something emotionless and raw in it as well. Avy is transfixed.)

MARTIN: Avy? Are you all right?

AVY: *(Momentarily moved by her.)* She's in pain . . .

MARTIN: How do you know?

AVY: Jesus! Can't you hear that?

(The Satyr shrieks again.)

MARTIN: What is she communicating to you?

AVY: Oh, God! Make her stop!

MARTIN: But what is she saying?

AVY: Nothing! She's . . . *screaming.* She's in pain.

MARTIN: Don't show fear —

(The Satyr shrieks again. This has now taken on an almost "baying-at-the-moon" kind of quality.)

AVY: You don't understand. I don't know how to help her.

MARTIN: It might be possible to make contact with her. To find out where she came from, what she looked like; what kind of life she led; why she now has a tail —

AVY: No, no — forget all that, I'm not hip to that AT ALL, my man — I just want the crazy trick out of my house! I want her out of here! I don't want any part of this. *(To the Satyr.) Get out of here!*

(At hearing this, the Satyr, now sad and dejected, begins to back away slowly, as the music ends. Lights change.)

MARTIN: *(Disappointed.)* Why did you do that? You said she's beautiful. With a tail.

AVY: Stop saying "tail", please! It makes me feel so dirty.

MARTIN: Is she still screaming?

AVY: No. She's gone.

MARTIN: *(After a beat.)* She's like an animal spirit.

AVY: She's not *like* an animal — she *is* an animal, dude. This is terrifying. *(A beat.)* Listen, Martin — you got to promise me you're not going to tell *anybody* about this, right?

MARTIN: Avy, I'm a professional. Everything you tell me will be held in the strictest confidence.

AVY: Yeah, yeah, I'm hip — I'm hip . . . But . . . listen . . . I gotta ask you something . . . and it's . . . um . . . kind of embarrassing . . .

MARTIN: What is it?

AVY: Well, this thing that's here, OK *that's* probably out of the question, of course, but . . . with a normal, regular kind of ghost . . . one with no furry, animal parts to her, I mean . . . I've been giving this some thought, and I've been wondering, uh . . . Say for instance, somehow if I were to have sex with a . . . you know . . . One of these . . . *beings* . . . Um . . . With a *ghost*, per se —

MARTIN: You can't have sex with a ghost.

AVY: No, no, no, no, no, no, no, no dude . . . dude — I'm saying, "what if", OK? *What if!* I'm not saying I'm going to do a damn thing.

MARTIN: You couldn't do anything even if you wanted to.

AVY: I know that, but —

MARTIN: You can't have sex with a ghost.

AVY: I hear you . . .

MARTIN: Besides, I thought you said you had a girlfriend.

AVY: I do! But again, see? That's my point. If I had sex with a ghost — it wouldn't be like I was cheating, you know what I'm saying? I mean, not really. Let's be honest . . . *(Moves in closer; conspiratorial.)* It's a *ghost*; the broad's dead.

MARTIN: What's your question?

AVY: Well, I was wondering, just *hypothetically*, of course . . . That if sexual relations were possible with a ghost, you know; spirit sex . . . Um . . . Would my dick just go right through her pussy and come out her ass? *(A beat. Martin stares at Avy.)*

MARTIN: I . . . I don't understand . . . ?

AVY: I mean, ghosts are see-thru, right? I mean, they are, right? I probably wouldn't even be able to get a grip on her ass, right? Because the ass would be almost *invisible*! Oh man, that is so *heavy* . . . I think if I had to see something like that, it would *really* blow my mind, you know what I'm saying? That would probably scare me worse than her being half-pony. I mean, that would be some pretty *intense shit*, you know? *(Another beat. Martin smiles at him. He begins to gather up all of his 'stuff.')*

MARTIN: Yeah — I'm hip. Here's my card. Call me again if she returns.

AVY: *(After a beat.)* Why do you think she's in pain?

MARTIN: I don't know, Avy. If you see her again you might try asking her. Maybe you'll have a little more luck next time, who knows? I'll see you later, alright?

(Martin exits. Now, we see that only Avy is left; he is alone on stage and he seems more like a sad, little boy lost.)

AVY: I'm a practical man.

I can be fair. I don't cheat.

I work hard. I want to enjoy my life . . . doesn't everyone? And I want to share my life with someone —

(Lights change. The Satyr has entered again. She slowly moves towards Avy. He sees her.)

AVY: *(Frightened.)* I'm telling you right now . . . ! *Get the hell away from me! (The Satyr calmly sits down on the floor. Her two goat hooves stick out in front of her. She smiles at him and pats the ground, signaling for him to sit down next to her. Avy is at a loss.)*

AVY: What? You want me to sit down?

(The Satyr smiles again and nods. A beat.)

Um . . . well . . . hell, I don't know if I should . . .

(The Satyr starts to look dejected again. She begins to cry.)

Aw come on — you have to give me a break! You cry too easily for a horse.

SATYR: *(Sobbing.) Ahhhwooowaaaaaheeeeyowooooo . . . !*

AVY: Come on. It's not so bad.

SATYR: *Ahhhwooowaaaaaheeeeyowooooo . . . !*

AVY: Aw, man . . . Look, I'm sorry, OK? I'm sorry I yelled at you. I'm sorry I said you were a little horse of the devil. And I'm sorry I brought that guy in with all the electrical stuff, but he offered to help me . . . you understand, don't you? I'm sure you do. I'm sure you're a very nice horse girl. *(The Satyr continues to motion for Avy to come nearer. He is reluctant to do so.)*

AVY: I think it might be a better idea if I just stay over here, all right? I mean, it's nothing personal.

(The Satyr frantically points to her goat hooves. He doesn't get it.)

What? What are you showing me?

(The Satyr continues pointing to her goat hooves.)

(Moves closer.) What? What do you want me to see?

SATYR: *(Sounds of a goat.) Baaah-Baaaah . . . !*

AVY: *(Looking back from her to the hooves.)* Alright. That sounds like sheep or a goat —

(The Satyr suddenly becomes very happy, continues making the goat sounds and points excitedly at Avy.)

Wait — OK . . . its like charades. OK, I think I got it. So, you're telling me that you're not a horse? You're a goat? *A goat?*

SATYR: *(Vigorous nod.) Baaah-Baaaah . . . !*

AVY: OK. You're a goat. Oh! You're a satyr. That's what they're called, right? Half-human, half-goat — a satyr.

(The Satyr laughs happily, pointing to her nose.)

I don't mean to be rude, but that's a little strange, too.

(The Satyr laughs happily again, and claps her hands like a small child.)

Hey! Yeah, I'm glad you're happy now. You're a nice . . . goat . . . girl.

(The Satyr motions for him to sit next to her. This time, he does.)

How did you get to be like this? I mean, were you always a . . . uh . . . a *Satyr*? I mean, how . . . ?

(The Satyr motions for him to be quiet. She leans over and gives him a slow, lingering kiss on the lips. Avy seems beside himself, but completely spellbound by her as well.)

I think I felt that! That was nice. Thank you. Look — I think you're very pretty and don't get me wrong . . . I'm flattered and I'm attracted to . . . to . . . to . . . but . . . I'm just not sure I'm into goats, you know?

SATYR: *(A drawn-out and softly plaintive cry.) Awoooooowahwahlata-datatatah!*

AVY: *(Attempting to make the same sound.)* Awoooowah —

SATYR: *Awoooooowahwahlatadatatatah!*

AVY: *(As though hypnotized.)* Awooowahwah —

(The Satyr begins to laugh at his attempts to impersonate her Satyr's cry. Avy smiles back at her; he begins to relax.)

AVY: Yeah, you like that, huh? You think that's funny? Maybe it is. Look . . . I know you probably speak Spanish, but can you speak English? Some English . . . ?

SATYR: English?

AVY: Yes, can you do that? I know you can do that. You can do that, can't you? Jesus, I hope you can. There's so much I want to tell you. I want to tell you everything. I feel like I can sit here and talk to you forever.

SATYR: *(Pointing at him; big smile.)* Talk. You talk. A lot.

AVY: *(Chuckles.)* Yeah . . . yeah . . . I do. I guess I do. Do you?

SATYR: *(Shrugs.)* Sometimes.

AVY: OK then . . . let's talk.

(Slow, steady fadeout as they continue to smile at one another. Complete blackout.)

END OF PLAY

Table for Four

Steven Korbar

Table for Four premiered in June, 2009 at the "Source Festival" in Washington DC. Director: Alexander Strain. Cast: First Man — Aaron Bliden; First Woman — Betsy Rosen; Second Man — Garrett Brennan; Second Woman — Magdelane Vick.

CHARACTERS

FIRST MAN, early to mid-twenties. Aggressive and bullying.
FIRST WOMAN, early to mid-twenties. Strong willed and Intelligent.
SECOND MAN, early to mid-twenties. Terrified and disoriented.
SECOND WOMAN, early to mid-twenties. Timid.

SETTING

A large table on a bare stage.

• • •

In darkness, we hear the muffled sound of a man crying and a young woman whispering the 23 psalms. As lights come up, we see four people cowering underneath a large wooden table; the kind you might find in a library. First Man is surrounded on either side by First Woman and Second Woman. Second Man is slightly behind the others, weeping softly. They are all college age and speak in urgent, terrified whispers.

SECOND WOMAN: Yea, though I walk through the valley of the shadow of death, I will fear no evil: for thou art with me; thy rod and thy staff they comfort me . . .

SECOND MAN: *(Sobbing quietly. Terrified and somewhat disoriented.)* Oh God, oh God, I'm so scared.

FIRST MAN: *(To Second Man.)* Will you shut up? Do want to get us killed?

FIRST WOMAN: I think it's over. I think that maybe it's over now.

FIRST MAN: How do you know that?

FIRST WOMAN: It's been really quiet ever since we got down here.

FIRST MAN: That doesn't mean shit; the guy could just be reloading or something.

SECOND WOMAN: *(Praying.)* Please, it's my little brother Elliot's birthday tomorrow, I'm not asking for myself but please don't do this to him.

FIRST WOMAN: Who ever did this probably isn't even on campus anymore. He probably shot himself by now, that's what they usually do.

FIRST MAN: Not all the time. Sometimes the cops have to take them out.

SECOND MAN: Are the police here?

FIRST WOMAN: They must be by now, they must know. We can't be alone here.

SECOND WOMAN: God is with us.

FIRST MAN: I knew I shouldn't have come to the library today, I fucking knew it. This is what I get for trying to study.

SECOND MAN: *(Sobbing too loudly.)* Oh God, there are so many people dead. So many people are dead!

FIRST MAN: Did you hear me say stop it? Try to man-up and show some balls!

FIRST WOMAN: I think he's right. I think when I was crawling under here I saw my Poli-Sci professor lying by the research desk. He always wears this same ugly jacket me and my friend make fun of and I could kind of see his . . .

(Unable to continue.)

SECOND WOMAN: Why would anybody do this?

FIRST MAN: I don't give a shit why. I just want to know how the fuck we're going to get out of here.

FIRST WOMAN: They'll come for us. We just have to wait a while and someone will come and get us.

FIRST MAN: He could come and get us too.

SECOND WOMAN: All these poor innocent people; what did they ever do?

FIRST MAN: Look, you see over there; that's the side door there. It can't be more than thirty feet. We could just make a run for it.

FIRST WOMAN: And what if who ever did this is out there now?

FIRST MAN: He wouldn't go out there; the cops would pick him off the minute he got out the door.

FIRST WOMAN: And they'd probably shoot us when we went running out too; how are they supposed to know the difference?

SECOND WOMAN: I think that we should pray. I think that we should all pray together right now.

FIRST MAN: Yeah, why don't we just sing a spiritual so the guy knows exactly where we are.

(Turning on Second Man, who is still crying.)

If he doesn't already with you crying like a God damned little girl.

SECOND MAN: I'm sorry.

FIRST WOMAN: How do you know it's a guy?

FIRST MAN: What?

FIRST WOMAN: Who ever did this, how do you know it's a guy?

SECOND WOMAN: *(Throwing a dirty look at First Man.)* It's always a guy.

FIRST WOMAN: How do you know, did you see him?

FIRST MAN: If I had I'd have bashed his head in.

SECOND WOMAN: I heard some girl scream "he's got a gun" right before it all started. I was so mad for a second; I just couldn't believe anyone would make a joke like that with all the terrible things going on in the world.

FIRST MAN: We've at least got to let somebody know we're here; let them know where to find us.

FIRST WOMAN: I'm sure they already know, somebody had to have called them by now.

(First Man and First Woman look at each other with the same thought.)

FIRST MAN: *(Frantically pulling his cellphone from his pocket.)* Oh shit! What the hell is wrong with us? I can't believe in the middle of all this, none of us even thought of our phones. Why didn't anyone think of it?

FIRST WOMAN: Why didn't you?

FIRST MAN: *(Impatiently listening.)* Com'on, com'on. Shit, I'm not getting any kind of a signal.

FIRST WOMAN: Who are you calling?

FIRST MAN: I can't get anything!

FIRST WOMAN: Who did you call; did you call 911?

FIRST MAN: . . . I will. I'll try them now. I'll try 911.

FIRST WOMAN: Well who did you just call?

FIRST MAN: Shit, I can't get any kind of signal at all!

SECOND MAN: *(Mimicking the TV commercial.)* "Can you hear me now?"

FIRST MAN: Are you kidding me!

SECOND WOMAN: I always have trouble getting reception in here. Something with the hills . . .

FIRST MAN: Do you have your phone?

FIRST WOMAN: No. I always keep it in my backpack.

SECOND WOMAN: Really? I keep mine in my backpack too.

FIRST MAN: God damn it; I could make a video of this for YouTube, but I can't get us any help!

SECOND WOMAN: I wouldn't want to call anyone now. I wouldn't want to leave one of those 9/11 messages. I'd never want my family to remember me that way.

FIRST MAN: They're not going to have to remember you. It's not some kind of freaking final phone call. Just stop acting like that. And will somebody please tell me what in the hell stinks so bad!?

FIRST WOMAN: What?

FIRST MAN: Something stinks. Can't you smell it? It reeks.

FIRST WOMAN: (*Sniffing. Distastefully.*) . . . Oh. I didn't notice it before. Oh . . .

SECOND WOMAN: . . . You don't think it's, you know . . . like, peoples bodies.

FIRST MAN: Oh don't be an idiot. It takes hours for that to happen; days. We've only been here a few minutes. It isn't anything like that.

SECOND MAN: I think it's me. I'm sorry. I couldn't help it.

FIRST MAN: *(A beat. Then with disgust.)* Oh Christ . . . you are just such a tool.

FIRST WOMAN: Leave him alone.

FIRST MAN: Shit!

FIRST WOMAN: He's scared.

FIRST MAN: Well this isn't exactly Spring break for me either, but I didn't crap my pants over it.

SECOND MAN: I didn't. I peed.

FIRST MAN: Jesus!

SECOND WOMAN: Oh don't mention peeing to me now.

SECOND MAN: My mom said when I was little, when I had to go to the bathroom and she asked me if I had to go number one or number two, I would always say I had to go number three. Isn't that funny, isn't that weird? I don't know if I meant that I had to do both together or something else or . . .

FIRST MAN: What in the fuck are you talking about?

FIRST WOMAN: Will you lay off him?

FIRST MAN: Jesus Christ, next thing he'll be telling us he wants his mommy.

FIRST WOMAN: Well I want mine. I want my mom really, really bad right now; don't you?

FIRST MAN: *(Stopped. A pause, unwilling to answer.)*

SECOND WOMAN: I do.

FIRST MAN: *(Regrouping.)* All I want is to get the thirty God damn feet to that door.

SECOND WOMAN: And will you please stop using the Lord's name like that.

FIRST MAN: Oh, like that is the biggest problem we have right. Do you really think it makes one damn bit of difference now what the hell any of us . . . *(Suddenly all four seem to hear a noise simultaneously. They convulsively draw together in shock and fear. Second Woman stifles a scream with her hand.)*

FIRST MAN: Fuck!

FIRST WOMAN: *(Breathlessly.)* What was that?

SECOND WOMAN: It sounded like it came from in here.

FIRST MAN: Fuck.

FIRST WOMAN: It sounded like something fell, or someone moved.

SECOND WOMAN: Maybe this is something to do with terrorism, some kind of terrorist attack.

FIRST MAN: Oh right. It's a Division III school, who the hell is going to bother? I'll bet you anything this is just another random, stupid thing. Just totally fucking senseless.

SECOND MAN: Now I think I may have shit myself too.

FIRST MAN: Has anybody got anything white?

FIRST WOMAN: White?

FIRST MAN: Something white, like cloth, something we can wave as we run out.

SECOND WOMAN: Do they even do that anymore?

FIRST MAN: There are security cameras all over this place, the cops would be scared to shoot us waving white; they'd get killed on CNN.

FIRST WOMAN: Forget it. It's too dangerous.

FIRST MAN: We just make a dash for it, all of us; the cops won't touch us.

SECOND MAN: I can't. I can't go; I'm too afraid.

FIRST MAN: Then we'll just go without you.

FIRST WOMAN: Don't say that. What is wrong with you; we're not leaving anybody behind.

FIRST MAN: If he's too much of a pussy to keep up it's not my fault.

SECOND MAN: I wish I could. I wish I was like you; I'm trying!

FIRST MAN: Will you just shut the fuck up!

SECOND MAN: *(With unexpected force.)* You shut up!

FIRST WOMAN: Just stop it. Why are you doing this? God, we're all in the same boat here. It doesn't help to bully people.

FIRST MAN: I'm just trying to get out of here alive.

FIRST WOMAN: And you think we're not?

SECOND WOMAN: It's in God's hands. Whatever happens is His will.

FIRST WOMAN: We can't lose it now. We can't turn on each other like we're in some dumb, lame old movie.

FIRST MAN: Then what should we do, just roll over like he is?

FIRST WOMAN: Roll over? Are you serious?! Do you think you're playing "Call of Duty" here?! This is real. Real people are lying all around us and they're not going to just get up and start again when the game is over. Do you know what could happen if we just left him here; do you want to be responsible for that? You can't treat people that way. I want to get out of here just as much as you do; just as much! But for whatever reason we're all under here together and we've all got to get out of here together too!

SECOND WOMAN: I just don't see how anyone could do this; maybe it *was* terrorists.

FIRST MAN: You know what; you just think whatever you want, it's fine with me. I will be responsible. I'm responsible for myself; just like everybody else is. You act like there's something wrong with trying to survive, but you know what, it's fucking normal. I didn't ask to be here; I didn't want to see this. I'd rather be home, I'd rather be watching the Rangers on TV with my Dad and . . . but I'm not even a little ashamed that I'm strong enough to get myself out of here. And if somebody else can't keep up, I'm sorry, but it's not going to stop me. And you can bet I'm going to knock him on his ass if he gets in my may too; because that's just the way the real world rolls. The rest of you can hide here if you want, but there's no way I'm going to end up being just another casualty of another random shooting. I am out of here!

(Preparing to run.)

FIRST WOMAN: (*Grabbing First Man's arm.*) Just wait a little bit longer. Just a few minutes.

SECOND MAN: Let him go. He's going to make it OK.

FIRST WOMAN: But this is just stupid.

FIRST MAN: You're the one being stupid.

SECOND MAN: He's right. It's better. You should all just go without me.

FIRST MAN: Hey, try growing a pair and maybe you wouldn't have to just sit here like a victim.

FIRST WOMAN: But for your own sake; think about what you're doing. What if the cops shoot first and ask questions later? Or how do you know you won't get out that door and just end up running straight into some maniac with a gun?!

SECOND MAN: . . . Because I dropped it somewhere. I'm such a total pussy. I dropped it somewhere.

(Second Man begins to sob again. The others look at him for a long, stunned moment. First Man smiles disbelievingly.)

FIRST MAN: . . . No way . . . No fucking way.

SECOND MAN: I think I'm going to pee again.

SECOND WOMAN: The Lord is my shepherd; I shall not want. He maketh me to lie down in green pastures: He leadeth me beside the still waters, He restoreth my soul: he leadeth me . . .

(Lights fade.)

END OF PLAY

Whack-a-Mole

Beth Lein

Whack-a-Mole was originally produced by Infiltrage! as part of a short play festival at the Flea Theatre, New York, New York. Cast: Charlotte — Hannah Bos; Brian — Oliver Henzler; Mom — Susan Finch; Robert — Charles Goforth; Mole Chorus — Joy Barrett, Shannon Black, and Justin McElfresh. Director: Gary Schwartz. Choreography: Nicole Berger. Sound: Dorsey Dunn.

CHARACTERS

CHARLOTTE, early twenties, a funky dresser with few social boundaries from Texas.

BRIAN, mid-twenties, a tortured writer.

MOM, fifties, native Brooklynite, saucy.*

ROBERT, fifties, Texan cowboy with a slow drawl.*

MOLE CHORUS, up to 10 actors with exceptional movement skills.

NOTES

Mom and Robert* are a part of the chorus. The actors in the chorus are dressed in all black and sit on small stools wearing neutral expressions. The moles are made from sock puppets on the arms of the actors. (You can get sock puppet making instructions all over the internet.) Robert needs a cowboy hat. Never underestimate the benefits of a good glue gun.

In the original production, there was a circus-like board outlined in lights that read "Whack-A-Mole" hanging above the chorus. The lights came on with the lighting cue in the script when Charlotte first introduces the game to Brian.

As in any good puppeteering, all the animation should be in the sock puppet, rather than the actor, who should remain facially neutral even when speaking. Charlotte and Brian speak to the puppet, not the puppeteer, unless indicated. The mole chorus should be extremely fun, but crisply and cleanly choreographed.

NOTES ON SOUND CUES

At the end of the first round, there should be a cacophony of bells, whistles, alarms, sirens, flashing lights, etc. In the original production, we used a sound track accompanied by musical toy instruments (kazoos, bells, whistles, those noisemakers they give you at New Years, etc.) that the mole chorus pulled out from under their stools.

There was also a sound track recorded that scored the entire piece that gave whacking sounds, bells, etc and digital music for the eighties break dancing and ballet segments. May your tech person be as meticulous as ours was. Have fun.

• • •

Blackout. There is one flashlight held by Charlotte who enters with Brian from the back of the theatre through the audience during the following, until the first lighting cue. Charlotte and Brian have just met earlier in the day. Brian is attracted to Charlotte's optimistic forthright nature which, although it can be jarring at times to his sensitive nature, is never sarcastic and purely sincere.

CHARLOTTE: Do you believe in love at first sight?

BRIAN: No.

CHARLOTTE: Me either. That's why I've been watching you for the past three months.

BRIAN: Oh, come on —

CHARLOTTE: Blue plaid is nearly always the Monday shirt, you always use hotel matches and I never see you on Thursdays.

BRIAN: Why?

CHARLOTTE: I have no idea, but I'll bet you have a job in that hotel.

BRIAN: No, I mean, why have you been watching me?

CHARLOTTE: Is it creeping you out?

BRIAN: I don't know.

CHARLOTTE: Yes. No?

BRIAN: No. Yes. Kind of. So what made you, um, watch me?

CHARLOTTE: Pure instinct.

BRIAN: Anything more specific?

CHARLOTTE: A certain look in your eyes. A slump in your shoulder. Black coffee, frequent cigarette breaks. Journal scribbling. Big giveaway.

BRIAN: God you make me sound like a cliche.

CHARLOTTE: *(Sincerely.)* Oh, I'm sorry . . . were you trying to be unique?

BRIAN: Well . . . no I wasn't *trying* to be anything. I guess I just like coffee, cigarettes, and being alone.

CHARLOTTE: There's a certain sensitivity that cafe in particular seems to attract, don't you think?

BRIAN: Never thought about it. I just know they'll let you stay there for hours on one cup of coffee.

CHARLOTTE: Oh please, drinking coffee is just the social coverup. It's literally written all over the walls.

BRIAN: You mean the graffitti in the bathroom?

CHARLOTTE: Come on, I know you read it.

BRIAN: Well, OK, yeah, sometimes. So?

CHARLOTTE: Sometimes? Let's see . . . *(Quoting.)* "Nothing is more seductive for man than his freedom of conscious, but nothing is a cause for greater suffering."

BRIAN: Wait, how did you —

CHARLOTTE: Try switching out just about anything for conscious and it's still true.

You had this incredibly satisfied smile on your face when you came back from the bathroom. You wrote it down in your journal and then went outside for a smoke.

BRIAN: You read my journal?

CHARLOTTE: You left it open on the table! I didn't read anything else, just that. I had to be sure and then I knew. It's why I asked you to come here today.

BRIAN: That's pretty disturbing. And where is *here*, by the way?

CHARLOTTE: I'm not exactly sure how to explain it. *(Lights up on the Whack-A-Mole Chorus. The actors sit with their puppets in a neutral position with blank expressions.)* I'm the only one who ever comes here and every time I leave I keep thinking I dreamed it all up. But then I come back and it's just where I left it.

BRIAN: *(Reading.)* Whack-A-Mole? This is where you wanted to take me?

CHARLOTTE: Don't let the name fool you, it's pretty intense. I've never made it to Level 2 . . . *(Flirtatiously.)* but I know I can with your help.

BRIAN: You lured me from the cafe to play Whack-a-Mole.

CHARLOTTE: Oh, yes.

BRIAN: This is . . . this not a good idea. I hate games. All of them. And no, it doesn't make me feel inferior or any less masculine, it's a fact with which I'm perfectly at ease. It's an eye-hand thing, there's a disconnect. I'm a reader of books.

CHARLOTTE: You're perfect.

BRIAN: No, I . . . can't . . . I really . . . And you know, *thank you* for inviting me out, and maybe I'll see you at the cafe, but I should get back. I have a deadline and —

CHARLOTTE: No! Wait! *(Pause.)* Um, look. I know you must think I'm crazy, but you should know . . . *(Charlotte comes closer to him and puts her hands on his chest.)* I just want you to know that I find you incredibly attractive —

BRIAN: *(Stunned. Not a common occurrence.)* Oh. Really?

CHARLOTTE: Like *smoking*. Hot.

BRIAN: Wow. Well, thanks —

CHARLOTTE: And I just . . . I just think that you're perfect, I mean not literally of course, but in this context, yes, and like I said, I've never made it to Level 2, but I know I can with your help and so I was hoping . . .

BRIAN: . . . You were hoping . . . that I'd play Whack-a-Mole?

CHARLOTTE: Yes!

(Charlotte comes in even closer.)

BRIAN: I see. So what is Level 2 exactly?

CHARLOTTE: *(Looking up at him, closely.)* Beats the hell out me, skee-ball?

BRIAN: OK . . . I mean, I guess if it's so important to you, I could . . . *try.*

(Charlotte pulls away and high fives him.)

CHARLOTTE: Yes! I'm really glad you agreed to come.

BRIAN: Yeah, its not like me, I don't usually —

CHARLOTTE: Take risks?

BRIAN: Well, it's just that I don't usually talk to anyone at that cafe. That's why I go there.

CHARLOTTE: What made you talk to me?

BRIAN: You bummed a cigarette.

CHARLOTTE: Is that all?

BRIAN: Then you asked me to join you outside in smoker solidarity and since you took my whole pack and my matches/

CHARLOTTE: I was going to give them back!

BRIAN: /I figured I'd better join you. And now somehow, I'm here.

CHARLOTTE: *(Seductively.)* Regrets?

BRIAN: *(He smiles. A beat.)* No.

(Charlotte smiles back then begins to look around the game for a mallet.)

CHARLOTTE: Good. You know it was more than that Dostoyevsky quote that told me you were the one.

BRIAN: Oh yeah?

CHARLOTTE: You're number 17.

BRIAN: What?

(She finds the mallet and holds it up.)

CHARLOTTE: Aha, *mallet.* Number 17. I've brought sixteen other guys here before you.

BRIAN: *(Flatly.)* Oh.

CHARLOTTE: But they never last.

BRIAN: Why?

CHARLOTTE: I don't know. But that's not important because 17 is my lucky number. In a way, I kind of knew they were just the stepping stones.

BRIAN: I see.

(Charlotte begins to swing the mallet in wide circles around her body.)

CHARLOTTE: I fell in love at seventeen. Have you ever been in love?

BRIAN: Well that depends on your definition.

CHARLOTTE: *(She stops.)* No it doesn't.

BRIAN: OK, then. No.

CHARLOTTE: I've only been in love once, but it wasn't reciprocated. He lied. *(Readies the mallet, take a few vicious swipes.)* God, I hate liars. OK so, I'll go first, but at a certain point yet to be determined, you'll jump in and help me out.

BRIAN: Help you "whack"?

CHARLOTTE: As far as I know. Like I said, I've never gotten very far, so I can't say, but I don't even think it's possible to get to Level 2 by yourself. There's this one point I can never seem to get past, I just kind of freak out, but don't be scared.

BRIAN: Why would I be scared? It seems fairly straightfoward.

CHARLOTTE: In an unpredictable sort of way, yeah. Oh and . . . there may be some *difficult* moles, but they're nothing a guy like you can't handle. So, ready to play?

BRIAN: Sure.

CHARLOTTE: Good. I think it's best just to plunge right in. OK. Here I'll show you how to start. *(She adopts a batter's stance, circles the mallet three times all the way around her body and yells at the top of her lungs.)* MOTHER FUCKING MOLES!!!

(Charlotte brings the mallet down immediately and the entire mole chorus pops up in synchronized time. As the play progresses, the Moles become craftier, as if they are "learning" how to out-smart the whacker. Charlotte begins whacking, expertly. See notes for music cues.)

BRIAN: Wow, you're really good at this.

CHARLOTTE: Thanks, but this is only the beginning. They're just baiting me now. You see that? Look: they're starting to organize. They're starting to come together. *(They are indeed organizing.)*

BRIAN: They do a seem a bit more —

They're really heating up here. They start to know all your moves and then — *(She scores a "out of bounds" mole.)* Ha! Don't even try it! Hey Brian, are you ready?

BRIAN: Is it my turn?

CHARLOTTE: It's coming. Are you ready?

BRIAN: I guess —

CHARLOTTE: Say yes!

BRIAN: Yes-

CHARLOTTE: You're going to be great. Here it comes! *(Charlotte begins to whack with rapid succession as the moles pull their fanciest moves yet. She hands him the mallet.) NOW!!*

(There is a sudden light change and the rest of the stage, including Charlotte and the game, goes entirely dark with a tight spotlight on Brian just as he grabs the mallet. At the same time, Mole number one "pops up." It is his mother.)

MOM: Hello Brian.

BRIAN: Holy shit. *Mom*? You're here? What —

MOM: *(Sarcastic.)* Such a bright child I've raised.

BRIAN: Hey, hey, hey — What the hell is this, Charlotte — ?

(Charlotte is nowhere to be seen, but calls from the darkness.)

CHARLOTTE: It's Mole number one.

(Mom motions for Brian to come closer.)

MOM: Get over here. We don't have much time and I think you know why I'm going to say.

BRIAN: No I don't.

MOM: Of course you do. Don't get smart with me. This girl you're with here. What's her name?

BRIAN: Charlotte.

MOM: Like the spider. OK fine. She'll do. So? You got some sort of problem?

BRIAN: What? What problem?

MOM: Offspring. Progeny. Issue. Stock. You're designed to sow the field, son. Where's the seed? Now I know you're not exactly a ladies man with your head in all those books, but she looks game and willing to me, a bit of a slut, but I'm not being choosy here, so no pansy-footing around. I want a *litter*, you got it?

BRIAN: Hey, OK Mom, that's —

MOM: You're the only one I got Brian. I wanted six, ten, twelve kids. I wanted a sea of dirty faces grabbing wet cereal and hair around the breakfast table. I wanted to be *prolific*. But of course, I married your father —

BRIAN: Mom . . .

MOM: — and if you got the same problem as he did, you better make hay while the sun shines. It's no small thing, no laughing matter. In all honesty that's one thing that led to our divorce.

BRIAN: I don't need to know this. *(Covers his ears.)*

MOM: *(Uncovers his ears.)* You need to know this more than anybody! If you got fear of *the failure* they got medicine for that now. You gotta learn to be a man of action Brian. Like your stepfather. Now there's a man who knows how to *fuck! (Guffaws brashly.)*

BRIAN: OK, Mom, stop it, that's enough!

(He tries to put his hands over her mouth but she ducks and he misses, they repeat this once again throught the following:)

MOM: Oh, so what? It's the perfect word, it sounds like what it means. Fuck, fuck, fuck, fuck, fuck. You were always such a little prude.

BRIAN: Stop!

(Brian remembers the mallet and brings it up over his head.)

MOM: You're the arrow, Brian, shoot the target. I mean for Christ's sake, when's the last time a woman touched your penis?

BRIAN: I said *STOP!*

(He whacks her and she recedes like the Wicked Witch on the following line:)

MOM: Don't whack your mother, Brian! *(She "disappears" out of the spotlight and there is another lighting change. "Mom" now sits and resumes a neutral expression, becoming a part of the anonymous mole-chorus. Charlotte beams at him as the moles "signal" the end of Round 1. Again, see sound cues at the end of script.)*

CHARLOTTE: I knew it, you're incredible.

BRIAN: *(He holds the mallet in his hand feeling the power.)* Man, you weren't kidding. So — this is it? This is . . .

CHARLOTTE: This is the game of Whack-a-Mole. And that was . . . ?!

BRIAN: That was my mother.

CHARLOTTE: Wow, I've never seen a Mom, it's always ex-girlfriends.

BRIAN: Yeah. Well she's a bit . . . but hey, I whacked her! This is really . . . *(Indicates the mallet.)* I'm glad I came. I can definitely see the benefit. *(The moles signal Level 2.)*

CHARLOTTE: Next round! Go on, you're way better than me.

(Brian grips the mallet. The mole chorus becomes very animated and organized, sychronizing in more circular motions that their previous angles.)

BRIAN: Wow. Look at them. They're incredible.

(He whacks one and then another. The moles have begun to break-dance.)

BRIAN: I guess they're eighties moles. *(He keeps whacking away.)*

CHARLOTTE: Pop-o-matic!

BRIAN: This is amazing. Hey look — hand/eye, I'm cured!

(Brian continues whacking away and begins to sort of dance along with them. He is winning and is really enjoying himself.)

CHARLOTTE: *(Begins to look around her.)* No one has made it this far before — I guess this is it . . . I guess this is . . . Brian, do you like me?

BRIAN: Well, I mean, I —

CHARLOTTE: Don't think — Yes. No. Which came first?

BRIAN: Yes!

CHARLOTTE: So promise me you won't leave . . . no matter what comes up.

BRIAN: *(Synchronized eighties moving with the moles.)* No, no . . . this is great.

CHARLOTTE: *Promise!*

BRIAN: OK . . . I promise.

CHARLOTTE: *(Smiles.)* Good, then I promise you right back.

(He smiles back at her. The moles continue to pop up around them as Charlotte moves to kiss him. Just as their lips touch, the lighting changes again, but this time the spotlight includes around both of them and the entire chorus. Robert then comes forward, inches from Charlotte's face, who jumps.)

CHARLOTTE: Robert!

(Charlotte and Brian break apart. Charlotte stands frozen, thouroughly shocked by his appearance. Brian suddenly remembers to whack the moles.)

ROBERT: *(To Charlotte.)* There she is . . . the one that got away. So who you got here this time, Charlotte?

CHARLOTTE: Oh, Brian, this is Robert. He used to date my mother.

ROBERT: Well, that's a least half of the truth, eh? *(Winks at her.)* Excellent mole-whacking there Brian.

BRIAN: *(Whacking away.)* It's all in the hand and eye.

ROBERT: *(Sleazy.)* Charlotte, you have grown into one *attractive* woman.

CHARLOTTE: What are you doing here? *(Suddenly realizes that Brian can hear.)* Oh, uh, listen, Brian, I'm sorry, I think maybe you should just go, it's been really, I'm sorry, I shouldn't have . . .

(Brian and the moles are now doing a sort of ballet.)

BRIAN: Ooooh no, too late. First you met my mother and then made me promise not to leave. *(He pirouettes and successfully whacks several moles, triumphantly.)* God, you're right, I am *really* good at this.

ROBERT: Charlotte brings all her boys here. How many you up to?

(The dance continues.)

BRIAN: Lucky 17.

ROBERT: I can see that he's lucky. Wish I could have been that lucky.

CHARLOTTE: You had every opportunity to be, but then you started dating my mother.

BRIAN: *(Off Charlotte.)* Oooooh. Um, I'll just be over here.

(As if cooperating, the moles begin to duck and recede and he has to hunt and search for them throughout the following.)

ROBERT: And as you can see she's always had an active imagination. Always exaggerating everything, just like your mother.

CHARLOTTE: You slept with her! You made me promise not to leave you and you promised me back and then you slept with my mother.

ROBERT: Oh now, Charlotte, you can't hold me to that after all this time. What's a man to do? Waiters used to ask me what my daughter wanted for dessert. People talk.

CHARLOTTE: You *promised* me.

ROBERT: Sometimes people have to break their promises, Charlotte. What about number 17 here? You think ol' journal scribbler's going to stay around just because you made him promise?

(Brian is struggling with the moles, who seem to be planning little attacks on him, plotting together. One by one they begin sneaking up behind him and tricking him to turn around. His whacking is a becoming more chaotic and out of control.)

BRIAN: Hey Charlotte, I'm not going anywhere!

ROBERT: You could have at least got one with a little more coordination.

(Brian tries swinging the mallet but he has become more entrapped by the moles.)

BRIAN: Oh fuck!

CHARLOTTE: What are you doing here?

ROBERT: *(Smiles.)* I'm always here.

CHARLOTTE: What are you doing here *now*?

ROBERT: Looking out for you, like I always have. Number 17 or 34 or 89 is always going to look different at FIRST, but in the end they're all the same.

(The moles have almost overpowered Brian.)

CHARLOTTE: *(Gives him a weak smile.)* You mean they'll never replace number one?

BRIAN: *(Deeply entagled in the moles.)* Charlotte?

(Robert steps in closer to Charlotte.)

ROBERT: People don't change as much as we'd like to believe they do. That includes ourselves.

CHARLOTTE: Maybe not.

ROBERT: My little Charlotte.

(The mole puppet touches her shoulder and slides down becoming a hand. She looks into the eyes of the actor now. Robert is becoming "real." Charlotte is entranced. The spotlight gets tighter. Brian is half-way eclipsed.)

ROBERT: You just keep puttin' the needle back on the record after the song is over and breakin' my heart all over again.

(Brian suddenly crawls out from the mass of moles that have crushed him. He frees himself and pushes the mallet towards her in the spotlight. The moles pursue him, hold him back.)

BRIAN: Charlotte . . . take the mallet. Do it!

(But Charlotte can't hear him, she's oblivious.)

ROBERT: Yes, mam. You've got to cut your losses and watch them float on behind you under the bridge.

BRIAN: *(To Robert.)* Oh man, that is really, really *bad.*

ROBERT: *(To Brian.)* You think Dovstoyevsky wasn't sentimental?

(Robert reaches in towards Charlotte to kiss her.)

BRIAN: Not about cliches.

(Charlotte doesn't respond. Brian breaks entirely free of the moles, dives behind Charlotte, puts the mallet in her hand, and raises it above her head.)

BRIAN: Come on, Charlotte, this is it. Time to hit the trail, Mr. Country and Western.

(They whack Robert. Robet recedes into the mole chorus.)

ROBERT: Don't worry little girl, I'll always be with you.

(Charlotte comes to. Brian stares at her.)

CHARLOTTE: Hi.

BRIAN: Hi.

CHARLOTTE: That was weird.

BRIAN: Yes it was. That was your *first love?*

CHARLOTTE: Umm . . . I guess it depends on your definition?

(The moles pounce upon them in a heap.)

BRIAN: Watch out!

(The moles swarm them, engulfing them. Brian continues with the mallet to go ballistic upon the entire mole chorus while Charlotte tries her best with her bare hands. The moles fight back spewing forth all sorts of one-liners:)

MOLES: He's such an angry boy. / He always had a temper. / Really? I thought he was a bit of a pussy. / Total pussy. / I'd like *her* pussy. / Psychological displacement. / I like *your* pussy. / Fuck, fuck, fuck, fuck. / Hit me. / Fuck me. / I want his father to fuck me. / Fuck me in the pussy. / Who wants to fuck his mother? / Coming right up! / Fuck, fuck, fuck, fuck fuck . . .

(Brian and Charlotte are successful and moles recede into a muted mass on the floor. Popping up only for the final "fuck, fuck, fuck, etc." like a dying machine.)

CHARLOTTE: *(Taking in the entire mess.)* Wow. We did it. He's gone. He's really gone.

ROBERT: *(Popping up in a final Southern drawl.)* Fu-u-u-u-ck . . .

(Robert dies.)

BRIAN: *(Looks around with an air of satisfaction.)* They're all gone.

(Charlotte smiles. A beat.)

CHARLOTTE: Look at you. You're a mole-whacking red-neck slayer.

BRIAN: I guess I am. And it looks like you're an officially reformed redneck.

(They smile.)

CHARLOTTE: Level 2?

(The lights blackout and Charlotte's flashlight pops on.)

END OF PLAY

Rights and Permissions

The Attractive Women on the Train © 2002 by P. Seth Bauer. Reprinted by permission of the author. For performance rights, contact Smith & Kraus, Inc. (www.smithandkraus.com).

The Bedmaker's Revenge © 2008 by Bekah Brunstetter. Reprinted by permission of the author. For performance rights, contact Derek Zasky, William Morris Endeavor Entertainment (dsz@wmeentertainment.com).

Bollywood Ending © 2009 by R. D. Murphy. Reprinted by permission of the author. For performance rights, contact Smith & Kraus, Inc. (www.smithandkraus.com).

Canadian Tuxedo © 2009 by Nicole Pandolfo. Reprinted by permission of the author. For performance rights, contact contact Smith & Kraus, Inc. (www.smithandkraus.com).

Carwash: or In This Town, You Are What You Drive © 2008 by Stephanie Hutchinson. Reprinted by permission of the author. For performance rights, contact Stephanie Hutchinson (pianovoice@roadrunner.com).

The Cooking King © 2009 by Sharon E. Cooper. Reprinted by permission of the author. For performance rights, contact Smith & Kraus, Inc. (www.smithandkraus.com).

Driving Green © 2009 by Martin Blank. Reprinted by permission of the author. For performance rights, contact Smith & Kraus, Inc. (www.smithandkraus.com).

The End of a Perfect Game © 2008 by Jay Rehak. Reprinted by permission of the author. For performance rights, contact Smith & Kraus, Inc. (www.smithandkraus.com).

For Our Mothers and Fathers © 2009 by Crystal Skillman. Reprinted by permission of the author. For performance rights, contact Smith & Kraus, Inc. (www.smithandkraus.com).

Goat © 2009 by Don Nigro. Reprinted by permission of the author. For performance rights, contact Samuel French, Inc., 45 W. 25th St., New York, NY 10010 (www.samuelfrench.com) (212-206-8990)

The Godot Variations © 2009 by Meron Langsner. Reprinted by permission of the author. For performance rights, contact Smith & Kraus, Inc. (www.smithandkraus.com).

Gunning for Life © 2009 by William Borden. Reprinted by permission of the author. For performance rights, contact Smith & Kraus, Inc. (www.smithandkraus.com).

Hands of Horror © 2009 by Ann Marie Healy. Reprinted by permission of the author. For performance rights, contact Mark Subias, Mark Subias Agency (mark@marksubias.com).

Hedge © 2009 by Jerrod Bogard. Reprinted by permission of the author. For performance rights, contact Jerrod Bogard (jerrodbogard@gmail.com).

High Speed Disconnect © 2009 by Chris Widney. Reprinted by permission of the author. For performance rights, contact Smith & Kraus, Inc. (www.smithandkraus.com).

His Daddy © 2008 by Cori Thomas. Reprinted by permission of the author. For performance rights, contact Ron Gwiazda, Abrams Artists Agency (ron.gwiazda@abramsartny.com).

His Last Fight © 2009 by Jacqueline Goldfinger. Reprinted by permission of the author. For performance rights, contact Smith & Kraus, Inc. (www.smithandkraus.com).

Jesse © 2004 by PJ Gibson. Reprinted by permission of the author. For performance rights, contact Smith & Kraus, Inc. (www.smithandkraus.com).

L.A. 8 A.M. © 2009 Mark Harvey Levine. Reprinted by permission of the author. For performance rights, contact Mark Harvey Levine (markle9@hotmail.com).

Labor Day Weekend © 2009 by Jon Spano. Reprinted by permission of the author. For performance rights, contact Smith & Kraus, Inc. (www.smithandkraus.com).

Ladybug Gonna Getcha © 2009 by Cara Lee Corthron. Reprinted by permission of the author. For performance rights, contact Beth Blickers and Morgan Jenness, Abrams Artists Agency (beth.blickers@abramsartny.com and morgan.jenness@abramsartny.com).

Let's Not Talk About Men © 2008 by Carla Cantrelle. Reprinted by permission of the author. For performance rights, contact Smith & Kraus, Inc. (www.smithandkraus.com).

Meatball Hero © 2009 by Richard Vetere. Reprinted by permission of the author. For performance rights, contact Smith & Kraus, Inc. (www.smithandkraus.com).

A Modest Proposal © 2010 by Steve Koppman. Reprinted by permission of the author. For performance rights, contact Smith & Kraus, Inc. (www.smithandkraus.com).

Mrs. Jansen Isn't Here Now © 2009 by Steven Korbar. Reprinted by permission of the author. For performance rights, contact Smith & Kraus, Inc. (www.smithandkraus.com).

Odysseus Swims for It © 2009 by Joshua H. Cohen. Reprinted by permission of the author. For performance rights, contact Smith & Kraus, Inc. (www.smithandkraus.com).

Off the Map © 2006 by Rich Orloff. Reprinted by permission of the author. For performance rights, contact Playscripts, Inc., 450 7th Ave. #803, New York, NY 10123. www.playscripts.com (phone 866-NEWPLAY).

Parachute Sillk © by Carson Kreitzer. Reprinted by permission of the author. For performance rights, contact Bruce Ostler, Bret Adams Ltd. (bostler@bretadamsltd.net).

Parental Consent © 2009 by S. D. Graubert. Reprinted by permission of the author. For performance rights, contact Smith & Kraus, Inc. (www.smithandkraus.com).

The Pickle Lady © 2007 by Sharyn Rothstein. Reprinted by permission of the author. For performance rights, contact Ian Polonsky, MacIntosh and Otis (ianpolonsky@macintoshandotis.com)

Public Relations © 2003 by Andrew Biss. Reprinted by permission of the author. For performance rights, contact Smith & Kraus, Inc. (www.smithandkraus.com).

Post Wave Spectacular © 2010 by Diana Grisanti. Reprinted by permission of the author. For performance rights, contact Smith & Kraus, Inc. (www.smithandkraus.com).

Pussy © 2009 by Laura Jacqmin. Reprinted by permission of the author. For performance rights, contact For performance rights, contact Derek Zasky, William Morris Endeavor Entertainment (dsz@wmeentertain ment.com).

Rainbow Sprinkles © 2001 by Stacey Lane. Reprinted by permission of the author. For performance rights, contact Stacey Lane (staceylaneplay wright@yahoo.com).

Rally © 2009 by Bridgette A. Wimberly. Reprinted by permission of the author. For performance rights, contact Smith & Kraus, Inc. (www.smithandkraus.com).

The Rental © 1998 by Mark Harvey Levine. Reprinted by permission of the author. For performance rights, contact Mark Harvey Levine (markle9@hotmail.com).

Revolutions © 2009 by Elaine Romero. Reprinted by permission of the author. For performance rights, contact Bruce Ostler, Bret Adams Ltd. (bostler@bretadamsltd.net).

Rightsized © 2009 by Kate McCamy. Reprinted by permission of the author. For performance rights, contact Smith & Kraus, Inc. (www.smithand kraus.com).

Ron Swoboda's Wish © 2009 by Anna Ziegler. Reprinted by permission of the author. For performance rights, contact Chris Till, Creative Artists Agency (ctill@caa.com).

Saguaro © 2007 by Philip Dawkins. Reprinted by permission of the author. For performance rights, contact Smith & Kraus, Inc. (www.smithand kraus.com).

Self Phone © 2008 by Brendon Etter. Reprinted by permission of the author. For performance rights, contact Smith & Kraus, Inc. (www.smithand kraus.com).

The Shore © 2006 by Daniel Talbott. Reprinted by permission of the author. For performance rights, contact Morgan Jenness, Abrams Artists Agency (morgan.jenness@abramsartny.com).

Small Portions © 2009 by Quinn D. Eli. Reprinted by permission of the author. For performance rights, contact Smith & Kraus, Inc. (www.smithandkraus.com).

Smile © 2008 by Nina Mansfield. Reprinted by permission of the author. For performance rights, contact Smith & Kraus, Inc. (www.smithand kraus.com).

Spirit Sex © 2009 by Desi Moreno-Penson. Reprinted by permission of the author. For performance rights, contact Bruce Ostler, Bret Adams Ltd. (bostler@bretadamsltd.net).

Steve © 2009 by Liz Bartucci. Reprinted by permission of Maura Teitelbaum, Abrams Artists Agency. For performance rights, contact Maura Teitelbaum (maura.teitelbaum@abramsartny.com).

Table for Four © 2009 by Steven Korbar. Reprinted by permission of the author. For performance rights, contact Smith & Kraus, Inc. (www.smithandkraus.com).

Use Unknown © 2009 by Ali Walton. Reprinted by permission of the author. For performance rights, contact Smith & Kraus, Inc. (www.smithandkraus.com).

Whack-a-Mole © 2009 by Beth Lein. Reprinted by permission of the author. For performance rights, contact Smith & Kraus, Inc. (www.smithandkraus.com).

Wish You Were Here © 2008 by Claudia Haas. Reprinted by permission of the author. For performance rights, contact Smith & Kraus, Inc. (www.smithandkraus.com).

Worse Things © 2009 by Mona Mansour. Reprinted by permission of the author. For performance rights, contact Smith & Kraus, Inc. (www.smithandkraus.com).